W9-AVA-452

"it's
finger lickin'
good"

everything

everything's an argument

everything's an argument

Fourth Edition

EVERYTHING'S AN argument

Andrea A. Lunsford

STANFORD UNIVERSITY

John J. Ruszkiewicz

UNIVERSITY OF TEXAS AT AUSTIN

BEDFORD / ST. MARTIN'S

BOSTON ◆ NEW YORK

For Bedford/St. Martin's

Developmental Editors: John Elliott, Genevieve Hamilton
Associate Editor: Laura King
Senior Production Editors: Shuli Traub, Karen Baart, Rosemary Jaffe
Senior Production Supervisor: Nancy Myers
Marketing Manager: Karita dos Santos
Editorial Assistant: Katherine Paarlberg
Production Assistants: Sarah Ulicny, Blake Royer, Kristen Merrill
Copyeditor: Alice Vigliani
Photo Research: Robin Raffer
Text Design: Anna Palchik
Cover Design: Donna Lee Dennison
Cover Photos: (clockwise from top) Copyright © Royalty-Free/Corbis; Copyright © Andersen Ross/Jupiter Images; Copyright © Bob Sacha/Corbis; Copyright © Ryan Red Corn from Red Hand Media; Copyright © Webstream/Alamy; Copyright © StockTrek/Getty Images; Copyright © Joseph Sohm, Chromo-Sohm, Inc./Corbis
Composition: Pine Tree Composition, Inc.
Printing and Binding: R.R. Donnelley & Sons Company

President: Joan E. Feinberg
Editorial Director: Denise B. Wydra
Editor in Chief: Karen S. Henry
Director of Marketing: Karen Melton Soeltz
Director of Editing, Design, and Production: Marcia Cohen
Managing Editor: Elizabeth M. Schaaf

Library of Congress Control Number: 2006925049

Manufactured in the United States of America.

1   0   9   8   7
f   e   d

For information, write: Bedford/St. Martin's, 75 Arlington Street, Boston, MA 02116   (617-399-4000)

ISBN 10: 0–312–44749–3
ISBN 13: 978–0–312–44749–6

Acknowledgments

PREFACE

Everything's an Argument remains a labor of love for us, a lively introduction to rhetoric drawn directly from our experiences teaching persuasive writing. The chapters still practically write themselves, and we take special pleasure in discovering fresh and provocative everyday arguments that illuminate the ways we all use language—both verbal and visual—to assert our presence in the world. Apparently, the book continues to strike a chord with many students and instructors who have made *Everything's an Argument* a best-seller in its field since its debut. We offer now a fourth edition, thoroughly revised to reach even more writers and instructors and to account for changes we see in the way arguments are framed and circulated throughout the world.

The purposefully controversial title of this text sums up three key assumptions we share. First, language provides the most powerful means of understanding the world and of using that understanding to help shape lives. Second, arguments seldom if ever have only two sides: rather, they present a dizzying array of perspectives, often with as many "takes" on a subject as there are arguers. Understanding arguments, then, calls for carefully considering a full range of perspectives before coming to judgment. Third, and most important, all language—including the language of sound and images or of symbol systems other than writing—is in some way argumentative or persuasive, pointing in a direction and asking for response. From the latest blog entry to the presidential seal, from the American flag to the Toyota Prius green-leaf logo, from the latest hip-hop hit to the brand identity of Nike, texts everywhere beckon for response. People walk, talk, and breathe persuasion very much as they breathe the air: *everything* is a potential argument.

So our purpose in *Everything's an Argument* is to present argument as something that's as natural and everyday as an old pair of sneakers, as something we do almost from the moment we are born (in fact, an infant's first cry is as poignant a claim as we can imagine), and as something that's worthy of careful attention and practice. In pursuing this goal, we try to use ordinary language whenever possible and to keep our use of specialized terminology to a minimum. But we also see argument, and want students to see it, as a craft both delicate and powerful. So we have designed *Everything's an Argument* to be itself an argument for argument, with a voice that aims to appeal to readers cordially but that doesn't hesitate to make demands on them when appropriate. To emphasize this point, we've added a new boxed activity in every chapter of the new edition: "If Everything's an Argument . . . " asks students to think critically about this book as itself an argument and to analyze rhetorical choices made by the authors and editors in such areas as cover images, examples and illustrations throughout the text, and the structure of chapters.

We also aim to balance attention to the critical *reading* of arguments (analysis) with attention to the *writing* of arguments (production). Moreover, we have tried to demonstrate both activities with lively—and realistic—examples, on the principle that the best way to appreciate an argument may be to see it in action. Indeed, we continue to work hard to try to enhance the power of the examples, expand the range of texts we present, and include works oriented toward the concerns of college students in all their diversity. In this edition, the six new full-length arguments (out of the ten such models in the book) include a student newspaper article on why *Napoleon Dynamite* became a cult film among young people and a student's detailed formal proposal to improve wheelchair access on her campus.

In the last two editions, we tried to broaden the use of visual media throughout. We've intensified that effort in this latest edition, with every chapter presenting new images and fresh argumentative situations. The new full-color design of the fourth edition allows us to integrate coverage of visual argument more thoroughly throughout each chapter and to include a new boxed visual analysis activity called "Not Just Words" in every chapter.

This fourth edition also features a reorganization and streamlining of the early chapters to focus more clearly and emphatically on *pathos, ethos,* and *logos,* giving students a firmer grounding in these central Aristotelian concepts before they begin to study and practice specific kinds of arguments. In particular, we have integrated much of the information from the former "Arguments Based on Values" chapter into the three chapters on these key concepts.

Based on advice from reviewers, we've added two new chapters to this fourth edition. Chapter 5, "Thinking Rhetorically," helps students put into practice what they've learned in Chapters 1–4; it models the skills of analysis and close reading of arguments and ends with a Guide to Writing a Rhetorical Analysis that provides students with detailed guidelines for carrying out rhetorical analyses of their own. Chapter 7, "Arguments of Fact," guides students in analyzing the kinds of factual assertions made by journalists, scientists, politicians, and others, and in writing their own compelling arguments based on factual claims. Throughout, we have tried to encourage students to be more critical in their evaluation of factual sources; and given the problems that reviewers of the book tell us students are having in judging potential source materials, we have added two "source maps" modeling evaluations of print and electronic sources in Chapter 19, "Evaluating and Using Sources."

Finally, we have paid particular attention in this revision to issues of style and presentation. The former chapter on figurative language and argument, retitled "Style in Arguments," now includes discussion of more basic elements of style such as syntax and punctuation. In addition, the former chapter on spoken arguments has been expanded into a new chapter called "Presenting Arguments," which discusses print and multimedia formats, such as blogs and Webcasts, as well as oral presentations.

Here is a summary of the key features that continue to characterize *Everything's an Argument* and of the major new features in this edition:

Key Features

- Student-friendly, easy-to-understand explanations in simple, succinct, everyday language, with many brief examples and a minimum of technical terminology.

- A uniquely wide-ranging scope, going beyond traditional pro/con verbal debates to show that argument is everywhere—from rap lyrics, news articles, and poems to advertisements, cartoons, posters, bumper stickers, billboards, Web sites, and blogs.

- Unique full chapters on intellectual property, humorous arguments, and arguments of fact.

- Thirteen full-length essays, including six by student writers, providing engaging models of extended verbal arguments over questions of fact, definition, evaluation, cause and effect, and proposals.

- Boxed discussions of "Cultural Contexts for Argument" that alert students to how ways of arguing differ from culture to culture and make this book more useful to both native and nonnative speakers of English.

New to This Edition

- A reorganization and streamlining of the early chapters to focus more strongly on the key concepts of *pathos, ethos,* and *logos.*
- A new full-color design that brings the images in the text to life and incorporates a "Not Just Words" visual analysis activity in each chapter.
- New chapters on "Arguments of Fact" and "Thinking Rhetorically."
- Six new full-length arguments, on topics ranging from why *Napoleon Dynamite* became a cult film to why literature matters.
- An expansion of the chapter on figurative language into a new "Style in Arguments" chapter that includes attention to word choice, sentence structure, and punctuation.
- An expansion of the chapter on oral arguments into a new "Presenting Arguments" chapter that includes Web-based and multimedia presentations and blogs.
- A new boxed activity in each chapter, "If Everything's an Argument . . . ," that helps students to think critically about the book itself as an argumentative text.

Acknowledgments

We owe a debt of gratitude to many people for making *Everything's an Argument* possible. Our first thanks must go to the students we have taught in our writing courses for nearly three decades, particularly first-year students at The Ohio State University, Stanford University, and the University of Texas at Austin, and to the six students whose fine argumentative essays appear in our chapters. Almost every chapter in this book has been informed by a classroom encounter with a student whose shrewd observation or perceptive question sent an ambitious lesson plan spiraling to the ground. (Anyone who has tried to teach claims and warrants on the fly to skeptical first-year students will surely appreciate why we have qualified our claims in the Toulmin chapter so carefully.) But students have also provided the motive for writing this book. More than ever, students need to know how to read and write arguments effectively if they are to secure a place in a world growing ever smaller and more rhetorically challenging.

We are grateful to our editors at Bedford/St. Martin's who contributed their talents to our book, beginning with Joan Feinberg and Nancy Perry, who have enthusiastically supported the project and provided us with the resources and feedback needed to keep us on track. Most of the day-to-day work on the project has been handled by the remarkably patient and perceptive and good-humored John Elliott. He prevented more than a few lapses of judgment yet understands the spirit of this book—which involves, occasionally, taking risks to make a memorable point. We have appreciated, too, his meticulous line editing as well as his ability to find just the right example when we were struggling to do so.

We are similarly grateful to others at Bedford/St. Martin's who contributed their talents to our book: Shuli Traub, Karen Baart, and Rosemary Jaffe who served as our superb production editors; Anna Palchik, who completely reworked her design of our book to accommodate color; Alice Vigliani, who meticulously copyedited this fourth edition; Laura King, who was indispensable in coordinating the entire art program for our book, researching images and writing captions throughout; Robin Raffer, who was our art researcher par excellence; Katie Paarlberg, the editorial assistant we could not have done without; Nancy Myers, who ably coordinated all our work with the printer; and Karita dos Santos, who served as our outstanding marketing manager.

We'd also like to thank the astute instructors and students who reviewed the third edition, among them Angela L. Berdahl of Portland Community College, Robert E. Cummings of the University of Georgia, Jodi Egerton of the University of Texas at Austin, Elaine Farrugia of Arizona State University, Shawn Keaton of the University of Central Florida, Susan K. Miller of Mesa Community College, Connie Pesce of the New England Institute of Technology, John Pinkerton of Mesa Community College, Lanette Pogue of the California State University at Sacramento, Sam Pritchard of Iowa State University, Rochelle Rodrigo of Mesa Community College, and Jacqueline Wheeler of Arizona State University.

Thanks, too, to Ben Feigert, who wrote some of the original exercises for *Everything's an Argument,* and to John Kinkade, who has again updated the instructor's manual for this edition.

We hope that *Everything's an Argument* responds to what students and instructors have said they want and need. And we hope readers of this text will let us know how we've done: please share your opinions and suggestions with us at <bedfordstmartins.com/everythingsanargument>.

Andrea A. Lunsford
John J. Ruszkiewicz

CONTENTS

**Part 2:
Writing Arguments**   137

Part 3:
Style and Presentation
in Arguments 367

Part 4:
Conventions of Argument 467

everything's an argument

PART 1

READING arguments

1
Everything Is an Argument

"Movie of the year!" blares the headline of an online ad for *Star Wars: Episode III–Revenge of the Sith.*

A professor interrupts a lecture to urge her students to spend less time on Instant Messaging and more in the company of thick, old books.

A senator tries to tell an irate C-SPAN caller that the Homeland Security Bill does not reduce citizens' constitutional rights or their privacy.

A nurse assures a youngster eyeing an approaching needle, "This won't hurt one bit."

A sports columnist blasts a football coach for passing on fourth down and two in a close game—even though the play produces a touchdown.

"Please let me make it through this chem exam!" a student silently prays.

● ● ●

These visual and verbal messages all contain arguments. From the clothes you wear to the foods you choose to eat to the groups you decide to join—all of these everyday activities make nuanced, sometimes implicit, arguments about who you are and what you value. Thus an argument can be any text—whether written, spoken, or visual—that expresses a point of view. Sometimes arguments can be aggressive, composed deliberately to change what people believe, think, or do. At other times your goals may be more subtle, and your writing may be designed to convince yourself or others that specific facts are reliable or that certain views should be considered or at least tolerated.

In fact, some theorists claim that language is itself inherently persuasive (even when you say "hi, how's it going?" for instance, in one sense you're arguing that your hello deserves a response) and hence *every* text is also an argument, designed to influence readers. For example, a poem that observes what little girls do in church may indirectly critique the role religion plays in women's lives, for good or ill:

> I worry for the girls.
> I once had braids,
> and wore lace that made me suffer.
> I had not yet done the things
> that would need forgiving.
>
> –Kathleen Norris, "Little Girls in Church"

To take another example, observations about family life among the poor in India may suddenly illuminate the writer's life and the reader's experience, forcing comparisons that quietly argue for change:

I have learned from Jagat and his family a kind of commitment, a form of friendship that is not always available in the West, where we have become cynical and instrumental in so many of our relationships to others.

–Jeremy Seabrook, "Family Values"

Even humor makes an argument when it causes readers to become aware—through bursts of laughter or just a faint smile—of the way things are and how they might be different. Take a look, for example, at an excerpt from the introduction to *Dave Barry Hits Below the Beltway*, along with its cover, which also makes a humorous argument:

> To do even a halfway decent book on a subject as complex as the United States government, you have to spend a lot of time in Washington, D.C. So the first thing I decided, when I was getting ready to write this book, was that it would not be even halfway decent.
>
> –Dave Barry, *Dave Barry Hits below the Beltway*

Dave Barry's humorous argument begins on his book's cover.

Not Just Words

Take a look at the two bumper stickers above. Each one makes a visual argument about President George W. Bush and about his relationship to the country and to the world. Spend some time working with one other student in your class to analyze these visual arguments. As simply as possible, state the claim you think each argument makes. Then write a paragraph that elaborates on that claim.

More obvious as arguments are those that make a claim and present evidence to support it. Such writing often moves readers to recognize problems and to consider solutions. Suasion of this kind is usually easy to recognize:

> Discrimination against Hispanics, or any other group, should be fought and there are laws and a massive apparatus to do so. But the way to eliminate such discrimination is not to classify all Hispanics as victims.
>
> –Linda Chavez, "Towards a New Politics of Hispanic Assimilation"

> [W]omen unhappy in their marriages often enter full-time employment as an escape. But although a woman's entrance into the workplace does tend to increase the stability of her marriage, it does not increase her happiness.
>
> –The Popular Research Institute, Penn State University

> Resistance to science is born of fear. Fear, in turn, is bred by ignorance. And it is ignorance that is our deepest malady.
>
> –J. Michael Bishop, "Enemies of Promise"

Purposes of Argument

If in some ways all language has an argumentative edge that aims to make a point, not all language use aims to win out over others. In contrast to the traditional Western concept of argument as being about fighting or combat, communication theorists such as Sonja Foss, Cindy Griffin, and Josina Makau describe an *invitational* argument, the kind that aims not to win over another person or group but to invite others to enter a space of mutual regard and exploration. In fact, as you'll see, writers and speakers have as many purposes for arguing as for using language, including—in addition to winning—to inform, to convince, to explore, to make decisions, even to meditate or pray.

Of course, many arguments *are* aimed at winning. Such is the traditional purpose of much writing and speaking in the political arena, in the business world, and in the law courts. Two candidates for office, for example, try to win out over each other in appealing for votes; the makers of one soft drink try to outsell their competitors by appealing to public tastes; and two lawyers try to defeat each other in pleading to a judge and jury. In your college writing, you may also be called on to make an argument that appeals to a "judge" and/or "jury" (your instructor and classmates). You might, for instance, argue that peer-to-peer file-sharing is legal because of the established legal precedent of fair use. In doing so, you may need to defeat your unseen opponents—those who oppose such file-sharing.

At this point, it may be helpful to acknowledge a common academic distinction between argument and persuasion. In this view, the point of *argument* is to discover some version of the truth, using evidence and reasons. Argument of this sort leads audiences toward conviction, an agreement that a claim is true or reasonable, or that a course of action is desirable. The aim of *persuasion* is to change a point of view or to move others from conviction to action. In other words, writers or speakers argue to discover some truth; they persuade when they think they already know it.

Argument (discover a truth) ⟶ conviction
Persuasion (know a truth)   ⟶ action

In practice, this distinction between argument and persuasion can be hard to sustain. It's unnatural for writers or readers to imagine their minds divided between a part that pursues truth and a part that seeks to persuade. And yet, you may want to reserve the term *persuasion* for writing that's aggressively designed to change opinions through the use of both reason and other appropriate techniques. For writing that sets out to persuade at all costs, abandoning reason, fairness, and truth altogether, the term *propaganda,* with all its negative connotations, seems to fit. Some would suggest that *advertising* often works just as well.

But, as we've already suggested, arguing isn't always about winning or even about changing others' views. In addition to invitational argument, another school of argument—called Rogerian argument, after the psychotherapist Carl Rogers—is based on finding common ground and establishing trust among those who disagree about issues, and on approaching audiences in nonthreatening ways. Writers who follow Rogerian approaches seek to understand the perspectives of those with whom they disagree, looking for "both/and" or "win/win" solutions (rather than "either/or" or "win/lose" ones) whenever possible. Much successful argument today follows such principles, consciously or not.

Some other purposes or goals of argument are worth considering in more detail.

Arguments to Inform

Many arguments, from street signs to notices of meetings to newspaper headlines, may not seem especially "argumentative" because their main purpose is just to inform members of an audience about something they didn't know. Other informative arguments are more obviously intended to persuade. For example, an essential step in selling anything, especially something new, is to inform or remind the customer that it exists, as in advertisements like the one for *Star Wars* mentioned at the very beginning of this chapter.

A visual argument to inform in Key West, Florida

Political campaigns use arguments to inform extensively, as well. Think of all the posters you've seen with names and smiling faces of candidates and the offices they're seeking: "Rice in 2008," "Lujan for Mayor." Of course, these verbal or visual texts are often aimed at winning out over an unnamed opponent, just as many ads are aimed at unnamed competing products. But on the surface, at least, they serve simply to give a candidate "name recognition" by informing voters that he or she is running for office.

Arguments to inform can be also more subtle than ads or signs. Consider how Joan Didion uses argument to inform readers about the artist Georgia O'Keeffe:

> This is a woman who in 1939 could advise her admirers that they were missing her point, that their appreciation of her famous flowers was merely sentimental. "When I paint a red hill," she observed coolly

Georgia O'Keeffe, *Rust Red Hills* (1930)

in the catalogue for an exhibition that year, "you say it is too bad that I don't always paint flowers. A flower touches almost everyone's heart. A red hill doesn't touch everyone's heart."

—Joan Didion, "Georgia O'Keeffe"

By giving specific information about O'Keeffe and her own ideas about her art, Didion in this passage argues that readers should pay closer attention to *all* the work of this artist.

Arguments to Convince

If you were writing a report that attempted to identify the causes of changes in global temperatures, you would likely be trying not to conquer opponents but to satisfy readers that you had thoroughly examined those causes and that they merit serious attention. As a form of writing, reports typically aim to persuade readers rather than win out over opponents. Yet the presence of those who might disagree is always implied, and it shapes a writer's strategies. In the following passage, for example, Paul Osterman argues to convince readers of the urgency surrounding jobs for all citizens:

Among employed 19- to 31-year-old high school graduates who did not go to college, more than 30 percent had not been in their position for even a year. Another 12 percent had only one year of tenure. The pattern was much the same for women who had remained in the

President George W. Bush was arguing to convince on May 1, 2003, when he landed on the USS *Abraham Lincoln* flight deck and announced "Mission Accomplished" in Iraq. Such pictures were later used against Bush, however, when it became clear that the announcement was, at best, premature.

> labor force for the four years prior to the survey. These are adults who, for a variety of reasons — a lack of skills, training, or disposition — have not managed to secure "adult" jobs.
>
> –Paul Osterman, "Getting Started"

Osterman uses facts to report a seemingly objective conclusion about the stability of employment among certain groups, but he's also arguing against those who find that the current job situation is tolerable and not worthy of concern or action.

Arguments to Explore

Many important subjects call for arguments that take the form of exploration, either on your own or with others. If there's an "opponent" in such a situation at all (often there is not), it's likely the status quo or a current trend that — for one reason or another — is puzzling. Exploratory arguments may be deeply personal, such as E. B. White's often-reprinted essay "Once More to the Lake," in which the author's return with his young son to a vacation spot from his own childhood leads him to reflect on time, memory, and mortality. Or the exploration may be aimed at addressing serious problems in society. James Fallows explores what he sees as "America's coming economic crisis" by projecting himself forward to the election of 2016—and then looking back to speculate on what might happen between 2005 and 2016. Along the way, he considers changes that may occur in education:

> . . . we could have shored up our universities. True, the big change came as early as 2002, in the wake of 9/11, when tighter visa rules . . . cut off the flow of foreign talent that American universities had channeled to American ends. In the summer of 2007 China applied the name "twenty Harvards" to its ambition, announced in the early 2000s, to build major research institutions that would attract international talent. It seemed preposterous (too much political control, too great a language barrier), but no one is laughing now. . . . The Historic Campus of our best-known university, Harvard, is still prestigious worldwide. But its role is increasingly that of the theme park, like Oxford or Heidelberg, while the most ambitious students compete for fellowships at the Har-Bai and Har-Bei campuses in Mumbai and Beijing.
>
> –James Fallows, "Countdown to a Meltdown"

Perhaps the essential argument in any such piece is the writer's assertion that a problem exists (in this case, the damage that tighter visa rules do to American economic competitiveness) and that the writer or reader needs to solve it. Some exploratory pieces present and defend solutions. Paul Goldberger, for example, takes on the question of how best to rebuild Ground Zero, exploring the false starts and what he argues is a massive "failure of imagination" that led to an unnecessarily elaborate plan for the Freedom Tower, a 2.6 million square foot office building. After exploring several possibilities, Goldberger concludes that a much smaller (but still very tall) memorial tower would solve the problem of how to commemorate the site by integrating the structure fully into housing and extensive cultural space:

> A great tower by Calatrava or another architect equally adept at turning engineering into poetic form would give New York the defiantly proud icon it has craved since the towers fell. And it wouldn't require anybody to live or work a hundred stories above the street. Most important, it would be a way of transcending the false divide between commemoration and renewal. A soaring tower can be made to coexist with apartments and museums. The planners at Ground Zero have

A digital rendering of the Freedom Tower designed by architects Michael Arad and Peter Walker

treated the sacred and the everyday as two distinct spheres. The answer isn't to split the site into a memorial sector and a business sector but, rather, to find ways to honor the dead while rejuvenating the city, to acknowledge the past while looking toward the future. Ground Zero is the first great urban-design challenge of the twenty-first century, and the noblest way to honor what happened here is to rebuild the site with the complexity and vitality that characterizes the best of Manhattan.

–Paul Goldberger, "Eyes on the Prize"

Arguments to Make Decisions

Closely allied to argument that explores is that which aims at making good, sound decisions. In fact, the result of many exploratory arguments may be to argue for a particular decision, whether that decision relates to the best computer for you to buy or the "right" person to choose as your life partner. For college students, choosing a major is a momentous decision, and one way to go about making that decision is to argue your way through several alternatives in your own mind as well as with friends, colleagues, maybe even your parents. By the time you've examined the pros and cons of each alternative, you should be at least a little closer to a good decision. In the following paragraphs, college   student   Jessica   Cohen reasons her way toward another momentous decision, asking should she, or should she not, become an egg donor for a wealthy couple:

> Early in the spring of last year a classified ad ran for two weeks in the *Yale Daily News*: "EGG DONOR NEEDED." The couple [Michelle and David] that placed the ad was picky, and for that reason was offering $25,000 for an egg from the right donor. . . . I kept dreaming about all the things I could do with $25,000. I had gone into the correspondence [with David and Michelle] on a whim. But soon, despite David's casual tone and the optimistic attitude of all the classifieds and information I read, I decided that this process was something I didn't want to be part of. I understand the desire for a child who will resemble and fit in with the family. But once a couple starts choosing a few characteristics, shooting for perfection is too easy—especially if they can afford it. The money might have changed my life for a while, but it would have led to the creation of a child encumbered with too many expectations.
>
> —Jessica Cohen, "Grade A: The Market for a Yale Woman's Eggs"

"I told my parents that if grades were
so important they should have paid
for a smarter egg donor."

Arguments to Meditate or Pray

Sometimes arguments can take the form of intense meditations on a theme, or of prayer. In such cases, the writer or speaker is most often hoping to transform something in him- or herself or to reach a state of equilibrium or peace of mind. If you know a familiar prayer or mantra, think for a moment of what it "argues" for and how it uses quiet meditation to accomplish that goal. Such meditations don't have to be formal prayers, however. Look, for example, at an excerpt from Michael Lassell's poem "How to Watch Your Brother Die." This poem, which evokes the confusing emotions of a man during the death of his gay brother, uses a kind of meditative language that allows the reader to reach an understanding of the speaker and to evoke meditative thought in others:

> Feel how it feels to hold a man in your arms
> whose arms are used to holding men.
> Offer God anything to bring your brother back.
> Know you have nothing God could possibly want.
> Curse God, but do not
> abandon Him.
>
> –Michael Lassell, "How to Watch Your Brother Die"

Another sort of meditative argument can be found in the stained-glass windows of churches and other public buildings. Dazzled by a spectacle of light, people pause to consider a window's message longer than they might were the same idea conveyed on paper. The window engages viewers with a power not unlike that of poetry (see p. 16).

As these examples suggest, the effectiveness of argument depends not only on the purposes of the writer but also on the context surrounding the plea and the people it seeks most directly to reach. Though we'll examine arguments of all types in this book, we'll focus chiefly on the kinds made in professional and academic situations.

Occasions for Argument

Another way of thinking about arguments is to consider the public occasions that call for them. In an ancient textbook of rhetoric, or the art of persuasion, the philosopher Aristotle provides an elegant scheme for classifying the purposes of arguments, one based on issues of time—past, future, and present. His formula is easy to remember and helpful

Rose and lancet windows in France's Chartres Cathedral

in suggesting strategies for making convincing cases. But because all classifications overlap with others to a certain extent, don't be surprised to encounter many arguments that span more than one category—arguments about the past with implications for the future, arguments about the future with bearings on the present, and so on.

Arguments about the Past

Debates about what has happened in the past are called forensic arguments; such controversies are common in business, government, and academia. For example, in many criminal and civil cases, lawyers interrogate witnesses to establish exactly what happened at an earlier time: *Did the defendant sexually harass her employee? Did the company deliberately ignore evidence that its product was deficient? Was the contract properly enforced?* The contentious nature of some forensic arguments is evident in this excerpt from a letter to the editor of *The Atlantic Monthly:*

> Robert Bryce's article on the U.S. military's gas consumption in Iraq ("Gas Pains," May *Atlantic*) is factually inaccurate, tactically misguided, and a classic case of a red herring.
> –Captain David J. Morris

In replying to this letter, the author of the article, Robert Bryce, disputes Morris's statements, introducing more evidence in support of his original claim. Obviously, then, forensic arguments rely on evidence and testimony to re-create what can be known about events that have already occurred.

Forensic arguments also rely heavily on precedents—actions or decisions in the past that influence policies or decisions in the present—and on analyses of cause and effect. Consider the ongoing controversy over Christopher Columbus: Are his expeditions to the Americas events worth celebrating, or are they unhappy chapters in human history—or a mixture of both? No simple exchange of evidence will suffice to still this debate; the effects of Columbus's actions beginning in 1492 may be studied and debated for the next five hundred years. As you might suspect from this example, arguments about history are typically forensic.

Forensic cases may also be arguments about character, such as when someone's reputation is studied in a historical context to enrich current perspectives on the person. Allusions to the past can make present arguments more vivid, as in the following text about Ward Connerly, head of an organization that aims to dismantle affirmative action programs:

> Despite the fact that Connerly's message seems clearly opposed to the Civil Rights Movement, some people are fond of pointing out that the man is black. But as far as politics goes, that is irrelevant. Before black suffrage, there were African Americans who publicly argued against their own right to vote.
> –Carl Villarreal, "Connerly Is an Enemy of Civil Rights"

Such writing can be exploratory and open-ended, the point of argument being to enhance and sharpen knowledge, not just to generate heat or score points.

Theodor de Bry's 1594 engraving tells one version of the Christopher Columbus story.

Arguments about the Future

Debates about what will or should happen in the future are called deliberative arguments. Legislatures, congresses, and parliaments are called deliberative bodies because they establish policies for the future: *Should two people of the same sex be allowed to marry? Should the United States build a defense against ballistic missiles?* Because what has happened in the past influences the future, deliberative judgments often rely on prior forensic arguments. Thus deliberative arguments often draw on evidence and testimony, as in this passage:

> The labor market is sending a clear signal. While the American way of moving youngsters from high school to the labor market may be imperfect, the chief problem is that, for many, even getting a job no longer guarantees a decent standard of living. More than ever, getting ahead, or even keeping up, means staying in school longer.
>
> –Paul Osterman, "Getting Started"

But since no one has a blueprint for what's to come, deliberative arguments also advance by means of projections, extrapolations, and reasoned guesses—*If X is true, Y may be true; if X happens, so may Y; if X continues, then Y may occur:*

> In 2000, according to a World Health Organization assessment, 1.1 billion people worldwide had no regular access to safe drinking water, and 2.4 billion had no regular access to sanitation systems. Lack of access to clean water leads to four billion cases of diarrhea each year. Peter Gleick, an expert on global freshwater resources, reveals that even if we reach the United Nations' stated goal of halving the number of people without access to safe drinking water by 2015, as many as 76 million people will die from water-borne diseases before 2020.
> —Pacific Institute for Studies in Development, Environment, and Security

Arguments about the Present

Arguments about the present are often arguments about contemporary values—the ethical premises and assumptions that are widely held (or contested) within a society. Sometimes called epideictic arguments or ceremonial arguments because they tend to be heard at public occasions, they include inaugural addresses, sermons, eulogies, graduation speeches, and civic remarks of all kinds. Ceremonial arguments can be passionate and eloquent, rich in anecdotes and examples. Martin Luther King Jr. was a master of ceremonial discourse, and he was particularly adept at finding affirmation in the depths of despair:

> Three nights later, our home was bombed. Strangely enough, I accepted the word of the bombing calmly. My experience with God had given me a new strength and trust. I know now that God is able to give us the interior resources to face the storms and problems of life.
> —Martin Luther King Jr., "Our God Is Able"

King argues here that the arbiter of good and evil in society is, ultimately, God. But not all ceremonial arguments reach quite so far.

More typical are values arguments that explore contemporary culture, praising what's admirable and blaming what's not. In the following argument, student Latisha Chisholm looks at rap after Tupac Shakur—and doesn't like what she sees:

> When I think about how rap music has changed, I generally associate the demise of my appreciation for the industry with the death of

Tupac. With his death, not only did one of the most intriguing rap rivalries of all time die, but the motivation for rapping seems to have changed. Where money had always been a plus, now it is obviously more important than wanting to express the hardships of Black communities. With current rappers, the positive power that came from the desire to represent Black people is lost. One of the biggest rappers now got his big break while talking about sneakers. Others announce retirement without really having done much for the soul or for Black people's morale. I equate new rappers to NFL players that don't love the game anymore. They're only in it for the money. . . . It looks like the voice of a people has lost its heart.

–Latisha Chisholm, "Has Rap Lost Its Soul?"

As in many ceremonial arguments, Chisholm here reinforces common values such as representing one's community honorably and fairly.

Kinds of Argument

Yet another way of categorizing arguments is to consider their status or stasis—that is, the kinds of issues they address. This categorization system is called stasis theory. In ancient Greek and Roman civilizations, rhetoricians defined a series of questions by which to examine legal cases. The questions would be posed in sequence, because each depended on the question(s) preceding it. Together, the questions helped determine the point of contention in an argument, the place where disputants could focus their energy and hence what kind of an argument they should make. A modern version of those questions might look like the following:

- Did something happen?
- What is its nature?
- What is its quality?
- What actions should be taken?

Here's how the questions might be used to explore a "crime."

DID SOMETHING HAPPEN?

Yes. A young man kissed a young woman against her will. The act was witnessed by a teacher and friends and acquaintances of both parties. The facts suggest clearly that something happened. If you were going

CULTURAL CONTEXTS FOR ARGUMENT

Considering What's "Normal"

If you want to communicate effectively with people across cultures, then you need to try to learn something about the norms in those cultures—and to be aware of the norms guiding your own behavior.

- Be aware of the assumptions that guide your own customary ways of arguing a point. Remember that most of us tend to see our own way as the "normal" or "right" way to do things. Such assumptions guide your thinking and your judgments about what counts—and what "works"—in an argument. Nevertheless, just because it seems "normal" to take a very aggressive stance in an argument, don't forget that others may find that aggression startling or even alarming.

- Keep in mind that if your own ways seem inherently right, then even without thinking about it you may assume that other ways are somehow less than right. It's "right" to drive on the right side of the road in the United States but on the left in England and Australia; arguing that one way is the only really right way would not get you very far. Such thinking makes it hard to communicate effectively across cultures.

- Remember that ways of arguing are influenced by cultural contexts and that they differ widely across cultures. Pay attention to the ways people from cultures other than your own argue, and be flexible and open to the many ways of thinking you'll no doubt encounter.

- Respect the differences among individuals within a given culture; don't expect that every member of a community behaves—or argues—in just the same way.

The best advice, then, might be *don't assume.* Just because you think wearing a navy blazer and a knee-length skirt "argues" that you should be taken seriously as a job candidate at a multinational corporation, such dress may be perceived differently in other settings. And if you're conducting an interview where a candidate doesn't look you in the eye, don't assume that this reflects any lack of confidence or respect; he or she may intend it as a sign of politeness.

Sexual harassment?

to write an argument about this event, this first stasis question proves not very helpful, since there's no debate about whether the act occurred. If the event were debatable, however, you could develop an argument of fact.

WHAT IS THE NATURE OF THE THING?

The act might be construed as "sexual harassment," defined as the imposition of unwanted or unsolicited sexual attention or activity on a person. The young man kissed the young woman on the lips. Kissing people who aren't relatives on the lips is generally considered a sexual activity. The young woman did not want to be kissed and complained to her teacher. The young man's act meets the definition of "sexual harassment." Careful analysis of this stasis question could lead to an argument of definition.

WHAT IS THE QUALITY OF THE THING?

Both the young man and young woman involved in the action are six years old. They were playing in a schoolyard. The boy didn't realize that kissing girls against their will was a violation of school policy;

school sexual harassment policies had not in the past been enforced against first-graders. Most people don't regard six-year-olds as sexually culpable. Moreover, the girl wants to play with the boy again and apparently doesn't resent his action. Were you to decide on this focus, you would be developing an argument of evaluation.

WHAT ACTIONS SHOULD BE TAKEN?

The case has raised a ruckus among parents, the general public, and some feminists and anti-feminists. The consensus seems to be that the school overreacted in seeking to brand the boy as a sexual harasser. Yet it is important that the issue of sexual harassment not be dismissed as trivial. Consequently, the boy should be warned not to kiss girls against their will. The teachers should be warned not to make federal cases out of schoolyard spats. With this stasis question as your focus, you would be developing a proposal argument.

As you can see, each of the stasis questions explores different aspects of a problem and uses different evidence or techniques to reach conclusions. You can use stasis theory to explore the aspects of any topic you're considering. In addition, studying the results of your exploration of the stasis questions can help you determine the major point you want to make and thus identify the type of argument that will be most effective.

Arguments of Fact—Did Something Happen?

An argument of fact usually involves a statement that can be proved or disproved with specific evidence or testimony. Although relatively simple to define, such arguments are often quite subtle, involving layers of complexity not apparent when the question is initially posed.

For example, the question of pollution of the oceans—*Is it really occurring?*—would seem relatively easy to settle. Either scientific data prove that the oceans are being polluted as a result of human activity, or they don't. But to settle the matter, writers and readers would first have to agree on a number of points, each of which would have to be examined and debated: *What constitutes pollution? How will such pollution be measured? Over what period of time? Are any current deviations in water quality unprecedented? How can one be certain that deviations are attributable to human action?* Nevertheless, questions of this sort can be disputed primarily on the facts, complicated and contentious as they may be. But should you choose to develop an argument of fact, be aware of how difficult it can sometimes be to establish "facts." (For more on arguments based on facts, see Chapter 4.)

Arguments of Definition—What Is the Nature of the Thing?

Just as contentious as arguments based on facts are questions of definition. An argument of definition often involves determining whether one known object or action belongs in a second—and more highly contested—category. One of the most hotly debated issues in American life today involves a question of definition: *Is a human fetus a human being?* If one argues that it is, then a second issue of definition arises: *Is abortion murder?* As you can see, issues of definition can have mighty consequences—and decades of debate may leave the matter unresolved.

Writer Christopher Hitchens defines a word familiar to almost everyone—then gives it a twist:

> On its own, the word "cowboy" is not particularly opprobrious. It means a ranch hand or cattle driver, almost by definition a mounted one, herding the steers in the general direction of Cheyenne and thus providing protein on the hoof. The job calls for toughness that has little appeal to the sentimental. A typical cowboy would be laconic, patient, somewhat fatalistic, and prone to spend his wages on brawling and loose gallantry. His first duty is to cattle, and he has to have an eye for weather. Unpolished, but in his way invaluable. A rough job but someone's got to do it. And so forth. . . .
>
> [But today] the word "cowboy" has a special relationship with the state of Texas, its "lone star" logo, and the name of its Dallas football team. . . . President Bush has played to this strength, if it is a strength, at least three times. . . .
>
> Boiled down, the use of the word "cowboy" expresses a fixed attitude and an expectation, on the part of non-Texans, about people from Texas. It's a competition between a clichéd mentality . . . and a cliché itself. How well—apart from some "with us or with the terrorists" rhetoric—does the president fit the stereotype?
>
> –Christopher Hitchens, "Cowboy"

Bob Costas, eulogizing Mickey Mantle, a great baseball player who had many universally human faults, advances his assessment by means of an important definitional distinction:

> In the last year, Mickey Mantle, always so hard upon himself, finally came to accept and appreciate the distinction between a role model and a hero. The first he often was not, the second he always will be.
>
> –Bob Costas, "Eulogy for Mickey Mantle"

But arguments of definition can be less weighty than these, though still hotly contested: *Is video game playing a sport? Is Lil' Kim an artist? Is the Subaru Outback an SUV?* To argue such cases, one would first have to put forth definitions, and then those definitions would have to become the foci of debates themselves. (For more about arguments of definition, see Chapter 8.)

Arguments of Evaluation — What Is the Quality of the Thing?

Arguments of definition lead naturally into arguments of quality — that is, to questions about quality. Most auto enthusiasts, for example, wouldn't be content merely to inquire whether the Corvette is a sports car. They'd prefer to argue whether it's a *good* sports car or a better sports car than, say, the Viper. Or they might want to assert

An artist — or not? Lil' Kim arriving at the 2005 MTV Video Music Awards

that it's the best sports car in the world, perhaps qualifying their claim with the caveat *for the price.*

Arguments of evaluation are so common that writers sometimes take them for granted, ignoring their complexity and importance in establishing people's values and priorities. For instance, the stasis question "What is the quality of the thing?" is at the heart of attempts to understand the nuclear capability of North Korea. Strategists working to develop U.S. policy toward North Korea need to use this stasis question to develop a compelling argument of evaluation.

Consider how Rosa Parks assesses Martin Luther King Jr. in the following passage. Though she seems to be defining the concept of "leader," she's actually measuring King against criteria she has set for "*true* leader," an important distinction:

Dr. King was a true leader. I never sensed fear in him. I just felt he knew what had to be done and took the leading role without regard to consequences. I knew he was destined to do great things. He had an elegance about him and a speaking style that let you know where you stood and inspired you to do the best you could. He truly is a role model for us all. The sacrifice of his life should never be forgotten, and his dream must live on.

–Rosa Parks, "Role Models"

Parks's comments represent a type of informal evaluation that's common in ceremonial arguments; because King is so well known, she doesn't have to burnish every claim with specific evidence. (See p. 19 for more on ceremonial arguments.) In contrast, Molly Ivins in praising Barbara Jordan makes quite explicit the connections between her claim and the evidence:

Barbara Jordan, whose name was so often preceded by the words "the first black woman to . . ." that they seemed like a permanent title, died Wednesday in Austin. A great spirit is gone. The first black woman to serve in the Texas Senate, the first black woman in Congress (she and Yvonne Brathwaite Burke of California were both elected in 1972, but Jordan had no Republican opposition), the first black elected to

Barbara Jordan addressing fellow members of Congress in 1978

Congress from the South since Reconstruction, the first black woman to sit on major corporate boards, and so on. Were it not for the disease that slowly crippled her, she probably would have been the first black woman on the Supreme Court—it is known that Jimmy Carter had her on his short list.

And long before she became "the first and only black woman to . . ." there was that astounding string of achievements going back to high school valedictorian, honors at Texas Southern University, law degree from Boston University. Both her famous diction and her enormous dignity were present from the beginning, her high school teachers recalled. Her precise enunciation was a legacy from her father, a Baptist minister, and characteristic of educated blacks of his day. Her great baritone voice was so impressive that her colleagues in the Legislature used to joke that if Hollywood ever needed someone to be the voice of the Lord Almighty, only Jordan would do.

–Molly Ivins, "Barbara Jordan: A Great Spirit"

An argument of evaluation advances by presenting criteria and then measuring individual people, ideas, or things against those standards. Both the standards and the measurement can be explored argumentatively. And that's an important way to think of arguments—as ways to expand what's known, not just to settle differences. (For more about arguments of evaluation, see Chapter 9.)

Proposal Arguments—What Actions Should Be Taken?

In arguments that propose action, writers first have to succeed in presenting a problem in such a compelling way that readers ask: *What can we do?* A proposal argument often begins with the presentation of research to document existing conditions. Thus if you're developing an argument about rising tuition costs at your college, you could use all of the stasis questions to explore the issue and to establish that costs are indeed rising. But the last question—"What actions should be taken?"—will probably be the most important, since it will lead you to develop concrete proposals to address the rise in fees. Knowing and explaining the status quo enable writers to explore appropriate and viable alternatives and then to recommend one preferable course of action. In examining a nationwide move to eliminate remedial education in four-year colleges, John Cloud considers one possible proposal to avoid such action:

Students age 22 and over account for 43% of those in remedial classrooms, according to the National Center for Developmental Education.

[. . . But] 55% of those needing remediation must take just one course. Is it too much to ask them to pay extra for that class or take it at a community college?

–John Cloud, "Who's Ready for College?"

Where a need is already obvious, writers may spend most of their energies describing and defending the solution. U.S. senators Barack Obama and Richard Lugar, for example, assume that one great threat to national security comes from the next flu pandemic. Here they detail the steps necessary to solve this problem:

We recommend that this administration work with Congress, public health officials, the pharmaceutical industry, foreign governments and international organizations to create a permanent framework for curtailing the spread of future infectious diseases. Among the parts of that framework could be these: Increasing international disease surveillance, response capacity and public education, especially in Southeast Asia; Stockpiling enough antiviral doses to cover high-risk populations and essential workers; Ensuring that, here at home, Health and Human Services and state governments put in place plans that address issues of surveillance, medical care, drug and vaccine distribution, communication, protection of the work force, and main-

Veterinarian holding chicken to be tested for avian flu

tenance of core public functions in case of a pandemic; Accelerating research into avian flu vaccines and antiviral drugs; Establishing incentives to encourage nations to report flu outbreaks quickly and fully. So far, [avian flu] has not been found in the United States. But in an age when you can board planes in Bangkok or Hong Kong and arrive in Chicago, Indianapolis, or New York in hours, we must face the reality that these exotic killer diseases are not isolated health problems half a world away, but direct and immediate threats to security and prosperity here at home.

–Barack Obama and Richard Lugar, "Grounding a Pandemic"

Americans in particular tend to see the world in terms of problems and solutions; indeed, many expect that almost any difficulty can be overcome by the proper infusion of technology and money. So proposal arguments seem especially appealing to Americans, even though quick-fix attitudes may themselves constitute a problem. (For more about proposal arguments, see Chapter 11.)

STASIS QUESTIONS AT WORK

Suppose you have an opportunity to speak at a student conference on the issue of global warming. The Campus Young Republicans are sponsoring the conference, but they've made a point of inviting students with varying perspectives to speak. You are concerned about global warming and are tentatively in favor of strengthening industrial pollution standards aimed at reducing global warming trends. You decide that you'd like to learn a lot more by investigating the issue more fully and preparing to speak on it. You use the stasis questions to get started.

- **Did something happen?** Does global warming exist? Many in the oil and gas industry and some scientists who've studied the issue insist that global warming isn't a worldwide phenomenon, or that it essentially doesn't exist, or that the evidence is still inconclusive. The Bush administration, which had previously expressed skepticism, appeared to accept the phenomenon as real in 2005, though it still refused to sign an international agreement aimed at reducing global warming. Most scientists who've studied the issue and most other governments, on the other hand, argue that the phenomenon

(continued)

(continued)

A glacier in Central Asia turning into a lake. Are human causes responsible?

does indeed exist and that it has reached very serious proportions. In coming to your own conclusion about global warming, you'll weigh the factual evidence very carefully, making sure that you can support your answer to the question "Does it exist?" and that you can point out problems associated with opposing arguments.

- **What is the nature of the thing?** Looking for definitions of global warming also reveals great disagreement. To the extent that the Bush administration and the oil and gas industry acknowledge the phenomenon as real, they tend to define it as largely a matter of naturally occurring events (periodic long-term fluctuations in climate), while most scientists and other governments base their definition mostly on human causes (emissions of carbon dioxide and methane). Thus you begin to consider questions of cause and effect and competing definitions very carefully: *How do the definitions these groups choose to use foster the goals of each group? What's at stake*

(*continued*)

Washington, D.C., turning into a lake. Even in proposal arguments, humor can help.

"Gentlemen, it's time we gave some serious thought
to the effects of global warming."

for the administration and the industry in promoting their definition of global warming? What's at stake for the scientists and governments who put forth the opposing definition? Exploring this stasis question will help you understand how the context of an argument shapes the claims that the argument makes.

- **What is the quality of the thing?** This question will lead you to examine claims that global warming is—or is not—harming our environment. Again, you quickly find that these charges are hotly contested, as the energy industry and the Bush administration largely dismiss the claims by most scientists and governments that the phenomenon is causing great environmental harm. Exploring these arguments will allow you to ask who or what entities are providing evidence in support of their claim and who stands to gain in this analysis. *Where does evidence for the dangers of global warming*

(*continued*)

(*continued*)

come from? Who stands to gain if the dangers are accepted as real and present, and who stands to gain if they aren't?

- **What actions should be taken?** In this case as well, you find wide disagreement. If global warming is a naturally occurring phenomenon, or may not be causing serious harm, then it's at least arguable that nothing needs to be done, that the problem will correct itself in time. Or perhaps those in the administration who have made these arguments ought to sponsor a new study of global warming, in an effort to prove once and for all that their understanding of global warming and its effects is the correct one. If, on the other hand, global warming is caused mainly by human activity and poses a clear threat to the quality of the environment, then the administration is bound to recommend implementing appropriate and effective responses to such danger (although not everyone agrees on precisely what such responses should be). You quickly discover that the definitions and assessment of harm being used directly shape the actions (or lack of action) that each side recommends. As you investigate the proposals being made and the reasons that underlie them, you come closer and closer to developing your own argument.

Using the stasis questions as a way to get into the topic of global warming adds up to a crash course on the subject. As you sort through the claims and counterclaims associated with each of the questions, you move toward identifying your own stance on global warming—and toward the claim you want to make about it for the student conference. You come to the conclusion that global warming does exist and that it does present a serious danger. Yet given the audience for the conference, you know that you still have quite a bit of work to do. Since many conference attendees will not agree with your conclusion, you begin to gather the most fair and evenhanded research available to make your case, and you begin working to establish your own credibility and to consider how best you can present your case to your specific audience.

Audiences for Arguments

No argument, of course, even one that engages stasis questions thoroughly, can be effective unless it speaks compellingly to others. Audiences for argument exist across a range of possibilities—from the flesh-and-blood person sitting right across the table from you, to the "virtual" participants in an online conversation, to the imagined ideal readers a written text invites.

The figure below may help you think about your own wide range of possible readers or audiences.

Readers and writers in context

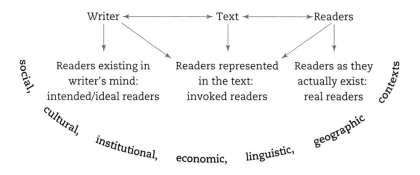

As a writer, you'll almost always be addressing an intended reader, one who exists in your own mind. As we write this textbook, we're certainly thinking of those who will read it: you are our intended reader, and ideally you know something about and are interested in the subject of this book. Though we don't know you personally, a version of you exists very much in us as writers, for we are *intending* to write for you. In the same way, the editors of student-produced *Soul Sistah* call out the audience they hope to address:

> *Soul Sistah* is a seasonal magazine dedicated to creatively exploring spirituality as it connects to black identity, womanhood, music, culture, and sexuality. Aiming to reach a multicultural readership and writership, *Soul Sistah* is addressed to everyone interested in understanding black women's experience as well as those seeking to explore their own spirituality. . . . By giving people a forum to express themselves honestly, *Soul Sistah* creates intimacy among readers, writers, and editors.
>
> –Editors of *Soul Sistah*

This passage reflects the editors' intention of talking to a certain group of people. But if texts—including visual texts—have intended readers (those the writer consciously intends to address), they also have invoked

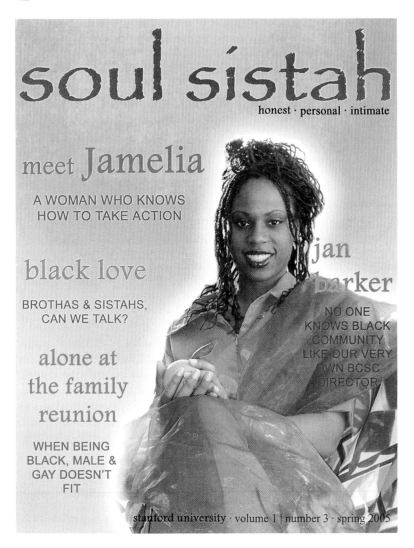

Soul Sistah, a campus magazine

readers (those who can be seen represented in the text). Later in this chapter, for example, "you" (our audience) are invoked as one who recognizes the importance of respecting readers. For another example, look at the first paragraph of this chapter; it invokes readers who are interested in the goals of argument, whether those goals are overt or subtle. And the editors of *Soul Sistah* also invoke particular readers—those interested in honest self-expression and spirituality.

Note that in spite of invoking a particular audience, the editors don't use the pronouns *we* or *us* but instead rely on *everyone*. Although the use of personal pronouns can often help make readers feel a connection to the writer, it can also be dangerous: if readers don't fit into the *us*, they can easily feel excluded from a text, and thus disaffected from it. Such is the risk that writer bell hooks takes in the passage below:

> The most powerful resource any of us can have as we study and teach in university settings is full understanding and appreciation of the richness, beauty, and primacy of our familial and community backgrounds.
>
> –bell hooks, "Keeping Close to Home: Class and Education"

This sentence reflects hooks's intention of talking to a certain *us*—"we [who] study and teach in university settings." Readers who don't fit into such an *us* may feel excluded from this group and thus from hooks's essay. And even those for whom this isn't an issue may feel alienated by hooks's celebration of "the richness, beauty, and primacy of our familial and community backgrounds." Readers who see their own backgrounds as lacking in richness or beauty—or those who came to college precisely to get away from the "primacy" of their families or communities—may well not read beyond the "our" to see how hooks develops this argument.

In addition to intended readers and the readers invoked by the text of the argument, any argument will have "real" readers—and these real people may not be the ones intended or even the ones that the text calls forth. You may pick up a letter written to someone else, for instance, and read it even though it's not intended for you. Even more likely, you may read email not sent to you but rather forwarded (sometimes unwittingly) from someone else. Or you may read a legal brief prepared for a lawyer and struggle to understand it, since you're neither the intended reader nor the knowledgeable legal expert invoked in the text. As these examples suggest, writers can't always (or even usually) control who the real readers of any argument will be. As a writer, then, you want to think carefully about these real readers and to summon up what you do know about them, even if that knowledge is limited.

When Julia Carlisle wrote an op-ed article for the *New York Times* about being "young, urban, professional, and unemployed," she intended to address readers who would sympathize with her plight; her piece invokes such readers through the use of the pronoun *we* and examples meant to suggest that she and those like her want very much to work at jobs that aren't "absurd." But Carlisle ran into many readers who felt not only excluded from her text but highly offended by it. One reader, Florence Hoff, made clear in a letter to the editor that she didn't sympathize with Carlisle at all. In fact, she saw Carlisle as self-indulgent, as feeling entitled to one kind of job while rejecting others—the jobs that Hoff and others like her are only too glad to hold. In this instance, Carlisle needed to think not only of her intended readers or of the readers her text invited in, but also of all the various "real" readers who were likely to encounter her article in the *Times*.

Considering Contexts

No consideration of readers can be complete without setting those readers in context. In fact, reading always takes place in what you might think of as a series of contexts—concentric circles that move outward from the most immediate context (the specific place and time in which the reading occurs) to broader and broader contexts, including local and community contexts, institutional contexts (such as school, church, or business) and cultural and linguistic contexts. Julia Carlisle's article, for instance, was written at a specific time and place (New York City in 1991), under certain economic conditions (increasing unemployment), and from the point of view of a white, college-educated, and fairly privileged person addressing an audience made up mostly of the same kind of people.

If Everything's an Argument . . .

Work with one or two members of your class to examine the front and back covers of this textbook. What arguments do you find being made there? How do these arguments shape your understanding of this text's purposes? What use do the covers make of emotional, ethical, and/or logical appeals? What other kinds of images or words might have been used to achieve this purpose more effectively? What audience do these covers seem to address—and how do they do so?

Thinking carefully about the context of an argument will almost always raise questions of value. Such is the case with Julia Carlisle's letter and the response it evoked: here we can see a clear clash of values, with Carlisle implicitly valuing and privileging white-collar jobs while Hoff's response calls Carlisle on her values and suggests that Hoff holds a different set of values that gives respect to blue-collar work as well. In fact, beliefs and values are often implicit rather than spelled out explicitly in arguments. But sometimes it's important to be very specific. Such was the case with Sharon Clahchischilliage, a Navajo woman who wanted to run for Secretary of State in New Mexico, even though doing so would require her to resist some of the values of her own culture. As a report in the *Washington Times* explains,

Fighting for honest elections!

Sharon
Clahchischilliage
Secretary of State

Sharon Clahchischilliage's campaign flyer

> By placing her face on billboards around the state and publicizing her justcallmesharon.com Web site, she is bucking tribal customs. Navajos as a rule do not stare people in the eyes, nor ask for money or boast about their capabilities.
>
> "I'm going against the norms of my culture," she admits, "just by being a candidate."
>
> –Julia Duin, "Navajo Woman Vies for Political Distinction"

As we have seen, such broader contexts and the values they entail always affect both you as a writer of arguments and those who will read and respond to your arguments. As such, they deserve your careful investigation. As you compose arguments of your own, you need to think carefully about the contexts that surround your readers—and to put your topic in context as well.

Appealing to Audiences

Twenty-five hundred years ago, Aristotle identified three key ways writers can appeal to their audiences in arguments; he labeled these appeals *pathos, ethos,* and *logos.* These general appeals are as effective today as they were in Aristotle's time, though we usually think of them in slightly different terms:

- pathos — emotional appeals or appeals to the heart
- ethos — ethical appeals or appeals based on the writer's authority and credibility
- logos — logical appeals or appeals to reason

Emotional Appeals

Human beings often respond strongly to emotional appeals that tug at the heartstrings. While facts and figures (or logical appeals) may convince us that the AIDS epidemic in Africa is real and serious, what elicits an outpouring of support is the emotional power of televised images and

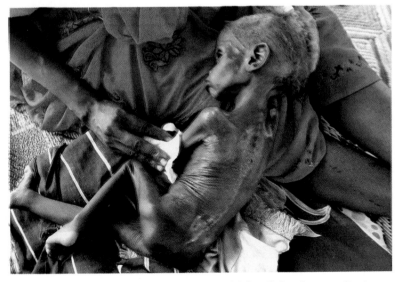

A starkly visual emotional appeal: a mother holds her ill daughter at a Doctors Without Borders clinic in Sudan, where violence and disease are killing tens of thousands.

newspaper accounts of suffering people. Concrete and descriptive language can paint pictures in readers' minds, thus building in emotional appeal, as in the following example from a student argument about providing better campus access for those using wheelchairs: "Marie inched her heavy wheelchair up the narrow, steep entrance ramp to the library, her arms straining to pull up the last twenty feet, her face pinched with the sheer effort of it." In addition, figurative language—metaphors, similes, analogies, and so on—can capture attention and appeal to emotions. In a scathing review of *Star Wars: Episode III*, reviewer Anthony Lane of the *New Yorker* uses a metaphor to stir an emotion in his readers—in this case, derision at how bad the movie is: "We already know the outcome—Anakin will indeed drop the killer-monk Jedi look and become Darth Vader, the hockey goalkeeper from hell." And, as we've already noted, visuals can make very powerful appeals to emotion. (For more about emotional appeals, see Chapter 2.)

Ethical Appeals

Equally important to an argument's success is the writer's ethos, or presentation of self. Audiences respond well to writers or speakers who seem authoritative or trustworthy. You can thus make ethical appeals to any audience by demonstrating that you're knowledgeable—you know what you're talking about and can make your case. In a researched article about the cost of protection against terrorism, for example, writer William Finnegan introduces a series of facts to support the argument that New York is having to protect itself with little help from the federal government: "In fiscal year 2004, Wyoming received $37.74 [in Homeland Security funds] per capita, and North Dakota $30.82, while New York got $5.41." Another good way to project authority is to mention your qualifications, though not in a boastful way: "My three-month observation of the communications procedures in a highly successful software firm demonstrates that. . . ."

In addition, you can build credibility in various other ways: by highlighting values that you and your audience share, by demonstrating that you're fair and evenhanded, and by showing that you respect your audience. A writer of an argument urging smokers to support a ban on smoking in restaurants might begin, for example, by saying, "For ten years I was a serious smoker, and I know how serious the addiction can be," thus demonstrating shared experiences and empathy for the audience. One final important aspect of establishing both your authority and your

U.S. Environmental Protection Agency

. . . to protect human health and the environment

A homepage that makes an ethical appeal

credibility is acknowledging opposing views and, if necessary, their strengths and the limitations of your own argument: "This proposal won't solve all the problems with the project, but it will at least put it on a more solid financial basis."

Visuals can make ethical appeals as well. For example, the banner on the homepage of the U.S. Environmental Protection Agency (above) aims to establish its credibility. The title emphasizes that this page has the authority of a U.S. government agency behind it. Underneath the title of the sponsoring agency are three pictures — of rows of healthy crops, a beautiful coastline, and a clean-looking city, each chosen to illustrate values Americans hold in common. The caption echoes the goal of protecting human health and the environment, thus making a strong ethical appeal in a very small space. (For more about ethical appeals, see Chapter 3.)

Logical Appeals

Appeals to logic are often given most prominence and authority in U.S. culture: "just the facts, ma'am," a famous early television detective used to say. Indeed, audiences respond well to the use of logic — to facts, statistics, credible testimony, cogent examples, even a narrative or story that embodies a good sound reason in support of an argument. Traditionally, logical arguments are identified as using either inductive or deductive reasoning, but in practice the two almost always work together. *Inductive reasoning* is the process of drawing a generalization on the basis of a number of specific examples: if you become sick on several occasions after eating shellfish, for instance, you'll likely draw the inductive conclusion that you're allergic to such food. *Deductive reasoning,* on the other hand, reaches a conclusion by assuming a general principle (called the major premise) and then applying that principle to a specific case (called the minor premise). The inductive generalization "Shellfish makes me ill," for example, could serve as the major premise

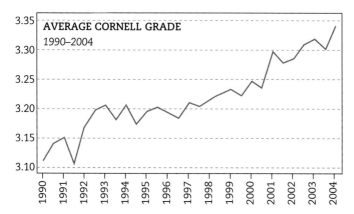

Grade inflation at Cornell. *Source:* "Society: Gut Check," *Atlantic Monthly,* June 2005, p. 44.

for a deductive chain of reasoning: "Since all shellfish makes me ill, I shouldn't eat the shrimp on this buffet." If you can draw sound inductive or deductive conclusions, and present them clearly in either words or images, they can exert strong appeals to your audience. The figure above shows a visual that makes a logical appeal about the existence of grade inflation at Cornell University. (For more about logical appeals, see Chapter 4.)

Arguments and Their Rhetorical Situations

In this chapter, we've been examining elements of argument one at a time, moving from purposes and kinds of arguments to identifying the crux of any argument (its stasis) and to ways to formulate arguments in ways that appeal to audiences. This discussion has emphasized the social nature of argument, the fact that even if we're arguing with ourselves there's some give-and-take involved, and that the argument exists in a particular context of some kind that influences how it can be shaped and how others will receive it. *The rhetorical situation* is a shorthand phrase for this entire set of concerns, and it can be depicted as a simple triangle. (See the figure on p. 42.)

It's important to think about your rhetorical situation as dynamic, since each element of it has the potential to affect all the other elements. A change of audience, for example, can lead you to reconsider all of your appeals. If you begin to think in this dynamic way, you'll be

The rhetorical triangle

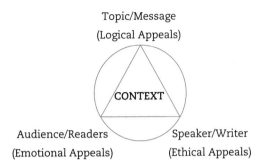

Topic/Message
(Logical Appeals)

CONTEXT

Audience/Readers   Speaker/Writer
(Emotional Appeals)   (Ethical Appeals)

developing a rhetorical turn of mind: you'll find yourself viewing any topic from a number of perspectives (*what might a different audience think of this?*) and hence develop greater critical engagement with the issues and ideas most important to you. Such a rhetorical frame of mind might even lead you to challenge the title of this textbook: Is everything *really an argument?*

RESPOND •

1. Can an argument really be any text that expresses a point of view? What kinds of arguments—if any—might be made by the following items?

   the embossed leather cover of a prayer book

   a Boston Red Sox cap

   a Livestrong bracelet

   the label on a best-selling rap CD

   the health warning on a package of cigarettes

   a belated birthday card

   the nutrition label on a can of soup

   the cover of a science fiction novel

   a colored ribbon pinned to a shirt lapel

   a Rolex watch

2. Write short paragraphs describing times in the recent past when you've used language to inform, to convince, to explore, to make decisions, and to meditate or pray. Be sure to write at least one paragraph

for each of these purposes. Then decide whether each paragraph describes an act of argument, persuasion, or both, and offer some reasons in defense of your decisions. In class, trade paragraphs with a partner, and decide whether his or her descriptions accurately fit the categories to which they've been assigned. If they don't, then work with your partner to figure out why. Is the problem with the descriptions? The categories? Both? Neither?

3. In a recent newspaper or periodical, find three editorials—one that makes a ceremonial argument, one a deliberative argument, and one a forensic argument. Analyze the arguments by asking these questions: *Who is arguing? What purposes are the writers trying to achieve? To whom are they directing their arguments?* Then consider whether the arguments' purposes have been achieved in each case. If they have, offer some reasons for the arguments' success.

4. What common experiences—if any—do the following objects, brand names, and symbols evoke, and for what audiences in particular?

   a USDA organic label

   the Nike swoosh

   the golden arches

   the Sean John label as seen on its Web site

a can of Coca-Cola

Sleeping Beauty's castle on the Disney logo

Oprah Winfrey

the Vietnam Veterans Memorial

Ground Zero

a dollar bill

5. Read the main editorial in your campus newspaper for three or four days. Then choose the most interesting one, and consider how the editor creates credibility, or ethos, in the editorial.

6. Take a look at the bumper sticker below, and then analyze it. What is its purpose? What kind of argument is it? Which of the stasis questions does it most appropriately respond to? What appeals does it make to its readers, and how?

2
Arguments from the Heart—*Pathos*

What makes you glance at a magazine ad long enough to notice a product? These days, it's probably an image or boldfaced words promising pleasure (a Caribbean beach), excitement (extreme diving on Maui), beauty (a model in low-rise jeans), security (a strong firefighter), or good health (more models). In the blink of an eye, ads can appeal to your emotions, intrigue you, perhaps even seduce you. Look closer, and you might find good logical reasons given for buying a product or service. But would you have even gotten there without an emotional tug to pull you into the page?

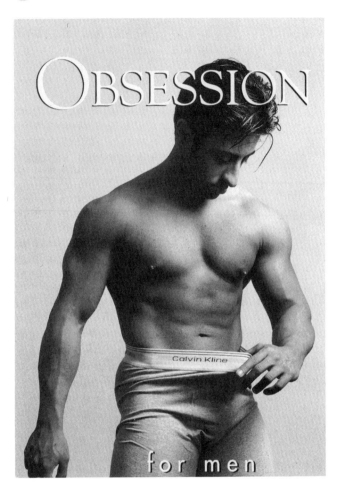

This image parodies ads that exploit one of the most powerful of emotional appeals.

Emotional appeals (sometimes called appeals to *pathos*) are powerful tools for influencing what people think and believe. We all make decisions—even important ones—based on our feelings. We rent funky apartments or buy zonked-out cars because we fall in love with some small detail. On impulse, we collect whole racks of shirts or shoes we're later too embarrassed to wear. We date, maybe even marry, people everyone else seemed to know are wrong for us — and sometimes it works out just fine.

That may be because we're not computers that use cost/benefit analyses to choose our friends or make our political decisions. Feelings belong in our lives. There's a powerful moment in Shakespeare's *Macbeth* when the soldier Macduff learns that his wife and children have been executed by the power-mad king. A well-meaning friend urges Macduff to "dispute it like a man." Macduff responds gruffly, "But I must also feel it as a man" (*Macbeth,* 4.3.219–21). As a writer, you must learn like Macduff to appreciate legitimate emotions, particularly when you want to influence the public. When you hear that formal or academic arguments should rely solely on facts, remember that facts alone often won't carry the day, even for a worthy cause. The civil rights struggle of the 1960s is a particularly good example of a movement that persuaded people equally by means of the reasonableness and the passion of its claims.

Of course, you don't have to look hard for less noble campaigns fueled with emotions such as hatred, envy, and greed. Democracies suffer when people use emotional arguments (and related fallacies such as personal attacks and name-calling) to drive wedges between groups, making them fearful and hateful. For that reason, writers can't use emotional appeals casually. (For more about emotional fallacies, see Chapter 17.)

Understanding How Emotional Arguments Work

You already know that words, images, and sounds can arouse emotions. In fact, the stirrings they generate are often physical. You've likely had the clichéd "chill down the spine" or felt something in the "pit of the stomach" when a speaker (or photograph or event) hits precisely the right note. On such occasions, it's likely that the speaker has you and people like you very purposefully in mind. At Stanford's Black Graduation ceremony in June 2005, graduating senior Efundunke Hughes was elected by her classmates to address the convocation of graduates, their parents, and friends. Speaking directly to them, Hughes called on all the students there to think not of their own achievements but rather of their ancestors, their grandparents, and especially their parents to whom they owed their success: "Stand with me today to acknowledge

Not Just Words

Take a look at this image, at first glance the familiar stars and stripes of the American flag. But a second glance reveals corporate logos rather than stars. Now look carefully at the picture, and then write for two or three minutes about the emotions that the image arouses in you. Do you respond first to the flag and then to the logos? What clash of emotional appeals do you see here, and how do you feel about that conflict? Try your hand at creating one or two possible titles or captions for this image.

and honor *them,* those who have loved and supported and nurtured us: only by standing on *their* strong shoulders have we been able to reach our dreams and goals. So stand now and begin to thank them." The audience at this commencement ceremony rose to their feet with long applause and loud cheers—for all those who had helped the students there.

Sometimes speakers are called upon to address not a particular group (such as a graduation gathering) but an entire nation, even the entire world. Such was the case during World War II when Prime Minister Winston Churchill spoke to the British House of Commons on June 4, 1940, seeking to raise British spirits and strengthen their resolve in resisting the German attacks:

> We shall not flag or fail. We shall go on to the end. We shall fight in France, we shall fight on the seas and oceans, we shall fight with growing confidence and growing strength in the air, we shall defend our island, whatever the cost may be, we shall fight on the beaches, we shall fight on the landing grounds, we shall fight in the fields and in the streets, we shall fight in the hills. We shall never surrender.
>
> —Winston Churchill, "We Shall Fight on the Beaches"

When writers and speakers can find the words and images to evoke certain emotions in people, they might also move their audiences to sympathize with ideas they connect to those feelings, and even to act on them. Make people aware of how much they owe to others, and they'll acknowledge that debt; make people hate an enemy, and they'll rally against him; help people to imagine suffering, and they'll strive to relieve it; make people feel secure or happy (or insecure or unhappy), and they'll buy products that promise such good feelings.

Arguments from the heart probably count more when you're persuading than when you're arguing. When arguing, you might use reasons and evidence to convince readers something is true—for instance, that preserving wetlands is a worthy environmental goal. When persuading, however, you want people to take action—to join an environmental boycott, contribute money to an organization dedicated to wetlands protection, or write a well-researched op-ed piece for the local paper about a local marsh threatened by development.

Argument (discover a truth) ———► conviction
Persuasion (know a truth)   ———► action

He Ain't Heavy, We're All Brothers.

Photo by Caroline Irby

In Sudan, where civil war has ravaged and emptied thousands of villages, we are bringing food, water, health care and protection to 350,000 children and families in 44 camps. Save the Children is the leading independent organization creating lasting change for children in need in the U.S. and around the world.

 **Save the Children.**

To learn more about our work, contact Fiona Hodgson
203-221-4002   fiona@savechildren.org   54 Wilton Road, Westport, CT 06880
www.savethechildren.org

Save the Children motivates contributors with a touching image and an inspiring story.

The practical differences between being convinced and acting on a conviction can be enormous. Your readers may agree that contributing to charity is a noble act, but that conviction may not be enough to persuade them to part with their spare change. You need a spur sharper than logic, and that's when emotion might kick in. You can embarrass readers into contributing to a good cause ("Change a child's life for the price of a pizza") or make them feel the impact of their gift ("Imagine the smile on that little child's face") or tell them a moving story ("In a tiny village in Central America . . ."). Doubtless, you've seen such techniques work.

Using Emotions to Build Bridges

You may sometimes want to use emotions to connect with readers, to assure them that you understand their experiences or, to use a famous political line, "feel their pain." Such a bridge is especially important when you're writing about matters that readers regard as sensitive. Before they'll trust you, they'll want assurances that you understand the issues in depth. If you strike the right emotional note, you'll establish an important connection.

That's what Apple founder Steve Jobs does in a 2005 commencement address, in which he tells the audience that he doesn't have a fancy speech, just three stories from his life:

> My second story is about love and loss. I was lucky. I found what I loved to do early in life. Woz and I started Apple in my parents' garage when I was twenty. We worked hard and in ten years, Apple had grown from just the two of us in a garage into a $2 billion company with over 4,000 employees. We'd just released our finest creation, the Macintosh, a year earlier, and I'd just turned thirty, and then I got fired. How can you get fired from a company you started? Well, as Apple grew, we hired someone who I thought was very talented to run the company with me, and for the first year or so, things went well. But then our visions of the future began to diverge, and eventually we had a falling out. When we did, our board of directors sided with him, and so at thirty, I was out, and very publicly out. . . .
>
> I didn't see it then, but it turned out that getting fired from Apple was the best thing that could have ever happened to me. The heaviness of being successful was replaced by the lightness of being a beginner again, less sure about everything. It freed me to enter one of the most creative periods in my life. During the next five years I started a company named NeXT, another company named Pixar and fell in love with an amazing woman who would become my wife. Pixar went on to create the world's first computer-animated feature

film, "Toy Story," and is now the most successful animation studio in the world.

–Steve Jobs, "You've Got to Find What You Love, Jobs Says"

In no obvious way is Jobs's recollection a formal argument. But it prepares his audience to accept the advice he'll give later in his speech, at least partly because he's speaking from deep personal experiences of his own.

A more obvious way to build an emotional tie is simply to help readers identify with your experiences. If, like Georgina Kleege, you were blind and wanted to argue for more sensible attitudes toward blind people, you might ask readers in the very first paragraph of your argument to confront their prejudices. Here Kleege, a writer and college instructor, makes an emotional point by telling a story:

> I tell the class, "I am legally blind." There is a pause, a collective intake of breath. I feel them look away uncertainly and then look back. After all, I just said I couldn't see. Or did I? I had managed to get there on my own—no cane, no dog, none of the usual trappings of blindness. Eyeing me askance now, they might detect that my gaze is not quite focused. . . . They watch me glance down, or towards the door where someone's coming in late. I'm just like anyone else.
>
> –Georgina Kleege, "Call It Blindness"

Given the way she narrates the first day of class, readers are as likely to identify with the students as with Kleege, imagining themselves sitting in a classroom, facing a sightless instructor, confronting their own prejudices about the blind. Kleege wants to put them on edge emotionally.

Let's consider another rhetorical situation: how do you win over an audience when the logical claims you're making are likely to go against what many in the audience believe? Once again, a slightly risky appeal to emotions on a personal level may work. That's the tack Michael Pollan takes in bringing readers to consider that "the great moral struggle of our time will be for the rights of animals." In introducing his lengthy exploratory argument, Pollan uses personal experience to appeal to his audience:

> The first time I opened Peter Singer's *Animal Liberation,* I was dining alone at the Palm, trying to enjoy a rib-eye steak cooked medium-rare. If this sounds like a good recipe for cognitive dissonance (if not indigestion), that was sort of the idea. Preposterous as it might seem to

A visual version of Michael Pollan's rhetorical situation

THE BIRTH OF A VEGETARIAN

supporters of animal rights, what I was doing was tantamount to reading *Uncle Tom's Cabin* on a plantation in the Deep South in 1852.

– Michael Pollan, "An Animal's Place"

In creating a vivid image of his first encounter with Singer's book, Pollan's opening builds a bridge between himself as a person trying to enter into the animal rights debate in a fair and open-minded, if still skeptical, way and readers who will surely be passionate about either side of this argument.

If Everything's an Argument . . .

Look at the opening pages of this chapter, and note the words and images that give, as the first paragraph puts it, an "emotional tug to pull you into the page." Given that these pages are trying to impress on college students the importance of emotional appeals in arguments, how well do they accomplish that goal? Are there other things the authors and editors might have done to make these pages even more emotionally appealing to this audience?

Using Emotions to Sustain an Argument

You can also use emotional appeals to make logical claims stronger or more memorable. That is, in fact, the way photographs and other images add power to arguments. In a TV attack ad, the scowling black-and-white photograph of a political opponent may do as much damage as the claim that his bank laundered drug money. Or the attractive skier in a spot for lip balm may make us yearn for brisk, snowy winter days. The technique is tricky, however. Lay on too much emotion—especially those like outrage, pity, or shame, which make people uncomfortable—and you may offend the very

Mukhtaran Bibi in September 2004

audiences you hoped to convince. But sometimes a strong emotion such as anger adds energy to a passage, as it does when columnist Nicholas Kristof berates the Pakistani government for imprisoning Mukhtaran Bibi—a woman who had done nothing except speak out against gang rape and the U.S. government for its refusal to condemn such actions—and accompanies his column with a picture of the woman he is trying to help. As you read the excerpt from Kristof's editorial, ask yourself why that particular picture was chosen to accompany the text. What does it add to the emotional pull of the argument? (Consider the positioning of the woman and her expression and gesture, as well as the use of color.)

> Excuse me, but Ms. Mukhtaran, a symbol of courage and altruism, is the best hope for Pakistan's image. The threat to Pakistan's image comes from President Musharraf for all this thuggish behavior.
>
> I've been sympathetic to Mr. Musharraf till now, despite his nuclear negligence. . . . So even when Mr. Musharraf denied me visas all this year, to block me from visiting Ms. Mukhtaran again and writing a follow-up column, I bit my tongue.
>
> But now President Musharraf has gone nuts.
>
> "This is all because they think they have the support of the U.S. and can get away with murder," Ms. Jahangir said. Indeed, on Friday, just as all this was happening, President Bush received Pakistan's foreign minister in the White House and praised President Musharraf's "bold leadership."

So, Mr. Bush, how about asking Mr. Musharraf to focus on finding Osama, instead of kidnapping rape victims who speak out? And invite Ms. Mukhtaran to the Oval Office—to show that Americans stand not only with generals who seize power, but also with ordinary people of extraordinary courage.

–Nicholas Kristof, "Raped, Kidnapped, and Silenced"

Here the challenge in Kristof's sarcasm becomes part of the argument: *If you act in the way President Musharraf has done, you open yourself to such a powerful response.*

In the same way, writers can generate emotions by presenting logical arguments in their starkest terms, stripped of qualifications or subtleties. Readers or listeners are confronted with core issues or important choices and asked to consider the consequences. It's hard to imagine an argument more serious than a debate about life and death, or one more likely to raise powerful feelings. Here is Andrew Sullivan on his blog in June 2005, commenting on the report that autopsy results on Terri Schiavo, the Florida woman whose family had fought bitterly over whether or not to

Demonstrators and politicians used highly charged language and images in their unsuccessful efforts to prevent Terri Schiavo's husband from removing her life support systems.

stop the life support systems that had been keeping her alive for over a decade, showed that she would never have been able to recover:

> 1:09 P.M. June 15, 2005. In her final days, Terri Schiavo was blind and her brain was about half its expected size. She wasn't in a PVS [Persistent Vegetative State]? Please. Bill Frist needs to acknowledge his reckless political opportunism at the time. The attempts of the fringe, theocon right to allege that her husband abused her have also been exposed as malicious falsehoods. Remember the lies that were told, the junk science that the theocons came up with, the endless slanders and misrepresentations? It's rare that we get an objective resolution of a fiercely disputed matter. We have now. And it ain't pretty.
>
> —Andrew Sullivan, "They Lied"

You might imagine how an opponent of suspending life support might respond: *Nothing can ever justify such an action.* Would a less in-your-face approach appeal more successfully to such an audience, or is Sullivan right to take the emotional issue head on—and with his own emotions clearly on display?

As you can see, it's difficult to gauge how much emotion will work in a given argument. Some issues—such as racism, date rape, abortion, gun control—provoke strong feelings and, as a result, are often argued on emotional terms. But even issues that seem deadly dull—such as funding for Medicare and Social Security—can be argued in emotional terms when proposed changes in these programs are set in human terms: *Cut benefits and Grandma will have to eat cat food; don't cut benefits and the whole health care system will go broke, leaving nothing for aging baby boomers.* Both alternatives might scare people into paying enough attention to take political action.

Using Humor

Humor has always played an important role in argument, sometimes as the sugar that makes the medicine go down. You can certainly slip humor into an argument to put readers at ease, thereby making them more open to a proposal you have to offer. It's hard to say "no" when you're laughing. Humor also makes otherwise sober people suspend their judgment and even their prejudices, perhaps because the surprise and naughtiness of wit are combustive: they provoke laughter or smiles, not reflection. That may be why TV sitcoms like *Sex and the City* or *Will & Grace* have become popular with mainstream audiences, despite their sometimes controversial subjects. Similarly, it's possible to make a point through humor that might not work at all in more sober writing. Consider the gross stereotypes about men that humorist Dave Barry presents here, tongue in cheek, explaining why people don't read the instructions that come with the products they buy:

> The third reason why consumers don't read manuals is that many consumers are men, and we men would no more read a manual than we would ask directions, because this would be an admission that the person who wrote the manual has a bigger . . . OK, a bigger grasp of technology than we do. We men would rather hook up our new DVD player in such a way that it ignites the DVDs and shoots them across the room—like small flaming UFOs—than admit that the manual-writer possesses a more manly technological manhood than we do.
> –Dave Barry, "Owners' manual Step No. 1: Bang head against the wall"

Our laughter testifies to a kernel of truth in Barry's observations and makes us more likely to agree with his conclusions.

A writer or speaker can use humor to deal with especially sensitive issues. For example, sports commentator Bob Costas, given the honor of eulogizing the great baseball player Mickey Mantle, couldn't ignore well-known flaws in Mantle's character. So he argues for Mantle's greatness by admitting the man's weaknesses indirectly through humor:

> It brings to mind a story Mickey liked to tell on himself and maybe some of you have heard it. He pictured himself at the pearly gates, met by St. Peter who shook his head and said "Mick, we checked the record. We know some of what went on. Sorry, we can't let you in. But before you go, God wants to know if you'd sign these six dozen baseballs."
> –Bob Costas, "Eulogy for Mickey Mantle"

Similarly, politicians use humor to admit problems or mistakes they couldn't acknowledge in any other way. Here, for example, is President Bush at the 2004 Radio & TV Correspondents Dinner discussing his much-mocked intellect:

> Those stories about my intellectual capacity do get under my skin. You know, for a while I even thought my staff believed it. There on my schedule first thing every morning it said, "Intelligence briefing."
> –George W. Bush

Not all humor is well intentioned. In fact, among the most powerful forms of emotional argument is ridicule—humor aimed at a particular target. Eighteenth-century poet and critic Samuel Johnson was known

for his stinging and humorous putdowns, such as this comment to an aspiring writer: "Your manuscript is both good and original, but the part that is good is not original and the part that is original is not good." Today, even bumper stickers can be vehicles for succinct arguments (see the figure above).

But ridicule is a two-edged sword that requires a deft hand to wield it. Humor that reflects bad taste discredits a writer completely, as does ridicule that misses its mark. Unless your target deserves assault and you can be very funny, it's usually better to steer clear of humor. (For more on humorous arguments, see Chapter 13.)

Using Arguments from the Heart

You don't want to play puppetmaster with people's emotions when you write arguments, but it's a good idea to spend some time early in your writing or designing process thinking about how you want readers to feel as they consider your persuasive claims. For example, would readers of your editorial about campus traffic policies be more inclined to agree with you if you made them envy faculty privileges, or would arousing their sense of fairness work better? What emotional appeals might persuade meat eaters to consider a vegan diet—or vice versa? Would sketches of stage props on a Web site persuade people to buy a season ticket to the theater, or would you spark more interest by featuring pictures of costumed performers?

Consider, too, the impact that telling a story can have on readers. Writers and journalists routinely use what are called human interest stories to give presence to issues or arguments. You can do the same, using a particular incident to evoke sympathy, understanding, outrage, or amusement. Take care, though, to tell an honest story.

RESPOND●

1. To what specific emotions do the following slogans, sales pitches, and maxims appeal?

"Just do it." (ad for Nike)

"Think different." (ad for Apple Computers)

"Reach out and touch someone." (ad for AT&T)

"In your heart, you know he's right." (1964 campaign slogan for U.S. presidential candidate Barry Goldwater, a conservative)

"It's the economy, stupid!" (1992 campaign theme for U.S. presidential candidate Bill Clinton)

"By any means necessary." (rallying cry from Malcolm X)

"Have it your way." (slogan for Burger King)

"You can trust your car to the man who wears the star." (slogan for Texaco)

"It's everywhere you want to be." (slogan for Visa)

"Know what comes between me and my Calvins? Nothing!" (tag line for Calvin Klein jeans)

"Don't mess with Texas!" (antilitter campaign slogan)

2. Bring a magazine to class, and analyze the emotional appeals in as many full-page ads as you can. Then classify those ads by types of emotional appeal, and see whether you can connect the appeals to the subject or target audience of the magazine. Compare your results with those of your classmates, and discuss your findings. For instance, do the ads in newsmagazines like *Time* and *Newsweek* appeal to different emotions and desires from the ads in publications such as *Cosmopolitan, Rolling Stone, Sports Illustrated, Automobile,* and *National Geographic?*

3. How do arguments from the heart work in different media? Are such arguments more or less effective in books, articles, television (both news and entertainment shows), films, brochures, magazines, email, Web sites, the theater, street protests, and so on? You might focus on a single medium, exploring how it handles emotional appeals, or compare different media. For example, why do Internet news groups seem to encourage angry outbursts? Are newspapers an emotionally colder source of information than television news programs? If so, why?

4. Spend some time looking for arguments that use ridicule or humor to make their point—check out your favorite Web sites; watch for bumper stickers, posters, or advertisements; and listen to popular lyrics. Bring one or two examples to class, and be ready to explain how the humor makes an emotional appeal and whether it's effective or not.

3
Arguments Based on Character—*Ethos*

It was a memorable moment—Massachusetts senator John Kerry walking up to the podium at the Democratic National Convention in 2004 to accept his party's nomination for president and beginning his speech with a smart military salute and these words:

"I'm John Kerry, and I'm reporting for duty."

It made a fine image too, suggesting powerfully that the Democratic Party had chosen a presidential candidate with real credentials to serve as commander-in-chief in time of war, unlike incumbent President George W. Bush, whose Air National Guard record during the

John Kerry at the Democratic National Convention, July 29, 2004

Vietnam era was regularly (if sometimes inaccurately) called into question by mainstream media. Kerry, in contrast, had actually fought in Vietnam and received three Purple Hearts. By his salute, Kerry affirmed that having served his country once, he was ready to do so again. He was making an argument based on character, or *ethos* — the presentation of self that a writer or speaker brings to an argument.

Audiences clearly pay attention to ethos. Before we'll listen to others, we usually must respect their authority, admire their integrity and motives, or at least acknowledge what they stand for. "Others," of course, can be a person, such as presidential candidate John Kerry; a group or organization, like the American Civil Liberties Union or Students for Academic Freedom; or an institution, such as a corporation, newspaper, or college. We observe people, groups, or institutions making and defending claims all the time and ask ourselves: *Should we pay attention to them? Can we trust them?* Establishing a persuasive ethos, however, is not simply a matter of seeming honest or likable but also of affirming an identity and sharing values with one's intended audiences.

Touch the photo to see which Swift officers support John Kerry, or click it to read more.

The purpose of this photo is to correct the misleading use of our images—
against our will—to further John Kerry's campaign.

Not Just Words

A group called Swift Vets and POWs for Truth used a number of visual arguments in an attempt to undermine Senator John Kerry's ethos during the presidential campaign of 2004. One argument involved a photograph the group claimed the Kerry campaign had used without authorization to suggest that all soldiers who fought with him in Vietnam supported his presidential bid. The group took advantage of the graphic capabilities of the Web to make its point.

- Do some research to explore the facts surrounding the use of the "Band of Brothers" photograph. How well does the visual

John Kerry's Band of Brothers?

presentation alone convey the complexities of the situation? You might explore campaign Web sites (many of which are archived) or coverage in newspapers and magazines, using such resources as LexisNexis and EBSCO.

- What issues of ethos does this visual argument raise? What questions does it raise about Kerry? What questions might it raise about the Swift Vets and POWs for Truth?

- Working in a group, imagine arguments that might use a similar technique, especially on issues of value or character. Choose one of the ideas, and create a full mock-up of the argument, either on paper or on the Web.

For example, although both Kerry and many entertainment celebrities were singing the same political tune in 2004, they attempted to reach different audiences. Kerry's very traditional military salute signaled his identification with the broad middle of the American political spectrum, while the band Green Day used a different and more charged, gesture—a revolutionary's raised fist clutching a heart-shaped grenade—on its 2004 CD *American Idiot* to connect with mainly younger voters interested in more sweeping change.

For the cover of its 2004 rock opera, Green Day used a traditional revolutionary gesture to support an alternative vision of American values.

Writers and speakers create their ethos in at least two ways. First, they shape themselves at the very moment they make any argument. They usually accomplish this self-fashioning through the language they use, the evidence they offer, the respect they show those with whom they disagree, and the way they tender themselves to an audience physically—through gestures, posture, eye contact, and tone of voice (or their equivalents in writing or imagery). Kerry's salute was just such a character-defining moment, crafted to affirm his stature and proclaim his values before a cheering convention and millions of TV viewers, a great many of whom may have not known much about him prior to his acceptance speech. Arguments of character frequently merge with issues of value in just this way because audiences tend to trust people with whom they can identify.

But writers and speakers also bring their previous lives, work, and reputations to the table when they make an argument. If they are well known, liked, and respected, that reputation will contribute to their persuasive power. If their character is problematic in any respect, they may have to use the speech to reshape an audience's perception. Some people in Kerry's audience were aware and worried that he was involved in Vietnam-era antiwar protests. The salute was possibly designed to reassure them that Kerry would be a trustworthy steward of the country's interests—one who respected the role of the military enough to begin his new role as an official presidential candidate by evoking its traditions and values.

Understanding How Arguments Based on Character Work

Because life is complicated, we often need shortcuts to help us make choices; we can't weigh every claim to its last milligram or trace every fragment of evidence to its original source. And we have to make such decisions daily: *Which college or university should I attend? Whom should I vote for in the next election? Which reviewers of Peter Jackson's* King Kong *will I believe? What are the real risks in taking prescription painkillers?* To answer the more serious questions, people typically turn to professionals for wise, well-informed, and frank advice: a doctor, lawyer, teacher, pastor. But people look to equally knowledgeable individuals to guide them in less momentous matters as well: a coach, a friend, maybe even a waiter (*Is the fish really fresh?*). Depending on the subject, an *expert* can be anyone with knowledge and experience, from a professor of nuclear physics at an Ivy League college to a short-order cook at the local diner.

Readers give people (or institutions) they know a hearing they might not automatically grant to a stranger or to someone who hasn't earned their respect or affection. That trust indicates the power of arguments based on ethos/character and accounts for why people will take the word of the "car guy" in their neighborhood more seriously than the reviews in *Consumer Reports*. And they'll believe *Consumer Reports* more readily than the SUV ads in *People*. Appeals or arguments about character often turn on claims such as the following:

- A person (or group) does or does not have the authority to speak to this issue.
- A person is or is not trustworthy or credible on this issue.
- A person does or does not have good motives for addressing this subject.

Claiming Authority

When you read an argument, especially one that makes an aggressive claim, you have every right to wonder about the writer's authority: *What does he know about the subject? What experiences does she have that make her especially knowledgeable? Why should I pay attention to this writer?*

When you offer an argument yourself, you have to anticipate pointed questions exactly like these and be able to answer them, directly or indirectly. Sometimes the claim of authority will be bold and personal, as it is when *Wall Street Journal* political writer Peggy Noonan responds to complaints by columnist Anna Quindlen that her political views provoke hate mail. What gives Noonan special expertise to speak on this subject? She too has taken the heat from those who dislike what she puts in her own columns:

> She [Anna Quindlen] said, as she has in the past—**she says it a lot, actually**—that she gets a lot of hate mail because of the views she holds. I don't doubt it. But when she speaks of it **she always seems to be suggesting she has a lot of courage to write what she writes.** *See what I have to put up with, and see how I persevere.* There's an air of indignation. *Do you believe what a nice liberal has to put up with from these right-wing primitives?*

Noonan dents Quindlen's ethos by suggesting that the columnist's complaints are a chronic form of heroic posturing.

Anna Quindlen

Peggy Noonan

Well Anna, . . . I have never written of this or even spoken of it, but let me tell you something.

My political philosophy is conservative. I am pro-life. I live in New York City, surrounded by modern people. They are mostly left-wing, they are all pro-choice, many of them passionately and even furiously so. I have written books saying Ronald Reagan is a great man and Hillary Clinton is a bad woman. I know something about being a target, and I know something about hate mail. I have received not hundreds but thousands of the most personal and obscene denunciations; I have received death threats; I have been threatened with blackmail; I have been informed that I do not deserve to live; I have received a three page typed double spaced letter with perfect grammar and syntax the first sentence of which was "Dr. Ms. Noonan, Let me explain to you why you are a . . ." and here I cannot suggest the word used. But damned if he didn't make a good case. I used to hear regularly from a woman who'd tell me she hopes I have a brain hemorrhage.

I have never talked about this because I would consider speaking of it both self-pitying and self-aggrandizing. But there's another reason. I'm a grownup. I know you pay a price for the stands you take.

It's a disputatious world. Rocks get thrown. I could make myself safer by changing my views, but why would I abandon what I think is true so that people I think are wrong will like me? That doesn't make sense. So I stand where I stand and pay. And you know what? Too bad. Tough. That's life. Nothing is free. If you hold a controversial position you will draw controversy and

Deliberately both comparing and contrasting herself with Quindlen, Noonan claims that she too has taken heat from readers, but in her case, without making an issue of it. Addressing her target directly by first name and with "Let me tell you something" creates an aggressively challenging ethos, one that risks arrogance but suits her point about harsh personal attacks.

The note of humor here probably enhances Noonan's credibility with readers.

Noonan claims the ethos of a responsible adult.

Even the sentence fragments here reinforce the toughness of the ethos Noonan creates.

its cousins: denunciation, dislike, etc. It's the price
you pay.

–Peggy Noonan, "Stand Up and Take It
Like an American"

Noonan is unusually blunt in the way she establishes her ethos in this column.

Writers typically establish their authority in other and less striking ways. We may not have lords and dukes in the United States, but many of us, it seems, have a job title that confers some clout. When writers attach such titles to their names, they're saying, "This is how I've earned the right to be heard"—they are medical doctors or have law degrees or have been board certified to work as psychotherapists. Similarly, writers can assert authority by mentioning who employs them—their institutional affiliations—and how long they've worked in a given field.

Bureaucrats often identify themselves with their agencies, and professors with their schools. As a reader, you'll likely pay more attention to an argument about global warming if it's offered by someone who identifies herself as a professor of atmospheric and oceanic science at the University of Wisconsin, Madison, than by your Uncle Sid who sells tools at Sears. But you'll prefer your uncle to the professor when you need advice about a reliable rotary saw.

When your readers are apt to be skeptical of both you and your claim—as is usually the case when your subject is controversial—you may have to be even more specific about your credentials. That's exactly the strategy Richard Bernstein uses to establish his right to speak on the delicate subject of teaching multiculturalism in American colleges and universities. At one point in a lengthy argument, he challenges those who make simplistic pronouncements about non-Western cultures, specifically "Asian culture." But what gives a New York writer named Bernstein the authority to write about Asian peoples? Bernstein tells us in a sparkling example of an argument based on character:

> The Asian culture, as it happens, is something I know a bit about, having spent five years at Harvard striving for a Ph.D. in a joint program called History and East Asian Languages and, after that, living either as a student (for one year) or a journalist (six years) in China and Southeast Asia. At least I know enough to know there is no such thing as the "Asian culture."
>
> –Richard Bernstein, *Dictatorship of Virtue*

Clearly, Bernstein understates the case when he says he knows "a bit" about Asian culture and then mentions a Ph.D. program at Harvard and years of living in Asia. But the false modesty may be part of his argumentative strategy, too.

When you write for readers who trust you and your work, you may not have to make an open claim to authority. But you should know that making this type of appeal is always an option. A second lesson is that it certainly helps to know your subject when you're making a claim.

Even if an author doesn't make an explicit effort to assert it, authority can be conveyed through tiny signals that readers may pick up almost subconsciously. Sometimes it comes just from a style of writing that presents ideas with robust confidence. For example, years ago when Allan Bloom wrote a controversial book about problems in American education, he used tough, self-assured prose to argue for what needed to be done. We've italicized the words that convey his confident ethos:

> *Of course,* the only *serious* solution [to the problems of higher education] is the one that is almost universally rejected: the *good old* Great Books approach. . . . I am *perfectly aware* of, and actually agree with, the objections to the Great Books Cult. . . . But *one thing is certain:* wherever the Great Books make up a central part of the curriculum, the students are excited and satisfied.
> –Allan Bloom, *The Closing of the American Mind* (emphasis added)

Establishing Credibility

Whereas authority is a measure of how much command someone has over a subject, credibility speaks to a writer's honesty and respect for the audience. The simplest way of establishing your credibility with an audience that doesn't know you is to make reasonable claims and then to back them up with evidence and documentation — or, in electronic environments, to link your claims to sites with reliable information. That is, authority is itself a good way to build credibility.

But there's a lot more to it than that. Consider that a number of studies over the years have shown that tall, thin, good-looking people have an advantage in getting a job or getting a raise. Apparently, employers make assumptions about such people's competence based on nothing more than good looks. You probably act the same way in some circumstances, even if you resent the practice. (A more recent study shows that good-looking instructors score significantly higher in teaching evaluations than their more unsightly colleagues.)

You might recall these studies when you make an argument, knowing that like it or not, readers and audiences are going to respond to how you

CULTURAL CONTEXTS FOR ARGUMENT

Ethos

In the United States, students writing arguments are often asked to establish authority by drawing on certain kinds of personal experience, by reporting on research they or others have conducted, and by taking a position for which they can offer strong evidence and support. But this expectation about student authority is by no means universal.

Indeed, some cultures regard student writers as novices who can most effectively make arguments by reflecting on what they've learned from their teachers and elders—those who are believed to hold the most important knowledge, wisdom, and, hence, authority. Whenever you're arguing a point with people from cultures other than your own, therefore, you need to think about what kind of authority you're expected to have:

- Whom are you addressing, and what is your relationship with that person?

- What knowledge are you expected to have? Is it appropriate or expected for you to demonstrate that knowledge—and if so, how?

- What tone is appropriate? If in doubt, always show respect: politeness is rarely if ever inappropriate.

present yourself as a person. In other words, be sure that your writing *visually* conveys your message as effectively as possible. Choose a medium that shows you at your best. Some writers love the written text, garnished with quotations, footnotes, charts, graphs, and bibliography. Others can make a better case online or in some purely visual form. Design arguments that assure readers they can trust you. And remember that even correct spelling counts.

You can also establish credibility by connecting your own beliefs and values to core principles that are well established and widely respected. This strategy is particularly effective when your position seems to be—at first glance, at least—a threat to traditional values. For example, when author Andrew Sullivan argues in favor of legalizing same-sex marriages, he does so in language that echoes the themes of family-values conservatives:

> Legalizing gay marriage would offer homosexuals the same deal society now offers heterosexuals: general social approval and specific

legal advantages in exchange for a deeper and harder-to-extract-yourself-from commitment to another human being. Like straight marriage, it would foster social cohesion, emotional security, and economic prudence. Since there's no reason gays should not be allowed to adopt or be foster parents, it could also help nurture children. And its introduction would not be some sort of radical break with social custom. As it has become more acceptable for gay people to acknowledge their loves publicly, more and more have committed themselves to one another for life in full view of their families and their friends. A law institutionalizing gay marriage would merely reinforce a healthy social trend. It would also, in the wake of AIDS, qualify as a genuine public health measure. Those conservatives who deplore promiscuity among some homosexuals should be among the first to support it.

–Andrew Sullivan, "Here Comes the Groom"

Yet another way to affirm your credibility as a writer is to use language that shows your respect for readers, addressing them neither above nor below their capabilities. Citing trustworthy sources and acknowledging them properly prove too that you've done your homework (another sign of respect) and suggests that you know your subject. So does presenting ideas clearly and fairly. Details matter: helpful graphs, tables, charts, or illustrations may carry weight with readers, as will the visual attractiveness of your work (or your Web site, for that matter). Again, even correct spelling counts.

Writers who establish their credibility this way seem trustworthy. But sometimes, to be credible, you have to admit limitations, too: *This is what I know; I won't pretend to understand more.* It's a tactic used by people as respected in their fields as was the late biologist Lewis Thomas, who in this example ponders whether scientists have overstepped their bounds in exploring the limits of DNA research:

> Should we stop short of learning some things, for fear of what we, or someone, will do with the knowledge? My own answer is a flat no, but I must confess that this is an intuitive response and I am neither inclined nor trained to reason my way through it.
>
> –Lewis Thomas, "The Hazards of Science"

When making an argument, many people would be reluctant to write "I suppose" or "I must confess," but those are the very concessions that might increase a reader's confidence in Lewis Thomas.

In fact, a very powerful technique for building credibility is to acknowledge outright any exceptions, qualifications, or even weaknesses

A classic "It's ugly, *but* . . ." campaign. Conceding your weaknesses can give a strong boost to your credibility.

Ugly is only skin-deep.

It may not be much to look at. But beneath that humble exterior beats an air-cooled engine. It won't boil over and ruin your piston rings. It won't freeze over and ruin your life. It's in the back of the car for better traction in snow and sand. And it will give you about 29 miles to a gallon of gas.

After a while you get to like so much about the VW, you even get to like what it looks like.

You find that there's enough legroom for almost anybody's legs. Enough headroom for almost anybody's head. With a hat on it. Snug-fitting bucket seats. Doors that close so well you can hardly close them. (They're so airtight, it's better to open the window a crack first.)

Those plain, unglamorous wheels are each suspended independently. So when a bump makes one wheel bounce, the bounce doesn't make the other wheel bump. It's things like that you pay the $1585* for, when you buy a VW. The ugliness doesn't add a thing to the cost of the car. That's the beauty of it.

©Volkswagen of America, Inc. *Suggested Retail Price, East Coast P.O.E. ($1663 West Coast P.O.E.), Local Taxes and Other Dealer Delivery Charges, if Any, Additional.

in your argument. Making such concessions to objections that readers might raise, called *conditions of rebuttal,* sends a strong signal to the audience that you've scrutinized your own position and can therefore be trusted when you turn to arguing its merits. Speaking to readers directly, using *I* or *you,* for instance, also enables you to come closer to them when that strategy is appropriate. Using contractions will have the same effect because they make prose sound more colloquial. Consider how linguist Robert D. King uses such techniques (as well as an admission that he might be wrong) to add a personal note to the conclusion of a serious essay arguing against the notion that language diversity is endangering the United States:

> *If I'm wrong,* then the great American experiment will fail—not because of language but because it no longer means anything to be an American; because we have forfeited that "willingness of the heart" that F. Scott Fitzgerald wrote was America; because we are no longer joined by Lincoln's "mystic chords of memory." We are not even close to the danger point. *I suggest* that we relax and luxuriate in our linguistic richness and our traditional tolerance of language differences. Language does not threaten American unity. Benign neglect is a good policy for any country when it comes to language, and *it's a good policy for America.*
> —Robert D. King, "Should English Be the Law?" (emphasis added)

In some situations, however, you may find that a more formal tone gives your claims greater authority. Choices like these are yours to make as you search for the ethos that best represents you in a given argument.

Coming Clean about Motives

When people are trying to sell us anything, whether it be a political idea or a trip to Cancun, it's only natural to question their motives. *Whose interests are they serving? How will they profit from their proposal?* Such suspicions go right to the heart of ethical arguments. It's not an accident that Jonathan Swift ends his satirical *A Modest Proposal* with his narrator claiming he will benefit in no way from what he suggests—that the people of eighteenth-century Ireland end their poverty by selling their infant children as the *other* white meat:

> I profess, in the sincerity of my heart, that I have not the least personal interest in endeavoring to promote this necessary work, having

no other motive than the public good of my country, by advancing our trade, providing for infants, relieving the poor, and giving some pleasure to the rich. I have no children by which I can propose to get a single penny; the youngest being nine years old, and my wife past childbearing.

–Jonathan Swift, *A Modest Proposal*

Even this monster of a narrator appreciates that his idea will gain no traction if his motives are suspect in the least.

He's also smart enough to discuss his potential conflicts of interest (his own children, his wife)—always a sensible strategy whenever your motives for offering an idea might seem driven by its potential advantage to yourself, or by your attachment to a particular class, gender, faction, or other group. Here, for example, in taking on the Bush administration's push to make the programming of public radio and TV less liberal, Michael Winship frankly admits that he has a long personal involvement with and stake in the issue:

As the *New York Times* led in its May 2 edition, "the Republican chairman of the Corporation for Public Broadcasting [Ken Tomlinson] is aggressively pressing public television to correct what he and other conservatives consider liberal bias, prompting some public broadcasting leaders—including the chief executive of PBS—to object that his actions pose a threat to editorial independence."

In the interest of full disclosure, for more than thirty years, off and on, I have toiled in the vineyards of public broadcasting, sometimes more fruitfully than others.

. . . One of Tomlinson's primary targets is PBS' Bill Moyers, of whom he has a "very vehement dislike," according to a former CPB employee, for his liberal point of view. (In the interest of even fuller disclosure, for that aforementioned thirty years and more, I have been, off and on, a colleague and/or employee of Bill's.)

–Michael Winship, "Speaking as a Public Broadcasting Stooge and Tool"

Note that even though Winship is writing for the Common Dreams News Center, a Web site that bills itself as "Breaking News and Views for the Progressive Community," he doesn't assume that just because most of his readers are likely to share his views he needn't mention these personal connections. Especially in online venues, writers have to expect that many of their readers will hold very different views and will be quick to point out unmentioned affiliations as serious drawbacks to credibility. In fact, attacks on such loyalties are common in political circles, where it's almost a sport to assume the worst about an opponent's motives and associations. But we all have connections and interests that, to use less pejorative language, represent the ties that bind us to other human beings. It makes sense that a woman might be concerned with women's issues or that investors might look out for their investments. So it can be good strategy to let your audiences know where your loyalties lie when such information does, in fact, shape your work.

There are other ways, too, to invite readers to regard you as trustworthy. Nancy Mairs, in an essay entitled "On Being a Cripple," wins the attention and probably the respect of her readers by facing her situation with a riveting directness:

> First, the matter of semantics. I am a cripple. I choose this word to name me. I choose from among several possibilities, the most common of which are "handicapped" and "disabled." I made the choice a number of years ago, without thinking, unaware of my motives for doing so. Even now, I am not sure what those motives are, but I recognize that they are complex and not entirely flattering. People— crippled or not—wince at the word "cripple," as they do not at "handicapped" or "disabled." Perhaps I want them to wince. I want them to see me as a tough customer, one to whom the fates/gods/viruses have not been kind, but who can face the brutal truth of her existence squarely. As a cripple, I swagger.
>
> –Nancy Mairs, "On Being a Cripple"

The paragraph takes some risks because the writer is expressing feelings that may make readers unsure how to react. Indeed, Mairs herself

If Everything's an Argument . . .

Analyze the ethos of the authors and editors of *Everything's an Argument* as they reveal themselves in this particular chapter. Look carefully at such elements as the language the authors use (formal? informal? condescending? chummy?), the examples and images they draw on (predictable? PC? fresh and imaginative? out-of-touch?), or the political and cultural attitudes they convey. Does the chapter suggest a coherent ethos, or do you find inconsistencies that surprise or confuse you? Write a page describing the ethos and the appeal it does or doesn't have for you, being sure to offer specific evidence for your claims.

admits that she doesn't completely understand her own feelings and motives. Yet the very admission of uncertainty helps her to build a bridge to readers.

RESPOND.

1. Consider the ethos of each of the following public figures. Then describe one or two public arguments, campaigns, or products that might benefit from their endorsements as well as several that would not.

   Oprah Winfrey—TV celebrity

   Ellen DeGeneres—comedian and talk-show host

   Dick Cheney—vice president

   Katie Holmes—actress

   Colin Powell—former secretary of state in the Bush administration

   Al Sharpton—civil rights activist and politician

   Queen Latifah—actress and rap artist

   Dave Chappelle—humorist and columnist

   Jeff Gordon—NASCAR champion

   Barbara Boxer—senator from California

   Bill O'Reilly—TV news commentator

   Marge Simpson—sensible wife and mother on *The Simpsons*

2 Voice is a choice. That is, writers modify the tone and style of their language depending on whom they want to seem to be. In the excerpts from this chapter, Allan Bloom wants to appear poised and confident; his language aims to convince us of his expertise. Peggy Noonan wants to appear mature, strong, and perhaps *personally* offended by the opinions offered by Anna Quindlen. In different situations, even when writing about the same topics, Bloom and Noonan would likely adopt different voices. Rethink and then rewrite the Noonan passage on p. 66, taking on the voice—the character—of someone who uses the pronoun "I" much less frequently than Noonan does, perhaps not at all. You may also need to change the way you claim authority, establish credibility, and demonstrate competence as you try to present a different and less personal ethos.

3. Opponents of Richard Nixon, the thirty-seventh president of the United States, once raised doubts about his integrity by asking a single ruinous question: *Would you buy a used car from this man?* Create

Public figures try to control their images for obvious reasons. Would you buy a used car from any of these distinguished men and women?

your own version of the argument of character. Begin by choosing an intriguing or controversial person or group and finding an image on-line. Download the image into a word-processing file. Create a caption for the photo modeled after the question asked about Nixon: *Would you give this woman your email password? Would you share a campsite with this couple? Would you eat lasagna this guy prepared?* Finally, write a serious 300-word argument that explores the character flaws or strengths of your subject(s).

4. A well-known television advertisement from the 1980s featured a soap-opera actor promoting a pain relief medication. "I'm not a doctor," he said, "but I play one on TV." Today, many celebrities, from athletes like Tiger Woods to actresses like Susan Sarandon, use their fame in pitches for products or political causes. One way or another, each case of celebrity endorsement relies on arguments based on character. Develop a one-page print advertisement for a product, service, or political position you use often—anything from soap to auto repair to cell phone service. There's one catch: Your advertisement should rely on arguments based on character, and you should choose as a spokesperson someone who would seem the least likely to use or endorse your product or service. The challenge is to turn an apparent disadvantage into an advantage by exploiting character.

4
Arguments Based on Facts and Reason—*Logos*

SPOCK: "Logic and practical information do not seem to apply here."

MCCOY: "You admit that?"

SPOCK: "To deny the facts would be illogical, Doctor."

—from *Star Trek* episode, "A Piece of the Action"

When writers need to persuade, they usually try their best to provide readers with good reasons to believe them. When the choice is between logic and emotion, many of us will side with *Star Trek*'s Dr. McCoy rather than the stern Spock. Most of us respect appeals to

Adlai Stevenson presents the American case at the United Nations during the Cuban Missile Crisis.

logos—arguments based on facts, evidence, and reason—but, like the good doctor, we're inclined to test the facts against our feelings and against the ethos of those making the appeal. Aristotle, among the first philosophers to write about persuasion, gives us a place to begin. He divided proofs based on facts and reason into two kinds: those derived from what we'd call *hard evidence* (Aristotle described these as *inartistic appeals*—facts, clues, statistics, testimonies, witnesses), and those based upon *reason and common sense* (what Aristotle termed *artistic appeals*). Though these categories overlap and leak (what, after all, is *common sense?*), they remain useful even today.

The differences can be observed in arguments presented forty years apart at the United Nations when American representatives charged other nations with harboring weapons of mass destruction. "Do you, Ambassador Zorin, deny that the U.S.S.R. has placed and is placing medium and intermediate range missiles and sites in Cuba?" American UN ambassador Adlai Stevenson famously asked on October 25, 1962, knowing that he had the hard evidence of spy photographs to prove his claim. The images showed the alleged construction beyond a reasonable doubt in an

**LIBERATING
IRAQI CHILDREN
FROM TYRANNY**

**IT'S CO$TING
TOO MUCH!**

www.protestwarrior.com

Not Just Words

Sometimes the difference between appeals isn't self-evident. What one person considers an appeal to reason may look like an emotional or ethical argument to another. Add in the element of irony or parody, and the categories scramble even more. Study the "Liberating Iraqi Children" poster on this page from the <ProtestWarrior.com> Web site. What kind of arguments does it make, and how exactly does it make them? You might answer this question first by listing all the claims you can take from it, both those that seem straightforward and any others that may be ironic or parodic. Then describe what you think the poster's point is. How does it make that point? Who is the target of the poster? Who is its audience? Finally, working within a group, discuss whether and why the poster does or doesn't represent an appeal to logic and reason.

era when doctoring photographs was no easy process. Ambassador Stevenson had more than a smoking gun: he had real missiles.

In contrast, Secretary of State Colin Powell did not have the same kind of open-and-shut case when he argued to the same Security Council on February 5, 2003, that Iraq was harboring weapons of mass destruction in contravention to UN resolutions. Instead, he had to assure his worldwide audience that "What you will see is an accumulation of facts and disturbing patterns of behavior." None of his materials — including some photographs — had the immediacy or transparency of the 1962 Cuban Missile Crisis images. So Powell had to hope that the pattern and weight of evidence offered in a lengthy presentation would make his claim seem compelling: "that Saddam Hussein and his regime are concealing their efforts to produce more weapons of mass destruction." Since no such weapons or weapon stockpiles were subsequently found in Iraq following a second Iraq War, one might infer (logically) that hard evidence is superior to reasoning aided by less-than-compelling inferences and probabilities. But hard evidence won't always be available, nor will it always be as overwhelming as the photographs Stevenson had to display. And yet decisions and choices have to be made.

Providing Hard Evidence

As the Stevenson/Powell examples suggest, people today usually prefer arguments based on facts and testimony to those grounded in reason. In a courtroom as well as in the popular media, for example, lawyers or reporters look for the "smoking gun" — the piece of hard evidence that ties a defendant or politician to a crime. It might be an audiotape, a fingerprint, a stained dress, or, increasingly, DNA evidence. Popular crime shows such as *CSI: Crime Scene Investigation* focus intensely on gathering this sort of "scientific" support for a prosecution. Less dramatically, the factual evidence in an argument might be columns of data carefully collected over time to prove a point about climate change or racial profiling or the effects of Title IX on collegiate sports. After decades of exposure to science and the wonders of technology, audiences today have more faith in claims that can be counted, measured, photographed, or analyzed than in those that are merely defended with words. If you live in a state where you can be ticketed after a camera catches you running a red light, you know what hard evidence means.

Factual evidence, however, takes many forms. Which ones you use will depend on the kind of argument you're writing. In fact, providing appropriate evidence ought to become a habit whenever you write an argument. The evidence makes your case plausible; it may also supply the details that make writing interesting. Consider Aristotle's claim that all arguments can be reduced to just two components:

Statement + Proof

Here's another way of naming those parts:

Claim + Supporting Evidence

In a scholarly article, you can actually see this connection between statements and proof in the text and the notes. As an example, we reprint a single page from a much-cited review of Michael Bellesiles's *Arming America: The Making of America's Gun Culture* by James Lindgren published in the *Yale Law Review* (see p. 83). Bellesiles had used evidence gathered from eighteenth-century documents to argue that gun ownership in frontier America was much rarer than advocates of the right to bear arms believed. Upon publication, *Arming America* was hailed by gun critics for weakening the claim of gun advocates today that the ownership of weapons has always been a part of American culture. But Lindgren, as well as many other critics and historians, found so many evidentiary flaws in Bellesiles's arguments that questions were soon raised about his scholastic integrity. Lindgren's review of *Arming America* runs for more than 50 meticulous pages (including an appendix of errors in Bellesiles's work) and contains 212 footnotes. You can see a factual argument in action just by looking at how Lindgren handles evidence on a single page. You may never write an argument as detailed as Lindgren's review, but you should develop the same respect for evidence.

Facts

"Facts," said John Adams, "are stubborn things," and so they make strong arguments, especially when readers believe they come from honest sources. Gathering such information and transmitting it faithfully practically define what we mean by professional journalism in one realm and scholarship in another. We'll even listen to people we don't agree with when they overwhelm us with evidence. On p. 84, for example, a reviewer for the conservative journal *National Review* praises the work of William Julius Wilson, a liberal sociologist, because of how well he presents his case.

This selection from James Lindgren's review of Michael Bellesiles's
Arming America first appeared in the *Yale Law Review,* vol. 111 (2002).

LINDGRENFINAL.DOC   APRIL 26, 2002 4/26/02 12:34 PM

B. *How Common Was Gun Ownership?*

The most contested portions of *Arming America* involve the book's
most surprising claim, that guns were infrequently owned before the mid-
1800s. As I show below, the claim that colonial America did not have a gun
culture is questionable on the evidence of gun ownership alone. Compared
to the seventeenth and eighteenth centuries, it appears that guns are not as
commonly owned today. Whereas individual gun ownership in every
published (and unpublished) study of early probate records that I have
located (except Bellesiles's) ranges from 40% to 79%; only 32.5% of
households today own a gun.[44] This appears to be a much smaller
percentage than in early America—in part because the mean household size
in the late eighteenth century was six people,[45] while today it is just under
two people.[46] The prevailing estimate of 40% to 79% ownership differs
markedly from Bellesiles's claim that only about 15% owned guns.[47] In the
remainder of this Section, I explain why.

1. *The Gun Censuses*

Bellesiles bases his claims of low gun ownership primarily on probate
records and counts of guns at militia musters.[48] He also discusses censuses
of all guns in private and public hands, but on closer examination, none of
these turns out to be a general census of all guns.

The trend is set in Bellesiles's first count of guns in an American
community—the 1630 count of all the guns in the Massachusetts Bay
Colony of about 1000 people. Bellesiles's account is quite specific: " In
1630 the Massachusetts Bay Company reported in their possession: '80
bastard musketts, . . . [10] Fowlinge peeces, . . . 10 Full musketts . . . .'
There were thus exactly one hundred firearms for use among seven towns

---

44. This results from my analysis of the March 2001 release of the National Opinion
Research Center's *General Social Survey, 2000* [hereinafter 2000 NORC GSS]. The data are also
available at Nat'l Opinion Research Ctr., General Social Survey, *at* http://www.icpsr.umich.edu/
GSS/ (last visited Apr. 8, 2002). According to the survey, 32.5% of households owned any gun,
19.7% owned a rifle, 18.6% owned a shotgun, and 19.7% owned a pistol or revolver. 2000 NORC
GSS, *supra.* Only 1.2% of respondents refused to respond to the question. *Id.*

45. Inter-Univ. Consortium for Political & Soc. Research (ICPSR), Census Data for the Year
1790, http://fisher.lib.virginia.edu/cgi-local/censusbin/census/cen.pl?year=790 (last visited Aug.
10, 2001).

46. 2000 NORC GSS, *supra* note 44.

47. BELLESILES, *supra* note 3, at 445 tbl.1.

> In his eagerly awaited new book, Wilson argues that ghetto blacks are
> worse off than ever, victimized by a near-total loss of low-skill jobs in
> and around inner-city neighborhoods. In support of this thesis, he
> *musters mountains of data, plus excerpts from some of the thousands of*
> *surveys and face-to-face interviews that he and his research team con-*
> *ducted among inner-city Chicagoans.* It is a book that deserves a wide
> audience among thinking conservatives.
>
> –John J. Dilulio Jr., "When Decency Disappears" (emphasis added)

In this instance, the facts are respected even above differences in political thinking or ideology.

When your facts are compelling, they may stand on their own in a
low-stakes argument, supported by little more than a tag that gives the
source of your information. Consider the power of phrases such as "reported by the *New York Times*," "according to CNN," or "in a book published
by Oxford University Press." Such sources gain credibility if they have, in
readers' experience, reported facts accurately and reliably over time. In
fact, one reason you document the sources you use in an argument is to
let the credibility of those sources reflect positively on you—a good reason to find the best, most reliable material to support your claims.

But arguing with facts also sometimes involves challenging the biases of reputable sources if they lead to unfair or selective reporting. You
don't have to search hard to find critics of the *Times* or CNN these days.
In recent years, bloggers and other online critics in particular have enjoyed pointing out the biases or factual mistakes of mainstream media
(MSM) outlets. Conservative columnist Peggy Noonan explores the consequences of this critical *new media:*

> Now anyone can take to the parapet and announce the news. This will
> make for a certain amount of confusion. But better that than one-
> party rule and one-party thought. Only 20 years ago, when you were
> enraged at what you felt was the unfairness of a story, or a bias on the
> part of the storyteller, you could do this about it: nothing. You could
> write a letter.
>
> When I worked at CBS a generation ago I used to receive those let-
> ters. Sometimes we read them, and sometimes we answered them,
> but not always. Now if you see such a report and are enraged you can
> do something about it: You can argue in public on a blog or on TV, you
> can put forth information that counters the information in the report.
> You can have a voice. You can change the story. You can bring down a
> news division. Is this improvement? Oh yes it is.
>
> –Peggy Noonan, "MSM Requiem"

In an ideal world, good information would always drive out bad. But you'll soon learn that such is not always the case. Sometimes bad information gets repeated in an echo chamber that amplifies the errors. Here is Colin Powell explaining subsequently how his UN presentation on Iraqi weapons of mass destruction could have been so far off the mark:

> When I made that presentation in February 2003, it was based on the best information that the Central Intelligence Agency made available to me. We studied it carefully; we looked at the sourcing in the case of the mobile trucks and trains. There was multiple sourcing for that. Unfortunately, that multiple sourcing over time has turned out to be not accurate. And so I'm deeply disappointed. But I'm also comfortable that at the time that I made the presentation, it reflected the collective judgment, the sound judgment of the intelligence community. But it turned out that the sourcing was inaccurate and wrong and in some cases, deliberately misleading. And for that, I am disappointed and I regret it.
>
> –Colin Powell, *Meet the Press*

Obviously, as a reader and researcher, you should look beyond headlines, bylines, and reputations, scrutinizing any facts you collect before passing them on yourself. Test their reliability, and admit any problems right at the start.

Statistics

Let's deal with a cliché right up front: *Figures lie and liars figure.* Like most clichés, it contains a grain of truth. It's possible to lie with numbers, even those that are accurate, because numbers rarely speak for themselves. They need to be interpreted by writers. And writers almost always have agendas that shape the interpretations.

For example, you might want to herald the good news that unemployment in the United States stands at just a little over 5 percent. That means 95 percent of Americans have jobs, an employment rate much higher than that of most other industrial nations. But let's spin the figure another way. In a country as populous as the United States, unemployment at 5 percent means that millions of Americans don't earn a daily wage. Indeed, *one out of every twenty adults* who wants work can't find it. Suddenly that's a sobering number. And, as you can see, the same statistic can be cited as a cause for celebration or shame.

We don't mean to suggest that numbers are meaningless or that you have license to use them in any way that serves your purposes. Quite the contrary. But you do have to understand the role you play in giving numbers a voice and a presence. Consider the way Armen Keteyian, writing for the *Sporting News,* raises serious questions about the safety of aluminum bats in high school and college sports, despite the insistence by many sports officials that they're safe. Keteyian makes his case by focusing on statistics and numbers—which we've highlighted—suggesting otherwise:

> Bat companies point to the NCAA's *annual injury report* ranking baseball as one of the safest collegiate sports. The report also shows "there is *no . . . significant increase in batted ball injuries.*" But last December, after *an 18-month study,* the U.S. Consumer Product Safety Commission released a report that called *the NCAA's injury statistics "inconclusive . . . and not complete enough"* to determine whether current aluminum bats are more dangerous than wood.
>
> "Let's be honest," says Anderson. "Bat manufacturers have been wonderful for college baseball. So you get caught up in that, the free product, the fact it's saving you money. But all of a sudden I see my young man lying on the ground, and I'm going, 'Is this the right thing?'"
>
> Birk [a college baseball player injured by a ball coming fast off of an aluminum bat] and many others were struck—and in some cases nearly killed—by balls hit off aluminum bats certified by the NCAA and the national high school federation. To be approved, an aluminum bat must not cause *a batted ball to travel any faster than the best wood bat does.* But there's a catch: Bats are tested in a laboratory on a machine *set at a 70 mph pitch speed and a 66 mph swing speed.* Why not test at far more realistic numbers, say, *85 mph pitches and 80 mph swings?*
>
> Simple, says MacKay: "It would scare people to death."
>
> Why? Reaction time. Experts say *the fastest batted ball a pitcher can defend against is about 97 mph.* Translation: *Less than four-tenths of a second.*
>
> *Ninety-seven mph also is the fastest a ball can be hit by a certified bat in the lab test.* Sounds safe, right? But what about on the field? Well, it turns out nobody officially tests balls hit by aluminum bats under game conditions.
>
> "We've seen some things on our radar gun—108 *miles per hour, 110 at different times,*" says Anderson. "*I've witnessed 114 myself.* Makes you question whether we are doing the right thing."
>
> I wanted to ask the NCAA about this and more but it refused comment.
>
> –Armen Keteyian, "Bats Should Crack, Not Skulls" (emphasis added)

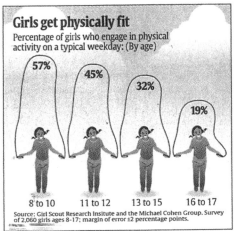

Girls get physically fit

Percentage of girls who engage in physical activity on a typical weekday: (By age)

57% 45% 32% 19%

8 to 10   11 to 12   13 to 15   16 to 17

Source: Girl Scout Research Insitute and the Michael Cohen Group. Survey of 2,060 girls ages 8-17; margin of error ±2 percentage points.

By Cindy Clark and Alejandro Gonzalez, USA TODAY

USA Today is famous for the tables, pie charts, and graphs it creates to present statistics and poll results. What claims might the evidence in this graph support? How does the design of the item influence your reading of it?

This is hardly the last word on aluminum bats. Proponents might cite different numbers and studies or argue that aluminum bats have advantages that outweigh exaggerated (to them, at least) safety concerns. The controversy is not likely to end anytime soon—unless the spike in injuries becomes more painfully obvious.

Surveys and Polls

Some of the most influential forms of statistics are those produced by surveys and polls. These measures play so large a role in people's political and social lives that writers, whether interpreting them or fashioning surveys themselves, need to give them special attention.

When they verify the popularity of an idea or proposal, surveys and polls provide persuasive appeals because, in a democracy, majority opinion offers a compelling warrant: *A government should do what most people want.* Polls come as close to expressing the will of the people as anything short of an election—the most decisive poll of all. (For more on warrants, see Chapter 6, p. 152.) However, surveys and polls can do much more than help politicians make decisions. They can also provide persuasive reasons for action or intervention. When surveys show, for example, that most American sixth-graders can't locate France or Wyoming on the map, that's an appeal for better instruction in geography. When polls suggest that consumer confidence is declining, businesses may have reason to worry about their bulging inventories.

It always makes sense, though, to push back against any poll numbers reported—especially, in fact, when they support your own point of view. Ask who commissioned the poll, who is publishing its outcome, who was surveyed (and in what proportions), and what stakes these parties might have in its outcome.

Are we being too suspicious? No. In fact, this sort of scrutiny is exactly what you should anticipate from your readers whenever you do surveys of your own to explore an issue. You should be confident that you've surveyed enough people to be accurate, that the people you chose for the study were representative of the selected population as a whole, and that you chose them randomly—not selecting those most likely to say what you hoped to hear.

The meaning of polls and surveys is also affected by the way questions are asked. Professional pollsters generally understand that their reputations depend on making their questions as neutral or unbiased as possible. But the exact wording of a poll or survey question can make a difference (as can the order and format of the questions). How much? Some would say a great deal. A group favoring school vouchers, for example, claims that poll results on the issue of providing tax-funded vouchers to parents for their children's education can vary more than twenty points, depending on how the question is asked (see the figure on p. 89). Of course, you should read this group's report with the same skepticism we're recommending that you approach any survey or poll with.

You must also read beyond the headlines to be sure you understand how the results of a poll are being interpreted. For instance, in late June 2005, *USA Today* chose the headline "Poll shows Americans 'generally in a funk'" for a story reporting on changing attitudes about terrorism and war. The poll asked questions such as the following:

- Do you approve or disapprove of the way George W. Bush is handling his job as president?

- How worried are you that you or someone in your family will become a victim of terrorism—very worried, somewhat worried, not too worried, or not worried at all?

- How likely is it that there will be further acts of terrorism in the United States over the next several weeks—very likely, somewhat likely, not too likely, or not at all likely?

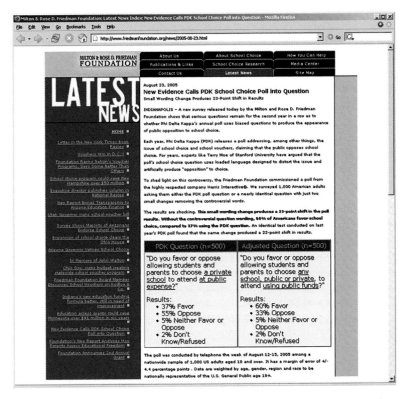

The Friedman Foundation finds that changing a poll's words changes its result.

- In general, do you approve or disapprove of the way the United States is treating the prisoners being held at Guantánamo Bay in Cuba?

The quotation marks around "generally in a funk" prove to be important. Why? Because the Americans responding to the *USA Today*/CNN/Gallup poll weren't actually queried about their general attitudes or overall mood. Instead, the headline reflects an *interpretation* of the poll numbers by Stephen Wayne, a professor of political science at George-town University, whose political leanings are not recorded. "Funk" is Wayne's term; another expert might have described the poll outcomes very differently since, for example, while public support for President Bush was declining slightly, so was fear of terrorism. A more neutral (and potentially accurate) headline might simply have noted contradictory attitudes.

Testimonies, Narratives, and Interviews

We don't want to give the impression that numbers and statistics make the only good evidence. Indeed, writers support arguments with all kinds of human experiences, particularly those they or others have undergone or reported. The testimony of reliable witnesses counts in almost any situation in which a writer seeks to make a case for action, change, or sympathetic understanding.

In a court, for example, decisions are often based on detailed descriptions of what happened. Following is a reporter's account of a court case in which a panel of judges decided, based on the testimony presented, that a man had been sexually harassed by another man. The narrative, in this case, supplies the evidence:

> The Seventh Circuit, in a 1997 case known as Doe v. City of Belleville, drew a sweeping conclusion allowing for same-sex harassment cases of many kinds. Title VII was sex-neutral, the court ruled; it didn't specifically prohibit discrimination against men or women. Moreover, the judges argued, there was such a thing as gender stereotyping, and if someone was harassed on that basis, it was unlawful. This case, for example, centered on teenage twin brothers working a summer job cutting grass in the city cemetery of Belleville, Ill. One boy wore an earring, which caused him no end of grief that particular summer — including a lot of menacing talk among his co-workers about sexually assaulting him in the woods and sending him "back to San Francisco." One of his harassers, identified in court documents as a large former marine, culminated a verbal campaign by backing the earring-wearer against a wall and grabbing him by the testicles to see "if he was a girl or a guy." The teenager had been "singled out for this abuse," the court ruled, "because the way in which he projected the sexual aspect of his personality" — meaning his gender — "did not conform to his co-workers' view of appropriate masculine behavior."
>
> –Margaret Talbot, "Men Behaving Badly"

Personal experience carefully reported can also support a claim convincingly, especially if a writer has earned the trust of readers. In the following excerpt, Christian Zawodniak describes his experiences as a student in a first-year college writing course. Not impressed by his instructor's performance, Zawodniak provides specific evidence of the instructor's failings:

> My most vivid memory of Jeff's rigidness was the day he responded to our criticisms of the class. Students were given a chance anonymously

to write our biggest criticisms one Monday, and the following Wednesday Jeff responded, staunchly answering all criticisms of his teaching: "Some of you complained that I didn't come to class prepared. It took me five years to learn all this." Then he pointed to the blackboard on which he had written all the concepts we had discussed that quarter. His responses didn't seem genuine or aimed at improving his teaching or helping students to understand him. He thought he was always right. Jeff's position gave him responsibilities that he officially met. But he didn't take responsibility in all the ways he had led us to expect.

                                   −Christian Zawodniak, "Teacher Power, Student Pedagogy"

This portrait of a defensive instructor gives readers details by which to assess the argument. If readers believe Zawodniak, they learn something about teaching. (For more on establishing credibility with readers, see Chapter 3.)

Personal revelations made in interviews can similarly provide the stuff of argument—the technique is a staple of some news shows such as *60 Minutes*. Following is an excerpt from a printed interview published in the *San Francisco Examiner* between writer Gregory Dictum and convicted arsonist Jeff Luers. Sentenced to serve twenty-two years and six months in the Oregon State Penitentiary for setting fire to three SUVs at an auto dealership, Luers uses the session with Dictum to justify what to him was an environmental protest:

DID YOU CONSIDER YOURSELF ENGAGED IN TERRORISM WHEN YOU SET FIRE TO THOSE SUVS?

No. Really, when you look at the use of the word today, terrorism is nothing more than a way to define armed struggles that you disagree with.

We were trying to draw attention to the use of resources in America that are contributing to climate change and global warming. Obviously, during an act of property destruction, objects are smashed, burned or demolished. That happens. But what makes an individual act of sabotage more heinous than crimes committed by governments and transnational corporations? If we're going to look at the definition of terrorism or the definition of violence, then we need to put it in its proper perspective. We certainly ought to open the definition up to corporate destruction of rivers, forests, oceans and all ecosystems, because those certainly aren't acts of love.

THE SUV CAPER WASN'T YOUR FIRST ATTEMPT TO BRING ATTENTION TO ENVIRONMENTAL ISSUES. WHAT OTHER EFFORTS HAD YOU BEEN INVOLVED IN PRIOR TO THAT ACTION?

I had been involved in civil-disobedience direct action. I spent a year and a half in an endangered old-growth forest outside of Eugene. I've done tree sits, roadblocks, lockdowns and some more confrontational things. I've been involved in street protests. I've met with and lobbied members of Congress. I've debated with timber-industry officials.

WAS BURNING THE SUVS THE MOST EXTREME THING YOU'D DONE?

Yeah, I'd say it was.

WERE YOU CONSCIOUS OF IT BEING A STEP IN A NEW DIRECTION FOR YOU?

I was trying to move into the realm of more radical actions. If you compare arson actions that have happened in the U.S., the majority of them were quite major. That's the goal that I was working toward—to be more of an underground guerrilla activist. The SUVs were kind of a baby step.

EVEN SO, THE JUDGE THREW THE BOOK AT YOU. WAS THIS AN EF-FORT TO MAKE AN EXAMPLE OF YOU, OR WAS IT JUST THE START OF TOUGHER SENTENCING IN GENERAL?

About six months ago, there was a man from Springfield who took his case to trial—he didn't take a plea bargain. He was accused of mul-tiple counts of arson in the City of Springfield [Oregon] for lighting apartment buildings on fire. And in every single one of his fires, people actually had to be evacuated. The fire department had to do door-to-door searches to ensure that no one was in the buildings. He very, very clearly put people in danger, and he was sentenced to 15 years—seven years less than me.

I'm obviously biased, but I have to say that my sentence is out of the norm. The only official explanation that has ever been given came from Kent Mortimore, chief deputy D.A. in Lane County [the county in which Eugene is located], who says, basically, bottom line, I'm a ter-rorist and I got what I deserved.

AT THE SAME TIME, THE SENTENCE HAS INCREASED YOUR PLAT-FORM AND YOUR NOTORIETY. I WOULDN'T BE TALKING TO YOU IF IT HADN'T BEEN SO UNUSUAL, FOR ONE THING.

Yeah, I think their idea backfired. I think the goal was to make me serve as a deterrent to anyone else that wanted to be involved in radi-cal actions and dissent. And I think that they failed to understand that all they did was galvanize my position.

With the growing trend toward ecotage in this country, I think that they looked upon me as representing that as a whole. But I didn't back down. I didn't plea out, and I didn't make apologies.

Luers is obviously defending his actions as an activist, resisting the label of eco-terrorist, and encouraging supporters who are protesting his lengthy prison sentence. And what about the interviewer? Does he play the role of neutral observer in presenting this story, or does he tip his hand? The interview, even in this brief excerpt, offers readers sensitive to nuances any number of pieces of evidence useful for arguments.

Using Reason and Common Sense

In the absence of hard facts, claims may be supported with other kinds of compelling reasons. The formal study of principles of reasoning is called *logic*, but few people—except perhaps mathematicians and philosophers—use formal logic to present their arguments. Many people might recognize the most famous of all syllogisms (a vehicle of deductive reasoning), but that's about the extent of what they know about formal logic:

> All human beings are mortal.
>
> Socrates is a human being.
>
> Therefore, Socrates is mortal.

Yet even as gifted a logician as Aristotle recognized that most people argue very well using informal logic (some might say *common sense*). Consciously or not, people are constantly stating claims, drawing conclusions, and making and questioning assumptions whenever they read or write. Mostly, people rely on the habits of mind and cultural assumptions they share with their readers or listeners.

In Chapter 6, we describe a system of informal logic you may find useful in shaping credible arguments—Toulmin argument. Here, we want briefly to examine some ways people use informal logic in their daily lives.

Once again, we begin with Aristotle, who used the term *enthymeme* to describe a very ordinary kind of sentence, one that includes both a claim and a reason:

> Enthymeme = Claim + Reason

Enthymemes are the sort of logical statements everyone manufactures almost effortlessly. The following sentences are all enthymemes:

Forecast at a Glance

A day for a picnic?

TODAY	TONIGHT	THURSDAY
Scattered Showers	Scattered Showers	Scattered Showers
Hi: 76°F	Lo: 62°F	Hi: 78°F
Pop: 40%	Pop: 40%	Pop: 40%

> We'd better cancel the picnic because it's going to rain.
>
> Flat taxes are fair because they treat everyone the same.
>
> I'll buy a PC laptop instead of a Mac because it's cheaper.
>
> NCAA football needs a real playoff to crown a real national champion.

On their own, enthymemes can be persuasive statements when most readers agree with the assumptions on which they're based. Sometimes the statements seem so obvious that readers don't realize they're drawing inferences when they agree with them.

Consider the first example:

> We'd better cancel the picnic because it's going to rain.

When a person casually makes such a claim, it's usually based on more specific information, so let's expand the enthymeme a bit to say more of what the speaker may mean:

> We'd better cancel the picnic this afternoon because the weather bureau is predicting a 70 percent chance of rain for the remainder of the day.

Embedded in this brief argument are all sorts of assumptions and fragments of cultural information that help make it persuasive:

> Picnics are ordinarily held outdoors.
>
> When the weather is bad, it's best to cancel picnics.
>
> Rain is bad weather for picnics.
>
> A 70 percent chance of rain means that rain is more likely to occur than not.

> When rain is more likely to occur than not, it makes sense to cancel picnics.
>
> The weather bureau's predictions are reliable enough to warrant action.

You'd sound ridiculous if you drew out all these inferences just to suggest that a picnic should be canceled. For most people, the original statement carries all this information on its own; it's a compressed argument, based on what audiences know and will accept. But sometimes your enthymemes aren't self-evident:

> Be wary of environmentalism because it's religion disguised as science.
>
> iPods are undermining civil society by making us even more focused on ourselves.
>
> It's time to make all public toilets unisex because to do otherwise is discriminatory.

In those cases, you'll have to work much harder to defend both the claim and the assumptions it's based on, drawing out the sort of inferences that seem self-evident in other enthymemes. And you'll likely also have to supply credible evidence. A simple declaration of fact won't suffice.

Cultural Assumptions and Values

Some of the assumptions in an argument will be based on shared values derived from culture and history. In the United States, for example, few arguments work better than those based on principles of fairness and equity. Most Americans will at least say that they believe all people should be treated the same way, no matter who they are or where they come from. That principle is announced in the Declaration of Independence.

Because fairness is culturally endorsed, in American politics and media enthymemes based on equity ordinarily need less support than those that challenge it. That's why, for example, both sides in debates over affirmative action programs seek the high ground of fairness: Proponents claim that affirmative action is needed to correct enduring inequities from the past; opponents suggest that the preferential policies should be overturned because they cause inequity today. Here's Linda Chavez drawing deeply on the equity principle:

> Ultimately, entitlements based on their status as "victims" rob Hispanics of real power. The history of American ethnic groups is one of overcoming disadvantage, of competing with those who were already here and proving themselves as competent as any who came before. Their fight was always to be treated the same as other Americans, never to be treated as special, certainly not to turn the temporary disadvantages they suffered into permanent entitlement. Anyone who thinks this fight was easier in the earlier part of this century when it was waged by other ethnic groups does not know history.
>
> –Linda Chavez, "Towards a New Politics of Hispanic Assimilation"

Chavez expects Hispanics to accept her claims because she believes they don't wish to be treated differently from other ethnic groups in the society.

Naturally, societies in other times and places have operated from very different premises—they may have privileged a particular race, gender, religion, or aristocratic birth. Such powerful culturally based assumptions may operate within smaller groups, especially those with long traditions. Indeed, *tradition* itself may be one such value. No doubt you've heard ideas or actions defended on the grounds that *we have always done it that way*. Understanding such core cultural assumptions is a key both to making successful arguments and to challenging the status quo.

Providing Logical Structures for Argument

Some types of argument are less tightly bound to cultural assumptions. Instead, they provide structures that can support very different, and sometimes even opposing, claims. In the second part of this book, we examine some of these patterns and strategies: *arguments of fact, arguments of definition, evaluations, causal arguments,* and *proposals*. Although we present them individually, you'll routinely blur their boundaries. Arguments should be consistent, but they needn't follow a single pattern.

In fact, there are many types of logical structures to build on—arguments that your readers will understand without the need for much explanation. In the following pages, we identify just a few.

Degree

Arguments based on degree—in all their endless permutations—are so common that people barely notice them. Nor do people pay much attention to how they work because they seem self-evident. Most audiences will readily accept that *more of a good thing or less of a bad thing is good*. In the novel *The Fountainhead,* novelist Ayn Rand asks: "If physical slavery is repulsive, how much more repulsive is the concept of servility of the spirit?" Most readers immediately comprehend the point Rand intends to make about slavery of the spirit because they already know that physical slavery is cruel and would reject any forms of slavery that were crueler still on the principle that *more of a bad thing is bad*. Rand may still have to offer evidence that "servility of the spirit" is, in fact, worse than bodily servitude, but she has begun with a structure readers can grasp. Here are other arguments that work similarly:

> If I can get a ten-year warranty on a humble Kia, shouldn't I get the same or better warranty from Lexus?
>
> The health benefits from using stem cells in research will surely outweigh the ethical risks.
>
> Better a conventional war now than a nuclear confrontation later.

Analogies

Analogies usually involve explaining one idea or concept by comparing it to something else. People understand comparisons intuitively. Indeed, people habitually think in comparative terms, through similes and metaphors: *Life is like a box of chocolates; war is hell.* An analogy is typically a complex or extended comparison. Following is an extended analogy that supports a controversial claim made in the very first sentence:

> Today, one of the most powerful religions in the Western World is environmentalism. Environmentalism seems to be the religion of choice for urban atheists. Why do I say it's a religion? Well, just look at the beliefs. If you look carefully, you see that environmentalism is in fact a perfect 21st century remapping of traditional Judeo-Christian beliefs and myths.
>
> There's an initial Eden, a paradise, a state of grace and unity with nature, there's a fall from grace into a state of pollution as a result of eating from the tree of knowledge, and as a result of our actions there is a judgment day coming for us all. We are all energy sinners, doomed to die, unless we seek salvation, which is now called sustainability.

Sustainability is salvation in the church of the environment. Just as organic food is its communion, that pesticide-free wafer that the right
people with the right beliefs, imbibe.

Eden, the fall of man, the loss of grace, the coming doomsday—
these are deeply held mythic structures. They are profoundly conservative beliefs. They may even be hard-wired in the brain, for all I
know. I certainly don't want to talk anybody out of them, as I don't
want to talk anybody out of a belief that Jesus Christ is the son of God
who rose from the dead. But the reason I don't want to talk anybody
out of these beliefs is that I know that I can't talk anybody out of them.
These are not facts that can be argued. These are issues of faith.

And so it is, sadly, with environmentalism. Increasingly it seems
facts aren't necessary, because the tenets of environmentalism are all
about belief.

–Michael Crichton, "Remarks to the Commonwealth Club"

Needless to say, environmentalists (a very large and diverse group)
would resist such a categorization and challenge the details of the analogy. And analogies of argument *are* routinely abused, so much so that
faulty analogy (see p. 511) is one of the most familiar fallacies of argument.

Precedent

Arguments from precedent are related to arguments of analogy in that
they both involve comparisons. Sometimes an argument of precedent
focuses on comparable institutions. Consider an assertion like the following:

If motorists in most other states can pump their own gas safely, surely
the state of New Jersey can trust its own drivers to be as capable. It's
time for New Jersey to permit self-service gas stations.

You could pull a lot of inferences out of this claim to explain its reasonableness: People in New Jersey are about as capable as people in other
states; people with equivalent capabilities can do the same thing; pump-
ing gas is not hard, and so forth. But you don't have to because most
readers would *get* the argument simply because of the way it is put
together.

Here's an excerpt from a more extended argument by a Yale law professor on the rather odd topic of single-sex toilets. It uses several arguments of precedent:

If Everything's an Argument . . .

Examine the examples cited in this chapter of *Everything's an Argument*, looking for patterns, tendencies, biases, habits, and so on, and then use those findings to support a factual claim about the chapter or its authors and editors. For example, do the examples habitually come from certain types of sources (academic more than popular), or do the authors favor some genres (Web pages) over others (blogs)? Do you detect political, cultural, racial, or gender biases in the examples? Or perhaps you find the authors and editors trying too hard to seem open-minded and inclusive. Are there kinds of examples you think *should* be included in a chapter on facts and reason that you do not find here? Do the examples seem dated or eccentric to you, perhaps suggesting that the authors and editors come from a specific generation (boomers, Generation Xers)? It's okay to reach a little beyond this chapter for your evidence: perhaps "Arguments Based on Facts and Reason" confirms a tendency you've already detected elsewhere in the book. Write a page or so defending your claim with the evidence you've gathered.

We don't have single-sex toilets at home, and we don't need them at the office. Then there's also the small question of efficiency. I see my male colleagues waiting in line to use the men's room, when the women's toilet is unoccupied. Which is precisely why Delta Airlines doesn't label those two bathrooms at the back of the plane as being solely for men and women. It just wouldn't fly.

The University of Chicago just got the 10 single-use restrooms on campus designated gender neutral. It's time Yale followed suit. And this is not just an academic problem. There are tens of thousands of single-use toilets at workplaces and public spaces throughout the nation that are wrong-headedly designated for a single-sex. All these single-use toilets should stop discriminating. They should be open to all on a first-come, first-lock basis. This is not just good sense. It's the law.

–Ian Ayres, "Looking Out for No. 2"

Other precedents deal with issues of time:

What was done in the past is a good/bad model for what we should do now.

For instance, every military action by the United States since the early 1970s has been ominously branded, at some moment and for persuasive reasons, as "another Vietnam." Cases in court are also routinely argued on precedents. What courts have decided in the past often determines how courts will rule on a similar or related issue. Even parents use precedents in dealing with their children:

We never let your older sister have a car while she was in high school, so we're not about to let you have one either.

It should be easy to appreciate the appeal in overturning precedents, particularly in a society as fond of rebellious stances as American culture. But there's no denying that you can support a claim effectively by showing that it's consistent with previous policies, actions, or beliefs.

You'll encounter additional kinds of logical structures as you create your own arguments. You'll find some of them in Chapter 6 on Toulmin argument and still more in Chapter 17, "Fallacies of Argument."

RESPOND•

1. Discuss whether the following statements are examples of hard evidence or rational appeals. Not all cases are clear-cut.

   "The bigger they are, the harder they fall."

   Drunk drivers are involved in more than 50 percent of traffic deaths.

   DNA tests of skin found under the victim's fingernails suggest that the defendant was responsible for the assault.

   Polls suggest that a large majority of Americans favor a constitutional amendment to ban flag burning.

   A psychologist testified that teenage violence could not be blamed on computer games.

   Honey attracts more flies than vinegar.

   History proves that cutting tax rates increases government revenues because people work harder when they can keep more of what they earn.

"We have nothing to fear but fear itself."

Air bags ought to be removed from vehicles because they can kill young children and small-framed adults.

2. We suggest in this chapter that statistical evidence becomes useful only when responsible authors interpret the data fairly and reasonably. As an exercise, go to the *USA Today* Web site or to the newspaper itself and look for the daily graph, chart, or table called the *USA Today* snapshot. (On the Web site, you'll have a series of these items to choose from.) Pick a snapshot, and use the information in it to support at least three different claims. See if you can get at least two of the claims to make opposing or very different points. Share your claims with classmates. (We don't mean to suggest that you learn to use data dishonestly, but it's important that you see firsthand how the same statistics can serve a variety of arguments.)

3. Testimony can be just as suspect as statistics. For example, check out the newspaper ads for some recent movies. How lengthy are the quotes from reviewers? A reviewer's stinging indictment of a shoot-'em-up film—"this blockbuster may prove to be a great success at the box office, but it stinks as filmmaking"—could be reduced to "A great success." Bring to class a full review of a recent film that you enjoyed. (If you haven't enjoyed any films lately, select a review of one you hated.) Using testimony from that review, write a brief argument to your classmates explaining why they should see that movie (or why they should avoid it). Be sure to use the evidence from the review fairly and reasonably, as support for a claim that you're making.

   Then exchange arguments with a classmate, and decide whether the evidence in your peer's argument helps convince you about the movie. What's convincing about the evidence? If it doesn't convince you, why not?

4. Choose an issue of some consequence, locally or nationally, and then create a series of questions designed to poll public opinion on the issue. But design the questions to evoke a range of responses. See if you can design a reasonable question that would make people strongly inclined to favor or approve an issue, a second question that would lead them to oppose the same proposition just as intensely, a third that tries to be more neutral, and additional questions that provoke different degrees of approval or disapproval. If possible, try out your questions on your classmates.

5
Thinking Rhetorically

When the thirty-second spot first aired in late March 2004, many viewers reacted with disbelief: *What the . . . ?! The guy with the mustache . . . and a sexy underwear model . . . it couldn't be . . . could it?*

But it was—counterculture folk legend, pop icon, and 1997 Kennedy Center honoree Bob Dylan crooning "Love Sick" in a TV ad for Victoria's Secret, a purveyor of sexy women's underclothes. Dylan, who had never before pitched a product other than his own recordings, now looked like a cross between Snidely Whiplash and

Salvador Dali as he traded glances with a winged vixen in high heels. The bard who'd penned "The Times They Are A-Changin'" and "Blowin' in the Wind" had sold his birthright, disillusioned critics charged, for—yikes—a bra and blue panties.

Media critic Seth Stevenson, writing in *Slate*, devoted a full column to analyzing the pitch, trying first to figure out why an artist of Dylan's stature would do a commercial—Money? Whimsy? Exposure? But then he turns to a question just as intriguing, especially if—thinking rhetorically—one is curious about how ads work their persuasive magic:

Why would a brand that's about sexiness, youth, and glamour want any connection at all with a decrepit, sixtysomething folksinger? The answer, my friend, is totally unclear. The answer is totally unclear.

Even if Victoria's Secret hopes to bring in more boomer women, do those women want their underwear to exude the spirit and essence of Bob Dylan? Or, conversely, is Bob Dylan the sort of man they're hoping to attract? Even if you're of the belief that men frequently shop at VS for their ladies, I still don't see the appeal of this ad. I, for instance, am a man, and I can assure you that Bob Dylan is not what I'm looking for in a woman's undergarment. (And if I found him there—man, would that be disturbing.)

Victoria's Secret wouldn't return my calls, but media reports say the idea of putting Dylan's face in the ad (they'd been using his song—"Love Sick"—in ads for the past year or so) came straight from corporate chief Les Wexner. To the company's surprise, Dylan

Bob Dylan and the products he pitches

accepted their offer. It's at this point that someone at Victoria's Secret should have stopped the madness. Just because you can hire Bob Dylan as the figurehead for your lingerie line, doesn't mean you should. Perhaps no one was willing to say no to the big boss, or perhaps they fully expected Dylan to say no. Joke's on them.

–Seth Stevenson, "Tangled Up in Boobs"

To pose the sort of questions Stevenson asks here is to perform (on a small scale) what's called a *rhetorical analysis,* a close reading of a text to find how and whether it works to persuade. In just these few paragraphs from a longer piece, Stevenson considers some of the basic strategies of argument explored in this book's preceding chapters. He first identifies the ethos of the company making the appeal (sexiness, youth, glamour) and finds it hard to reconcile with the ethos of the celebrity in the ad (decrepit, sixtysomething). He considers the emotional pull the TV commercial might have, maybe enticing dirty old men to buy expensive underwear for their ladies, but then rejects the logic of that approach: even men who shop for underwear at Victoria's Secret certainly don't want to think about Dylan when they do. Then Stevenson takes a step beyond the ad itself to consider the rhetorical world in which it might have been created—one in which it would seem so cool to have a superstar spokesperson like Bob Dylan that you don't think about the messages you might be sending. Stevenson's conclusion? "Joke's on them."

Whenever you encounter a similarly puzzling, troubling, or even successful appeal, try subjecting it to a rhetorical analysis of your own, asking yourself what strategies the piece employs to move your heart, win your trust, and change your mind—and why it does or doesn't do so. Here's how.

Composing a Rhetorical Analysis

Arguments have many strategies. But exactly how does a Bose ad make you want to buy new speakers or an op-ed piece in the *Washington Post* suddenly change your thinking about school vouchers? A rhetorical analysis might help you understand. You perform a rhetorical analysis by analyzing how well the components of an argument work together to persuade or move an audience. You can study arguments of any kind— advertisements, as we've seen, or editorials, political cartoons, perhaps even movies or photographs. (If everything really is an argument, then just about any communication can be opened up rhetorically.)

Because arguments have many aspects, you may need to focus a rhetorical analysis on elements that stand out or make the piece intriguing or problematic. You could begin by exploring issues such as the following:

- What is the purpose of this argument? What does it hope to achieve?
- Who is the audience for this argument?
- What appeals or techniques does the argument use—emotional, logical, ethical?
- Who is making the argument? What ethos does it create, and what values does it assume?
- How does it try to make the writer or creator seem trustworthy?
- What authorities does the argument rely on or appeal to?
- What facts are used in the argument? What logic? What evidence? How is the evidence arranged and presented?
- What claims are advanced in the argument? What issues are raised, and which ones are ignored or, perhaps, evaded?
- What are the contexts—social, political, historical, cultural—for this argument? Whose interests does it serve? Who gains or loses by it?
- What shape does the argument take? How is the argument presented or arranged? What media do the argument use?
- How does the language or style of the argument work to persuade an audience?

Questions like these should get you thinking. But don't just describe techniques and strategies in a rhetorical analysis. Instead, show how the key devices in an argument actually make it succeed or fail. Quote language freely from a written piece, or describe the elements in a visual argument. (Annotating a visual text is one option.) Show readers where and why an argument makes sense and where it seems to fall apart (just as Stevenson does in the Victoria's Secret ad). If you believe that an argument startles audiences or challenges them, insults them, or lulls them into complacency, explain precisely why that's so and provide evidence. Don't be surprised when your rhetorical analysis itself becomes an argument. That's what it should be.

Understanding the Purpose of an Argument

To understand how well any argument works, ask what its purpose might be: To sell shoes? To advocate Social Security reform? To push a political agenda? In many cases, that purpose may be obvious, or at least seem so. A conservative newspaper will likely advance a right-wing agenda on its editorial page; ads from a baby food company will show happy infants delighted with stewed prunes and squash. But some projects may be coy about their persuasive intentions or blur the lines between types of argument. Perhaps you've responded to a mail survey or telephone poll only to discover that the questions are leading you to switch your cell phone service. Does such a stealthy argument succeed? That may depend on whether you're more intrigued by the promise of cheaper phone rates than offended by the bait-and-switch. The deception could provide material for a thoughtful rhetorical analysis in which you measure the strengths, risks, and ethics of such strategies.

Genre can be important in determining how to assess an argument. You probably know the difference between different types (or *genres*) of arguments—say, between an op-ed column and a bumper sticker. You'd have every right to challenge an argument in an editorial if it lacked sufficient evidence; you'd look foolish making the same complaint about a bumper sticker. But you could still expect that a bumper sticker meet the expectations of *its* genre: compressed, attention-getting, sometimes clever or sarcastic argument.

 Funny, offensive, or both?

Understanding Who Makes an Argument

Knowing *who* is claiming *what* is key to any analysis. That's why you'll usually find the name of a person or an institution attached to an argument or persuasive appeal. Remember the statements included in TV ads during the last federal election campaign: "Hello, I'm Jane Doe and I approved this ad"? Federal law requires such statements so that viewers can tell the difference between ads actually endorsed by candidates and those sponsored by special interest groups not always affiliated with the campaigns. Their interests and motives might be very different.

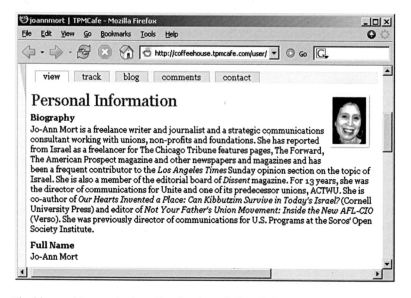

The blogger bio: required reading for rhetorical analysis

Of course, knowing an author's name is just a starting place for a serious analysis. You need to dig deeper whenever you don't recognize the author of an argument or the institution sponsoring it—and sometimes even when you do. You could do worse than to google the Internet to discover more about such people or groups. What else have they produced? By whom have they been published—the *Wall Street Journal,* the blog DailyKos, or, perhaps, *Spin?* Big difference. If a group has a Web site, what can you learn about its goals, policies, contributors, and, very important, funding? These days, you can't afford to be naïve about who's asking for your ear. Nor do you have an excuse for ignoring the biases, special interests, and conflicts of interest in people competing for your attention. The information is out there for you to find.

Identifying and Appealing to Audiences

Audience is the third person of the rhetorical Trinity, after author and purpose. Most arguments are composed with specific audiences in mind, and their success depends, in part, on how well their strategies, content,

tone, and language meet the expectations of readers or viewers. In analyzing an argument, you must first identify its target audience(s), remembering how complex that notion can be (see "Audiences for Arguments"
on pp. 32–37). But you can usually make an educated judgment because
most arguments have contexts that, one way or another, describe whom
they intend to reach and in what ways. Both a photocopied sheet stapled
to a bulletin board in a college dorm ("Why You Should Be a Socialist")
and a forty-foot billboard for Bud Lite might be aimed at the same general population—college students. But each will adjust its appeals for the
different moods of that group in different moments. The political screed
will likely be deliberately simple in layout and full of earnest language
("We live in a world of obscene inequality . . .") to appeal to students in a
serious vein, while the liquor ad will be visually stunning and virtually
text-free to connect with students when they aren't quite so worried
about uniting the workers of the world. Your rhetorical analysis might
make a case for the success or failure of such audience-based strategies.

You might also examine how a writer or an argument establishes
credibility with an audience. One very effective means of building credibility, you will discover, comes through a seven-letter word made famous by Aretha Franklin: *respect*. Respect is crucial in arguments that
invoke audiences who don't agree on critical issues or who may not have
thought carefully about the issues presented. In introducing an article
on problems facing African American women in the workplace, editor-
in-chief of *Essence* Diane Weathers considers the problems she faced
with respecting *all* her potential readers:

> We spent more than a minute agonizing over the provocative cover
> line for our feature "White Women at Work." The countless stories we
> had heard from women across the country told us that this was a
> workplace issue we had to address. From my own experience at sev-
> eral major magazines, it was painfully obvious to me that Black and
> White women are not on the same track. Sure, we might all start out
> in the same place. But early in the game, most sisters I know become
> stuck—and the reasons have little to do with intelligence or drive. At
> some point we bump our heads against that ceiling. And while White
> women may complain of a glass ceiling, for us, the ceiling is concrete.
>
> So how do we tell this story without sounding whiny and paranoid,
> or turning off our White-female readers, staff members, advertisers
> and girlfriends? Our solution: Bring together real women (several of
> them highly successful senior corporate executives), put them in a
> room, promise them anonymity and let them speak their truth.
>
> —Diane Weathers, "Speaking Our Truth"

Both paragraphs affirm Weathers's determination to treat audiences fairly *and* to deal honestly with a difficult subject. The strategy would merit attention in any rhetorical analysis.

Look, too, for signals that writers share values with readers or at least understand an audience. In the following passage, writer Jack Solomon is very clear about one value he hopes readers have in common—a preference for "straight talk":

> There are some signs in the advertising world that Americans are getting fed up with fantasy advertisements and want to hear some straight talk. Weary of extravagant product claims and irrelevant associations, consumers trained by years of advertising to distrust what they hear seem to be developing an immunity to commercials.
> –Jack Solomon, "Masters of Desire: The Culture of American Advertising"

It's a pretty safe assumption, isn't it? Who favors doubletalk or duplicity? But writers or advertisers can manage even more complex appeals to values, talking the talk to target specific groups and their experiences, values, and perceptions. Here's media critic Seth Stevenson again, first summarizing ads in a new anti-smoking campaign directed specifically at teens:

> The spots: *They appear to be episodes of a sitcom called "Fair Enough." In this series of 30-second segments, a team of tobacco executives brainstorms new ways to market to teens. Among their ideas: fruit-flavored chewing tobacco, tobacco in the form of a gum ball, and an effort to win influence with the "hipster" crowd by giving them free packs of smokes.*
> –Seth Stevenson, "How to Get Teens Not to Smoke"

Then he does a rhetorical analysis, explaining why the particular TV spot will resonate with its target audience. The creators of the ad clearly knew what might motivate teens to give up cigarettes—insecurity:

> In fact, the ultimate adolescent nightmare is to appear in any way unsavvy—like an out-of-it rookie who doesn't know the score. These "Fair Enough" ads isolate and prey on that insecurity, and they do a great job. With a dead-on, rerun sitcom parody (jumpy establishing shot; upbeat horn-section theme song ending on a slightly unresolved note; three-wall, two-camera set; canned laugh track), the ads first establish their own savvy, knowing coolness before inviting us to join them in ridiculing big tobacco's schemes. The spots are darkly comic, just the way teens like it. And rather than serving up yet more boring evidence that smoking is deadly (something that all teens, including

> ### If Everything's an Argument . . .
>
> Choose another chapter in this textbook, and read it with a special eye for how it addresses its readers. Do the authors follow the guidelines offered here—that is, do they demonstrate knowledge and respect their readers? How do they use pronouns to establish a relationship between themselves and their readers? What other strategies for connecting with readers can you identify? Write a page summarizing your observations.

the ones who smoke, already know) the ads move on to the far more satisfying step: kicking big tobacco in the groin.

Examining Arguments from the Heart: *Pathos*

Arguments from the heart appeal to readers' emotions and feelings. Some emotional appeals are, in fact, just ploys to win readers over with a pretty face, figurative or real. You've seen ads promising an exciting life and attractive friends if only you drink the right beer or wear designer clothes. Are you fooled by such claims? Probably not, if you pause to think about them. But that's the strategy, isn't it—to distract you from thought just long enough to make a bad choice. It's a move worth commenting upon in a rhetorical analysis. Yet you might also want to applaud illogical appeals that nonetheless work brilliantly. Consider the stylish iPod TV spots, just silhouettes of people dancing to the tunes from their white ear buds. How do these spots make their case, and is the emotional spike they create suited to the product?

Emotions can add real muscle to arguments, too. For example, persuading people not to drink and drive by making them fear death, injury, or arrest seems like a fair use of an emotional appeal. That's exactly what the Texas Department of Transportation did in 2002 when it created a memorable ad campaign (see the figure on p. 111) featuring the image of a formerly beautiful young woman horribly scarred in a fiery accident caused by a driver who'd had too much to drink. In an analysis, you might note the impact of the headline right above the gut-wrenching image: "Not everyone who gets hit by a drunk driver dies."

In analyzing emotional appeals, judge whether the emotions raised—be they anger, sympathy, fear, envy, joy, or love—advance the claims

Jacqueline Saburido was 20 years old when the car she was riding in was hit by a drunk driver. Today, at 24, she is still working to put her life back together.
Learn more at www.TexasDWI.org

DON'T DRINK & DRIVE

Texas Department of Public Safety · Texas Alcoholic Beverage Commission · Texans Standing Tall · Partnership for a Drug-Free Texas · Texas Commission on Alcohol and Drug Abuse
© 2003 Texas Department of Transportation

Images and words combine to create an unforgettable emotional appeal.

offered. Consider how Paul Begala, a media commentator and former advisor to President Clinton, uses graphic language (*lynch-dragged; crucified; bludgeoned*) and deliberate repetition (*it's red*) to provoke revulsion against states that had just voted Republican in a recent presidential election:

> You see the state where James Byrd was lynch-dragged behind a pickup truck until his body came apart—it's red. You see the state where Matthew Shepard was crucified on a split-rail fence for the

crime of being gay—it's red. You see the state where right-wing extremists blew up a federal office building and murdered scores of federal employees—it's red. The state where an Army private who was thought to be gay was bludgeoned to death with a baseball bat, and the state where neo-Nazi skinheads murdered two African-Americans because of their skin color, and the state where Bob Jones University spews its anti-Catholic bigotry: they're all red too.

–Paul Begala, "Banana Republicans"

Does the passion here move you, or does it suggest an argument out of control, damaging its own case? Your task in a rhetorical analysis would be to study an author's words, the emotions they evoke, and the claims they support, and then to make such a judgment.

Examining Arguments Based on Character: *Ethos*

It should come as no surprise: readers believe writers who seem honest, wise, and trustworthy. So in examining the effectiveness of an argument, look for evidence of these traits. Does the writer have the experience or authority to write on this subject? Are all claims qualified reasonably? Is evidence presented in full, not tailored to the writer's agenda? Are important objections to the author's position acknowledged and addressed? Are sources documented? Above all, does the writer sound trustworthy? Here, in a paragraph from a lengthy argument about church/state conflicts in the United States, Professor Noah Feldman of the New York University School of Law hits just the right notes to sound concerned, thoughtful, and above all, evenhanded in balancing the rights of both "values evangelicals" who see a role for religion in the political arena and "legal secularists" who would rather keep religion out of public deliberations.

The solution I have in mind rests on the basic principle of protecting the liberty of conscience. So long as all citizens have the same right to speak and act free of coercion, no adult should feel threatened or excluded by the symbolic or political speech of others, however much he may disagree with it. If many congressmen say that their faith requires intervening to save Terri Schiavo, that is not a violation of the rules of political debate. The secular congresswoman who thinks

Feldman offers a personal proposal based on a principle both sides will likely accept.

He insists that political debate must allow for people of faith to base their arguments on their deeply held principles.

Schiavo should have the right to die in peace can express her contrary view and explain why it is that she believes a rational and legal analysis of the situation requires it. She may lose the vote, but she is not excluded from the process or from the body that votes against her, any more than a Republican would be "excluded" from a committee controlled by Democrats.

Then he applies the same principle to secularists, treating both sides with fairness and respect.

–Noah Feldman, "A Church-State Solution"

In performing such an analysis, pay attention to the details, right down to the choice of words or, in a visual argument, the shapes and colors. The modest, tentative tone of "[t]he solution I have in mind," in Feldman's argument, is an example of the kind of choice that can shape an audience's perception of ethos. But these details need your interpretation. Language that's hot and extreme can mark a writer as either passionate or loony. Work that's sober and carefully organized might suggest that an institution is either competent or anal. Technical terms and abstract phrases can make a writer seem either knowledgeable or pompous.

Examining Arguments Based on Facts and Reason: *Logos*

In judging most arguments, you'll have to decide whether an argument makes a plausible claim and offers good reasons for you to believe it.

Not all arguments you read will package such claims in a single neat sentence, or *thesis*—nor should they. A writer may tell a story from which you have to infer the claim; think of the way many films make a social or political statement by dramatizing an issue, whether it be political corruption, government censorship, or economic injustice. Visual arguments may work the same way: viewers have to assemble the parts and draw inferences before they get the point.

In some conventional arguments, the sort you might find on an editorial page, arguments may be perfectly obvious. Writers stake out a claim and then offer the reasons you should consider; or they work in the opposite direction, laying out a case that leads you toward a conclusion. Consider the following examples. The first is a provocative opening paragraph by economist Paul Krugman previewing the contents of his

caglecartoons.com/español

What argument does this editorial cartoon by Antonio Neri Licon, "Nerilicon," make? What elements come together to constitute the claim? It may be helpful to look at the Not Just Words box on p. 116 along with the cartoon, which originally appeared in *El Economista,* Mexico City, on March 29, 2005.

column in the *New York Times;* the second occurs nearer the conclusion of a lengthy article defending the car against its many snobbish critics:

> Fifteen years ago, when Japanese companies were busily buying up chunks of corporate America, I was one of those urging Americans not to panic. You might therefore expect me to offer similar soothing words now that the Chinese are doing the same thing. But the Chinese challenge — highlighted by the bids for Maytag and Unocal — looks a lot more serious than the Japanese challenge ever did.
> —Paul Krugman, "The Chinese Challenge"

> But even if we do all the things that can be done to limit the social costs of cars, the campaign against them will not stop. It will not stop because so many of the critics dislike everything the car stands for and everything society constructs to serve the needs of its occupants.
> —James Q. Wilson, "Cars and Their Enemies"

Think of claims like these as vortices of energy in an argument. You need to identify any such statements and then examine a text carefully to see how (sometimes *whether*) they're supported by good reasons and reliable evidence. A lengthy essay may, in fact, contain a series of claims, each developed to support an even larger point. Indeed, every paragraph in an argument may develop a specific and related idea. In a rhetorical analysis, you need to track down all these separate propositions and examine the relationships among them. Are they solidly linked? Are there inconsistencies that the writer should acknowledge? Does the end of the piece support what the writer said (and promised) at the beginning?

Since many logical appeals rely heavily on data and information from sources, you'll also need to examine the quality of the information presented in an argument, assessing how accurately such information is reported, how conveniently it's displayed (in charts or graphs, for example), and how well the sources cited represent a range of *respected* opinion on a topic.

Knowing how to judge the quality of sources is more important now than ever because the electronic pathways, where increasing numbers of writers find their information, are clogged with junk. The computer terminal may have become the equivalent of a library reference room in certain ways, but the sources available online vary much more widely in quality. As a consequence, both readers and writers of arguments today must know the difference between reliable, firsthand, or fully documented sources and those that don't meet such standards. (For more on using and documenting sources, see Chapters 19 and 20.)

Examining the Shape and Media of Arguments

Arguments have a structure. Aristotle carved the structure of logical argument to its bare bones when he observed that it had only two parts:

- statement
- proof

You could do worse, in examining an argument, than just to make sure that every claim a writer makes is backed by sufficient evidence.

Most arguments you read and write, however, will be more than mere statements followed by proofs. Some writers will lay their cards on the table immediately; others may lead you carefully through a chain of claims toward a conclusion. Writers may even interrupt their arguments to offer background information or cultural contexts for readers. Sometimes they'll tell stories or provide anecdotes that make an argumentative point. They'll qualify the arguments they make, too, so they don't bite off more than they can chew. Smart writers may even pause to admit that other points of view are plausible, though they might also spend time undercutting such contrary opinions or evidence. In other words, there are no formulas or acceptable patterns that fit all successful

Not Just Words

New media such as Web sites and blogs have practically made a sport out of analyzing the stories and arguments offered by traditional mainstream media (MSM) such as newspapers, TV network news, and print publishers. It's no surprise that the MSM have pushed back, providing readers with uncharacteristically lively examples of rhetorical analyses as part of the daily news.

In September 2005, the *San Francisco Chronicle,* usually regarded as a liberal news source, included in its coverage of an anti–Iraq War demonstration a memorable close-up photograph of a youth at the protest, with the following caption: "Jasmine Williams, 17, a student with the leadership group Youth Together, joins the Iraq war protest in San Francisco."

The image provoked the ire of a presumably more conservative blogger at <zombietime.com.> Zombie, who had also photographed the event and even the same girl, but at a wider angle, found the *Chronicle*'s shot disingenuous, omitting details such as Palestinian flags in the background. Here are some of Zombie's photographs and commentary:

Now we can see that the girl is just one of several teenagers, all wearing terrorist-style bandannas covering their faces. But, as you'll notice, the bandannas are all printed with the same design. Was this a grassroots protest statement the teenagers had come up with all by themselves? To find out, let's take a look at another photo in the series, taken at the same time:

Oops—it looks like they're actually being stage-managed by an adult, who is giving them directions and guiding them toward the front of the march. But who is she? The last picture in the series reveals all. It turns out that the woman giving directions belongs to one of the Communist groups organizing the rally—if her t-shirt is to be believed, since it depicts the flag of Communist Vietnam, which has been frequently displayed by such groups at protest rallies in the U.S. for decades. The *San Francisco Chronicle* featured the original photograph on its front Web page in order to convey a positive message about the rally—perhaps that even politically aware teenagers were inspired to show up and rally for peace, sporting the message, "People of Color say 'No to War!'" And that served the *Chronicle*'s agenda. But this simple analysis reveals the very subtle but insidious type of bias that occurs in the media all the time. The *Chronicle* did not print an inaccuracy, nor did it doctor a photograph to misrepresent the facts. Instead, the *Chronicle* committed the sin of omission: it told you the truth, but it didn't tell you the *whole* truth.

As you might expect, shortly after Zombie's photos and observations made their way around the Web, the *Chronicle* offered a rebuttal. Here's a brief portion of that newspaper's rhetorical analysis of the situation, offered by "readers' representative" Dick Rogers:

So the *Chronicle* photo didn't exactly shout "Middle America." It was far more dramatic and displayed the protester in far more detail. If the newspaper was setting out to "de-radicalize" the scene, it did a pretty lame job. If the paper wants to sanitize a protest, it should forget tight shots of radicals in disguise and go for pictures of suburban moms with young children. Now that's centrist.

The accompanying story, by the way, noted the Palestinian angle, the arrests of members of an anarchist group and the presence of counter-demonstrators, one of whom called for "patriotism instead of a socialist revolution."

Readers should ponder what they don't see in pictures, just as they should critically judge what they do see. Photographs are representations of reality, and small slices of it at that.

But a wide-angle view isn't necessarily a bigger slice of reality. It's true that, in some cases, a story is told in more detail by stepping back. In other cases, an image is more powerful and vivid by coming in close.

–Dick Rogers, "Picturing the Debate"

Study the photographs and the contrary rhetorical analyses here. Do you have a problem with the original photograph published in the *Chronicle,* or might one of Zombie's images more accurately represent the protest? Can you make such a judgment without more information? How could you find out more about this controversy?

Apply what you learn from this exercise to your own analysis of several news photographs selected from current newspapers, news magazines, or Web sites. Do the images you've chosen provide the facts you need to make a judgment about a story, or do you suspect something may have been left out of them? Do the images provoke strong emotional responses because of their careful composition, or do they manipulate your feelings? Do you have reason to trust the source offering the images, or might the ethos of that source be suspect? Select one or two of the images, and present your rhetorical analysis of them to your class.

arguments. Many are written on the fly in the heat of a moment. In writing a rhetorical analysis, you'll have to assess the organization of a persuasive text on its own merits.

It's fair, however, to complain about what may be *absent* from an argument. Most arguments of proposal (see Chapter 11), for example, include a section that defends the feasibility of a new idea, explaining how it might be funded or managed. In a rhetorical analysis, you might fault an editorial that supports a new stadium for a city without addressing feasibility issues. Similarly, analyzing a movie review that reads like off-the-top-of-the-head opinion, you might legitimately ask what criteria of evaluation are in play (see Chapter 9).

You also may find that an argument benefits from strong transitions, helpful headings, or a confident voice that makes navigating the claims easy. Don't take such an accomplishment for granted. Nor should you ignore the way a writer or institution uses media in an argument. Would an argument originally made in an editorial, for instance, work better as a cartoon (or vice versa)? Would a lengthy paper have more power if it included more images? Or do you find that images distract from a written argument, diminishing its substance? These are important issues you might comment on or connect to other aspects of an argument, such as its style.

Finally, be open to the possibility of new or nontraditional structures of arguments. The visual arguments you analyze may defy conventional principles of logic or arrangement—for example, making juxtapositions rather than logical transitions between elements; or using quick cuts, fades, or other devices to link ideas. Quite often, these nontraditional structures will also resist the neatness of a thesis, leaving it up to readers to construct at least a part of the argument in their heads. Advertisers are growing quite fond of these sorts of soft-sell multimedia productions that can seem more like games or entertainments than what they really are—product pitches. We're asked not just to buy a product but also to live its lifestyle. Is that a reasonable or workable strategy for an argument? Your analysis might entertain such possibilities.

Looking at Style

Even a coherent argument flush with evidence may not connect with readers if it's dull, off-key, or offensive. Readers naturally judge the credibility of arguments in part by how stylishly the case is made—even when they don't know exactly what *style* is. Consider how these simple, blunt sentences from the opening of an argument shape your image of the author and probably determine whether you're willing to continue to read the whole piece:

> We are young, urban and professional. We are literate, respectable, intelligent and charming. But foremost and above all, we know what it's like to be unemployed.
>
> –Julia Carlisle, "Young, Privileged and Unemployed"

Now consider how you'd approach an argument that begins like the following, responding to a botched primary election in Florida following the electoral disaster of 2000:

> The question you're asking yourself is: Does South Florida contain the highest concentration of morons in the entire world? Or just in the United States? The reason you're asking this, of course, is South Florida's performance in Tuesday's election. This election was critical to our image, because of our performance in the 2000 presidential election—the one that ended up with the entire rest of the nation watching, impatiently, as clumps of sleep-deprived South Florida election officials squinted at cardboard ballots, trying to figure out what the hell the voters were thinking when they apparently voted for two presidents, or no presidents, or part of a president, or, in some cases, simply drooled on the ballot.
>
> –Dave Barry, "How to Vote in 1 Easy Step"

Both styles probably work, but they signal that the writers are about to make very different kinds of cases. Style alone tells readers what to expect.

Manipulating style also enables writers to shape readers' responses to their ideas. Devices as simple as repetition and parallelism can give sentences remarkable power. Consider this sentence from Andrew Sullivan, who argues for greater tolerance of homosexuals in American culture:

> Growing up homosexual was to grow up normally but displaced; to experience romantic love, but with the wrong person; to entertain grand ambitions, but of the unacceptable sort; to seek a gradual self-awakening, but in secret, not in public.
>
> –Andrew Sullivan, "What Are Homosexuals For?"

The balanced style of this sentence asks readers to pay attention and perhaps to sympathize. But the entire argument can't be presented in this key without exhausting readers—and it isn't. Style has to be modulated almost like music to keep readers tuned in.

In a rhetorical analysis, you can explore many stylistic choices. Why does a formal style work for discussing one type of subject matter, but

 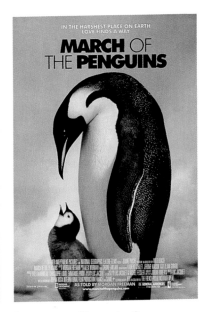

How does *look* support *message* in these documentary film posters?

not another? How does a writer use humor or irony to underscore an important point or to manage a difficult concession? Do stylistic choices, even something as simple as the use of contractions, bring readers comfortably close to a writer, or do a highly technical vocabulary and impersonal voice signal that an argument is for experts only?

To describe the stylistic effects of visual arguments, you may use a different vocabulary, talking about colors, camera angles, editing, balance, proportion, fonts, perspective, and so on. But the basic principle is this: the look of an item—whether it be a poster, an editorial cartoon, or a film documentary—can support the message it carries, undermine it, or muddle it. In some cases, the look will *be* the message. In a rhetorical analysis, you can't ignore style.

Examining a Rhetorical Analysis

Following is an argument in defense of free speech by Derek Bok, a distinguished scholar and past president of Harvard University—credentials that certainly add to his ethos. Responding to it with a detailed analysis is Milena Ateya, a college student who reveals in her piece that she, too, brings unique credentials to this case.

Protecting Freedom of Expression at Harvard

DEREK BOK

March 25, 1991

For several years, universities have been struggling with the problem of trying to reconcile the rights of free speech with the desire to avoid racial tension. In recent weeks, such a controversy has sprung up at Harvard. Two students hung Confederate flags in public view, upsetting students who equate the Confederacy with slavery. A third student tried to protest the flags by displaying a swastika.

These incidents have provoked much discussion and disagreement. Some students have urged that Harvard require the removal of symbols that offend many members of the community. Others reply that such symbols are a form of free speech and should be protected.

Different universities have resolved similar conflicts in different ways. Some have enacted codes to protect their communities from forms of speech that are deemed to be insensitive to the feelings of other groups. Some have refused to impose such restrictions.

It is important to distinguish between the appropriateness of such communications and their status under the First Amendment. The fact that speech is protected by the First Amendment does not necessarily mean that it is right, proper, or civil. I am sure that the vast majority of Harvard students believe that hanging a Confederate flag in public view — or displaying a swastika in response — is insensitive and unwise because any satisfaction it gives to the students who display these symbols is far outweighed by the discomfort it causes to many others.

I share this view and regret that the students involved saw fit to behave in this fashion. Whether or not they merely wished to manifest their pride in the South — or to demonstrate the insensitivity of hanging Confederate flags, by mounting another offensive symbol in return — they must have known that they would upset many fellow students and ignore the decent regard for the feelings of others so essential to building and preserving a strong and harmonious community.

To disapprove of a particular form of communication, however, is not enough to justify prohibiting it. We are faced with a clear example of the conflict between our commitment to free speech and our desire to foster a community founded on mutual respect. Our society has wrestled with this problem for many years. Interpreting the First Amendment, the Supreme Court has clearly struck the balance in favor of free speech.

While communities do have the right to regulate speech in order to uphold aesthetic standards (avoiding defacement of buildings) or to protect the public from disturbing noise, rules of this kind must be applied across the board and cannot be enforced selectively to prohibit certain kinds of messages but not others.

Under the Supreme Court's rulings, as I read them, the display of swastikas or Confederate flags clearly falls within the protection of the free speech clause of the First Amendment and cannot be forbidden simply because it offends the feelings of many members of the community. These rulings apply to all agencies of government, including public universities.

Although it is unclear to what extent the First Amendment is enforceable against private institutions, I have difficulty understanding why a university such as Harvard should have less free speech than the surrounding society—or than a public university.

One reason why the power of censorship is so dangerous is that it is extremely difficult to decide when a particular communication is offensive enough to warrant prohibition or to weigh the degree of offensiveness against the potential value of the communication. If we begin to forbid flags, it is only a short step to prohibiting offensive speakers.

I suspect that no community will become humane and caring by restricting what its members can say. The worst offenders will simply find other ways to irritate and insult.

In addition, once we start to declare certain things "offensive," with all the excitement and attention that will follow, I fear that much ingenuity will be exerted trying to test the limits, much time will be expended trying to draw tenuous distinctions, and the resulting publicity will eventually attract more attention to the offensive material than would ever have occurred otherwise.

Rather than prohibit such communications, with all the resulting risks, it would be better to ignore them, since students would then have little reason to create such displays and would soon abandon them. If this response is not possible—and one can understand why—the wisest course is to speak with those who perform insensitive acts and try to help them understand the effects of their actions on others.

Appropriate officials and faculty members should take the lead, as the Harvard House Masters have already done in this case. In talking with students, they should seek to educate and persuade, rather than resort to ridicule or intimidation, recognizing that only persuasion is likely to produce a lasting, beneficial effect. Through such effects, I believe that we act in the manner most consistent with our ideals as an educational institution and most calculated to help us create a truly understanding, supportive community.

A Curse and a Blessing

MILENA ATEYA

Connects article to personal experience to create ethical appeal.

In 1991, when Derek Bok's essay "Protecting Freedom of Expression at Harvard" was first published in the Boston Globe, I had just come to America to escape the oppressive Communist regime in Bulgaria. Perhaps my background explains why I support Bok's argument that we should not put arbitrary limits on freedom of expression.

Provides brief overview of Bok's argument.

States Bok's central claim.

Bok wrote the essay in response to a public display of Confederate flags and a swastika at Harvard, a situation that created a heated controversy among the students. As Bok notes, universities have struggled to achieve a balance between maintaining students' right of free speech and avoiding racist attacks. When choices must be made, however, Bok argues for preserving freedom of expression.

Transition sentence.

In order to support his claim and bridge the controversy, Bok uses a variety of rhetorical strategies. The author first immerses the reader in the controversy by vividly describing the incident: two Harvard students had hung Confederate flags in public view, thereby "upsetting students who equate the Confederacy with slavery" (51). Another student, protesting the flags, decided to display an even more offensive symbol—the swastika. These actions provoked heated discussions among students. Some students believed that school officials should remove the offensive symbols, whereas others suggested that the symbols "are a form of free speech and should be protected" (51). Bok establishes common ground between the factions: he regrets the actions of the offenders but does not believe we should prohibit such actions just because we disagree with them.

Examines the emotional appeal the author establishes through description.

Links author's credibility to use of logical appeals.

The author earns the reader's respect because of his knowledge and through his logical presentation of the issue. In partial support of his position, Bok refers to U.S.

Supreme Court rulings, which remind us that "the display of swastikas or Confederate flags clearly falls within the protection of the free speech clause of the First Amendment" (52). The author also emphasizes the danger of the slippery slope of censorship when he warns the reader, "If we begin to forbid flags, it is only a short step to prohibiting offensive speakers" (52). Overall, however, Bok's work lacks the kinds of evidence that statistics, interviews with students, and other representative examples of controversial conduct could provide. Thus, his essay may not be strong enough to persuade all readers to make the leap from this specific situation to his general conclusion.

Reference to First Amendment serves as warrant for Bok's claim.

Comments critically on author's evidence.

Throughout, Bok's personal feelings are implied but not stated directly. As a lawyer who was president of Harvard for twenty years, Bok knows how to present his opinions respectfully without offending the feelings of the students. However, qualifying phrases like "I suspect that," and "Under the Supreme Court's rulings, as I read them" could weaken the effectiveness of his position. Furthermore, Bok's attempt to be fair to all seems to dilute the strength of his proposed solution. He suggests that one should either ignore the insensitive deeds in the hope that students might change their behavior, or talk to the offending students to help them comprehend how their behavior is affecting other students.

Examines how Bok establishes ethical appeal.

Identifies qualifying phrases that may weaken claim.

Analyzes author's solution.

Nevertheless, although Bok's proposed solution to the controversy does not appear at first reading to be very strong, it may ultimately be effective. There is enough flexibility in his approach to withstand various tests, and Bok's solution is general enough that it can change with the times and adapt to community standards.

Raises points that suggest Bok's solution may work.

In writing this essay, Bok faced a challenging task: to write a short response to a specific situation that represents a very broad and controversial issue. Some people may find that freedom of expression is both a curse and a blessing because of the difficulties it creates. As one who has lived under a regime that permitted very limited,

Returns to
personal
experience in
conclusion.

censored expression, I am all too aware that I could not
have written this response in 1991 in Bulgaria. As a result,
I feel, like Derek Bok, that freedom of expression is a
blessing, in spite of any temporary problems associated
with it.

Work Cited

Bok, Derek. "Protecting Freedom of Expression on the
Campus." <u>Current Issues and Enduring Questions</u>. Eds.
Sylvan Barnet and Hugo Bedau. 6th ed. Boston: Bedford,
2002. 51–52. Rpt. of "Protecting Freedom of Expression
at Harvard." <u>Boston Globe</u> 25 May 1991.

GUIDE | to writing a rhetorical analysis

● Finding a Topic

A rhetorical analysis is usually assigned work: you're asked to describe how an argument works or to assess its effectiveness. When that's the case and you're free to choose your own subject for analysis, look for one or more of the following qualities:

- a verbal or visual argument that challenges you—or rankles, excites, amazes, impresses
- a verbal or visual argument rich enough to give you stuff to analyze
- a text that raises current or enduring issues of substance
- a text that you believe should be taken more seriously

Look for arguments of all kinds. Obvious places for public arguments are the editorial/op-ed pages of any newspaper, political magazines such as *The Nation* or *The New Republic*, Web sites of organizations and interest groups, political blogs such as <DailyKos.com> or <Powerline.com>, corporate Web sites that post their TV ad spots, and so on.

● Researching Your Topic

Once you've selected a text to analyze, you should find out all you can about it. Use the library or resources of the Web to explore:

- who the author(s) is/are and what credentials they have (or claim)
- if the author is an institution, what it does; what its sources of funding are; who belongs; and so on
- who is publishing or sponsoring the piece, and what they typically publish
- what the leanings or biases of authors and publishers might be
- what the context of the argument is—what preceded or provoked it; how others responded to it

● Formulating a Claim

Begin a rhetorical analysis with a hypothesis in mind. A full thesis might not become evident until after you've looked at the document closely. Your final thesis should reflect the complexity of the piece you're studying, not just state that "the editorial has good pathos and ethos, but lousy logos." In developing a thesis, consider questions such as the following:

- How can I describe what this argument achieves?
- Does the argument have a clear purpose, and does it accomplish it?
- Does the argument have a clear intended audience?
- For what audiences does it work/not work?
- Which of its rhetorical features will likely influence readers most? Audience connections? Emotional appeals? Style?
- Do some aspects of the argument work better than others?
- How do the rhetorical elements interact?

You don't actually have to address these questions in your thesis. Rather, they're offered to take you inside the argument you're studying. Once you're in and you begin to deal with the issues it raises, you'll likely discover the point you need to make.

Here's the hardest part for most writers of rhetorical analyses: whether you agree or disagree with an argument doesn't matter in a rhetorical analysis. You've got to stay out of the fray and pay attention only to how well the argument—even one you dislike—works. That's tough to do. Keep your distance as you write a rhetorical analysis.

● Examples of Possible Claims for a Rhetorical Analysis

- Many people today who admire the inspiring language and elevated style of John F. Kennedy's inaugural address might be uneasy with the claims he actually makes.
- Today's editorial in the *Daily Collegian* about campus crimes may scare first-year students, but its anecdotal reporting doesn't get down to hard numbers—and for a good reason. Those statistics don't back the position taken by the editors.
- Powerline has become an influential blog because its admittedly partisan authors show great respect for the intelligence of readers. In particular, they check sources meticulously and immediately acknowledge and correct any errors.
- VW's "Think Small" spot may be the finest print ad of all time, not because it sold a product well (which it did) but because it actually invoked an audience that wasn't there yet: consumers who weren't comfortable with excessive consumption.

- The original design of New York's Freedom Tower, with its torqued surfaces and evocative spire, made a stronger argument about American values than will its last-minute replacement, a fortress-like skyscraper stripped of imagination and unable to make any statement except "I'm 1,776 feet tall."

● Preparing a Proposal

If your instructor asks you to prepare a proposal for your project, here's a format you might use:

- Provide a copy of the work you intend to analyze, whether it's a printed text or available in some other medium. (You might have to furnish a photograph, digital image, or URL, for instance.)
- Offer a working hypothesis or tentative thesis.
- Indicate which rhetorical components seem, at the outset of the study, especially compelling and worthy of detailed study. Also note where you see potential connections between elements. For example, does the piece seem to emphasize facts and logic so much that it becomes disconnected from potential audiences? If so, hint at that possibility in your proposal.
- Indicate what background information — about the author, institution, and contexts (political, economic, social, religious) of the argument — you intend to research.
- Define the audience you imagine for the analysis. If you're responding to an assignment, you may be writing primarily for a teacher and classmates. But they make up a complex audience in themselves. If you can do so, within the spirit of the assignment, imagine that your analysis will be published in a local newspaper, on a Web site, or in a blog.
- Suggest the media that you might use in your analysis. Will a traditional paper work? Could you use highlighting or other word-processing tools to focus attention on stylistic details? Would it be possible to use balloons or other callouts to annotate a visual argument?
- Conclude by briefly discussing the key challenges you anticipate in preparing your analysis.

● Thinking about Content and Organization

Your rhetorical analysis may take various forms, but it's likely to include elements such as the following:

- facts about the text you're analyzing: author; title or name of the work; where published, located, or seen; date of publication or viewing.

- contexts for the argument. Readers need to know what the text is doing, to what it may be responding, in what controversies it might be embroiled, and so on. Don't assume writers can infer the important contextual elements.

- a synopsis of the text you're analyzing. If you can't actually attach the argument, you must summarize it in enough detail so that a reader can imagine it. Even if you do attach a copy of the piece, the analysis should include a summary.

- some claim(s) about the rhetorical effectiveness of the work. It might be a straightforward evaluative claim or something more complex. The claim can come early in the paper, or you might work toward it steadily, providing the evidence that leads toward the conclusion you've reached.

- a detailed analysis of the argument. Although you'll analyze various rhetorical components and dimensions separately, don't let your analysis become a dull roster of emotional, ethical, and logical appeals. Your rhetorical analysis should be an argument itself that supports a claim; a simple list of rhetorical appeals won't make much of a point.

- evidence for every part of the analysis.

- an assessment of alternative views and counterarguments to your own analysis.

● Getting and Giving Response

If you have access to a writing center, discuss the text you intend to analyze with a consultant there before you write the paper. Try to find people who both agree with the argument and others who disagree, and take note of their observations. Your instructor may assign you to a peer group for the purpose of reading and responding to each other's drafts; if not, share your draft with someone on your own. You can use the following questions to evaluate a draft. If you're evaluating someone else's draft, be sure to illustrate your points with examples. Specific comments are always more helpful than general observations.

The Claim

- Does the claim address the rhetorical effectiveness of the argument itself, not the opinion or position it takes?

- Is the claim significant enough to interest readers?

- Does the claim indicate important relationships between various rhetorical components, not just list them?

- Would the claim be one that the author or creator of the piece might regard as serious criticism?

Evidence for the Claim

- Is enough evidence furnished to explain or support all claims you make? If not, what kind of additional evidence is needed?

- Is the evidence in support of the claim simply announced, or are its significance and appropriateness analyzed? Is a more detailed discussion needed?

- Do you use the right kind of evidence, drawn either from the argument itself or from other materials?

- Are any objections readers might have to the claim, criteria, or evidence, or to the way the analysis is conducted, adequately addressed?

- What kinds of sources might you use to explain the context of the argument? Do you need to use sources to check factual claims made in the argument?

- Are all quotations introduced with appropriate signal phrases (such as "As Peggy Noonan points out"), and do they merge smoothly into your sentences?

Organization and Style

- How are the parts of the argument organized? Is this organization effective, or would some other structure work better?

- Will readers understand the relationships among the original text you're analyzing, the claim(s) you're making, your supporting reasons, and the evidence you've gathered—both from the text you're analyzing and any other sources you've used? If not, what could be done to make those connections clearer? Are more transitional words and phrases needed? Would headings or graphic devices help?

- Are the transitions or links from point to point, paragraph to paragraph, and sentence to sentence clear and effective? If not, how could they be improved?

- Is the style suited to the subject and appropriate to your audience? Is it too formal? Too casual? Too technical? Too bland?

- Which sentences seem particularly effective? Which ones seem weakest, and how could they be improved? Should some short sentences be combined, or should any long ones be separated into two or more sentences?
- How effective are the paragraphs? Do any seem too skimpy or too long? Do they break the analysis at strategic points?
- Which words or phrases seem particularly effective, accurate, and powerful? Do any seem dull, vague, unclear, or inappropriate for the audience or your purpose? Are definitions provided for technical or other terms that readers might not know?

Spelling, Punctuation, Mechanics, Documentation, Format

- Check the spelling of the author's name, and make sure the name of any institution involved with the work is correct. Note that the names of many corporations and institutions use distinctive spelling and punctuation.
- Get the name of the text you're analyzing right.
- Are there any errors in spelling, punctuation, capitalization, and the like?
- Does the assignment require a specific format? Check the original assignment sheet to be sure.

RESPOND•

1. Describe a persuasive moment you can recall from a speech, an article, an editorial, an advertisement, or your personal experience. Alternatively, research one of the following famous moments of persuasion and then describe the circumstances of the appeal: what the historical situation was, what issues were at stake, what the purpose of the address was, and what made the particular speech memorable.

   Abraham Lincoln's "Gettysburg Address" (1863)

   Elizabeth Cady Stanton's draft of the "Declaration of Sentiments" for the Seneca Falls Convention (1848)

   Franklin Roosevelt's inaugural address (1933)

   Winston Churchill's addresses to the British people during the early stages of World War II (1940)

   Martin Luther King Jr.'s "Letter from Birmingham Jail" (1963)

   Ronald Reagan's tribute to the *Challenger* astronauts (1986)

   Toni Morrison's speech accepting the Nobel Prize (1993)

   George Bush's speech to Congress following the 9/11 terrorist attack (2001)

2. Find a written argument on the editorial page or op-ed section in a recent newspaper. Analyze this argument rhetorically, drawing upon the principles discussed in this chapter. Analyze the elements of the argument that best explain why it succeeds, fails, or does something else entirely. Perhaps you can show that the author is unusually successful in connecting with readers, but then has nothing to say. Or perhaps you discover that the strong logical appeal is undercut by a contradictory emotional argument. Upon finishing your analysis, readers should feel that they've learned something about the essay you've taken as your subject. Be sure that the analysis does include a summary of the essay and provided basic publication information: written by whom, published where, by whom?

3. Browse a magazine, newspaper, or Web site to find an example of a powerful emotional argument that's made visually, either alone or using words as well. Then, in a paragraph, defend a claim about how the argument works. For example, does an image itself make a claim, or does it draw you in to consider a verbal claim? What emotion does the argument generate? How does that emotion work to persuade you?

4. Find a recent example of a visual argument, either in print or on the Internet. Analyze this argument rhetorically. Even though you may

have a copy of the image, describe the argument carefully in your paper on the assumption that your description is all readers may have to go on. Then make a judgment about the effectiveness of the visual argument, supporting your claim with clear evidence from the "text."

5. Make one of the other chapters in *Everything's an Argument* the subject of a full-blown rhetorical analysis. Follow the advice in this chapter, particularly in the Guide to Writing on pp. 129–134. Pay particular attention to the ethos the authors try to project and the audiences intended and evoked in the chapter you select for study. Your biggest challenge may be to identify what *argument(s)* the chapter makes.

PART 2

WRITING
arguments

6
Structuring Arguments

"Don't put the cart before the horse."

"Get your ducks in a row."

"Stop beating around the bush!"

"And your point is?"

● ● ●

These familiar idiomatic sayings all suggest the importance of getting things in the right order, or structuring them in the best way, to make a clear, persuasive point.

Pepsi-Cola advertisements, 1954 and 2005

"Don't put the cart before the horse" is particularly good advice for writers of arguments—as long as it's clear which part of the argument is the cart and which the horse. Advertisements usually put the cart before the horse by featuring the product in the foreground and linking it to reasons we should purchase. Take a look at the two advertisements for Pepsi-Cola, one from 1954, the other from 2005: note the way each is structured and designed, what the focal point of the image is, and what reasons are provided or implied in support of the argument the advertisements make.

If arguments are carefully structured in advertisements, and they are, then more traditional arguments also pay very careful attention to the design or structure of their cases. You no doubt recognize the words of the 1776 Declaration of Independence proclaiming the sovereignty of the United States:

> When in the Course of human events, it becomes necessary for one people to dissolve the political bands which have connected them with another, and to assume among the powers of the earth, the separate and equal station to which the Laws of Nature and of Nature's God entitle them, a decent respect to the opinions of mankind requires that they should declare the causes which impel them to the separation.
>
> We hold these truths to be self-evident, that all men are created equal, that they are endowed by their Creator with certain unalienable Rights, that among these are Life, Liberty, and the pursuit of

Happiness—that to secure these rights, Governments are instituted among Men, deriving their just powers from the consent of the governed—That whenever any Form of Government becomes destructive to these ends, it is the Right of the People to alter or to abolish it and to institute new Government, laying its Foundation on such principles and organizing its powers in such form, as to them shall seem most likely to effect their Safety and Happiness. Prudence, indeed, will dictate that Governments long established should not be changed for light and transient causes; and accordingly all experience hath shewn that mankind are more disposed to suffer, while evils are sufferable, than to right themselves by abolishing the forms to which they are accustomed. But when a long train of abuses and usurpations, pursuing invariably the same Object evinces a design to reduce them under absolute Despotism, it is their right, it is their duty, to throw off such Government and to provide new Guards for their future security. — Such has been the patient sufferance of these Colonies; and such is now the necessity which constrains them to alter their former Systems of Government. The history of the present King of Great Britain is a history of repeated injuries and usurpations, all having in direct object the establishment of an absolute Tyranny over these States. To prove this, let Facts be submitted to a candid world.

–Declaration of Independence, July 4, 1776

The Declaration then lists the "long train of abuses and usurpations" by King George III, details the colonists' unsuccessful attempts at reconciliation with the British, and ends by asserting the central claim: "That these United Colonies are, and of Right ought to be FREE AND INDEPENDENT STATES."

The authors might have organized this argument in a different way—for example, by beginning with the last two sentences of the excerpt and then listing the facts intended to prove the king's abuse and tyranny. But by choosing first to explain the purpose and "self-evident" assumptions behind their argument and only then moving on to demonstrate how these "truths" have been denied by the British, the authors forge an immediate connection with readers and build to a more memorable and compelling conclusion.

A little over seventy years after the Declaration of Independence, Elizabeth Cady Stanton and Lucretia Mott gathered a group of people together to issue a new Declaration, one that—with great irony—followed the precise structure of the framing document to make a strong argument about women's rights:

When, in the course of human events, it becomes necessary for one portion of the family of man to assume among the people of the earth a position different from that which they have hitherto occupied, but one to which the laws of nature and of nature's God entitle them, a decent respect to the opinions of mankind requires that they should declare the causes that impel them to such a course.

We hold these truths to be self-evident: that all men and women are created equal; that they are endowed by their Creator with certain inalienable rights; that among these are life, liberty, and the pursuit of happiness; that to secure these rights governments are instituted, deriving their just powers from the consent of the governed. Whenever any form of government becomes destructive of these ends, it is the right of those who suffer from it to refuse allegiance to it, and to insist upon the institution of a new government, laying its foundation on such principles, and organizing its powers in such form, as to them shall seem most likely to effect their safety and happiness. Prudence, indeed, will dictate that governments long established should not be changed for light and transient causes; and accordingly all experience hath shown that mankind are more disposed to suffer while evils are sufferable, than to right themselves by abolishing the forms to which they are accustomed. But when a long train of abuses and usurpations, pursuing invariably the same object, evinces a design to reduce them under absolute despotism, it is their duty to throw off such government, and to provide new guards for their future security. Such has been the patient sufferance of the women under this government, and such is now the necessity which constrains them to demand the equal station to which they are entitled. The history of mankind is a history of repeated injuries and usurpations on the part of man toward woman, having in direct object the establishment of an absolute tyranny over her. To prove this, let facts be submitted to a candid world.
    – "The Declaration of Sentiments: Seneca Falls Conference, 1848"

Such beautifully structured point/counterpoint arguments abound in American history, a part of the fabric of free speech and democracy. Consider celebrations of the Declaration, for instance, which from the very beginning included patriotic proclamations that were an important part of political and social commentary of the day. For example, the Not Just Words box on p. 143 shows the title page of such a speech given by John Quincy Adams in 1793, part of a genre that began right after 1776 and continues to the present day.

Most Fourth of July speeches follow a pattern of praising the Revolutionary heroes and emphasizing freedom, democracy, and liberty. Sometimes, however, orators have sounded a different note. Frederick Douglass certainly had this tradition of celebratory speeches in mind when, in 1852, he delivered his own Fourth of July oration. Note his use

AN

ORATION,

PRONOUNCED

JULY 4th, 1793,

AT THE

REQUEST OF THE INHABITANTS

OF THE

TOWN OF *BOSTON*;

IN COMMEMORATION

OF THE

ANNIVERSARY OF

AMERICAN INDEPENDENCE.

BY JOHN QUINCY ADAMS.

O NOMEN DULCE LIBERTATIS !   *Cit.*

YE shades of ancient heroes ! Ye who toil'd,
Through long succesive ages to build up
A labouring plan of state ; behold at once
The wonder done !   THOMSON.

[THE SECOND EDITION.]

BOSTON:
PRINTED BY BENJAMIN EDES & SON, in *Kilby-Street.*
M,DCC,XCIII,

Not Just Words

Take a close look at the page above, announcing a Fourth of July celebratory oration. Note how it is designed and structured. If you were revising it to announce a speech in celebration of July 4 in the twenty-first century, what changes would you make to the design, layout, and so on?

of questions to structure what follows and to secure the close attention of his (white) audience:

> Fellow-citizens, pardon me, allow me to ask, why am I called upon to speak here today? What have I, or those I represent, to do with your national independence? Are the great principles of political freedom and natural justice, embodied in the Declaration of Independence, extended to us? And am I, therefore, called upon to bring our humble offering to the national altar, and to confess the benefits and express devout gratitude for the blessings resulting from your independence to us?...I say it with a sad sense of the disparity between us. I am not included within the pale of this glorious anniversary! Your high independence only reveals the immeasurable distance between us. The blessings in which you, this day, rejoice, are not enjoyed in common. The rich inheritance of justice, liberty, prosperity and independence, bequeathed by your fathers, is shared by you, not by me. The sunlight that brought life and healing to you, has brought stripes and death to me. This Fourth of July is yours, not mine. You may rejoice, I must mourn.
>
> –Frederick Douglass, "What to the Slave Is the Fourth of July?"

Just eleven years later, President Abraham Lincoln issued the Emancipation Proclamation, a document intended to respond in some ways to Douglass's and other abolitionists' arguments for full rights for all citizens (see the figure on p. 145). Unlike the documents you've seen in previous pages, this one is handwritten in a flowing and formal script. Its title, "By the President of the United States of America, a Proclamation," announces its power and authority and calls all Americans to attention. Yet this famous statement—one of the most important documents in U.S. history—actually provided quite limited freedom for slaves, since it applied only to the states that had seceded from the Union and even exempted parts of them. As a result, the Proclamation itself underscores the deep irony that infused Douglass's earlier speech.

Speaking at the foot of the Lincoln Memorial in Washington, D.C., one hundred years later, on August 28, 1963, Martin Luther King Jr. clearly had both Douglass's address and the Emancipation Proclamation in mind in the opening of his "I Have a Dream" speech:

> Five score years ago, a great American, in whose symbolic shadow we stand today, signed the Emancipation Proclamation. This momentous decree came as a great beacon light of hope to millions of Negro slaves who had been seared in the flames of withering injustice. It came as a joyous daybreak to end the long night of their captivity.

By the President of the United States of America:

A Proclamation.

Whereas, on the twenty-second day of September, in the year of our Lord one thousand eight hundred and sixty-two, a proclamation was issued by the President of the United States, containing, among other things, the following, to wit:

"That on the first day of January, in the
"year of our Lord one thousand eight hundred
"and sixty-three, all persons held as slaves within
"any State or designated part of a State, the people
"whereof shall then be in rebellion against the
"United States, shall be then, thenceforward, and
"forever free; and the Executive Government of the
"United States, including the military and naval
"authority thereof, will recognize and maintain
"the freedom of such persons, and will do no act
"or acts to repress such persons, or any of them,
"in any efforts they may make for their actual
"freedom.
"That the Executive will, on the first day

Emancipation Proclamation, January 1, 1863

But one hundred years later, the Negro still is not free. One hundred years later, the life of the Negro is still sadly crippled by the manacles of segregation and the chains of discrimination. One hundred years later, the Negro lives on a lonely island of poverty in the midst of a vast ocean of material prosperity. One hundred years later, the Negro is still languished in the corners of American society and finds himself an exile in his own land.

–Martin Luther King Jr., "I Have a Dream"

King went on to delineate in detail the many injustices still characteristic of U.S. society—and then in one of the most brilliant perorations in the history of speechmaking, he invoked his dream of a future in which the United States would live up to its highest ideals, such as those articulated in the Declaration of Independence. Once this happened, King said, the following would be the outcome:

. . . when we allow freedom to ring, when we let it ring from every village and every hamlet, from every state and every city, we will be able to speed up that day when *all* of God's children, black men and white men, Jews and Gentiles, Protestants and Catholics, will be able to join hands and sing in the words of the old Negro spiritual: "Free at last! Free at last! Thank God Almighty, we are free at last!"

–Martin Luther King Jr., "I Have a Dream"

Martin Luther King Jr. on the steps of the Lincoln Memorial

These examples all illustrate the deep complexity and layered quality of most important national arguments, which, as you've seen, can span hundreds of years. In recognition of this complexity, we won't pretend that learning how to make (or analyze) an argument is easy. Nor will we offer any foolproof guidelines for structuring persuasive arguments, because such arguments are as complicated and different as the people who make them. Five-step plans for changing minds or scoring big on *The Daily Show* won't work.

But making effective arguments isn't a mystery either. As you'll see shortly, you already understand, almost intuitively, most of the basic moves in arguing successfully. But it helps to give them names and to appreciate how they work. When you can recognize a reasonable claim, you can make one of your own. When you know that claims need to be supported with sound reasons and reliable evidence, you'll expect to see both in what you read and what you write yourself. You'll also see that all arguments rest on assumptions, some far more controversial than others. And when you do, you'll be prepared to air your differences with a considerable degree of confidence.

Toulmin Argument

To look at argument, we'll borrow some of the key terms and strategies introduced by British philosopher Stephen Toulmin in *The Uses of Argument* (1958). Toulmin was looking for a method that accurately de-scribed the way people make convincing and reasonable arguments. Because Toulmin argument takes into account the complications in life — all those situations when people have to qualify their thoughts with words such as *sometimes, often, presumably, unless,* and *almost* — his method isn't as airtight as formal logic, the kind that uses syllogisms (see Chapter 4, p. 93). But for exactly that reason, Toulmin logic has be-come a powerful and, for the most part, practical tool for understanding and shaping argument in the real world.

You'll find Toulmin argument especially helpful as a way to come up with ideas and test them. Moreover, it will help you understand what goes where in many kinds of arguments. Perhaps most important, you'll acquire good critical thinking habits when you think in Toulmin's terms.

Making Claims

In the Toulmin model, arguments begin with *claims*, which are debatable and controversial statements or assertions you hope to prove. Notice that in this model the arguments depend on conditions set by others — your audience or readers. *It's raining* might be an innocent statement of fact in one situation; in another, it might provoke a debate: *No, it's not. That's sleet.* And so an argument begins, involving a question of definition.

Claims worth arguing tend to be controversial; there's no point wor-rying about points on which most people agree. For example, there are assertions in the statements *Twelve inches make a foot* and *Earth is the third planet from the sun.* But except in unusual circumstances, such claims aren't worth the time it takes to argue over them.

Claims should also be debatable; they can be demonstrated using logic or evidence, the raw material for building arguments. Sometimes the line between what's debatable and what isn't can be thin. You push back your chair from the table in a restaurant and declare, *That was delicious!* A debatable point? Not really. If you thought the meal was out of sight, who can challenge your taste, particularly when your verdict affects no one but yourself?

But now imagine you're a restaurant critic working for the local newspaper, leaning back from the same table and making the same observation. Because of your job, your claim about the restaurant's cannelloni would have different status and wider implications. People's jobs—including your own—might be at stake. *That was delicious!* suddenly becomes a claim you have to support, bite by bite.

Many writers stumble when it comes to making claims because facing issues squarely takes thought and guts. A claim answers the question *So what's your point?* Some writers would rather ignore the question and avoid taking a stand. But when you make a claim worth writing about, you step slightly apart from the crowd and ask that it notice you.

Is there a danger that you might oversimplify an issue by making too bold a claim? Of course. But making that sweeping claim is a logical first step toward eventually saying something more reasonable and subtle. Here are some fairly simple, undeveloped claims:

> The filibuster system has outlived its usefulness.
>
> It's time to legalize medical use of marijuana.
>
> NASA should launch a human expedition to Mars.
>
> Vegetarianism is the best choice of diet.
>
> Same sex unions deserve the same protections as those granted to marriage between a man and a woman.

Note that these claims are statements, not questions. There's nothing wrong with questions per se; in fact, they're what you ask to reach a claim:

> Questions   What should NASA's next goal be? Should the space agency establish a permanent moon base? Should NASA launch more robotic interstellar probes? Should NASA send people to Mars or Venus?
>
> Statement   NASA should launch a human expedition to Mars.

Don't mistake one for the other.

Good claims often spring from personal experience. Almost all of us know enough about something to merit the label *expert*—though we don't always realize it. If you're a typical first-year college student, for example, you're probably an expert about high school. You could make trustworthy claims (or complaints) about a range of consequential issues, from competency testing to the administration of athletic programs. And if you aren't a typical college student, what makes you different—perhaps your experiences at work, in the military, or with a family—could make claims fairly leap to mind. Whether you're a typical or nontypical college student, you might also know a lot about music or urban living or retail merchandising, or inequities in government services and so on—all of them fertile ground for authoritative, debatable, and personally relevant claims.

CULTURAL CONTEXTS FOR ARGUMENT

Being Explicit

In the United States, many people (especially those in the academic and business worlds) expect a writer to "get to the point" as directly as possible and to articulate that point efficiently and unambiguously. Student writers are typically expected to make their claims explicit, leaving little unspoken. Such claims usually appear early on in an argument, often in the first paragraph. But not all cultures take such an approach. Some prefer that the claim or thesis be introduced subtly and indirectly, expecting that readers "read between the lines" to understand what's being said. Some even save the thesis until the very end of a written argument. Here are a couple of questions that might help you think about how explicitly you should (or shouldn't) make your points:

- What general knowledge does your audience have about your topic? What information do they expect or need you to provide?

- Do members of your audience tend to be very direct, saying explicitly what they mean? Or are they more subtle, less likely to call a spade a spade? Look for cues to determine how much responsibility you have as the writer and how you can most successfully argue your points.

Offering Evidence and Good Reasons

A claim is just a lonely statement hanging out there in the wind—until it teams up with some evidence and good reasons. You can begin developing a claim simply by drawing up a list of reasons to support it or finding evidence that backs up the point. In doing so, you'll likely generate still more claims in need of more support; that's the way arguments work.

One student writer, for instance, wanted to gather good reasons in support of an assertion that his college campus needed more officially designated spaces for parking bicycles. He had been doing some research—gathering statistics about parking space allocation, numbers of people using particular designated slots, and numbers of bicycles registered on campus. Before he went any further with this argument, however, he decided to list the primary reasons he had identified for more bicycle parking:

- *Personal experience:* At least twice a week for two terms, he had been unable to find a designated parking space for his bike.
- *Anecdotes:* Several of his friends told similar stories; one had even sold her bike as a result.
- *Facts:* He had found out that the ratio of car to bike parking spaces was 100 to 1, whereas the ratio of cars to bikes registered on campus was 25 to 1.
- *Authorities:* The campus police chief had indicated in an interview with the college newspaper that she believed a problem existed for students trying to park bicycles legally.

On the basis of his preliminary listing of possible reasons in support of the claim, this student decided that his subject was worth still more research. He was on the way to amassing a set of good reasons sufficient to support his claim.

In some arguments you read, claims might be widely separated from the reasons offered to support them. In shaping your own arguments, try putting claims and reasons together early in the writing process to create what Aristotle called *enthymemes,* or arguments in brief. Think of these enthymemes as test cases or even as topic sentences:

> Bicycle parking spaces should be expanded because the number of bikes on campus far exceeds the available spots.
>
> It's time to lower the drinking age because I've been drinking since I was fourteen and it hasn't hurt me.
>
> Legalization of the medical use of marijuana is long overdue since it has been proven an effective treatment for symptoms associated with cancer.
>
> Violent video games should be carefully evaluated and their use monitored by the industry, the government, and parents because these games cause addiction and psychological harm to players.

As you can see, attaching a reason to a claim often spells out the major terms of an argument. In rare cases, the full statement is all the argument you'll need:

> Don't eat that mushroom—it's poisonous.
>
> We'd better stop for gas because the gauge has been reading empty for more than thirty miles.

Anticipate challenges to your claims.

"I know your type, you're the type who'll
make me prove every claim I make."

More often, your work is just beginning when you've put a claim together with its supporting reasons and evidence. If your readers are capable — and you should always assume they are — they'll then begin to question your statement. They might ask whether the reasons and evidence you're offering really do support the claim: *Should the drinking age be changed simply because you've managed to drink since you were fourteen? Should the whole state base its laws on what's worked for you?* They might ask pointed questions about your evidence: *Exactly how do you know the number of bikes on campus far exceeds the number of spaces available?* Eventually, you've got to address both issues: quality of assumptions and quality of evidence. The connection between claim and reason(s) is a concern at the next level in Toulmin argument. (For more on enthymemes, see Chapter 4, p. 93.)

Determining Warrants

Crucial to Toulmin argument is appreciating that there must be a logical and persuasive connection between a claim and the reasons and data supporting it. Toulmin calls this connection the *warrant*; it answers the question *How exactly do I get from the claim to the data?* Like the warrant in legal situations (a search warrant, for example), a sound warrant in an argument gives you authority to proceed with your case.

The warrant tells readers what your (often unstated) assumptions are — for example, that any practice that causes serious disease should be banned by the government. If readers accept your warrant, you can then present specific evidence to develop your claim. But if readers dispute your warrant, you'll have to defend it before you can move on to the claim itself.

When you state a warrant accurately, you sometimes expose a fatal flaw in an argument. However, stating warrants can be tricky because they can be phrased in various ways. What you're looking for is the general principle that enables you to justify the move from a reason to a specific claim, the bridge connecting them. The warrant is the assumption that makes the claim seem plausible. It's often a value or principle you share with your readers. Let's demonstrate this logical movement with an easy example:

Don't eat that mushroom—it's poisonous.

The warrant supporting this enthymeme can be stated in several ways, always moving from the reason (*It's poisonous*) to the claim (*Don't eat that mushroom*):

That which is poisonous shouldn't be eaten.

If something is poisonous, it's dangerous to eat.

Here's the relationship, diagrammed:

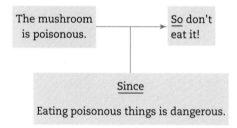

Perfectly obvious, you say? Exactly—and that's why the statement is so convincing. If the mushroom in question is indeed a death cap or destroying angel (and you might still need expert testimony to prove that's what it is), the warrant does the rest of the work, making the claim it supports seem logical and persuasive.

Let's look at a similar example, beginning with the argument in its basic form:

We'd better stop for gas because the gauge has been reading empty for more than thirty miles.

In this case, you have evidence so clear (a gas gauge reading empty) that the reason for getting gas doesn't even have to be stated: the tank is

POCKET NATURALIST™

MUSHROOMS

AN INTRODUCTION
TO FAMILIAR NORTH
AMERICAN SPECIES

Fly Agaric
Amanita muscaria
To 7 in. (18 cm)
Cap: Yellow to red-orange cap
has white warts
Stalk: Whitish, frilled collar
Gills: Free, white to yellow
Spore Print: White
Habitat: Oak and coniferous forests.
Was once used, mixed with milk,
to poison house flies.

Ravenel's
Stinkhorn

Fading Scarlet
Waxy Cap

Parasol
Mushroom

Destroying Angel
Amanita virosa
To 10 in. (25 cm)
Cap: White, smooth
Stalk: Basal bulb, collar
Gills: Free
Spore Print: White
Habitat: Mixed forests.
Young caps resemble edible
Agaricus mushrooms.

Chanterelle

Turkey Tail

Death Cap
Amanita phalloides
To 5 in. (13 cm)
Cap: Smooth, greenish-yellow
Stalk: Widest at base, collar near top
Gills: Free
Spore Print: White
Habitat: All woods, especially under
oaks and conifers.

WATERFORD PRESS

In a pocket field guide, a simple icon —a skull and crossbones—makes a visual
argument that implies a claim, a reason, and a warrant.

almost empty. The warrant connecting the evidence to the claim is also compelling and pretty obvious:

> **If the fuel gauge of a car has been reading empty for more than thirty miles, that car is about to run out of gas.**

Since most readers would accept this warrant as reasonable, they would also likely accept the statement the warrant supports.

Naturally, factual information might undermine the whole argument—the fuel gauge might be broken, or the driver might know from previous experience that the car will go another fifty miles even though the fuel gauge reads empty. But in most cases, readers would accept the warrant.

Let's look at a third easy case, one in which stating the warrant confirms the weakness of an enthymeme that doesn't seem convincing on its own merits:

> **Grades in college should be abolished because I don't like them!**

Moving from stated reason to claim, we see that the warrant is a silly and selfish principle:

> **What I don't like should be abolished.**

Most readers won't accept this assumption as a principle worth applying generally. It would produce a chaotic or arbitrary world, like that of the Queen of Hearts in *Alice's Adventures in Wonderland* ("Off with the heads of anyone I don't like!"). So far, so good. But how does understanding warrants make you better at writing arguments? The answer is simple: warrants tell you what arguments you have to make and at what level you have to make them. If your warrant isn't controversial, you can immediately begin to defend your claim. But if your warrant is controversial, you must first defend the warrant—or modify it or look for better assumptions on which to support the claim. Building an argument on a weak warrant is like building a house on a questionable foundation. Sooner or later, the structure will crack.

Let's consider how stating and then examining a warrant can help you determine the grounds on which you want to make a case. Here's a political enthymeme of a familiar sort:

> **Flat taxes are fairer than progressive taxes because they treat all taxpayers in the same way.**

Examples of Claims, Reasons, and Warrants

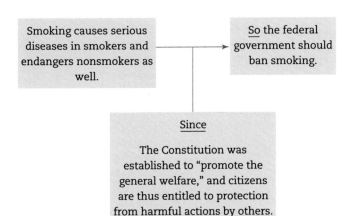

Smoking causes serious diseases in smokers and endangers nonsmokers as well. ⟶ <u>So</u> the federal government should ban smoking.

<u>Since</u>

The Constitution was established to "promote the general welfare," and citizens are thus entitled to protection from harmful actions by others.

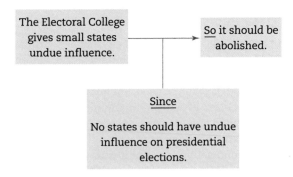

The Electoral College gives small states undue influence. ⟶ <u>So</u> it should be abolished.

<u>Since</u>

No states should have undue influence on presidential elections.

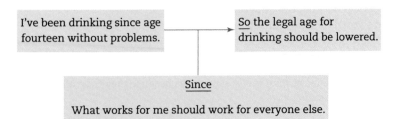

I've been drinking since age fourteen without problems. ⟶ <u>So</u> the legal age for drinking should be lowered.

<u>Since</u>

What works for me should work for everyone else.

Warrants that follow from this enthymeme have power because they appeal to a core American value—equal treatment under the law:

> **Treating people equitably is the American way.**
>
> **All people should be treated in the same way.**

You certainly could make an argument on these grounds. But stating the warrant should also raise a flag if you know anything about tax policy. If the principle is so obvious and universal, why are federal and many state income taxes progressive, requiring people at higher levels of income to pay at higher tax rates than people at lower income levels? Could it be that the warrant isn't as universally popular as it might seem at first glance? To explore the argument further, try stating the contrary claim and warrants:

> **Progressive taxes are fairer than flat taxes because people with more income can afford to pay more, benefit more from government, and can shelter more of their income from taxes.**
>
> **People should be taxed according to their ability to pay.**
>
> **People who benefit more from government and can shelter more of their income from taxes should be taxed at higher rates.**

Now you see how different the assumptions behind opposing positions really are. In a small way, we've stated one basic difference between political right and political left, between Republicans and Democrats. If you decided to argue in favor of flat taxes, you'd be smart to recognize that some members of your audience might have fundamental reservations about your position. Or you might even decide to shift your entire argument to an alternative rationale for flat taxes:

> **Flat taxes are preferable to progressive taxes because they simplify the tax code and reduce the likelihood of fraud.**

Here you have two stated reasons, supported by two new warrants:

> **Taxes that simplify the tax code are desirable.**
>
> **Taxes that reduce the likelihood of fraud are preferable.**

Whenever possible, you'll choose your warrant knowing your audience, the context of your argument, and your own feelings. Moreover, understanding how to state a warrant and how to assess its potential makes subsequent choices better informed.

Be careful, though—especially if you're citing more than one reason for your claim—that you don't give your audience the impression you're just appealing to whatever warrant(s) you think might work with them. This was one difficulty the Bush administration ran into when it began offering reasons for its invasion and occupation of Iraq after some of the original ones proved unsupported by evidence. Switching arguments— from the dangers of weapons of mass destruction, to Saddam Hussein's supposed connection with Al Qaeda, to spreading democracy and women's rights in the Middle East, to the need to "stay the course" in order to retroactively justify the invasion—left many Americans confused about what the reason or reasons for this war actually were. Likewise, if your readers suspect that the warrant of your argument for flat taxes amounts merely to *My own taxes would be lower than they are under progressive taxes,* your credibility may suffer a fatal blow.

Offering Evidence: Backing

As you might guess, claims and warrants provide only the skeleton of an argument. The bulk of a writer's work—the richest, most interesting part—remains to be done after the argument has been outlined. Claims and warrants clearly stated do suggest the scope of the evidence you have yet to assemble.

An example will illustrate the point. Here's an argument in brief— suitably debatable and controversial, if somewhat abstract:

> **NASA should launch a human expedition to Mars because Americans need a unifying national goal.**

Here's the warrant that supports the enthymeme, at least one version of it:

> **What unifies the nation ought to be a national priority.**

To run with this claim and warrant, a writer needs, first, to place both in context because most points worth arguing have a rich history. Entering an argument can be like walking into a conversation already in progress. In the case of the politics of space exploration, the conversation has been a lively one, debated with varying intensity since the launch in 1957 of the Soviet Union's *Sputnik* satellite (the first man-made object to orbit the earth) and sparked again after the 1986 death of all seven crew members in the *Challenger* disaster and, more recently, after the *Columbia* shuttle broke up on reentry in 2003, killing all aboard. A writer stumbling into this dialogue without a sense of history won't get far. Acquiring background knowledge (through reading, conversation, inquiry of all kinds) is the price you have to pay to write on the subject. Without a minimum amount of information on this—or any comparable subject— all the moves of Toulmin argument won't do you much good. You've got to do the legwork before you're ready to make a case. (See Chapter 3 for more on gaining authority.)

If you want examples of premature argument, just listen to talk radio or C-SPAN phone-ins for a day or two. You'll soon learn that the better callers can hold a conversation with the host or guests, fleshing out their basic claims with facts, personal experience, and evidence. The weaker callers usually offer a claim supported by a morsel of data. Then such callers begin to repeat themselves, as if saying over and over again that "Republicans are fascists" or "Democrats are traitors" will make the statement true.

As noted earlier, there's no point defending any claim until you've satisfied readers that any questionable warrants (like those about Republicans and Democrats above) the claim is based on are, in fact, defensible. In Toulmin argument, evidence you offer to support a warrant is called *backing*.

WARRANT

What unifies the nation ought to be a national priority.

BACKING

On a personal level, Americans want to be part of something bigger than themselves. (Emotional appeal as evidence)

In a country as regionally, racially, and culturally diverse as the United States, common purposes and values help make the nation stronger. (Ethical appeal as evidence)

In the past, enterprises such as westward expansion, World War II, and the Apollo moon program enabled many—though not all— Americans to work toward common goals. (Logical appeal as evidence)

In addition to evidence necessary to support your warrant (backing), you'll need evidence to support your claim.

ARGUMENT IN BRIEF (ENTHYMEME / CLAIM)

NASA should launch a human expedition to Mars because Americans need a unifying national goal.

EVIDENCE

> The American people are politically divided along lines of race, ethnicity, religion, gender, and class. (Fact as evidence)
>
> A common challenge or problem often unites people to accomplish great things. (Emotional appeal as evidence)
>
> Successfully managing a Mars mission would require the cooperation of the entire nation—financially, logistically, and scientifically. (Logical appeal as evidence)
>
> A human expedition to Mars would be a valuable scientific project for the nation to pursue. (Appeal to values as evidence)

As these examples show, you can draw from the full range of argumentative appeals to provide support for your claims. Appeals to values and emotions might be just as appropriate as appeals to logic and facts, and all such claims will be stronger if a writer presents a convincing ethos. Although it's possible to study such appeals separately, they work together in arguments, reinforcing each other. (See Chapter 3 for more on ethos.)

Finally, understand that arguments can quickly shift downward from an original set of claims and warrants to deeper, more basic claims and reasons. In a philosophy course, for example, you might dig many layers deep to reach what seem to be first principles. In general, however, you need to pursue an argument only as far as your audience demands, always presenting readers with adequate warrants and convincing evidence. There comes a point, as Toulmin himself acknowledges, at which readers have to agree to some basic principles or else the argument becomes pointless.

Using Qualifiers

What makes Toulmin's system work so well in the real world is that it acknowledges that *qualifiers*—words and phrases that place limits on claims, such as *usually, sometimes, in many cases*—play an essential role in arguments. By contrast, formal logic requires universal premises: *All humans are mortal*, for example. Unfortunately, life doesn't lend itself well to many such sturdy truths. If we could argue only about these types of sweeping claims, we'd be silent most of the time.

Toulmin logic, in fact, encourages you to limit your responsibilities in an argument through the effective use of qualifiers. You can save time if you qualify a claim early in the writing process. But you might not figure out how to limit a claim effectively until after you've explored your subject or discussed it with others.

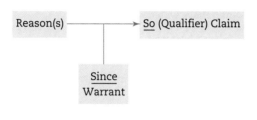

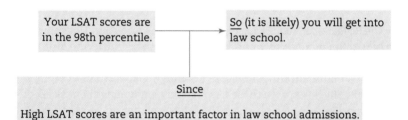

Experienced writers cherish qualifying expressions because they make writing more precise and honest.

Qualifiers

few	more or less	often
it is possible	in some cases	perhaps
rarely	many	under these conditions
it seems	in the main	possibly
some	routinely	for the most part
it may be	most	if it were so
sometimes	one might argue	

Never assume that readers understand the limits you have in mind. By spelling out the terms of the claim as precisely as possible, you'll have less work to do, and your argument will seem more reasonable. In the following examples, the first claim in each pair would be much harder to argue convincingly and responsibly—and tougher to research—than the second claim. (Notice that the second qualified claim above doesn't use terms from the list above but instead specifies and limits the actions proposed.)

Unqualified Claim	People who don't go to college earn less than those who do.
Qualified Claim	*In most cases,* people who don't go to college earn less than those who do.
Unqualified Claim	Welfare programs should be cut.
Qualified Claim	*Ineffective federal* welfare programs should be *identified, modified,* and, *if necessary, eliminated.*

Understanding Conditions of Rebuttal

In *The Reader over Your Shoulder,* Robert Graves and Alan Hodge advise writers to imagine a crowd of "prospective readers" hovering over their shoulders, asking hard questions. At every stage in Toulmin argument—making a claim, offering a reason, or studying a warrant—you might consider conversing with those nosy readers, imagining them as skeptical, demanding, even a bit testy. They may well get on your nerves. But they'll likely help you foresee the objections and reservations real readers will have regarding your arguments.

In the Toulmin system, potential objections to an argument are called *conditions of rebuttal.* Understanding and reacting to these conditions are essential not only to buttress your own claims where they're weak, but also to understand the reasonable objections of people who see the world differently. For example, you may be a big fan of the Public Broadcasting Service (PBS) and the National Endowment for the Arts (NEA) and prefer that federal tax dollars be spent on these programs. So you offer the following claim:

Claim	The federal government should support the arts.

Of course, you need reasons to support this thesis, so you decide to present the issue as a matter of values:

Argument in Brief	The federal government should support the arts because it also supports the military.

Now you've got an enthymeme and can test the warrant, or the premises of your claim:

Warrant	If the federal government can support the military, it can also support other programs.

But the warrant seems frail—something's missing to make a convincing case. Over your shoulder you hear your skeptical friends wondering what wouldn't be fundable according to your very broad principle. They restate your warrant in their own mocking fashion: *Because we pay for a military, we should pay for everything!* You could deal with their objection in the body of your paper, but revising your claim might be a better way to parry the objections. You give it a try:

Revised Argument	**If the federal government can spend huge amounts of money on the military, it can afford to spend moderate amounts on arts programs.**

Now you've got a new warrant, too:

Revised Warrant	**A country that can fund expensive programs can also afford less expensive programs.**

This is a premise you feel more able to defend, believing strongly that the arts are just as essential to the well-being of the country as a strong military. (In fact, you believe the arts are more important; but remembering those readers over your shoulder, you decide not to complicate your case by overstating it.) To provide backing for this new and more defensible warrant, you plan to illustrate the huge size of the federal budget and the proportion of it that goes to various programs.

Although the warrant seems solid, you still have to offer strong grounds to support your specific and controversial claim. Once again you cite statistics from reputable sources, this time comparing the federal budgets for the military and the arts; you break them down in ways readers can visualize, demonstrating that much less than a penny of every tax dollar goes to support the arts.

But once more you hear those voices over your shoulder, pointing out that the "common defense" is a federal mandate; the government is constitutionally obligated to support a military. Support for public television or local dance troupes is hardly in the same league. And the nation still has a huge federal debt.

Hmmm. You'd better spend a paragraph explaining all the benefits the arts provide for the very few dollars spent, and maybe you should also suggest that such funding falls under the constitutional mandate to "promote the general welfare." Though not all readers will accept these grounds, they'll at least see that you haven't ignored their point of view. You gain credibility and authority by anticipating a reasonable objection.

As you can see, dealing with conditions of rebuttal is a natural part of argument. But it's important to understand rebuttal as more than mere opposition. Anticipating objections broadens your horizons and likely makes you more open to change. One of the best exercises for you or for any writer is to learn to state the views of others in your own favorable words. If you can do that, you're more apt to grasp the warrants at issue and the commonalities you may share with others, despite differences.

Fortunately, today's wired world is making it harder to argue in isolation. Newsgroups and blogs on the Internet provide quick and potent responses to positions offered by participants in discussions. Email and Instant Messaging make cross-country connections feel almost like face-to-face conversations. Even the links on Web sites encourage people to think of communication as a network, infinitely variable, open to many voices and different perspectives. Within the Toulmin system, conditions of rebuttal—the voices over the shoulder—remind us that we're part of this bigger world. (For more on arguments in electronic environments, see Chapters 14 and 15.)

Outline of a Toulmin Argument

Consider the claim mentioned earlier:

Claim	The federal government should ban smoking.
Qualifier	The ban would be limited to public spaces.
Good Reasons	Smoking causes serious diseases in smokers. Nonsmokers are endangered by second-hand smoke.
Warrants	The Constitution promises to "promote the general welfare." Citizens are entitled to protection from harmful actions by others.
Backing	The United States is based on a political system that is supposed to serve the basic needs of its people, including their health.
Evidence	Numbers of deaths attributed to second-hand smoke Lawsuits recently won against large tobacco companies, citing the need for reparation for smoking-related health care costs Examples of bans already imposed in many public places

Authority	Cite the surgeon general.
Conditions of Rebuttal	Smokers have rights too.
	Smoking laws should be left to the states.
	Such a ban could not be enforced.
Response	The ban applies to public places; smokers can smoke in private.
	The power of the federal government to impose other restrictions on smoking, such as warning labels on cigarettes and bans on cigarette advertisements on television, has survived legal challenges.
	The experience of New York City, which has imposed such a ban, suggests that enforcement would not be a significant problem.

A Toulmin Analysis

You might wonder how Toulmin's method holds up when applied to an argument longer than a few sentences. Do such arguments really work the way Toulmin predicts? After all, knowledgeable readers often won't agree even on what the core claim in a piece is, let alone on what its warrants are. Yet such an analysis can be rewarding because it can't help raising basic questions about purpose, structure, quality of evidence, and rhetorical strategy. The following short argument by Alan Dershowitz, a professor at Harvard Law School, is responding to a proposal by the school in late 2002 to impose a speech code on its students. Dershowitz's piece, originally published in the *Boston Globe* newspaper, is followed by an analysis of it in Toulmin's terms. Keep in mind what you've learned about analyzing arguments as you read this article.

If Everything's an Argument . . .

Perform a Toulmin analysis of either the introduction to this chapter (pp. 139–147) or the section "Understanding Conditions of Rebuttal" (pp. 162–165). What central claim are the authors making, and what reasons and evidence do they provide? Do they use any qualifiers? What warrants and backing are involved? Write a page or two summarizing your analysis.

Testing Speech Codes

ALAN M. DERSHOWITZ

We need not resort to hypothetical cases in testing the limits of a proposed speech code or harassment policy of the kind that some students and faculty members of Harvard Law School are proposing. We are currently experiencing two perfect test cases.

The first involves Harvard's invitation to Tom Paulin to deliver a distinguished lecture for which it is paying him an honorarium. Paulin believes that poetry cannot be separated from politics, and his politics is hateful and bigoted.

He has urged that American Jews who make aliya to the Jewish homeland and move into the ancient Jewish quarters of Jerusalem or Hebron "should be shot dead." He has called these Jews "Nazis" and has expressed "hatred" toward "them." "Them" is many of our students and graduates who currently live on land captured by Israel during the defensive war in 1967 or who plan to move there after graduation.

The Jewish quarters of Jerusalem and Hebron have been populated by Jews since well before the birth of Jesus. The only period in which they were Judenrein was between 1948 and 1967, when it was under Jordanian control, and the Jordanian government destroyed all the synagogues and ethnically cleansed the entire Jewish populations.

Though I (along with a majority of Israelis) oppose the building of Jewish settlements in Arab areas of the West Bank and Gaza, the existence of these settlements—which Israel has offered to end as part of an overall peace—does not justify the murder of those who believe they have a religious right to live in traditional Jewish towns such as Hebron.

Paulin's advocacy of murder of innocent civilians, even if it falls short of incitement, is a paradigm of hate speech. It would certainly make me uncomfortable to sit in a classroom or lecture hall listening to him spew his murderous hatred. Yet I would not want to empower Harvard to censor his speech or include it within a speech code or harassment policy.

Or consider the case of the anti-Semitic poet Amiri Baraka, who claims that "neo-fascist" Israel had advance knowledge of the terrorist attack on the World Trade Center and warned Israelis to stay away. This lie received a standing ovation, according to *The Boston Globe,* from "black students" at

Wellesley last week. Baraka had been invited to deliver his hate speech by Nubian, a black student organization, and [was] paid an honorarium with funds provided by several black organizations. Would those who are advocating restrictions on speech include these hateful and offensive lies in their prohibitions? If not, would they seek to distinguish them from other words that should be prohibited?

These are fair questions that need to be answered before anyone goes further down the dangerous road to selective censorship based on perceived offensiveness. Clever people can always come up with distinctions that put their cases on the permitted side of the line and other people's cases on the prohibited side of the line.

For example, Paulin's and Baraka's speeches were political, whereas the use of the "N-word" is simply racist. But much of what generated controversy at Harvard Law School last spring can also be deemed political. After all, racism is a political issue, and the attitudes of bigots toward a particular race is a political issue. Paulin's and Baraka's poetry purports to be "art," but the "N-word" and other equally offensive expressions can also be dressed up as art.

The real problem is that offensiveness is often in the eyes and experiences of the beholder. To many African Americans, there is nothing more offensive than the "N-word." To many Jews, there is nothing more offensive than comparing Jews to Nazis. (Ever notice that bigots never compare Sharon to Pinochet, Mussolini, or even Stalin, only to Hitler!)

It would be wrong for a great university to get into the business of comparing historic grievances or experiences. If speech that is deeply offensive to many African Americans is prohibited, then speech that is deeply offensive to many Jews, gays, women, Asians, Muslims, Christians, atheists, etc. must also be prohibited. Result-oriented distinctions will not suffice in an area so dominated by passion and historical experience.

Unless Paulin's and Baraka's statements were to be banned at Harvard—which they should not be—we should stay out of the business of trying to pick and choose among types and degrees of offensive, harassing, or discriminatory speech. Nor can we remain silent in the face of such hate speech. Every decent person should go out of his or her way to condemn what Tom Paulin and Amiri Baraka have said, just as we should condemn racist statements made last spring at Harvard Law School.

The proper response to offensive speech is to criticize and answer it, not to censor it.

ANALYSIS

Dershowitz uses an inverted structure for his argument, beginning with his evidence—two extended examples—and then extracting lessons from it. Indeed, his basic claim occurs, arguably, in the final sentence of the piece, and it's supported by three major reasons—although the third reason might be seen as an extension of the second:

> The proper response to offensive speech is to criticize and answer it, not to censor it, [because]
>
> - Clever people can always come up with distinctions that put their cases on the permitted side of the line and other people's cases on the prohibited side of the line.
> - It would be wrong for a great university to get into the business of comparing historic grievances or experiences.
> - [W]e should stay out of the business of trying to pick and choose among types and degrees of offensive, harassing, or discriminatory speech.

As Dershowitz presents them, the cases of Tom Paulin and Amiri Baraka suggest that smart people can always find reasons for defending the legitimacy of their offensive speech.

The closest Dershowitz gets to stating a warrant for his argument may be in the following sentence:

> The real problem is that offensiveness is often in the eyes and experiences of the beholder.

He doesn't want individuals dictating the limits of free speech because if they did, freedom would likely be restrained by the "eyes and experiences" of specific people and groups, not protected by an absolute and unwavering principle. Dershowitz doesn't actually offer such a warrant, perhaps because he assumes that most readers will understand that protecting free speech is a primary value in American society.

Dershowitz establishes his ethos by making it clear that although he's powerfully offended by the speech of both Paulin and Baraka, he wouldn't censor them—even though Paulin especially says things offensive to him. An implicit ethical appeal is that if Dershowitz himself is willing to experience such hate speech on his own campus, surely the law school should be able to show such tolerance toward its students.

What Toulmin Teaches

Just as few arguments you read are expressed in perfectly sequenced claims or clearly agreed-upon warrants, you might not think of Toulmin's terms yourself as you build arguments. Once you're into your subject, you'll be too eager to make a point to worry about whether you're qualifying a claim or finessing a warrant. That's not a problem if you appreciate Toulmin argument for what it teaches:

- *Claims should be stated clearly and qualified carefully.* Arguments in magazines or newspapers often develop a single point, but to make that point they may run through a complex series of claims. They may open with an anecdote, use the story to raise the issue that concerns them, examine alternative perspectives on the subject, and then make a half-dozen related claims only as they move toward a conclusion. You have the same freedom to develop your own arguments, as long as you make sure that your claims are clear and reasonable.

- *Claims should be supported with evidence and good reasons.* Remember that a Toulmin structure provides just the framework of an argument. Most successful arguments are thick with ideas and different kinds of evidence. You may not think of photographs or graphs as evidence, but they can serve that purpose. So can stories, even those that go on for many paragraphs or pages. Once you acquire the habit of looking for reasons and evidence, you'll be able to separate real supportive evidence from filler, even in arguments offered by professional writers. When you write arguments, you'll discover that it's far easier to make claims than to back them up.

- *Claims and reasons should be based on assumptions readers will likely accept.* Toulmin's focus on warrants confuses a lot of people, but that's because it forces readers and writers to think about their assumptions— something they would often just as soon skip. It's tough for a writer, particularly in a lengthy argument, to stay consistent about warrants. At one point a writer might offer a claim based on the warrant that makes "free speech" an absolute principle. But later he might rail against those who criticize the president in wartime, making national morale a higher value than free speech. Because most people read at the surface, they may not consciously detect the discrepancy—although they may nonetheless sense at some level that something's wrong with the argument. Toulmin pushes you to probe into the values that support any argument and to think of those values as belonging to particular audiences. You can't go wrong if you're both thoughtful and aware of your readers when you craft an argument.

- *Effective arguments respectfully anticipate objections readers might offer.* In the United States, public argument seems more partisan than ever today. Yet there's still plenty of respect for people who can make a powerful, even passionate, case for what they believe without dismissing the objections of others as absurd or idiotic. They're also willing to admit the limits of their own knowledge. Toulmin argument appreciates that any claim can crumble under certain conditions, so it encourages a complex view of argument, one that doesn't demand absolute or unqualified positions. It's a principle that works for many kinds of successful and responsible arguments.

It takes considerable experience to write arguments that meet all these conditions. Using Toulmin's framework brings them into play automatically; if you learn it well enough, constructing good arguments can become a habit.

Beyond Toulmin

Useful as it is, Toulmin's system isn't the only way to go about developing and constructing an argument. For thousands of years, writers and speakers have depended on a system developed by ancient Greek and Roman orators. This so-called *classical system* provides one way to go beyond Toulmin in terms of structuring an argument. Here's an outline of how arguments are organized in the classical system:

1. Introduction
   - Gains readers' attention and interest
   - Establishes your qualifications to write about your topic
   - Establishes some common ground with your audience
   - Demonstrates that you're fair and evenhanded
   - States your claim

2. Background
   - Presents any necessary information, including personal narrative, that's important to your argument

3. Lines of argument
   - Presents good reasons, including logical and emotional appeals, in support of your claim

4. Alternative arguments

   • Examines alternative points of view / opposing arguments
   • Notes advantages and disadvantages of these views
   • Explains why your view is better than others

5. Conclusion

   • Summarizes the argument
   • Elaborates on the implications of your claim
   • Makes clear what you want the audience to think or do
   • Reinforces your credibility

CULTURAL CONTEXTS FOR ARGUMENT

Organization

As you think about how to organize your writing, remember that cultural factors are at work: the patterns that you find satisfying and persuasive are probably ones that are deeply embedded in your culture. The organizational patterns favored by U.S. engineers in their writing, for example, hold many similarities to the system recommended by Cicero some two thousand years ago. It's a highly explicit pattern, leaving little or nothing unexplained: introduction and thesis, background, overview of the parts that follow, evidence, other viewpoints, and conclusion. If a piece of writing follows this pattern, Anglo-American readers ordinarily find it "well organized."

In contrast, writers who are accustomed to different organizational patterns may not. Those accustomed to writing that's more elaborate or that sometimes digresses from the main point may find the U.S. engineers' writing overly simple, even childish. Those from cultures that value subtlety and indirectness tend to favor patterns of organization that display these values instead.

When arguing across cultures, think about how you can organize material to convey your message effectively. Here are a couple of points to consider:

• Determine when to state your thesis: At the beginning? At the end? Somewhere else? Not at all?

• Consider whether digressions are a good idea, a requirement, or an element that's best avoided.

RESPOND •

1. Following is a claim followed by five possible supporting reasons. State the warrant that would support each of the arguments in brief. Which of the warrants would need to be defended? Which one would a college audience likely accept without significant backing?

   We should amend the Constitution to abolish the Electoral College

   — because a true democracy is based on the popular vote, not the votes of the usually unknown electors.

   — because under the Electoral College system the votes of people who have minority opinions in some states end up not counting.

   — because then Al Gore would have won the 2000 election.

   — because the Electoral College is an outdated relic of an age when the political leaders didn't trust the people.

   — because the Electoral College skews power toward small and mid-size states for no good reason.

2. Claims aren't always easy to find; sometimes they're buried deep within an argument, and sometimes they're not present at all. An important skill in reading and writing arguments is the ability to identify claims, even when they aren't obvious.

   Collect a sample of eight to ten letters to the editor of a daily newspaper (or a similar number of argumentative postings from a political blog). Read each item, and then identify every claim the writer makes. When you've compiled your list of claims, look carefully at the words the writer or writers use when stating their positions. Is there a common vocabulary? Can you find words or phrases that signal an impending claim? Which of these seem most effective? Which ones seem least effective? Why?

3. At their simplest, warrants can be stated as *X is good* or *X is bad*. Return to the letters to the editor or blog postings that you analyzed in exercise 2, this time looking for the warrant behind each claim. As a way to start, ask yourself these questions: *If I find myself agreeing with the letter writer, what assumptions about the subject matter do I share with the letter writer? If I disagree, what assumptions are at the heart of that disagreement?* The list of warrants you generate will likely come from these assumptions.

4. Using a paper you're writing for this class—it doesn't matter how far along you are in the process—do a Toulmin analysis of the argument. At first, you may struggle to identify the key elements, and you might not find all the categories easy to fill. When you're done, see which elements of the Toulmin scheme are represented. Are you short of evi-

dence to support the warrant? Have you considered the conditions of rebuttal? Next, write a brief revision plan: How will you buttress the argument in the places where it is weakest? What additional evidence will you offer for the warrant? How can you qualify your claim to meet the conditions of rebuttal? Having a clearer sense of the logical structure of your argument will help you revise more efficiently.

It might be instructive to show your paper to a classmate and have him or her do a Toulmin analysis, too. A new reader will probably see your argument in a very different way and suggest revisions that may not have occurred to you.

5. Take a look at the General Electric advertisement below, which was featured in a number of magazines during summer 2005. Do a Toulmin analysis of this advertisement, trying to identify as many claims, reasons, warrants, evidence, and qualifiers as possible. What, if anything, do the Toulmin terms leave out of the argument made by the advertisement?

General Electric's "Lapland Longspur and Freight Train: Choo-Choo Tweetus Tweetus" ad. The text at the bottom reads "The Evolution is the cleanest GE locomotive ever made. Just one way ecoimagination is creating a better world," followed by the GE logo and the slogan "Imagination at work."

7
Arguments of Fact

A varsity wrestler stops his teammate from ordering the grilled chicken sandwich at a fast food restaurant. "It's more fattening than the burgers," he warns. Could that possibly be true?

For the umpteenth time, the *Times* is carrying a feature story about the *real* authorship of Shakespeare's plays. All the familiar claimants are mentioned: Francis Bacon, Christopher Marlowe, Ben Jonson, even Edward de Vere, seventeenth Earl of Oxford. But isn't it more likely that the author of *Hamlet, Macbeth,* and *Twelfth*

Night was the person that audiences who first saw those plays thought wrote them—William Shakespeare of Stratford-upon-Avon?

Members of the faculty council are outraged to learn that the Athletic Department aims to raise $100 million to build an addition to the football stadium. The chair of the council complains in an editorial in the campus paper that the professionalization of college sports—football in particular—is not consistent with the educational mission of the university as stated in its charter.

When an instructor announces a tough new attendance policy for her course, a student objects on the grounds that there is no evidence that students who regularly attend their lecture classes perform any better than those who do not. The instructor begs to differ.

A nutritionist notes that many people think that taking Vitamin E daily will prevent colon cancer, heart attacks, cataracts, impotence in men, and wrinkles. The evidence available in many scientific studies suggests they are probably wrong.

● ● ●

Understanding Arguments of Fact

Given the pressure on natural environments throughout the world, it's a triumph whenever a threatened plant or animal, such as the American alligator, the Peregrine falcon, or, soon, the gray wolf, recovers enough to be removed from the endangered species list. Far more typically, species depart the list because they have become extinct. So imagine the excitement in April 2005 when an article in *Science* magazine carried the good news that the ivory-billed woodpecker, a strikingly handsome bird not seen for more than sixty years in American forests, had been spotted in Arkansas. The *Science* article staked its claim on the evidence of at least seven sightings by searchers and a brief, blurry videotape of a bird resembling the ivory-billed woodpecker flying away from a naturalist's canoe (see the video image on p. 176).

(Top) The ivory-billed woodpecker by J. J. Audubon, American naturalist and painter (1785–1851). (Bottom) Frame from a videotape that may show the bird in flight.

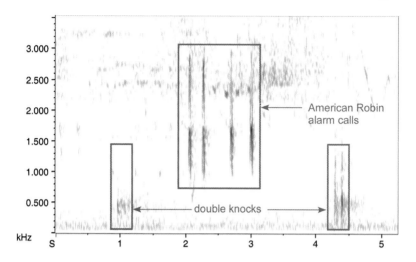

Ornithologists carefully analyzed what may have been the characteristic sounds of the ivory-billed woodpecker, recorded in an Arkansas wood. Like the videotape on the facing page, the evidence was made available for public scrutiny on the Web site of the Cornell Lab of Ornithology.

Was the argument sound? At least a few ornithologists remained doubtful, worried that too-eager colleagues may actually have mistaken a pileated woodpecker, a common bird with similar markings, for the extinct species.

Some of these skeptics withdrew their objections to the claim after hearing audiotapes recorded in an Arkansas bottomland forest carrying the distinctive call and double-rap sound of the ivory-bill (see the figure above). But blue jays or nuthatches might have made the noises, experts also admitted.

What would it take to seal the deal, to assure scientists and birders alike that the ivory-billed woodpecker really did survive in the wilds of Arkansas? As in the heyday of species collection during the eighteenth and nineteenth centuries, a specimen of the bird, dead and mounted, could confirm its existence. But that practice wouldn't be acceptable today, especially with an endangered animal whose numbers might be down to just a few breeding pairs. "What we need, what we need is a photo," said Russell Chariff of the Cornell Lab of Ornithology to the *New York Times*, discussing the burden of proof as it existed in late 2005. True, a photograph might be faked, especially a digital image. But a clear shot of the woodpecker by a reputable researcher could indeed be the clincher—given all the other tantalizing but not quite conclusive evidence in this case.

Ornithologists and amateurs will doubtless continue to scour the Arkansas woods hoping to bring this argument to a conclusion by confirming the bird's existence. Their dilemma will be like that of anyone trying to make a factual argument: to find sufficient evidence for a claim to satisfy a reasonably skeptical audience, in this case of scientists, naturalists, and birders.

Factual arguments come in many varieties with different standards of proof. What they have in common is an attempt to establish whether something is or is not so—that is, whether a thing exists (*the ivory-bill*) or whether claims made about something are true (*The poverty rate is higher in New Mexico than in Texas*). At first glance, you might object that these aren't arguments at all, but just a matter of looking things up and writing a report. And you'd be right to an extent: people don't ordinarily argue factual matters that are settled or agreed upon (*The earth orbits the sun*) or that might be decided with simple research (*Manuel Deodoro da Fonseca was the first president of Brazil*) or the equivalent of a rule (*One foot equals 0.3048 meters*).

Transmitting facts, it would seem, should be a dispassionate activity, free of the pressures and biases of argument. Yet facts become arguments when they're controversial in themselves or when they're used to educate people, challenging or changing their beliefs. A factual argument about the existence of a woodpecker has a kind of clean scientific logic to it, but there's passion in the debate if only because so many researchers *want* the bird to survive. And so there's resistance too among those who don't want to rush to judgment until the evidence is definitive—as it could be in this case.

Arguments of fact do much of the heavy lifting in our world. Some of them do the important task of reporting on what has been recently discovered or become known. Such arguments may also explore the implications of that new information and the conflicts that may follow from it. In recent years, for instance, we've seen plenty of contrary medical reports that raise questions about the safety or efficacy of prescription drugs, vitamin regimens, or surgical procedures. Such news has become so routine that the public is asking increasingly sophisticated questions about the studies, such as who sponsored them, who or what exactly was studied, over how many years, and among which populations. Healthy skepticism is the common attitude now, rather than simple acceptance of what the scientific community reports.

Some factual arguments make the public aware of information that's already available to anyone willing to do the work of finding it and studying its implications. Malcolm Gladwell, author of *The Tipping Point* and *Blink,* has become the go-to author for using research to expose patterns in our cultural behavior that seem obvious once he's pointed them out. *Blink,* for example, highlights the important fact that people routinely use gut feelings to make sound (as well as dubious) judgments, an argument with important repercussions for business, education, even the military—if Gladwell is right.

But serious factual arguments almost always have consequences, especially those that touch on public issues. *Can we rely on hydrogen to solve our energy needs? Will the Social Security trust fund really go broke? (Does such a fund even exist?) Does your school have the resources to open a new program in nursing?* Various publics, national or local, need well-reasoned factual arguments on subjects of this kind in order to make well-informed decisions. Such arguments educate audiences.

For the same reason, we need arguments that correct or challenge beliefs and assumptions held widely within a society on the basis of inadequate or incomplete information. Corrective arguments appear daily in the national media, often based on more detailed studies by scientists, researchers, or thinkers that the public may not encounter. Many people, for example, believe that talking on a cell phone while driving is no different from listening to the radio. But that's an intuition not based on hard information: what more and more scientific studies suggest is that using a cell phone in a car is comparable to driving under the influence of alcohol—something the public clearly needs to know.

Factual arguments also routinely address broader questions about the history or myths societies want to believe about themselves. For example, are the accounts we have of the American founding, or the Civil War and slavery, or the heroics of the revolutionary Che Guevara, indeed accurate? Or do the facts we believe in reflect the perspectives and prejudices of earlier times or ideologies? Scholars and historians frequently claim to be completing the historical record or looking both for new information and for new ways of interpreting evidence. Such revisionist history is almost always controversial and rarely settled: The British and Americans will always tell different versions of what happened in North

You've worn the T-shirt, but do you know the man? Writer Alvaro Vargas Llosa argues that Che Guevara doesn't deserve the adulation he receives in some circles, describing him as a megalomaniac in "The Killing Machine," an article in *The New Republic,* July 11, 2005.

America in 1776; Anglos and Latinos will write different histories of the Rio Grande border regions.

It's especially important to have factual arguments that flesh out or correct what's narrowly or mistakenly reported — whether by various news media, corporations, or branches of government. If there has been any growth in factual arguments in the last decade, it may have been in this area because readers on Web sites and blogs can find (or dredge up) obscure facts and information on just about any subject, correcting or expanding the coverage in the mainstream media or elsewhere. For good or ill, the words of public figures and the actions of institutions, from churches to news organizations, are now always *on record* and searchable. When, for example, the *New York Times* criticized federal officials for cutting money for flood control measures in the Mississippi Delta prior to the New Orleans hurricane of 2005, critics of the *Times* quickly located editorials from the same paper in 1993 and 1997 criticizing spending proposals for flood control. Corrective arguments can sometimes play like a game of "Gotcha!" but they broaden readers' perspectives and help them make judgments on the basis of better information. (They also suggest that our institutions are often just as inconsistent, fallible, and petty as the rest of us.)

As you probably suspect, factual arguments have a way of adding interest and complexity to our lives, taking what at one time seems simple and adding new dimensions to it. In many situations, they're the precursors to other forms of analysis, especially causal and proposal arguments. Before we can explore causes or solve problems, we need to know the facts on the ground.

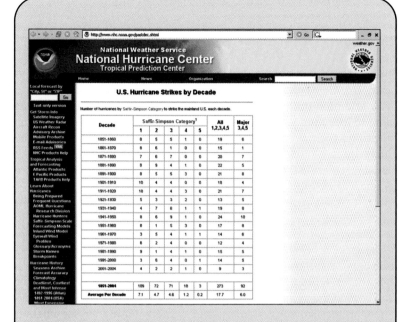

National Weather Service
National Hurricane Center
Tropical Prediction Center

Home   News   Organization   Search

Local forecast by
"City, St" or "ZIP"   Go

Text-only version
Get Storm Info
Satellite Imagery
US Weather Radar
Aircraft Recon
Advisory Archive
Mobile Products
E-mail Advisories
RSS Feeds
NHC Products Help
Tropical Analysis
and Forecasting
Atlantic Products
E Pacific Products
TAFB Products Help
Learn About
Hurricanes
Being Prepared
Frequent Questions
AOML Hurricane
Research Division
Hurricane Hunters
Saffir-Simpson Scale
Forecasting Models
Inland Wind Model
Eyewall Wind
Profiles
Glossary/Acronyms
Storm Names
Breakpoints
Hurricane History
Seasons Archive
Forecast Accuracy
Climatology
Deadliest, Costliest
and Most Intense
1492-1996 (Atlan)
1851-2004 (USA)
Most Expensive

U.S. Hurricane Strikes by Decade

Number of hurricanes by Saffir-Simpson Category to strike the mainland U.S. each decade.

Decade	Saffir-Simpson Category[1]					All 1,2,3,4,5	Major 3,4,5
	1	2	3	4	5		
1851-1860	8	5	5	1	0	19	6
1861-1870	8	6	1	0	0	15	1
1871-1880	7	6	7	0	0	20	7
1881-1890	8	9	4	1	0	22	5
1891-1900	8	5	5	3	0	21	8
1901-1910	10	4	4	0	0	18	4
1911-1920	10	4	4	3	0	21	7
1921-1930	5	3	3	2	0	13	5
1931-1940	4	7	6	1	1	19	8
1941-1950	8	6	9	1	0	24	10
1951-1960	8	1	5	3	0	17	8
1961-1970	3	5	4	1	1	14	6
1971-1980	6	2	4	0	0	12	4
1981-1990	9	1	4	1	0	15	5
1991-2000	3	6	4	0	1	14	5
2001-2004	4	2	2	1	0	9	3
1851-2004	109	72	71	18	3	273	92
Average Per Decade	7.1	4.7	4.6	1.2	0.2	17.7	6.0

Not Just Words

Above is a table on the Web site of the National Hurricane Center that received much attention following the destruction caused by Hurricane Katrina along the American Gulf Coast in summer 2005. Study the table closely, and then try to offer several different factual claims that might be supported by the data you find there. Or locate a statistical study on a subject, and then offer a variety of claims. You can find an enormous variety of statistical information—including many similar tables—by beginning your search at <http://www. fedstats.gov> or <http://www.census.gov/statab/www/>.

Characterizing Factual Arguments

Factual arguments tend to be driven by perceptions and evidence. A writer first notes something new or different or mistaken and wants to draw attention to that fact. Or researchers notice a pattern that leads them to look more closely at some phenomenon or behavior, exploring questions such as *What if?* or *How come?* They're also motivated by simple human curiosity or suspicion: *If being fat is so unhealthy, why aren't mortality rates rising? Just how different are the attitudes of people in so-called red and blue states?*

Such observations can lead quickly toward hypotheses, that is, toward tentative and plausible statements of fact whose merits need to be examined more closely. *Maybe being a little overweight isn't so bad for people as we've been told? Maybe the differences between blue and red staters have been exaggerated by media types looking for a story?* To support such hypotheses, writers would then have to uncover evidence that reaches well beyond the observations (often quite casual or accidental) that triggered the initial interest—like a news reporter motivated to see whether there's a verifiable story behind a source's tip. For instance, the authors of *Freakonomics*, Stephen J. Dubner and Steven Levitt, were intrigued by the National Highway Traffic Safety Administration's claim that car seats for children were 54 percent effective in preventing deaths in auto crashes for children below the age of four. In a *New York Times* op-ed column entitled "The Seat Belt Solution," they posed an important question about that factual claim:

> But 54 percent effective compared with what? The answer, it turns out, is this: Compared with a child's riding completely unrestrained.

Their initial question about that claim would lead them to a more focused inquiry, then to a database on auto crashes, and then to a surprising conclusion: For kids above age 24 months, those in car seats might be statistically safer than those without any protection, but they apparently weren't any safer than those confined by much simpler, cheaper, and more readily available devices—seat belts. Looking at the statistics every which way, the authors wonder if children that age wouldn't be just as well off physically—and their parents less stressed and better off financially—if the government mandated seat belts rather than car seats for them.

Safer than a seat belt?

Truth be told, a great many factual arguments begin with people actively looking for a problem or working within a framework that will turn one up. Such factual arguments come close to representing what's been called spin, in which the only arguments offered are favorable to one's own side and evidence is either made to conform to this pre-determined claim or wholly ignored when it doesn't suit the party line. For instance, you wouldn't look to the Web site of the Republican National Committee for facts about how well the economy is doing during a Democratic administration (or vice versa); instead, you could be fairly confident of finding statistical analyses and anecdotal evidence all putting the most negative spin on the national situation. PR people on someone's payroll might get away with selective reporting of this kind, but no reputable writer wants to be known for using facts or evidence incorrectly in arguments.

Just what kinds of evidence typically appear in sound factual arguments? The simple answer might be "all sorts," but a case can be made that factual arguments rely on "hard evidence" more than on logic and reason (see Chapter 4). Even so, some pieces of evidence will be harder and more convincing than others. Very early in the twentieth century, for example, astronomer Percival Lowell suspected that there might be a ninth planet wandering out there beyond the orbit of Neptune. Why? Oddities in the orbits of the outer planets Uranus and Neptune, Lowell surmised, could be explained by the gravity of yet another orbital body pulling on these objects. Yet while these orbital irregularities were sufficient to persuade astronomers to hypothesize about an undiscovered Planet X, the argument wasn't closed until twenty-four-year-old astronomer Clyde Tombaugh actually spotted Pluto in 1930. His photographic evidence for the new planet was more direct than Lowell's inferences from orbital paths—the difference between hearing what *might* be the call of an ivory-billed woodpecker and actually capturing the bird's image compellingly on film. (Oddly enough, it turned out that Pluto had nothing to do with the anomalies in the orbits of Uranus and Neptune.)

Does the Pluto example mean that you can't make a factual argument without hard evidence? Of course not. In fact, in many factual arguments, no single piece of evidence will function as a clincher. For example, what *single* piece of evidence would prove that global warming is actually occurring or that students today are less conscientious readers than those in the recent past? In both cases, you might point to lots of evidence drawn from various sources, but no one item would close the case. Instead, you'd be arguing from the preponderance of evidence that you are probably, not certainly, correct. But *probably* right is good enough in many everyday situations and all the assurance readers will be able to expect in many circumstances.

Developing a Factual Argument

Factual arguments on the same subject can bubble with outrage and anger or speak with the dispassionate drone of science. Here are two claims that circulated in the media shortly after Hurricane Katrina struck the Gulf Coast; they suggest the range of factual argument in both substance and style. The first, by Ross Gelbspan, shows the sweeping claims and pithy style of fact-based editorial commentary. It's angry and speculative:

> **The hurricane that struck Louisiana and Mississippi on Monday was nicknamed Katrina by the National Weather Service. Its real name is global warming. . . .**

Although Katrina began as a relatively small hurricane that glanced off southern Florida, it was supercharged with extraordinary intensity by the high sea surface temperatures in the Gulf of Mexico.

The consequences are as heartbreaking as they are terrifying.

Unfortunately, few people in America know the real name of Hurricane Katrina because the coal and oil industries have spent millions of dollars to keep the public in doubt about the issue.

The reason is simple: To allow the climate to stabilize requires humanity to cut its use of coal and oil by 70 percent. That, of course, threatens the survival of one of the largest commercial enterprises in history.

–Ross Gelbspan, "Hurricane Katrina's Real Name"

The second claim, by William M. Gray and Philip J. Klotzback, writing for the Department of Atmospheric Science at Colorado State University, addresses much the same issue but provides its answers in a different style:

Many individuals have queried whether the unprecedented landfall of four destructive hurricanes in a seven-week period during August–September 2004 and the landfall of two more major hurricanes in the early part of the 2005 season is related in any way to human-induced climate changes. There is no evidence that this is the case. If global warming were the cause of the increase in United States hurricane landfalls in 2004 and 2005 and the overall increase in Atlantic basin major hurricane activity of the past eleven years (1995–2005), one would expect to see an increase in tropical cyclone activity in the other storm basins as well (i.e., West Pacific, East Pacific, Indian Ocean, etc.). This has not occurred. When tropical cyclones worldwide are summed, there has actually been a slight decrease since 1995. In addition, it has been well documented that the measured global warming during the 25-year period of 1970–1994 was accompanied by a downturn in Atlantic basin major hurricane activity over what was experienced during the 1930s through the 1960s.

–William M. Gray and Philip J. Klotzback, "Forecast of Atlantic
Hurricane Activity for September and October 2005
and Seasonal Update through August"

Clearly, the shape of any factual argument you might compose, from how you state your claim to how you present evidence and the language you use, will be shaped by the occasion for the argument and the audiences you intend to reach. But we can offer some general advice to get you started.

Identifying an Issue

Before you can offer a factual argument, you need to identify an issue or problem that may already have the attention of potential readers or, in your opinion, should have their attention. Or look for anomalies in local or national communities, that is, situations or phenomena out of the ordinary in the expected order of things. You might note, for example, the rapid increase in Native American–owned gambling casinos and resorts in your state. What's going on, and is it important? Or you might notice that many people you know are deciding not to attend college. How widespread is this change, and who are the people making this choice? Or you might explore questions that many people have already formulated but haven't found the time to examine in detail—such as whether cell phones are really as safe as claimed, or whether we'll discover twenty years from now that a generation of Americans has slow-cooked its gray matter.

Whole books get written when authors decide to pursue factual questions, even those that have been explored before. But you do want to be careful not to argue matters that pose no challenge to you or your audiences. You've got nothing new to offer if you try to persuade readers that smoking is harmful to their health. But could you uncover information about smoking on your campus that might provoke thoughtful examinations of the issue? Perhaps you suspect that smoking is correlated in interesting ways to academic majors, sexual orientation, or ethnic identity. Would it be important to recognize these facts—if indeed you could prove them?

Some quick preliminary research and reading might make it possible for you to move from an intuition, hunch, or mere interest to a *hypothesis,* a tentative statement of your claim: *Women in the liberal arts are the heaviest smokers on campus.* A hypothesis like this might seem frivolous at first, or it may provoke enough controversy and resistance to merit the research necessary to support it. Where might such a claim lead if you could find evidence to support it? As noted earlier, factual arguments often provoke other kinds of analysis. Here, you might find yourself moving irresistibly toward arguments about the cause of the phenomenon, but not until you had established its basis in fact.

On the other hand, you might discover, from the sheer number of butts on the ground outside the business school, that your hypothesis is questionable. It may be that men in accounting and marketing blacken their lungs as thoroughly as do women in philosophy. What do you do now? Abandon your hypothesis or modify it. That's what hypotheses are for. They are works in progress.

If Everything's an Argument . . .

Some of the factual arguments in this chapter may seem to you much more like reports or scientific studies than persuasive pieces. Study the examples of factual arguments throughout these pages, and then try ranking them on a scale from most factual to most argumentative. Does such a scale make sense when you try to apply it? Does this chapter increase your faith in the title of the book, or does it raise doubts? Explain.

Researching Your Hypothesis

How and where you research your subject will depend, naturally, on your subject. You'll certainly want to review Chapter 16, "What Counts as Evidence," and Chapter 19, "Evaluating and Using Sources," before constructing an argument of fact. Libraries and the Web will provide you deep resources on almost every subject. Your task will typically be to separate the best sources from all the rest, *best* here having many connotations. Some reputable sources may be too technical for your audiences; some accessible sources may be pitched too low or be too far removed from the actual facts.

You'll be making judgments like this routinely. But don't hesitate to go to primary sources whenever you can. For example, when gathering a comment from a source on the Web, trace it whenever possible to its original site and read the comment in its full context. When statistics are quoted, follow them back to the source that originally offered them to be sure that they're recent and reputable. Instructors and librarians can help you appreciate the differences. Understand that even sources with pronounced biases can furnish useful information, provided that you know how to use them, take their limitations into account, and then share what you know about the sources with your readers.

Sometimes, you'll be able to do primary research on your own, especially when your subject is local and you have the resources to do it. You might be able to conduct a competent survey of campus opinions and attitudes, for example, or you could study budget records to determine trends in faculty salaries, tuition, student fees, and so on. Primary research of this sort can be challenging because even the simplest surveys or polls have to be intelligently designed and executed in a way that samples a representative population (see Chapter 4). But the work could pay off in an argument that brings new information to readers.

Refining Your Claim

As you learn more about your subject, your hypothesis may turn into an actual claim, revised to reflect what you've discovered. In many cases, these revised hypotheses will grow increasingly complex and specific. Following are three versions of essentially the same claim, with each iteration offering more information to help readers assess its merit:

> Americans really did land on the moon, despite what some people think!

> Since 1969, when the *Eagle* supposedly landed on the moon, some people have been skeptical about the success of the USA's Apollo program.

> Despite plentiful hard evidence to the contrary—from *Saturn* V launches witnessed by thousands, to actual moon rocks tested by independent labs worldwide—some people persist in believing that NASA's moon landings were actually filmed on deserts in the American Southwest as part of a massive propaganda fraud.

As you advance in your research, your hypothesis or thesis will likely pick up even more qualifying words and expressions, which help you to make reasonable claims. They'll be among your most valuable tools—words and phrases such as *some, most, few, for most people, for a few users, under specific conditions, usually, occasionally, seldom,* and so on.

It may be important sometimes, too, to set your claim into a context that helps explain it to others who may find it untenable or hostile. For instance, Professor of English Vincent Carretta anticipated strong objections after he uncovered evidence that the author of *The Interesting Narrative* (1789), a much-cited autobiographical account of Olaudah Equiano's Middle Passage voyage and subsequent life as a slave, may have been born in South Carolina, not in west Africa. Speaking to the *Chronicle of Higher Education*, Carretta explains why Equiano may have made up African origins to serve a larger cause—a growing antipathy to slavery and slave markets:

> "... Whether [Equiano] invented his African birth or not, he knew that what that movement needed was a first-person account. And because they were going after the slave trade, it had to be an account of some-

New details about a subject often lead to new ways to support or refute a claim about it. Conspiracy theorists point to the absence of visible stars in photographs of the moon landing as evidence that it was staged, but photographers know that the camera exposure needed to capture the foreground—astronauts in their bright space suits—would have made the stars in the background too dim to see.

> one who had been born in Africa and was brought across the Middle Passage. An African-American voice wouldn't have done it."
>
> —Jennifer Howard, "Unraveling the Narrative"

Thus Carretta asks readers to see that the new facts he has discovered about *The Interesting Narrative* do not diminish the work's historical significance. If anything, his work has added new dimensions to its meaning and interpretation.

Deciding Which Evidence to Use

In this chapter, we've been blurring the distinction somewhat between factual arguments aimed at scientific and technical audiences and those offered for more public consumption in media such as editorials, magazines, and Web sites. In the former, you might find exhaustive appendices of information, including charts, graphs, and full databases. Scientific claims themselves are usually stated with great economy and precision, followed by a thorough account of methods and results. The article reporting the discovery of the ivory-billed woodpecker makes its point in two sentences: "The ivory-billed woodpecker (*Campephilus principalis*), long suspected to be extinct, has been rediscovered in the Big Woods region of eastern Arkansas. Visual encounters during 2004 and 2005, and analysis of a video clip from April 2004, confirm the existence of at least one male." The evidence then follows.

Less scientific factual arguments—claims about our society, institutions, behaviors, habits, and so on—are seldom this clean and could draw on evidence from a great many different sources. For example, when the National Endowment for the Arts (NEA) published a study entitled "Reading at Risk" in June 2004 to report "the declining importance of literature to our populace," it drew its conclusion by studying a variety of phenomena in a large population:

> This survey investigated the percentage and number of adults, age 18 and over, who attended artistic performances, visited museums, watched broadcasts of arts programs, or read literature. The survey sample numbered more than 17,000 individuals, which makes it one of the most comprehensive polls of art and literature consumption ever conducted.
>
> –National Endowment for the Arts

Still, you could imagine other ways to measure an interest in literature, some of which might include nontraditional (graphic novels, for instance) or electronic forms not examined in the NEA study. A phenomenon as broad as "literature" is difficult to define factually because few people can agree on its dimensions. So any study would have to make choices about what evidence to draw from and be prepared to defend those choices.

By contrast, a factual argument about a specific literary work (rather than the larger phenomenon of reading) might be a significantly easier task to manage because you could find much of your evidence in the poem, play, or novel itself, supplemented by historical and biographical information on the life and times of the author. For instance, is *Frankenstein* (1831) really a story about the growing impact of science and industrialism on Europe? To answer the question, you could refer to passages in Mary Shelley's novel itself and to information from his-

David B.'s *Epileptic* is a graphic novel written, according to *Publisher's Weekly,* with "wrenching psychological depth." Is it literature?

tories of the period during which it was written showing a society experiencing rapid technological change.

Quite often, you may have only so many words or pages to make a factual argument. What do you do then? Obviously, you need to present your best evidence as powerfully as possible. But that's not as difficult a task as it may seem. It has been widely noticed that you can make a persuasive factual case with just a few examples—three or four often suffice to make a point. Indeed, going on too long or presenting even good data in a way that makes it seem uninteresting or pointless can undermine a claim.

Presenting Your Evidence

In *Hard Times* (1854), British author Charles Dickens poked fun at a pedagogue he named Thomas Gradgrind, who preferred hard facts before all things human or humane: "A man of realities. A man of fact and calculations. A man who proceeds upon the principle that two and two are four, and nothing over, and who is not to be talked into allowing for anything over." When poor Sissy Jupe (designated "girl number twenty" in his classroom) is unable at his command to define a horse, Gradgrind turns to his star pupil:

> "Bitzer," said Thomas Gradgrind. "Your definition of a horse."
> "Quadruped. Graminivorous. Forty teeth, namely twenty-four grinders, four eyeteeth, and twelve incisive. Sheds coat in the spring; in marshy countries, sheds hoofs, too. Hoofs hard, but requiring to be shod with iron. Age known by marks in mouth." Thus (and much more) Bitzer.
> "Now girl number twenty," said Mr. Gradgrind. "You know what a horse is."
>
> —Charles Dickens, *Hard Times*

But does Bitzer? Rattling off facts about a subject isn't quite the same thing as knowing it, especially when your goal is, as it will be in an argument of fact, to educate and persuade audiences. So you must take care how you present your evidence.

Factual arguments, like any others, do take many forms. They can be as simple and pithy as a letter to the editor (or Bitzer's definition of a

American and other backgrounds increased between 1982 and 2002. In contrast, the number of white Americans reading literature fell by more than 6 million between 1982 and 2002. In summary, because of the changing demographics of the U.S., there was an increase in the number of literary readers from all ethnic and racial groups *except* white Americans.

These changes in the number of literary readers are highlighted in Table 22. White Americans represented 80 percent of literary readers in 2002, down from 87 percent in 1982. African Americans constituted 9 percent of literary readers in 2002, a slight increase from 8 percent in 1982. Hispanic Americans comprised 6 percent of literary readers in 2002, up from 4 percent in 1982. Finally, Americans from other ethnic and racial groups represented 4 percent of literary readers in 2002, an increase from 2 percent in 1982.

Education

Figure 7 illustrates that the literary reading rate

decreased significantly for people with all levels of educational attainment. In fact, the literary reading rate decreased by 15 percentage points or more for those in all except the lowest education group (grade school only).

Table 23
Literary Reading by Education, 1982, 1992, and 2002
(Millions of U.S. Adults)

	1982	1992	2002	Change	% change
Grade school	4.2	2.4	1.6	-2.5	-60.9 %
Some high school	9.9	7.6	4.7	-5.2	-52.6
High school graduate	33.1	32.6	24	-9.1	-27.5
Some college	26.1	27.2	30	4	15.2
College graduate / Graduate school	23.5	31.1	35.6	12.2	52.0

The gap between the literary reading rates of college graduates and high school graduates remained large but stable between 1982 and 2002. In 1982, the difference between the reading rates of college graduates (82 percent) and high school graduates (54 percent) was about 28 percentage points. By 2002, after a significant drop in the literary reading rates of both groups, the gap was 29 percentage points.

Despite the sharp decreases in literary reading at all education levels, rising levels of education in American society led to an increase in the number of literary readers who had some college education or a college degree. Table 23 shows that the number of readers with a college degree or graduate education increased by about 12 million. The number of literary readers with some college education increased by about 4 million. There were decreases in the number of literary readers at the three other education levels. In particular, the number of literary readers with a high school education decreased by 9 million.

Figure 7: Literary Reading Rates by Education, 1982, 1992, and 2002
Americans 18 years of age or older

Source: 2002 Survey of Public Participation in the Arts

This page from the National Endowment for the Arts report "Reading at Risk" illustrates its use of tables and charts to make information accessible.

horse) or as comprehensive and formal as a senior thesis or even a dissertation. The National Endowment for the Arts 2004 report on literary reading, for example, has all the trappings of a formal scientific report, with no fewer than twenty-five tables and eight figures that present all its numerical findings in a form readers can process easily. Like many studies, it includes a title page, a table of contents, a preface, an executive summary, several chapters of analysis (including a conclusion), and three appendices. All these elements also have the function of supporting the ethos of the work, making it seem serious and credible, well conceived and thorough.

Considering Design and Visuals

Precisely because factual arguments so often rely on evidence that can be measured, counted, computed, or illustrated, they benefit from thoughtful, even artful, presentation of data. So when you prepare a factual argument, consider how its design can enhance the evidence you have to offer. If you have an argument that can be translated into a table, chart, or graph (see Chapter 14), try it. If you have lots of examples, you might present them in a list (bulleted or otherwise) and keep the language in each item roughly parallel. That's what Thomas Jefferson and his coauthors did almost 250 years ago in enumerating factual charges against King George III in the American Declaration of Independence (1776).

Photos and images have many uses in factual arguments, from technical illustration to imaginative re-creation. We know, of course, that

> He has refused his Assent to Laws, the most wholesome and necessary for the public Good.
>
> He has forbidden his Governors to pass Laws of immediate and pressing Importance, unless suspended in their Operation till his Assent should be obtained ; and when so suspended, he has utterly neglected to attend to them.
>
> He has refused to pass other Laws for the Accommodation of large Districts of People, unless those People would relinquish the Right of Representation in the Legislature, a Right inestimable to them, and formidable to Tyrants only.
>
> He has called together Legislative Bodies at Places unusual, uncomfortable, and distant from the Depository of their public Records, for the sole Purpose of fatiguing them into Compliance with his Measures.
>
> He has dissolved Representative Houses repeatedly, for opposing with manly Firmness his Invasions on the Rights of the People.
>
> He has refused for a long Time, after such Dissolutions, to cause others to be elected ; whereby the Legislative Powers, incapable of Annihilation, have returned to the People at large for their exercise ; the State remaining, in the mean Time, exposed to all the Dangers of Invasion from without, and Convulsions within.

An early printed version of the Declaration of Independence uses paragraph breaks to highlight the list of grievances against King George III.

even amateurs can manipulate digital images today the way only spy agencies could in the not-so-distant past, erasing people from photographs. But images retain their power to illustrate precisely what readers might otherwise have to imagine—whether it be actual conditions of drought, poverty, or disaster in some part of the world today, or the dimensions of the Roman forum as it existed in the time of Julius Caesar. These days, readers will expect the arguments they read to include visual elements, and there's little reason not to offer this assistance.

Finally, consider how your opportunities for presenting information increase when you take an argument to the Web or use presentation software such as PowerPoint or Keynote. Not only can you use still images and illustrations, but you have access to video and audio resources as well. Readers interested in the ivory-billed woodpecker controversy, for example, could download both the video that purported to show the bird in flight and the audios of its call and knock.

Key Features of Factual Arguments

In drafting a factual argument, make sure you do the following:

- Describe a situation that leads you to raise questions about what the facts in a given situation might be.
- Make a claim that addresses the status of the facts as they're known. You'll usually be establishing, challenging, or correcting them. Your claim can be presented tentatively as a hypothesis, or more boldly as a thesis.
- Offer substantial and authoritative evidence to support your claims.

In academic situations, a claim typically comes first, with the evidence trailing after. But it's not unusual for arguments of fact to present evidence first and then build toward a claim or thesis. Such a structure invites readers to participate in the process by which a factual claim is made (or challenged). The argument unfolds with the narrative drive of a mystery story, with readers eager to know what point the evidence is leading to.

GUIDE | **to writing an argument of fact**

● Finding a Topic

You're entering an argument of fact when you:

- make a claim about fact or existence that's controversial or surprising: *Global warming is threatening Arctic species, especially polar bears.*

- correct an error of fact: *The overall abortion rate is not increasing in the United States, though rates are increasing in some states.*

- challenge societal myths: *Many Mexicans fought alongside Anglos in battles that won Texas its independence from Mexico.*

● Researching Your Topic

Solid research is the basis for most factual arguments. Use both a library and the Web to locate the information you need. One of your most valuable resources may be a research librarian. Take advantage of other human resources, too: don't hesitate to call experts or talk with eyewitnesses who may have special knowledge. For many factual arguments, you can begin research by consulting the following types of sources:

- newspapers, magazines, reviews, and journals (online and print)
- online databases
- government documents and reports
- Web sites, blogs, and listservs or newsgroups
- books
- experts in the field, some of whom might be right on your campus

In addition, your topic may require field research: a survey, a poll, systematic observation.

● Formulating a Hypothesis

Don't rush into a thesis when developing a factual argument. Instead, begin with a hypothesis that expresses your beliefs at the beginning of the project, but that may change as your work proceeds. You might even begin with a question to which you don't have an answer, or with a broad, general interest in a subject:

- **Question:** Have higher admissions standards at BSU reduced the numbers of entering first-year students from small, rural high schools?
- **Hypothesis:** Higher admissions standards at BSU are reducing the number of students admitted from rural high schools, which tend to be smaller and less well funded than those in suburban and urban areas.
- **Question:** Have the iPod and the convenience of its iTunes and comparable music sites reduced the amount of illegal downloading of music?
- **Hypothesis:** The iPod and its iTunes Web site may have done more than lawsuits by record companies to discourage illegal downloads of music.
- **Question:** How are prison guards who work on death row affected by their jobs?
- **Hypothesis:** A death-row assignment will desensitize prison guards to the prisoners held there.

● Examples of Arguable Factual Claims

- The fact that a campus survey shows that far more students have read *Harry Potter and the Prisoner of Azkaban* than *Hamlet* indicates that our current core curriculum lacks depth.
- Evidence suggests that the European conquest of the Americas may have had more to do with infectious diseases than any superiority in technology or even weaponry.
- In the long run, dieting may be more harmful than moderate overeating.

● Preparing a Proposal

If your instructor asks you to prepare a proposal for your project, here's a format that may help:

State your thesis completely. If you are having trouble doing so, try outlining it in Toulmin terms:

Claim:

Reason(s):

Warrant(s):

- Explain why the issue you're examining is important, and provide the context for raising the issue. Are you introducing new information, making available information better known, correcting what has been reported incorrectly, or complicating what has been understood more simply?

- Identify and describe those readers you most hope to reach with your proposal. Why is this group of readers most appropriate for your proposal? What are their interests in the subject?

- Discuss the kinds of evidence you expect to use in the project and the research the paper will require.

- Briefly identify the major difficulties you foresee in researching your argument.

- Describe the format or genre you expect to use: An academic essay? A formal report? A Web site? A wiki? Will you need charts, tables, graphs, other illustrations?

● Thinking about Organization

Factual arguments can be arranged many different ways. The simplest structure is to make a claim and then prove it. But even so basic an approach will likely need an introductory section that provides a context for the claim and a concluding section that assesses the implications of the argument. A factual argument that corrects an error or provides an alternative view of some familiar concept or historical event will also need a section early on explaining what the error or the common belief is. Don't be stingy with details: be sure your opening answers the *who, what, where, when, how,* and (maybe) *why* questions readers will bring to the case.

Some factual arguments offered in academic fields follow formulas and templates. For example, a typical paper in psychology will include an abstract, a review of literature, a discussion of method, an analysis, and a references list. You may be expected to follow a pre-existing pattern for factual arguments or reports in many fields.

When you have more flexibility in the structure of your argument, pay particular attention to the arrangement of evidence and the transitions between key points. In many cases, it makes sense to lead with a strong piece of evidence or striking example to get readers interested in your subject and then to conclude with your strongest evidence.

Even if your argument isn't correcting an error or challenging a common belief, anticipate objections to it and find a place for them in the body of your argument. Ordinarily, you wouldn't want to end a factual argument in a public venue—in an op-ed piece or letter to the editor, for example—with your concessions and/or refutations. Such a strategy leaves readers thinking about the potential problems with your claim at the point they should be impressed with its strengths instead. But an acknowledgment earlier in an argument of any problems in your analysis will usually enhance your ethos.

● Getting and Giving Response

All arguments benefit from the scrutiny of others. Your instructor may assign you to a peer group for the purpose of reading and responding to each other's drafts; if not, get some response on your own from serious readers or consultants at a writing center. You can use the following questions to evaluate a draft. If you're evaluating someone else's draft, be sure to illustrate your points with examples. Specific comments are always more helpful than general observations.

The Claim

- Does the claim clearly raise a serious and arguable factual issue?
- Is the claim as clear and specific as possible?
- Is the claim qualified? If so, how?

Evidence for the Claim

- Is enough evidence provided to get the audience to believe the claim? If not, what kind of additional evidence is needed? Does any of the evidence provided seem inappropriate or otherwise ineffective? Why?
- Is the evidence in support of the claim simply announced, or are its significance and appropriateness analyzed? Is a more detailed discussion needed?
- Are any objections readers might have to the claim or evidence adequately addressed?
- What kinds of sources are cited? How credible and persuasive will they be to readers? What other kinds of sources might be more credible and persuasive?
- Are all quotations introduced with appropriate signal phrases (such as "As Ehrenreich argues,") and blended smoothly into the writer's sentences?
- Are all visuals titled and labeled appropriately? Have you introduced them and commented on their significance?

Organization and Style

- How are the parts of the argument organized? Is this organization effective, or would some other structure work better?

- Will readers understand the relationships among the claims, supporting reasons, warrants, and evidence? If not, what could be done to make those connections clearer? Are more transitional words and phrases needed? Would headings or graphic devices help?

- How might you use visual design elements to make your proposal more effective?

- Are the transitions or links from point to point, paragraph to paragraph, and sentence to sentence clear and effective? If not, how could they be improved?

- Is the style suited to the subject? Is it too formal? Too casual? Too technical? Too bland? How can it be improved?

- Which sentences seem particularly effective? Which ones seem weakest, and how could they be improved? Should some short sentences be combined, or should any long ones be separated into two or more sentences?

- How effective are the paragraphs? Do any seem too skimpy or too long? How can they be improved?

- Which words or phrases seem particularly effective, vivid, and memorable? Do any seem dull, vague, unclear, or inappropriate for the audience or the writer's purpose? Are definitions provided for technical or other terms that readers might not know?

Spelling, Punctuation, Mechanics, Documentation, Format

- Are there any errors in spelling, punctuation, capitalization, and the like?

- Is an appropriate and consistent style of documentation used for parenthetical citations and the list of works cited or references? (See Chapter 20.)

- Does the paper or project follow an appropriate format? Is it appropriately designed and attractively presented? How could it be improved? If it's a Web site, do all the links work?

RESPOND●

1. For each topic in the following list, decide whether the claim is worth arguing to a college audience and explain why or why not:

   Hurricanes are increasing in number and ferocity.

   Many people die annually of cancer.

   Fewer people would die of heart disease each year if more of them paid attention to their diets.

   Japan might have come to terms more readily in 1945 if the Allies hadn't demanded unconditional surrender.

   Boys would do better in school if there were more men teaching in elementary and secondary classrooms.

   The ever-increasing number of minorities in higher education is evidence that racial problems have just about ended in the United States.

   There aren't enough high-paying jobs for college graduates these days.

   Hydrogen may never be a viable alternative to fossil fuels because it takes too much energy to change hydrogen into a useable form.

   Only one of the first forty-three presidents of the United States was a Catholic.

   Political activists have grossly exaggerated the effects of the USA Patriot Act on free expression.

2. Working with a group of colleagues, generate a list of favorite "mysteries" explored on cable TV shows or in dorm-room bull sessions or tabloid newspapers. Aim for twenty. Here are three to get you started: the alien crash landing at Roswell, the existence of Atlantis, the uses of Area 51. Then decide which—if any—of these mysteries might be resolved or explained in a reasonable factual argument and which ones remain eternally mysterious and improbable. Why are people attracted to such topics?

3. The Annenberg Public Policy Center at the University of Pennsylvania hosts <FactCheck.org>, a Web site dedicated to separating facts from opinion or falsehood in the area of politics. It claims to be politically neutral. Analyze one of its cases, either a recent controversial item listed on its homepage or another from its archives. Carefully study the FactCheck case you've chosen. Pay particular attention to the devices FactCheck uses to suggest or ensure objectivity and how it handles facts and statistics. Then offer your own brief factual argument about the site's objectivity. A full case from <FactCheck.org> appears at the end of this chapter as a sample reading.

4. Because digital and electronic technologies have made still and video cameras cheap, small, and durable, they're being increasingly used in many situations to provide factual evidence. Security cameras survey more and more public spaces, from convenience stores to subway stations, to deter assaults or catch criminals in the act. Video recorders on police cars routinely tape encounters between officers and the public, putting both groups under scrutiny. Even responsible citizens can occasionally get tickets in some states from cameras that catch them speeding or entering intersections after traffic lights have turned red. And, of course, the National Football League and some college leagues rely on instant replay to check calls by the officials that are disputed or questionable.

Police in New Orleans were videotaped arresting and beating a man they accused of being disorderly and drunk, a charge the former teacher strongly disputed. The police were subsequently charged with battery.

In all these circumstances, the cameras record what individuals on their own may not see or not remember well, presumably providing a better—though far from perfect—account of an event. (Overturning a call in a Big 10 football game, for example, requires "indisputable video evidence"; otherwise, the call by the referee stands.)

Does all this surveillance enhance our society or undermine it in some ways? Study just one type of surveillance, including any others you think of not mentioned here (baby monitors? cameras on cell phones?). Read up on the subject in the library or on the Web, and then make a factual argument based on what you uncover. For example, you might show whether and how people benefit from the technology, how it's being abused, or both.

The Psychological Experience of Security Officers Who Work with Executions

MICHAEL OSOFSKY

The Louisiana and Alabama "Execution Teams" were interviewed in order to understand the roles, experiences, and effects of carrying out the death penalty. One hundred twenty out of a possible one hundred twenty-four correctional officers were interviewed. Of those questioned, one hundred fifteen completed mental health inventories. The subjects were grouped based on their roles in order to gain a broader picture of the steps and their impact in carrying out the death penalty. Our results show that participants in the execution process stress "caring professionalism." There is an overwhelming emphasis on carrying out one's job at a high level. At the same time, officers are neither dehumanized nor callous, describing acting with respect and decency toward all involved. While their job is their prima facie duty, they experience stress and emotional reactions, frequently having a hard time carrying out society's "ultimate punishment."

An abstract summarizes Osofsky's research. Abstracts are usually required in journal articles.

Working with Professor Philip G. Zimbardo, Michael Osofsky wrote "The Psychological Experience of Security Officers Who Work with Executions" while he was a junior at Stanford University. His essay was published in the Spring 2002 edition of the *Stanford Undergraduate Research Journal*. The paper provides an example of a factual argument with an indirect thesis: the study produces surprising insights into the lives and attitudes of officers who work with prisoners on death row. But it doesn't open with a thesis or even a hypothesis about the security officers. If the piece has a point of view to defend, it may lie in its opening account of arguments for and against the death penalty. Osofsky offers one rationale and a single sentence for the majority position in favor of the death penalty; he provides four arguments and a full paragraph to explicating the position of those who oppose the death penalty. Note that the documentation style in the paper does not conform to conventional MLA or APA styles.

The research essay opens by briefly examining arguments for and against the death penalty— setting the context for Osofsky's study of correctional officers involved in executions.

The topic of state-ordered executions invokes strong emotions from many people throughout the United States and around the world. In the past decade alone, dozens of countries have either placed a moratorium on executions or abolished the death penalty altogether.[1] Simultaneously, ambivalence is the term that best describes the overall attitude towards the death penalty.[2] On the one hand, the majority of the American public believes that serious offenders should be punished to the extent that they inflicted pain and suffering, namely retributive justice or the biblical concept of "an eye for an eye."[3]

Alternatively, a growing minority is horrified by the idea of state-ordered killing, regardless of the heinous nature of the crimes committed. In fact, an ABC Poll conducted in early 2001 found that public support for the death penalty had declined to 63%, a drop from 77% in 1996.[4] Many question whether the death penalty has any positive deterrent effect, citing evidence comparing states with and without capital punishment.[5] Others worry about the economic discrimination against the poor and even racist tendencies associated with the death penalty.[6] Additional opponents of capital punishment feel the punishment to be appalling, arguing that innocent individuals can be put to death.[7] Finally, many individuals question the lengthy appeals process that allows inmates to be executed years after their convictions. Over the course of ten, fifteen, or even twenty years on death row, inmates can be rehabilitated, the family of the victim(s) receive no closure, and prison guards can form a relationship with the inmate.[8–9]

A great deal of intrigue surrounds the members of an execution team. From stereotypes of a hooded executioner to the notion of multiple executioners with only one possessing the deadly bullet, little knowledge exists about the actual nature of how executions are carried out.[10–11]

Our interviews of execution team members at the Louisiana State Penitentiary at Angola and Holman State Prison in Alabama utilize an unprecedented number of subjects through full and uninhibited access to the staff involved. The current study was undertaken in order to gain more understanding about the unusual responsibilities and experiences of those who are directly involved with the legal termination of the lives of others.

One hundred and twenty correctional officers at the Louisiana State Penitentiary at Angola and Holman State Prison in Alabama were interviewed anonymously in order to understand broad areas of the execution process. The one to two hour interviews were conducted over the summers of 2000 and 2001. During 2000, interviews were conducted of fifty of fifty-two members of the Louisiana execution team. During 2001, fifty interviews were conducted of security officers who either work on Death Row or are a part of the execution process in Louisiana. An additional twenty interviews were carried out involving correctional officers who have worked with executions in Alabama. In addition to gathering demographic and background information, a number of questions were asked about the following topics: (1) The execution experience, including roles, reactions, preparation, emotions experienced, and changes over time; (2) Stresses related to their job and methods to cope with stress; (3) Support network and influence of work on relationships; (4) Aftermath of execution experience for the officer. Based on our interviews, we were able to recreate the step-by-step process of carrying out an execution. The process was largely similar in the two states, but differed due to both situational factors with the two facilities as well as the mode of execution employed in each state. (Louisiana uses lethal injection while Alabama is one of two remaining states still employing the electric chair as its sole means of execution.)

The point of the study is explicit: "to gain more understanding" of death row guards and the work they do.

The research methodology is described in detail.

Questions posed to death row officers examine their reactions to the "execution process." Osofsky seems to anticipate emotional reactions and stress.

The security officers were asked to complete three separate measures. During 2000, subjects completed the Beck Depression Inventory (BDI) and the first page of a Clinician Administered Post Traumatic Stress Disorder Scale (CAPS 1) for the DSM-IV, a life events checklist. The reported results from these two measures are primarily descriptive due to our desire to understand the execution process and psychological impacts of carrying out the death penalty. During 2001, we asked the officers to complete a questionnaire pertaining to issues of moral disengagement employed throughout the process. Interviews were tape recorded (without their names on the tapes) in order to guarantee that quotes, reactions, and attributed material were accurate.

After completing the interviews, we classified subjects into one of twelve roles: Wardens, classifications personnel, death row guards, death house/front gate security, liaisons to the press, mental health professionals, spiritual advisors, officers who sit with the victim's family, officers who sit with the inmate's family, the strapdown team, emergency medical technicians, and the Executioner.

Responses to the interviews suggest that guards reflect majority opinion about the death penalty in the United States.

Interview responses conveyed an interesting perspective on the death penalty relative to the existing literature on the subject. Consistent with current national polls, approximately two-thirds of officers indicate general support for the death penalty, stressing the heinous nature of the inmates' crimes and the impact on the victims and their families.

All but three do not believe the death penalty is racially motivated. However, an equal number raised concerns that social class and poverty play major roles in determining who is executed.

Officers do question the equity of the punishment.

"I've never seen a rich man executed," Death Row guard Willie W. asserted. The inmates on Death Row tend to come from poor, underprivileged backgrounds in which they had little access to basic necessities.

Sarah S., the deputy warden, pointed out, "If they had educational opportunities, they wouldn't be here."

The execution team also noted that certain districts within the state are more likely to hand down a death sentence. This variation by district is a function of the District Attorneys, judges, and juries—standards that vary by city and state. A considerable number of the officers discussed their concern that many "lifers" have committed crimes that are as horrific as those committed by the inmates on Death Row. For this reason alone, several members of the execution team argued that either the sentences of those on Death Row should be commuted to life in prison or others should be on Death Row.

Further, we repeatedly heard that the death penalty simply takes too long to be carried out. Some described their identification with the inmates' pain in living and awaiting execution. Others discussed the high monetary cost to the state of the lengthy appeals process. Some worried that the victims cannot receive closure until the inmate is dead.

Ultimately, nearly every person we interviewed echoed two main components of the execution process. On the one hand, and most importantly, the security officers stressed their professionalism. Their duty is to carry out the laws of the United States, whatever those may be. They believe in their jobs, and try to do them as well as they possibly can. On the other hand, they act with decency and humanity toward the inmates. In their efforts to adjust and function successfully, they struggle internally. Although most attempt to suppress painful feelings, they state that if it ever becomes easy to participate in an execution, they would worry about themselves and their loss of humanity. Some deal with their stress by disassociative mechanisms. Some overtly exhibit their distress through transient or persistent stress, guilt, and even depression. Although many officers view Death Row

Osofsky gives ample attention to a critical view of the death penalty expressed by "several" execution team members.

Study is not specific here about numbers. No charts or graphs summarize responses to interview questions.

Factual results here might furnish material for subsequent arguments: guards support implementation of the law yet struggle with the nature of their work.

inmates as the "worst of the worst," all describe treating the inmates with decency. Death Row guard Charles S. said, "I treat them as I would want to be treated. I help them when I can and when my job permits." Strapdown team member Robert A. concurred, "They are people and deserve to be treated as such." While some prisoners do not repent or do so only superficially, the officers describe how many change, becoming cooperative in the process.

Osofsky finds that most officials do, indeed, approach their stressful work with death row inmates humanely and reflectively.

Certainly there are exceptions to the almost universal decency of the officers in this study; wrongful emotional and physical abuse can occur in a maximum-security penitentiary. Some guards have inappropriate motives for working at a prison. From our discussions it appears that most voluntarily leave or are weeded out over time. However, the officers we interviewed did not display hostility toward the inmates, but were concerned with maximizing humanity and dignity. Within the constraints needed to maintain security, they describe being kind to the inmates. Some describe feeling good about a number of inmates who shortly before their execution thank them for their compassion. If anything, after being involved on the death team, correctional officers become more reflective and take their job more seriously than ever.

Works Cited

Osofsky provides notes keyed to the text rather than the alphabetical bibliography more typical of a works cited page.

1. Prokosch E. *Human Rights v. The Death Penalty: Abolition and Restriction in Law and Practice.* Amnesty International, 1998.
2. Finckenauer JO. Public Support for the Death Penalty: Retribution as Just Deserts or Retribution as Revenge? *Justice Quarterly* 1988; 5:81–100.
3. Gale ME. Retribution, Punishment and Death. *UC Davis Law Review* 1985; 18:973–1035.
4. Ellsworth P, Ross L. Public Opinion and Capital Punishment: A Close Examination of the Views of Abolitionists and Retentionists. *Crime and Delinquency* 1983; 29:116–169.

5. Reiman JH. *The Rich Get Richer and the Poor Get Prison*, 4th ed. Boston: Allyn and Bacon, 1985.

6. Jackson J. *Legal Lynching: Racism, Injustice and the Death Penalty*. New York: Marlowe, 1996.

7. Radelet ML, Bedau HA, Putnam CE. *In Spite of Innocence: Erroneous Convictions in Capital Cases*. Boston: Northeastern University Press, 1992.

8. Radelet ML, Vandiver M, Berardo F. Families, Prisons, and Men with Death Sentences: The Human Impact of Structured Uncertainty. *J of Family Issues* 1983; 4:595–596.

9. Goldhammer GE. *Dead End*. Brunswick: Biddle Publishing Company, 1994.

10. Mailer N. *The Executioner's Song*. Boston: Little, Brown, 1979.

11. Elliot RG. *Agent of Death: The Memoirs of an Executioner*. New York: Dutton, 1940.

Abortion Distortions:
Senators from both sides make
false claims about *Roe v. Wade.*

SUMMARY

July 18, 2005

As President Bush considers exactly whom to nominate to succeed Justice Sandra Day O'Connor on the Supreme Court, Senators Barbara Boxer and Rick Santorum both have distorted some facts about the effect of *Roe v. Wade.*

Boxer, a Democrat, claimed that repeal of *Roe* "means a minimum of 5,000 women a year will die" from illegal abortions. But that's a 69-year-old figure dating to a time before penicillin and the birth-control pill. Experts say nowhere near that many women were dying from abortion complications even in the years just before *Roe* made abortions legal nationwide.

On the other side of the abortion debate, Republican Santorum says that suicides by women, and also crime, "got worse, much worse" after *Roe.* But in fact, the female suicide rate is one-third lower now than in 1973. And the Justice Department's annual survey on crime victimization shows a 69 percent drop in property crime and a 53 percent drop in violent crime since *Roe.*

ANALYSIS

Boxer's False Statistic

On July 5, Sen. Boxer claimed that overturning *Roe v. Wade* would cost the lives of more than 5,000 pregnant women a year. That <u>might</u> have been true before the invention of penicillin and the birth control pill, but it's

---

"Abortion Distortions" is from the Web site <FactCheck.org>, which provides this statement of its mission: "We are a nonpartisan, nonprofit, 'consumer advocate' for voters that aims to reduce the level of deception and confusion in U.S. politics. We monitor the factual accuracy of what is said by major U.S. political players in the form of TV ads, debates, speeches, interviews, and news releases. Our goal is to apply the best practices of both journalism and scholarship, and to increase public knowledge and understanding." The site is sponsored by the Annenberg Public Policy Center at the University of Pennsylvania. Note that this article does include a list of sources, but they are not listed or cited within the text in any conventional way, such as MLA or APA style.

not true now. The best evidence indicates that the annual deaths from illegal abortions would number in the hundreds, not thousands.

Boxer made the claim to support her position that the repeal of *Roe* would be the sort of "extraordinary circumstance" that could justify use of the filibuster to stop the confirmation of a nominee to the Supreme Court. The *Associated Press* quoted her this way:

Boxer: It means a minimum of 5,000 women a year will die.

So all options are on the table.

But Boxer was just wrong. The figure comes from a 1936 study by Dr. Frederick Taussig who estimated that abortion claimed the lives of 5,000 to 10,000 women a year. It is impossible to know if his figures are accurate, given that no reliable records exist on the total number of illegal abortions that occurred, much less the number of deaths. Taussig extrapolated the data from trends in New York City and Germany.

His estimate is at least plausible. Women had few means to prevent unwanted pregnancies, and illegal abortions were often performed in less than sanitary settings. Furthermore, penicillin wasn't in use until World War II, and not widely available to the civilian population until after the war ended in 1945. And Enovid, the first oral contraceptive, wasn't available until 1957. But whether Taussig's estimate was accurate or not, the conditions of the 1930s don't apply today.

From the 1940s through the 1960s, in fact, the best available evidence shows a dramatic decline in abortion-related deaths occurring even <u>before</u> the first states liberalized abortion laws in 1967. The *Journal of the American Medical Association* quotes official estimates from the National Center for Health Statistics showing an 89 percent decrease in abortion-related deaths by 1966. That is based on counting the number of death certificates that listed complications from abortion as the cause of death. The numbers reported for any given year are assuredly low since doctors could easily misstate the cause of death to protect the family. Still, these are the only figures that allow comparisons over time. There's no reason to think that the rate of under-reporting would vary from one year to another, and so little reason to doubt that a steep downward trend took place long before *Roe* was decided.

Christopher Tietze, one of the leading experts on abortion trends, wrote in 1969 that it was plausible that 5,000 women a year died from abortion in the 1930s, but concluded that it cannot be anywhere near the true rate now. He said that, although the 235 formally listed on death certificates in 1965 was too low, "in all likelihood it (the actual number) was under 1,000." An abortion statistics expert at the Guttmacher Institute, Stanley Henshaw, is studying abortion rates during the first part of the century. Though his data collection is unfinished, Henshaw concurred that Tietze's estimate of fewer than 1,000 deaths is "reasonable."

Boxer would have been correct to say that <u>some</u> increase in deaths of pregnant women would result should abortions be made illegal. But the number is much lower than she claimed. In 1972, the last year before *Roe v. Wade* legalized abortion nationwide, CDC counted only 39 deaths from illegal abortions based on surveys of health care providers, medical examiners' reports, state and national records, and news reports. However, Henshaw said it's difficult to quantify the number of deaths that could result today if *Roe* were overturned. For one thing, it is not clear how many states would actually make abortions illegal again. And Henshaw noted it is unlikely that the numbers of deaths would be as high as they were before 1973 due to medical advances and emergency services available today. In any case, Boxer's 5,000 figure was nearly 70 years out of date, and clearly wrong.

Santorum's Overreaching

Republican Senator Rick Santorum of Pennsylvania claims in a new book that a number of social ills got "much worse" after *Roe* was decided in 1973. He's clearly right about some, but wrong on at least one, female suicide, and possibly on another, crime.

The book is *It Takes a Family: Conservatism and the Common Good*, released on July 4. It devotes several chapters to abortion, and one of them includes this argument:

> **Santorum, p. 250:** Back before 1973, there were all sorts of claims in favor of legal abortion. Legal abortion would lead to less domestic violence, since young women would not be forced into unhealthy and inappropriate marriages. Fewer desperate women would commit suicide. There would be fewer out-of-wedlock births. There would be fewer divorces. There would be fewer children in poverty, less crime, and less child abuse, since all children would be wanted and grow up in stable families. **None of this happened. Not a single social ill improved as a result of legal abortion: in fact, they all got worse, much worse.**

Santorum is right on some things: The percentage of children living in poverty is up, according to the Census Bureau. It was 14.4 percent in 1973 and 17.6 percent in 2003, the most recent year on record. The birth rate among unmarried women aged 15–44 has increased as well. It went from 24.5 per 1,000 unmarried women in 1973 to about 44 most recently, according to the Center for Disease Control's National Center for Health Statistics. And Santorum has a strong case regarding divorce: the number of divorced persons has risen from 3 percent of the adult population before *Roe* to 10 percent most recently. The divorce rate (per 1,000 population) rose for several years after *Roe* and didn't dip back below pre-*Roe* levels until 1999, according to Census Bureau figures.

Santorum <u>may</u> also be right about child abuse and domestic violence. We could find no reliable statistics on either that allow comparisons with 1973, and Santorum's Senate staff did not respond to several requests from us to say where he is getting his information. As things stand, we consider those claims unverified.

But not all the social problems Santorum cited have gotten worse since the Supreme Court decided *Roe v. Wade*. And at least one has actually gotten better.

Suicide Rates

Santorum says suicides by "desperate women" got "much worse" since 1973. Actually, the suicide rate for women has <u>dropped</u> by one-third since *Roe* was decided. According to the Center for Disease Control, the rate was 6.5 per every 100,000 women in 1973, and had fallen to 4.06 by 2001, the most recent year on record.

As seen in this chart, it is true that the female suicide rate went up after *Roe,* but only slightly—by 0.4 percent. It peaked in 1977 before plunging.

And those numbers refer only to the raw rate of suicides per 100,000 women. The National Center for Health Statistics also publishes an "age-adjusted" suicide rate. Statistics show that women in their 40's are more than twice as likely to commit suicide as women in their 20's, and the age-adjusted rates attempt to cancel out changes in the overall rate that might be due simply to a greater concentration of women in the population who have reached a suicide-prone age. The age-adjusted figure offers even less support for Santorum, however. It shows an even more dramatic decrease

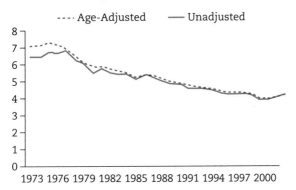

**Female suicide rate
(per 100,000 women)**

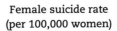

since *Roe*—a decline of 41 percent, compared to a decline of 34 percent for the unadjusted rate. Either way, Santorum was way off.

Crime

Santorum's claim that crime has gotten worse since *Roe* is also doubtful, though here the picture is a bit muddled.

According to the FBI's Uniform Crime Reporting (UCR) Program the overall rate of crimes <u>reported to police</u> is actually 2 percent lower now, though it rose after *Roe* and is still higher for some categories of crime. But according to an annual survey conducted by the Department of Justice, the number of <u>people saying they were crime victims</u> has shown a huge and steady drop since 1973. The survey may be the more accurate, since it attempts to capture the large number of crimes that go unreported to police.

Santorum would be correct to say that the FBI's crime rate rose in the first years after *Roe,* continuing a trend that had been evident for more than a decade. But it plunged starting in 1992 and was about 2 percent <u>below</u> the 1973 level in 2003, the most recent year on record. And it is true that <u>violent</u> crimes reported to police are still 14 percent higher than in 1973, although reported crimes against <u>property</u> are down 3 percent, according to the FBI's statistics.

By another official measure, crime decreased dramatically since 1973 in <u>both</u> categories. The Bureau of Justice Statistics (BJS) National Crime Victimization Survey shows that **crime rates in 2003 are at the lowest levels recorded since the survey's inception,** which coincidentally was the year *Roe* was decided. According to this annual survey, the number of people saying they were victims of <u>property</u> crime dropped steadily after *Roe* to, most recently, about 69 percent below 1973 levels. Meanwhile, the number of people who say they were victimized by <u>violent</u> crime has decreased by 53 percent since 1973. Furthermore, by this measure the rate of violent crime was actually stable between 1973 and 1977, the first several years following *Roe*.

How can the FBI's statistics show an increase in violent crime while the Bureau of Justice Statistics survey shows it dropping by half? There's reason to believe that persons are simply more likely now than in 1973 to report certain crimes to police.

The survey collects responses from a statistical sample of the population, and is not an actual count of crime reports. It attempts to measure the large number of crimes that were never reported to police, as well as those that were. Even now, half of all violent crime goes unreported. Furthermore, the increase in the FBI's violent crime rate is due entirely to big jumps in the numbers of reported rapes and aggravated assaults, which may simply reflect that women are less likely to keep silent about such crimes than they were 30 years ago. The FBI's murder rate, meanwhile, has dropped more than 39 percent since 1973. That's one category of violent crime that is almost always reported, since a dead body is hard to ignore.

In any case, even using the FBI's crime statistics, there is less crime today overall than there was in 1973, contrary to Santorum's claim.

Santorum would have been correct to say that many of the arguments for legalizing abortion proved to be unfounded. But he doesn't have the facts to include female suicide and crime among his examples.

These false claims by Boxer and Santorum show that whoever is named to the current Supreme Court vacancy, truth is already a casualty in the confirmation fight.

—by *Jennifer L. Ernst and Matthew Barge*

———————————

Correction, Aug. 22, 2005: In our original article we said the poverty rate for children was 15.1 percent in 1973. Actually, it was 14.4 percent. So the rise in child poverty after *Roe* has been even more pronounced than we originally stated.

Footnote, Aug 22, 2005: Many of our visitors have written to fault us for failing to observe that changes in such things as suicide rates or child poverty rates don't constitute evidence that *Roe* was or was not the <u>cause</u> of those changes. We agree entirely. However, Santorum didn't claim *Roe* was the cause, he said the other side did. We have no quarrel with his logic, only some of his facts.

Sources

Justin M. Norton, "Boxer: Filibuster to Block Anti-abortion Supreme Court Candidate," *The Associated Press*, 5 July 2005.

Christopher Tietze and Sarah Lewit, "Abortion," *Scientific American*: January 1969, 220(1).

Frederick J. Taussig, M.D., F.A.C.S., *Abortion: Spontaneous and Induced* (St. Louis: C.V. Mosby Co., 1936) 25–28.

"Induced Termination of Pregnancy before and after Roe v. Wade," *Journal of the American Medical Association*, 268 (Dec. 1992): 3231–3239.

Suzanne White Junod, Ph.D., "FDA's Approval of the First Oral Contraceptive, Enovid," *Update,* Food and Drug Law Institute: (July–August 1998).

Ricki Lewis, Ph.D., "*The Rise of Antibiotic-Resistant Infections*," FDA Consumer Magazine, September 1995.

"Abortion Surveillance — United States, 2001," *Morbidity and Mortality Weekly Report*, Center for Disease Control: 26 Dec. 2004.

"Criminal Victimization, 2003," National Crime Victimization Survey, Bureau of Justice Statistics, September 2004.

"Criminal Victimization, 1973–1995," National Crime Victimization Survey, Bureau of Justice Statistics, April 1997.

"National Crime Victimization Survey Violent Crime Trends, 1973–2003," Bureau of Justice Statistics, website, 12 September 2004.

"National Crime Victimization Survey Property Crime Trends, 1973–2003," Bureau of Justice Statistics, website, 12 September 2004.

"Crime in the United States," Federal Bureau of Investigation, website, undated.

Michael R. Rand and Callie M. Rennison, "True Crime Stories? Accounting for Differences in Our National Crime Indicators," *Chance* Vol. 15, No. 1, 2002.

"Reducing Suicide: A National Imperative," Institute of Medicine, 2002.

"Leading Causes of Death 1900–1998," Center for Disease Control, website, undated.

"*Age-Adjusted Rates for 69 Selected Causes by Race and Sex Using Year 2000 Standard Population: United States, 1968–78*," National Vital Statistics System, Center for Disease Control/National Center for Health Statistics, undated.

"*Age-Adjusted Death Rates for 72 Selected Causes by Race and Sex Using Year 2000 Standard Population: United States, 1979–98*," National Vital Statistics System, Center for Disease Control/National Center for Health Statistics, 2002.

Center for Disease Control, Web-based Injury Statistics Query and Reporting System, website, accessed July 2005.

8

Arguments of Definition

A traffic committee must define what a small car is in order to enforce parking restrictions in a campus lot where certain spaces are marked "Small Car Only!" Owners of compact luxury vehicles, light trucks, and motorcycles have complained that their vehicles are being unfairly ticketed.

A panel of judges must decide whether computer-enhanced images will be eligible in a contest for landscape photography. At what point is an electronically manipulated image no longer a photograph?

A scholarship committee must decide whether the daughter of two European American diplomats, born while her parents were assigned to the U.S. embassy in Nigeria, will be eligible to apply for grants designated specifically for "African American students."

A young man hears a classmate describe hunting as a "blood sport." He disagrees and argues that hunting for sport has little in common with "genuine blood sports" such as cockfighting.

A committee of the student union is accused of bias by a conservative student group, which claims that the committee has brought a disproportionate share of left-wing speakers to campus. The committee defends its program by challenging the definition of "left wing" used to classify its speakers.

In a book, an eminent historian distinguishes between *patriotism* and *nationalism:* "Patriotism is the love of a particular land with its particular traditions; nationalism is the love of something less tangible, of the myth of a 'people,' and is often a political and ideological substitute for religion."

● ● ●

Understanding Arguments of Definition

In the wake of devastating Hurricane Katrina in 2005, thousands of New Orleans residents fled their homes to try to find shelter. As the crisis deepened and the failures of the Federal Emergency Management Authority became evident, the media were full of reports about those who had retreated from the storm's horrors. But what to call these people? In some early reports, those who had left New Orleans were labeled *refugees.* But that term rankled many of them (and others) who were native-born American citizens and were, after all, still in their home country. How, they asked, could they be *refugees,* the term commonly used for people legally admitted to the United States from other countries?

As the media hastened to change its terminology to *evacuees,* however, some foreign refugees began voicing their own feelings of being insulted by the implication that *refugees* was a derogatory term. The matter got even more complicated when some reporters pointed out that any legally designated foreign refugees who had been affected by the hurricane would be eligible for many benefits not available to other Katrina victims. In this case, the definition of one word could mean a great deal for thousands of displaced people. While the debate raged on, some "refugee" agencies leapt into action, sending their services to New Orleans.

In a class on Contemporary Issues of Identity, a student group in charge of the day's discussion arrived early to try an experiment: all around the room, on white boards or on posters on the wall, they displayed racial and sexual labels, most of them slurs, and made sure that there were chairs placed under each one. When members of the class arrived, the student group asked them to choose a seat under a label that was close to something they had been called—or had used to label someone else. The students complied at first, but as they took seats they were visibly uncomfortable: they found that sitting under a label *defined* them in ways they found offensive and hurtful. Instead of discussing the impact of such stereotyping slurs on identity formation, class members found themselves silently but intently removing every word from the walls and white boards. Only when the room was completely free of them did they begin to discuss the strong effect this experience had had on them. Among other things, they learned that labels and stereotypes can make for very bad definitions. In short, what you call something matters. That's what arguments of definition are all about.

In many creation stories, the world and its inhabitants are called into being as a result of being named. In the Jewish and Christian bible, for example, when Adam names the animals he gains authority over them because to name things is, partly, to control them. That's why arguments of definition are so important and so very contentious. They can wield the power to say what someone or something is or can be. As such, they can also be arguments that include or exclude: *A creature is an endangered species or it isn't; an act was harassment or it wasn't; a person deserves official refugee status or doesn't.* Another way of approaching definitional arguments, however, is to think of what comes between *is* and *is not*. In fact, the most productive definitional arguments probably occur in this murky realm.

Consider the controversy over how to define human intelligence. Some might argue that human intelligence is a capacity measured by tests of verbal and mathematical reasoning. In other words, it's defined by IQ and SAT scores. Others might define intelligence as the ability to perform specific practical tasks. Still others might interpret intelligence in emotional terms, as a competence in relating to other people. Any of

Not Just Words

Take a look at the images on this page and the facing one. What definition of *patriotism* can you induce from each one?

these positions could be defended reasonably, but perhaps the wisest approach would be to construct a definition of intelligence rich enough to incorporate all these perspectives—and maybe more. In fact, one well-known theorist has posited a theory of "multiple intelligences," arguing that human intelligence is too varied and protean to be marked by any one standard.

Actually, it's important to realize that many political, social, and scientific definitions are constantly "under construction," reargued and reshaped whenever they need to be updated for the times. After horrifying photographs of U.S. soldiers holding Iraqi prisoners on leashes and otherwise abusing and humiliating them became public, and reports indicated that other detainees in Iraq and elsewhere had endured even harsher treatment, a fierce debate over what constituted torture broke out. Amnesty International defines torture as "the deliberate infliction of severe pain or suffering by state agents, or similar acts by private individuals for which the state bears responsibility through consent, acquiescence or inaction. We also use the term *torture* to refer to deliberate pain or suffering inflicted by members of armed political groups." Under this definition, many of the abuses at Abu Ghraib and elsewhere would be deemed torture. Others, however, argued for a different definition, saying that these acts were primarily "the use of traditionally unconventional methods of interrogation."

Attempts to redefine words go on all around us. Just a few weeks after the attacks of 9/11, for example, Peter Ferrara, a law professor at George Mason University, thought it was appropriate to refine the meaning of the word *American* in response to a call in Pakistan to kill all people of that nationality. Here are the opening and conclusion of what proved to be an "extended definition" of the term—a lengthy exploration of the many dimensions of the word, some of which people might have not considered earlier:

> You probably missed it in the rush of news last week, but there was actually a report that someone in Pakistan had published in a newspaper there an offer of a reward to anyone who killed an American, any American.
>
> So I just thought I would write to let them know what an American is, so they would know when they found one.
>
> An American is English . . . or French, or Italian, Irish, German, Spanish, Polish, Russian or Greek. An American may also be African, Indian, Chinese, Japanese, Australian, Iranian, Asian, or Arab, or Pakistani, or Afghan.

An American is Christian, or he could be Jewish, or Buddhist, or Muslim. In fact, there are more Muslims in America than in Afghanistan. The only difference is that in America they are free to worship as each of them chooses.

An American is also free to believe in no religion. For that he will answer only to God, not to the government, or to armed thugs claiming to speak for the government and for God. . . .

So you can try to kill an American if you must. Hitler did. So did General Tojo and Stalin and Mao Tse-Tung, and every bloodthirsty tyrant in the history of the world. But in doing so you would just be killing yourself. Because Americans are not a particular people from a particular place. They are the embodiment of the human spirit of freedom.

Everyone who holds to that spirit, everywhere, is an American.

–Peter Ferrara, "What Is an American?"

Clearly, Ferrara's definition is in fact an argument in favor of American values and principles. The definition makes an unabashed political point.

In case you're wondering, you usually can't resolve important arguments of definition by consulting dictionaries. (Ferrara certainly wouldn't have found any of his definitions of an American in *Webster's*.) Dictionaries themselves just reflect the way particular groups of people used words at a specified time and place. And, like any form of writing, these reference books mirror the prejudices of their makers—as shown, perhaps most famously, in the entries of lexicographer Samuel Johnson (1709–1784), who gave the English language its first great dictionary. Johnson, no friend of the Scots, defined *oats* as "a grain which in England is generally given to horses, but in Scotland supports the people." (To be fair, he also defined *lexicographer* as "a writer of dictionaries, a harmless drudge.") Thus it's quite possible to disagree with dictionary definitions or to regard them merely as starting points for arguments.

Kinds of Definition

Because there are different kinds of definitions, there are also different ways to make a definition argument. Fortunately, identifying a particular type of definition is less important than appreciating when an issue of definition is at stake. Let's explore some common definitional issues.

Formal Definitions

Formal definitions are what you find in dictionaries. Such definitions involve placing a term in its proper genus and species—that is, first determining the larger class to which it belongs and then identifying the features that distinguish it from other members of that class. That sounds complicated, but a definition will help you see the principle. A *hybrid car* might first be identified by placing it among its peers—vehicles that combine two or more sources of power. Then the formal definition would go on to identify the features necessary to distinguish hybrid cars from other multiply powered vehicles such as mopeds or locomotives—four wheels, a mixture of gasoline and electricity, energy efficient, five-passenger capacity, family-friendly interior, and so on.

Is the 2006 Ford Escape a real hybrid?

People can make arguments from either part of a formal definition, from the genus or the species, so to speak. Does a category of objects or ideas (the "species" of hybrid cars) really belong to the larger class (the "genus" of multiply powered vehicles) to which it could be assigned? *Are all hybrids really powered by two sources, or are some of them just gussied-up versions of the regular gasoline car?* That's the genus argument. Or maybe a particular object or idea doesn't have all the features required to meet the species definition. *Is the new Ford Escape Hybrid efficient enough to count as a genuine hybrid?* That's the species argument.

Questions Related to Genus

- Is tobacco a drug or a crop?
- Do tabloids report the news or sensationalize it?
- Is hate speech a right protected by the First Amendment?

Questions Related to Species

- Is tobacco a harmless drug? A dangerously addictive one? Something in between?
- Is *On the Record with Greta Van Susteren* a news program? A tabloid? Both?
- Is using a racial epithet always an instance of hate speech?

Before downloading a video clip from *On the Record,* visitors to the Fox News Web site can browse the catalog of photogenic murder victims, missing persons, and suspects featured on the show. Is it a news program, a tabloid, or something in between?

Operational Definitions

Operational definitions identify an object or idea not by what it is so much as by what it does or by the conditions that create it. In an article called "Moms Know . . . All about Operational Definitions," Kathy Parker gives this example: "From the age of six on, I knew the essence of an operational definition, even if the term itself was not known to me. I knew that chores were not considered 'complete' until I had taken the linens off my bed and put them in the laundry hamper, picked up toys and vacuumed my room. I also knew that there would be consequences, if I ignored the definition of 'complete.'" Here's another operational definition used by the American Psychological Association: "Sexual Abuse is any incident of sexual contact involving a child that is inflicted or allowed to be inflicted by the person responsible for the child's care." You'll get arguments that arise from operational definitions when people debate what the conditions are that define something or whether these conditions have been met. (See also the discussion of stasis theory in Chapter 1, p. 20.)

Questions Related to Conditions

- Must sexual imposition be both unwanted and unsolicited to be considered harassment?
- Can institutional racism occur in the absence of individual acts of racism?
- Is a volunteer who is paid still a volunteer?
- Does someone who uses steroids to enhance home-run-hitting performance deserve the title Hall of Famer?

Questions Related to Fulfillment of Conditions

- Was the act really sexual harassment if the accused believed the interest was mutual?
- Has the institution supported traditions or policies that have led to racial inequities?
- Was the compensation given to the volunteer really "pay" or just "reimbursement" for expenses?
- Should Player X, who used steroids prescribed for a medical reason, be ineligible for the Hall of Fame?

Definitions by Example

Resembling operational definitions are definitions by example, which define a class by listing its individual members. For example, one might define *planets* by listing all nine major bodies in orbit around the sun, or *heirloom tomatoes* by listing all those available at the local farmer's market.

Arguments of this sort focus on who or what may be included in a list that defines a category: *great movies, worst natural disasters, groundbreaking painters*. Such arguments often involve comparisons and contrasts with the items most readers would agree from the start belong in this

A definition of *heirloom tomatoes* would include the Brandywine but not the New Jersey Beefsteak.

list. One might, for example, wonder why planet status is denied to asteroids, when both planets and asteroids are bodies in orbit around the sun. A comparison between planets and asteroids might suggest that size is one essential feature of the nine recognized planets that asteroids don't meet.

Questions Related to Membership in a Named Class

- Is any pop artist today in a class with Chuck Berry, Elvis Presley, the Beatles, or Aretha Franklin?
- Are comic books, now sometimes called graphic novels, literature?
- Who are the Madame Curies or Albert Einsteins of the current generation?
- Does Washington, D.C., deserve the status of a state?

Other Issues of Definition

Many issues of definition cross the line among the types described here and some other forms of argument. For example, if you decided to explore whether banning pornography on the Internet violates First

Amendment guarantees of free speech, you'd first have to establish definitions of pornography and free speech—either legal ones already settled on by, let's say, the Supreme Court, or other definitions closer to your own beliefs. Then you'd have to argue that types of pornography on the Internet are (or are not) in the same class or share (or do not share) the same characteristics as types of speech that you're arguing are protected by the First Amendment. In doing so, you'd certainly find yourself slipping into an evaluative mode because matters of definition are often also questions of value. (See Chapter 9.)

When exploring or developing an idea, you shouldn't worry about such slippage—it's a natural part of the process of writing. But do try to focus an argument on a central issue or question, and appreciate the fact that any definition you care to defend must be examined honestly and rigorously. Be prepared to explore every issue of definition with an open mind and with an acute sense of what will be persuasive to your readers.

Developing a Definitional Argument

Definitional arguments don't just appear out of the blue; they evolve out of the occasions and conversations of daily life, both public and private. You might get into an argument over the definition of *ordinary wear and tear* when you return a rental car with some battered upholstery. Or you might be asked to write a job description for a new position to be created in your office: you have to define the position in a way that doesn't step on anyone else's turf on the job. Or maybe employees on your cam-

If Everything's an Argument . . .

This chapter itself defines three different kinds of definitions: formal definitions, operational definitions, and definitions by example. Which kind(s)—formal, operational, or examples—have the authors used in defining the three kinds and distinguishing among them? How well do you think they've made their argument? Are there ways they could have made the individual definitions clearer or more distinct from one another? Are there any kinds of definitions you can think of that don't fit into one of these categories?

pus object to being defined as *temporary workers* when they've held their same jobs for years. Or someone derides one of your best friends as *just a nerd*. In a dozen ways every day, you encounter situations that turn out to be issues of definition. They're so frequent and indispensable that you barely notice them for what they are.

Formulating Claims

In addressing matters of definition, you'll likely formulate tentative claims — declarative statements that represent your first response to such situations. Note that these initial claims usually don't follow a single definitional formula.

Claims of Definition

- A person paid to do public service is not a volunteer.
- Institutional racism can exist — maybe even thrive — in the absence of overt civil rights violations.
- Torture has clearly been used by the U.S. military at Guantánamo Bay.
- A municipal fee is often the same darn thing as a tax.
- *Napoleon Dynamite* is one of the latest independent film to achieve cult status.

None of the claims listed here could stand on its own. Such claims often reflect first impressions and gut reactions. That's because stating a claim of definition is typically a starting point, a moment of bravura that doesn't last much beyond the first serious rebuttal or challenge. Statements of this sort aren't arguments until they're attached to reasons, data, warrants, and evidence. (See Chapter 6.)

Finding good reasons to support a claim of definition usually requires formulating a general definition by which to explore the subject. To be persuasive, the definition must be broad and not tailored to the specific controversy:

- A volunteer is . . .
- Institutional racism is . . .
- Torture is . . .
- A tax is . . .
- A cult film is . . .

Now consider how the following claims might be expanded with a general definition in order to become full-fledged definitional arguments:

Arguments of Definition

- Someone paid to do public service is not a volunteer because volunteers are people who . . .

- Institutional racism can exist even in the absence of overt violations of civil rights because, by definition, institutional racism is . . .

- Harsh treatment of detainees becomes torture when . . .

- A municipal fee is the same darn thing as a tax. Both fees and taxes are . . .

- *Napoleon Dynamite* has achieved all the criteria of cult status: . . .

Notice, too, that some of the issues can involve comparisons between things — such as taxes and fees.

Crafting Definitions

Imagine that you decide to tackle the concept of *paid volunteer* in the following way:

> Participants in the federal AmeriCorps program are not really volunteers because they are paid for their public service. Volunteers are people who work for a cause without compensation.

In Toulmin terms, the argument looks like this:

Claim	Participants in AmeriCorps aren't volunteers . . .
Reason	. . . because they are paid for their service.
Warrant	People who are compensated for their services are, ordinarily, employees.

As you can see, the definition of *volunteers* will be crucial to the shape of the argument. In fact, you might think you've settled the matter with this tight little formulation. But now it's time to listen to the readers over your shoulder (see Chapter 6) pushing you further. Do the terms of your definition account for all pertinent cases of volunteerism — in particular, any related to the types of public service AmeriCorps volunteers might be involved in? Consider, too, the word *cause* in your original statement of the definition:

> Volunteers are people who work for a cause without compensation.

Cause has political connotations that you may or may not intend. You'd better clarify what you mean by *cause* when you discuss its definition in your paper. Might a phrase such as *the public good* be a more comprehensive or appropriate substitute for *a cause?* And then there's the matter of compensation in the second half of your definition:

Volunteers are people who work for a cause without compensation.

Aren't people who volunteer to serve on boards, committees, and commissions sometimes paid, especially for their expenses? What about members of the so-called all-volunteer military? They're financially compensated for their years of service, and they enjoy substantial benefits after they complete their tour of duty.

As you can see, you can't just offer up a definition as part of your argument and assume that readers will understand or accept it. Every part of the definition has to be weighed, critiqued, and defended. That means you'll want to investigate your subject in the library, on the Internet, and in conversation with others, including experts on your term. You might then be able to present your definition in a single paragraph, or you may have to spend several pages coming to terms with the complexity of the core issue.

After conducting research of this kind, you might be in a position to write an extended definition well enough informed to explain to your readers what you believe makes a volunteer a volunteer, a tax a tax, and so on. At the end of this chapter, writer Lynn Peril provides just such a definition of the mind-set she claims is imposed on women in this country, what she calls "Pink Think."

Matching Claims to Definitions

Once you've formulated a definition readers will accept—a demanding task in itself—you might need to look at your particular subject to see if it fits that general definition, providing evidence to show that:

- it is a clear example of the class defined,
- it clearly falls outside the defined class,
- it falls between two closely related classes or fulfills some conditions of the defined class but not others, *or*
- it defies existing classes and categories and requires an entirely new definition.

It's possible that you might have to change your original claim at this point if the evidence you've gathered suggests that qualifications are necessary. It's amazing how often seemingly cut-and-dry issues of definition become blurry—and open to compromise and accommodation—

when you learn more about them. That has proved to be the case as various campuses across the country have tried to define *hate speech* or *sexual harassment*—very tricky matters. And even the Supreme Court has never quite been able to say what *pornography* is. Just when matters seem settled, new legal twists develop. Should virtual child pornography created with software be as illegal as the real thing? Is a virtual image—even a lewd one—an artistic expression, protected like other works of art by the First Amendment?

Considering Design and Visuals

In thinking about how to present your argument of definition, don't forget that design issues—such as boldface and italics, headings, or links in online text—can make a powerful contribution to (or detract seriously from) how credible and persuasive it is. Remember, too, that visuals like photographs, drawings, and graphs can also help make your case. A graph or chart, for example, might help you show visually the hierarchy of a "genus" and "species" relationship in a formal definition. Or photographs might help demonstrate that the conditions for a definition have been met. If you're working with a definitional claim about torture, for example, your choice to introduce an Abu Ghraib prison photograph that circulated widely on the Web might become a focal point of emphasis in your definition, especially if you argue that the photograph perfectly represents your definition of *torture*.

Hooded and wired prisoner at Abu Ghraib

Key Features of Definitional Arguments

In writing an argument of definition of your own, consider that it's likely to include the following parts:

- a claim involving a question of definition
- a general definition of some key concept
- a careful look at your subject in terms of that general definition
- evidence for every part of the argument, including visual evidence if appropriate
- a consideration of alternative views and counterarguments
- a conclusion, drawing out the implications of the argument

It's impossible, however, to predict what emphasis each of those parts might receive or what the ultimate shape of an argument of definition will be.

Whatever form your definitional argument takes, be sure to share your draft with others who can examine its claims, evidence, and connections. It's remarkably easy for a writer in isolation to think narrowly—and not to imagine that others might define *volunteer* or *institutional racism* in a completely different way. Thus it's important to keep a mind open to criticism and suggestions. Look very carefully at the terms of any definitions you offer. Do they really help readers distinguish one concept from another? Are the conditions offered sufficient or essential? Have you mistaken accidental features of a concept or object for more important features?

Don't hesitate to look to other sources for comparisons with your definitions. You can't depend on dictionaries to offer the last word about any disputed term, but you can at least begin with them. Check the meaning of terms in encyclopedias and other reference works. And search the Web intelligently to find how your key terms are presented there. (In searching for the definition of *wetland,* for example, you could type *wetland definition* into a search engine like Google and get a limited number of useful hits.)

Finally, be prepared for surprises in writing arguments of definition. That's part of the delight in expanding the way you see the world. "I'm not a pig, I'm a sheep dog," thinks Babe in the 1995 film by the same name. Babe then goes right on to win a sheep dog competition. Such is the power of definition.

GUIDE to writing an argument of definition

● Finding a Topic

You're entering an argument of definition when you:

- formulate a controversial or provocative definition: *Today, the American Dream means a McMansion in a gated community with a deferential maid, gardener, and personal chef.*

- challenge a definition: *For most Americans today, the American Dream involves not luxury but the secure pensions, health insurance, and vacations that workers in the 1950s and 1960s enjoyed.*

- try to determine whether something fits an existing definition: *Expanding opportunity is (or is not) central to the American Dream.*

Look for issues of definition in your everyday affairs — for instance, in the way jobs are classified at work; in the way key terms are described in your academic major; in the way politicians characterize the social issues that concern you; in the way you define yourself or others try to define you. Be especially alert to definitional arguments that may arise whenever you or others deploy adjectives such as *true, real, actual,* or *genuine: a true Texan; real environmental degradation; actual budget projections; genuine rap music.*

● Researching Your Topic

You can research issues of definition by using the following sources:

- college dictionaries and encyclopedias

- unabridged dictionaries

- specialized reference works and handbooks, such as legal and medical dictionaries

- your textbooks (check their glossaries)

- newsgroups and listservs that focus on particular topics

Be sure to browse in your library reference room. Also, use the search tools of electronic indexes and databases to determine whether or how often controversial phrases or expressions are occurring in influential materials: major online newspapers, journals, and Web sites.

● Formulating a Claim

After exploring your subject, begin to formulate a full and specific claim, a thesis that lets readers know where you stand and what issues are at stake. In moving toward this thesis, begin with the following types of questions of definition:

- questions related to genus: *Is assisting in suicide a crime?*
- questions related to species: *Is marijuana a harmful addictive drug or a useful medical treatment?*
- questions related to conditions: *Must the imposition of sexual attention be both unwanted and unsolicited to be considered sexual harassment?*
- questions related to fulfillment of conditions: *Has our college kept in place traditions or policies that might constitute racial discrimination?*
- questions related to membership in a named class: *Is any pop artist today in a class with Bob Dylan, the Beatles, Aretha Franklin, or the Rolling Stones?*

Your thesis should be a complete statement. In one sentence, you need to make a claim of definition and state the reasons that support your claim. In your paper or project itself, you may later decide to separate the claim from the reasons supporting it. But your working thesis should be a fully expressed thought. That means spelling out the details and the qualifications: *Who? What? Where? When? How many? How regularly? How completely?* Don't expect readers to fill in the blanks for you.

● Examples of Definitional Claims

- Assisting a gravely ill person to commit suicide should not be considered murder when the motive behind the act is to ease a person's suffering, not to do harm or to benefit from the death.
- Although marijuana is somewhat addictive, it should not be classified as a dangerous drug because its immediate effects are far less damaging to the individual and society than those of heroin or cocaine and because it is effective in helping people with life-threatening diseases.
- Flirting with the waitstaff in a restaurant should be considered sexual harassment when the activity is repeated, unsolicited, and obviously unappreciated.

- Giving college admission preference to children of alumni is an example of class discrimination because most such policies privilege families that are rich and already advantaged.

● Preparing a Proposal

If your instructor asks you to prepare a proposal for your project, here's a format that may help:

State your thesis completely. If you're having trouble doing so, try outlining it in Toulmin terms:

Claim:

Reason(s):

Warrant(s):

- Explain why this argument of definition deserves attention. What's at stake? Why is it important for your readers to consider?
- Specify whom you hope to reach through your argument and why this group of readers would be interested in it.
- Briefly discuss the key challenges you anticipate in preparing your argument: Defining a key term? Establishing the essential and sufficient elements of your definition? Demonstrating that your subject will meet those conditions?
- Determine what strategies you'll use in researching your definitional argument. What sources do you expect to consult: Dictionaries? Encyclopedias? Periodicals? The Internet?
- Determine what visuals you will include in your definitional argument. How will each one be used?
- Consider what format you expect to use for your project: A conventional research essay? A letter to the editor? A Web page?

● Thinking about Organization

Your argument of definition may take various forms, but it's likely to include elements such as the following:

- a claim involving a matter of definition: *Labeling Al Qaeda and similar groups as representatives of "Islamic fascism" is understandable but misleading.*

- an attempt to establish a definition of a key term: *Genuine fascism is a mass movement within a nation resulting from democracy gone wrong.*

- an explanation or defense of the terms of the definition: *Scholars agree that fascism is a modern mass movement distinguished by the primacy of the nation over the individual, the elimination of dissent, the creation of a single-party state, and the glorification of violence on behalf of a national cause.*

- an examination of the claim in terms of the definition and all its criteria: *Fascism is highly nationalistic, but Islam is hostile to nationalism; Islam is a religious movement, but fascism is a secular movement that is usually quite hostile to religion.*

- a consideration of alternative views and counterarguments: *It is true that Osama bin Laden appeals to violence on behalf of his cause of restoring the medieval Islamic empire and that some fascist regimes (like Franco's Spain) were closely allied to religious authorities. . . .*

● Getting and Giving Response

All arguments benefit from the scrutiny of others. Your instructor may assign you to a peer group for the purpose of reading and responding to each other's drafts; if not, get some response on your own from serious readers or consultants at a writing center. You can use the following questions to evaluate a draft. If you're evaluating someone else's draft, be sure to illustrate your points with examples. Specific comments are always more helpful than general observations.

The Claim

- Is the claim clearly an issue of definition?
- Is the claim significant enough to interest readers?
- Are clear and specific criteria established for the concept being defined? Do the criteria define the term adequately? Using this definition, could most readers identify what's being defined and distinguish it from other related concepts?

Evidence for the Claim

- Is enough evidence furnished to explain or support the definition? If not, what kind of additional evidence is needed?

- Is the evidence in support of the claim simply announced, or are its significance and appropriateness analyzed? Is a more detailed discussion needed?

- Are all the conditions of the definition met in the concept being examined?

- Are any objections readers might have to the claim, criteria, or evidence, or to the way the definition is formulated, adequately addressed?

- What kinds of sources, including visual sources, are cited? How credible and persuasive will they be to readers? What other kinds of sources might be more credible and persuasive?

- Are all quotations introduced with appropriate signal phrases (such as "As Himmelfarb argues,") and blended smoothly into the writer's sentences?

Organization and Style

- How are the parts of the argument organized? Is this organization effective, or would some other structure work better?

- Will readers understand the relationships among the claims, supporting reasons, warrants, and evidence? If not, what could be done to make those connections clearer? Is the function of every visual clear? Have you related each visual to a particular point in your essay and explained its significance? Are more transitional words and phrases needed? Would headings or graphic devices help?

- Are the transitions or links from point to point, paragraph to paragraph, and sentence to sentence clear and effective? If not, how could they be improved?

- Is the style suited to the subject? Is it too formal? Too casual? Too technical? Too bland? How can it be improved?

- Which sentences seem particularly effective? Which ones seem weakest, and how could they be improved? Should some short sentences be combined, or should any long ones be separated into two or more sentences?

- How effective are the paragraphs? Do any seem too skimpy or too long? How can they be improved?

- Which words or phrases seem particularly effective, vivid, and memorable? Do any seem dull, vague, unclear, or inappropriate for the audience or the writer's purpose? Are definitions provided for technical or other terms that readers might not know?

Spelling, Punctuation, Mechanics, Documentation, Format

- Are there any errors in spelling, punctuation, capitalization, and the like?

- Is an appropriate and consistent style of documentation used for parenthetical citations and the list of works cited or references? (See Chapter 20.)

- Does the paper or project follow an appropriate format? Is it appropriately designed and attractively presented? How could it be improved? If it's a Web site, do all the links work?

RESPOND •

1. Briefly discuss the criteria you might use to define the italicized terms in the following controversial claims of definition. Compare your definitions of the terms with those of your classmates.

   Graphic novels are *serious literature*.

   Burning a nation's flag is a *hate crime*.

   The Bushes have become America's *royal family*.

   Matt Drudge and Larry Flynt are legitimate *journalists*.

   College sports programs have become *big businesses*.

   Plagiarism can be an act of *civil disobedience*.

   Satanism is a *religion* properly protected by the First Amendment.

   Campaign contributions are acts of *free speech*.

   The District of Columbia should have all the privileges of an American *state*.

   Committed gay and lesbian couples should have the legal privileges of *marriage*.

2. This chapter opens with sketches of six rhetorical situations that center on definitional issues. Select one of these situations, and write definitional criteria using the strategy of formal definition. For example, identify the features of a photograph that make it part of a larger class (art, communication method, journalistic technique). Next, identify the features of a photograph that make it distinct from other members of that larger class. Then use the strategy of operational definition to establish criteria for the same object: what does it do? Remember to ask questions related to conditions (*Is a computer-scanned photograph still a photograph?*) and questions related to fulfillment of conditions (*Does a good photocopy of a photograph achieve the same effect as the photograph itself?*).

3. In an essay at the end of this chapter entitled "Pink Think," Lynn Peril makes a variety of claims about a concept she identifies as *pink think,* which she defines in part as "a set of ideas and attitudes about what constitutes proper female behavior." After reading this selection carefully, consider whether Peril has actually defined a concept that operates today. If you think "pink think" still exists, prove it by showing how some activities, behaviors, products, or institutions meet the definition of the concept. Write, too, about the power this concept has to define behavior.

   Alternatively, define a concept of your own that applies to a similar kind of stereotypical behavior—for example, *chick think* or *surfer think* or *geek think*. Then argue that your newly defined concept does, in fact, influence people today. Be sure to provide clear and compelling examples of the concept in action as it shapes the way people think and behave.

The Offbeat Allure of Cult Films

SAYOH MANSARAY

Opening paragraph includes a parodic definition of "great skills."

On a Saturday afternoon in February junior Clare Marshall and her family sit in her living room watching a film that Marshall is an avid fan of: *Napoleon Dynamite.* Marshall and her family say quotes along with the movie and laugh aloud at the hilarious parts. "Girls only want boyfriends who have great skills," Clare says, imitating Napoleon's trademark throaty drawl. "You know, like nun chuck skills, bow hunting skills . . . computer hacking skills."

Marshall is not the only teenager who likes films that are completely different from most movies in theaters. The teen followings of nonmainstream films like *Napoleon Dynamite* and *Donnie Darko* show that today's teens are looking for films that are "off the beaten path," according to English and Literature as Film teacher Mike Horne. Teens are gravitating toward these quirky movies, raising some of them to a cult-like status.

A tentative definition of "cult film" is offered.

The consensus among Blazers is that a cult movie is a quirky, different film that did not do well in theaters but has since gained a strong and faithful following on DVD or video. In recent years the definition of cult films has begun to evolve and broaden to include films that did not actually flop in theaters. Regardless of the specific definition, recent cult films are attracting teen fans.

Sayoh Mansaray wrote this article for *Silver Chips Online,* the online newspaper of Montgomery Blair High School in Silver Spring, Maryland, where she served as public relations co-director and factcheck supervisor. *Silver Chips Online,* which has won a number of awards, is all student-run and is partially sponsored by the *Washington Post.* Note that the article, like most pieces published in newspapers, does not document sources in any formal way.

A still from *Napoleon Dynamite,* starring Jon Heder (center)

"It Feels Real"

As Marshall continues to watch the film, a scene plays in which Napoleon talks to a girl on the phone. The girl has been forced by her mother to thank Napoleon for a picture he drew of her in hopes of getting a date. "It took me like three hours to finish the shading on your upper lip," Napoleon says to the girl, as Marshall quotes along with him.

Another characteristic of cult films is offered: They are "not formulaic" and they "require thought."

Many teens, Marshall included, like cult films because they differ from other films in theaters. Horne says that teens gravitate to cult movies because they are not formulaic. "They are a little bit different, and they require some thought or interpretation," he says.

Reasons for the popularity of cult films are given.

Junior Katrina Jabonete likes *Donnie Darko,* a film about a teen who is teetering on the edge of schizophrenia, because it is so beautifully twisted and darkly weird that the film opens itself to a thousand different interpretations. She believes that teens are drawn to cult movies because they aren't as clean or processed as mainstream flicks and because cult films are less likely to offer a concrete conclusion. Basically, they are more like real life. "[They] deal with problems and emotions in a different, real way," she explains. "Teens relate to [these movies] because it feels real to them."

TIME WARP

While recent movies are gaining cult status, some students remain exclusively faithful to the classics, becoming part of groups that view their cult favorites over and over again.

Junior Linda Dye fits into this category. She thinks a cult movie is a film that is "so bad it's good." Take her favorite cult film, *The Rocky Horror Picture Show,* a 1975 musical about a group of gender-bending, quasi-alien, quasi-vampire, raving-lunatics-in-drag. "Ever since I first saw it, I've been completely in love with it," she gushes.

Example of a classic cult film is provided.

Dye is drawn to the film partially because the close-knit following allows her to interact with people she might never have known before. When Dye attended the annual *Rocky Horror* screening at the University of Maryland, she dressed up as one of the film's characters. In a bustier, a feather boa, and heels, Dye, along with the rest of the audience, yelled dialogue to the screen and made up her own lines as the movie played.

For Dye, this energy is what keeps her love for the film and its following alive. "You're sitting with these people you've never met, [but] by the end of the movie there's an energy—you're a community," she says.

"IF I HAD A TUMOR, I'D NAME IT MARLA"

Regardless of whether a movie is a classic or a recent hit, movie fans often display their love of films by quoting them. On snowy days, senior Robin Weiss likes to write one-liners from *Fight Club* like, "If I had a tumor, I'd name it Marla" and "We are a generation of men raised by women" on the icy windshields of random cars.

Marshall likes to answer questions with *Napoleon Dynamite* quotes. If a friend asks, "What are you doing today, Clare?" she might respond with a Napoleon line: "Whatever I feel like doing—gosh!"

Quotable dialogue is a defining characteristic of a cult film.

Horne says that a major component of cult films is quotable dialogue. "Half the fun is reliving it with your friends," he says, smiling. Some fans can quote most of a movie, he adds. Senior Walker Davis, for example, knows most of the lines from *The Big Lebowski*.

Low-budget aspect of cult films, first mentioned in third paragraph, is reiterated here.

According to Davis, cult films are never big budget productions, and no movie studio ever sets out to create a cult film—it just happens.

Many teens, like Marshall, just can't get enough of these films. Horne says that cult films are often bizarre, random, and edgy, which adds to their appeal. He says that people who watch cult films may have different motives than other moviegoers. "Many people look to film as an escape, [but] others are looking to find different thoughts," he says.

Pink Think

LYNN PERIL

From the moment she's wrapped in a pink blanket, long past the traumatic birthday when she realizes her age is greater than her bust measurement, the human female is bombarded with advice on how to wield those feminine wiles. This advice ranges from rather vague proscriptions along the lines of "nice girls don't chew gum/swear/wear pants/fill-in-the-blank," to obsessively elaborate instructions for daily living. How many women's lives, for example, were enriched by former Miss America Jacque Mercer's positively baroque description of the proper way to put on a bathing suit, as it appeared in her guide *How to Win a Beauty Contest* (1960)?

> [F]irst, roll it as you would a girdle. Pull the suit over the hips to the waist, then, holding the top away from your body, bend over from the waist. Ease the suit up to the bustline and with one hand, lift one breast up and in and ease the suit bra over it. Repeat on the other side. Stand up and fasten the straps.

Instructions like these made me bristle. I formed an early aversion to all things pink and girly. It didn't take me long to figure out that many things young girls were supposed to enjoy, not to mention ways they were supposed to behave, left me feeling funny—as if I was expected to pound my square peg self into the round hole of designated girliness. I didn't know it at the time, but the butterflies in my tummy meant I had crested the first of many hills on the roller coaster ride of femininity—or, as I soon referred to it, the other f-word. Before I knew what was happening, I was hurtling down its track, seemingly out of control, and screaming at the top of my lungs.

After all, look what I was up against. The following factoids of femininity date from the year of my birth (hey, it wasn't *that* long ago):

- In May of 1961, Betsy Martin McKinney told readers of *Ladies' Home Journal* that, for women, sexual activity commenced with intercourse

---

Lynn Peril is the publisher of the 'zine *Mystery Date*. This essay is excerpted from the introduction to *Pink Think*, a book that examines the influence of the feminine ideal.

and was completed with pregnancy and childbirth. Therefore, a woman who used contraceptives denied "her own creativity, her own sexual role, her very femininity." Furthermore, McKinney asserted that "one of the most stimulating predisposers to orgasm in a woman may be childbirth followed by several months of lactation." (Mmm, yes, must be the combination of episiotomy and sleep deprivation that does it.) Politely avoiding personal examples, she neglected to mention how many little McKinneys there were.

- During the competition for the title of Miss America 1961, five finalists were given two questions to answer. First they were asked what they would do if "you were walking down the runway in the swimsuit competition, and a heel came off one of your shoes?" The second question, however, was a bit more esoteric: "Are American women usurping males in the world, and are they too dominant?" Eighteen-year-old Nancy Fleming, of Montague, Michigan, agreed that "there are too many women working in the world. A woman's place is in the home with her husband and children." This, along with her pragmatic answer to the first question ("I would kick off both shoes and walk barefooted") and her twenty-three-inch waist (tied for the smallest in pageant history), helped Nancy win the crown.

- In 1961, toymaker Transogram introduced a new game for girls called Miss Popularity ("The True American Teen"), in which players competed to see who could accrue the most votes from four pageant judges — three of whom were male. Points were awarded for such attributes as nice legs, and if the judges liked a contestant's figure, voice, and "type." The prize? A special "loving" cup, of course! Who, after all, could love an unpopular girl?

These are all prime examples of "pink think." Pink think is a set of ideas and attitudes about what constitutes proper female behavior; a groupthink that was consciously or not adhered to by advice writers, manufacturers of toys and other consumer products, experts in many walks of life, and the public at large, particularly during the years spanning the mid-twentieth century—but enduring even into the twenty-first century. Pink think assumes there is a standard of behavior to which all women, no matter their age, race, or body type, must aspire. "Femininity" is sometimes used as a code word for this mythical standard, which suggests that women and girls are always gentle, soft, delicate, nurturing beings made of "sugar and spice and everything nice." But pink think is more than a stereotyped vision of girls and women as poor drivers who are afraid of mice and snakes, adore babies and small dogs, talk incessantly on the phone, and are incapable of keeping secrets. Integral to pink think is the belief that one's success as a woman is grounded in one's allegiance to such behavior. For example, a woman who fears mice isn't necessarily following the dictates of pink think. On the other hand, a woman who isn't afraid of mice but pretends to be because she thinks such helplessness adds to her appearance of femininity is toeing the pink think party line. When you hear the words "charm" or "personality" in the context of successful womanhood, you can almost always be sure you're in the presence of pink think.

While various self-styled "experts" have been advising women on their "proper" conduct since the invention of the printing press, the phenomenon defined here as pink think was particularly pervasive from the 1940s to the 1970s. These were fertile years for pink think, a cultural mindset and consumer behavior rooted in New Deal prosperity yet culminating with the birth of women's liberation. During this time, pink think permeated popular books and magazines aimed at adult women, while little girls absorbed rules of feminine behavior while playing games like the aforementioned Miss Popularity. Meanwhile, prescriptions for ladylike dress, deportment, and mindset seeped into child-rearing manuals, high school home economics textbooks, and guides for bride, homemaker, and career girl alike.

It was almost as if the men and women who wrote such books viewed proper feminine behavior as a panacea for the ills of a rapidly changing modern world. For example, myriad articles in the popular press devoted to the joys of housewifery helped coerce Rosie the Riveter back into the kitchen when her hubby came home from the war and expected his factory job back. During the early cold war years, some home economics texts seemed to suggest that knowing how to make hospital corners and a good tuna casserole were the only things between Our Way of Life and communist incursion. It was patriotic to be an exemplary housewife. And pink-thinking experts of the sixties and seventies, trying to maintain this ideal, churned out reams of pages that countered the onrushing tide of both the sexual revolution and the women's movement. If only all women behaved like our Ideal Woman, the experts seemed to say through the years, then everything would be fine.

You might even say that the "problem with no name" that Betty Friedan wrote about in *The Feminine Mystique* (1963) was a virulent strain of pink-thinkitis. After all, according to Friedan, "the problem" was in part engendered by the experts' insistence that women "could desire no greater destiny than to glory in their own femininity"—a pink think credo.

The pink think of the 1940s to 1970s held that femininity was necessary for catching and marrying a man, which was in turn a prerequisite for childbearing—the ultimate feminine fulfillment. This resulted in little girls playing games like Mystery Date long before they were ever interested in boys. It made home economics a high school course and college major, and suggested a teen girl's focus should be on dating and getting a boyfriend. It made beauty, charm, and submissive behavior of mandatory importance to women of all ages in order to win a man's attention and hold his interest after marriage. It promoted motherhood and housewifery as women's only meaningful career, and made sure that women who worked outside the home brought "feminine charm" to their workplaces lest a career make them too masculine.

Not that pink think resides exclusively alongside antimacassars and 14.4 modems in the graveyard of outdated popular culture: Shoes, clothing, and movie stars may go in and out of style with astounding rapidity, but attitudes have an unnerving way of hanging around long after they've outlived their usefulness—even if they never had any use to begin with.

9
Evaluations

"We don't want to go *there* for Tex-Mex. Their tortillas aren't fresh, their quesadillas are mush, and they get their salsa from New York City!"

The campus Labor Action Committee has been co-chaired for four years by three students whose leadership has led to significant improvements in the way the university treats its workers. Now they're all graduating at once, leaving a leadership vacuum; so the group calls a special meeting to talk about what qualities it needs in its next leaders.

A senior is frustrated by the "C" she received on an essay written for a history class, so she makes an appointment to talk with the teaching assistant who graded the paper. "Be sure to review the assignment sheet first," the TA warns. The student notices that the sheet, on its back side, includes a checklist of requirements for the paper; she hadn't turned it over before.

"We have a lousy homepage," a sales representative observes at a district meeting. "What's wrong with it?" the marketing manager asks. "Everything," the sales rep replies, then quickly changes the subject when she notices the manager's furrowed brow. But the manager decides to investigate the issue. Who knows what an effective Web site looks like these days?

You've just seen *Citizen Kane* for the first time and want to share the experience with your roommate. Orson Welles's masterpiece is playing at the Student Union for only one more night, but *The War of the Worlds* is featured across the street in THX sound. Guess which movie your roomie wants to see? You intend to set him straight.

● ● ●

Understanding Evaluations

Kristin Cole has a problem. The holiday break is approaching, she's headed out of town, and she still hasn't found a pet-sitter for Baldrick, her lovable cockatiel. When her first email appeal to colleagues in a large academic department fails to turn up a volunteer, she tries a second, this one more aggressively singing the praises of her companion:

> Apologies for all the duplications, folks! Since nobody's stepped forward to birdsit for me from 15–30 or 31 December, I must repeat my plea.
>
> Please take my bird for this time. I'll pay. If you have other pets, all I ask is that your little darlings can't get at my little darling.
>
> And let me repeat that Baldrick could be the poster child for birds: he's quiet, loves people, and couldn't be happier than to sit on your shoulder while you go about your day. He'll whistle and make kissy noises in your ear, since he's a huge flirt. I must admit that he loves to chew paper and pens, but that's controllable. And he loves feet—that can be positive, negative, or neutral, depending on you.

He's much easier than a cat or dog—no litter boxes, walks, or poop in the yard. And his food smells like candy. He's pretty much allergy-free, and the mess he makes is easily vacuumable with the dustbuster I'll lend you. He just needs contact with people and a fair amount of supervised out-of-cage time per day.

Please do let me know if you can help me out. He's a great pet—he converted me, who had always thought a proper pet needed fur and four legs!

In just a few lines, Kristin offers about a half-dozen reasons for birdsitting Baldrick, many of them based on the evaluative claim "he's a great pet." The claim deploys several different lines of argument, including appeals to the heart ("he's a huge flirt"), the head ("He's much easier than a cat or dog"), and even credibility ("he converted me, who had always thought a proper pet needed fur and four legs"). About the only potential device Kristin misses is a visual argument—for example, a photo of Baldrick, which she might have attached to the email easily enough.

Kristin makes Baldrick seem lovable and charming for a reason: to persuade someone to board the cockatiel over the holidays. In this

Baldrick: the poster child for birds

respect, her strategy is typical of many arguments of evaluation. They're written to clarify or support other decisions in our lives: what to read, who to hire, what to buy, which movies to see, who to vote for. (In case you're wondering, Kristin's email worked.)

Evaluations are everyday arguments. By the time you leave home in the morning, you've likely made a dozen informal evaluations. You've selected dressy clothes because you have a job interview in the afternoon with a law firm; you've chosen low-fat yogurt and shredded wheat over the pancakes, butter, and syrup you really love; you've queued up just the perfect play list on your iPod for your hike to campus. In each case, you've applied criteria to a particular problem and then made a decision.

Some professional evaluations require much more elaborate standards, evidence, and paperwork (imagine what an aircraft manufacturer has to do to certify a new jet for passenger service), but such work doesn't differ structurally from the simpler choices that people make routinely. And, of course, people do love to voice their opinions, and they always have: a whole mode of ancient rhetoric—called the ceremonial, or epideictic—was devoted entirely to speeches of praise and blame. (See Chapter 1.)

The famously fashionable Gwyneth Paltrow frequently tops best-dressed lists.

Today, rituals of praise and blame are a significant part of American life. Adults who'd choke at the very notion of debating causal or definitional claims will happily spend hours appraising the Tampa Bay Buccaneers or the Boston Red Sox or the Detroit Pistons. Other evaluative spectacles in our culture include awards shows, beauty pageants, most-valuable-player presentations, lists of best-dressed or worst-dressed celebrities, "sexiest people" magazine covers, literary prizes, political opinion polls, consumer product magazines, and—the ultimate formal public gesture of evaluation—elections. Indeed, making evaluations is a form of entertainment in America—one that generates big audiences (think of *American Idol*) and revenues.

Criteria of Evaluation

Whether arguments of evaluation produce simple rankings and winners or lead to more profound decisions about our lives, they involve standards. The particular standards we establish for judging anything—whether an idea, a work of art, a person, or a product—are called *criteria of evaluation*. Sometimes criteria are pretty self-evident. You probably know that a truck that gets ten miles per gallon is a gas hog or that a piece of fish that's served charred and rubbery should be returned. But criteria are often more complex when a potential subject is more abstract: *What makes a judge or a teacher effective? What features make a film a classic? What constitutes a living wage? How do we measure a successful foreign policy or college education?* Struggling to identify such difficult criteria of evaluation can lead to important insights into your values, motives, and preferences.

Why make such a big deal about criteria when many acts of evaluation seem almost effortless? Because we should be most suspicious of our judgments precisely when we start making them carelessly. It's a cop-out simply to think that everyone's entitled to an opinion, however stupid and uninformed it might be. Evaluations always require reflection. And when we look deeply into our judgments, we sometimes discover important "why" questions that typically go unasked:

- You may find yourself willing to challenge the grade you received in a course, but not the practice of grading itself.
- You argue that Miss Alabama would have been a better Miss America than the contestant from New York, but perhaps you don't wonder loudly enough whether such competitions make sense at all.
- You argue passionately that a Republican Congress is better for America than a Democratic alternative, but you fail to ask why voters get only two choices.
- You can't believe people take Britney Spears seriously as a singer, but you never consider what her impact on young girls might be.

Push an argument of evaluation hard enough, and even simple judgments become challenging and intriguing.

In fact, for many writers, grappling with criteria is the toughest step in producing an evaluation. They've got an opinion about a movie or book or city policy, but they also think that their point is self-evident and widely shared by others. So they don't do the necessary work to specify the criteria for their judgments. If you know a subject well enough to evaluate it, your readers should learn something from you when you offer an opinion. Do you think, for instance, that you could explain what (if anything) makes a veggie burger *good?* The following criteria offered on the *Cooks Illustrated* Web site show that they've given the question quite a bit of thought:

> Store-bought veggie burgers border on inedible, but most homemade renditions are a lot of work. Could we develop a recipe that was really worth the effort? We wanted to create veggie burgers that even meat eaters would love. We didn't want them to taste like hamburgers, but we did want them to act like hamburgers, having a modicum of chew, a harmonious blend of savory ingredients, and the ability to go from grill to bun without falling apart.
>
> *–Cooks Illustrated*

After a lot of experimenting, *Cooks Illustrated* came up with a recipe that met these criteria.

Though many people have eaten veggie burgers, they probably haven't thought about them this carefully. But to evaluate them convincingly, it's not enough to claim merely that a good veggie burger is juicy or tasty. Such a claim is also not very interesting.

Criteria of evaluation aren't static either. They differ according to time and audience. Much market research, for example, is designed to find out what particular consumers want now and in the future—what their criteria for buying a product are. Consider what the researchers at Honda discovered when they asked Y-generation men—a targeted demographic of consumers who generally don't consider Honda products—what they wanted in a new car. The answer, reported in the *New York Times,* was surprising:

> The Honda group found that young adults wanted a basic, no-nonsense vehicle with lots of space—and they didn't seem to care much about the exterior style. "We found that vehicles, in this generation, were not the top priority," Mr. Benner said. "They're the means, not the end. The car is a tool." . . . What distinguishes younger buyers, all car companies seem to agree, is that they don't seem to care as

Young people think a car should be a tool. Does this Honda Element meet that criterion?

much about cars as young people used to—putting more stock in the style of their cellphones or P.D.A.'s than in the style of what they drive.
—Phil Patton, "Young Man, Would You Like That in a Box?"

Such an evaluation of criteria actually led Honda to build the Element, a boxy—some would say homely—truck with swing-out side doors and an easily reconfigurable interior designed to be a "place" more than a vehicle. The Element did win fans, but less from among the X-generation Honda originally targeted than from their baby boomer parents!

Characterizing Evaluation

One way of understanding evaluative arguments is to consider the types of evidence they use. A distinction we explored in Chapter 4 between hard evidence and arguments based on reason is helpful here. You may recall that we defined hard evidence as facts, statistics, testimony, and other kinds of arguments that can be measured, recorded, or even found—the so-called smoking gun in a criminal investigation. Arguments based on reason are those shaped by language, using various kinds of logic.

We can study arguments of evaluation the same way, looking at some as *quantitative* and others as *qualitative*. Quantitative arguments of evaluation rely on criteria that can be measured, counted, or demonstrated in some mechanical fashion—something is taller, faster, smoother, quieter, more powerful than something else. In contrast, qualitative arguments rely on criteria that must be explained through words, relying on such matters as values, traditions, and even emotions: something is more ethical, more beneficial, more handsome, more noble. Needless to say, a claim of evaluation might be supported by arguments of both sorts. We separate them below merely to present them more clearly.

Quantitative Evaluations

At first glance, quantitative evaluations would seem to hold all the cards, especially in a society as enamored of science and technology as our own. Once you've defined a quantitative standard, making judgments should be as easy as measuring and counting—and in a few cases, that's the way things work out. *Who's the tallest or heaviest or loudest person in your class?* If your colleagues allow themselves to be measured, you could find out easily enough, using the right equipment and internationally sanctioned standards of measurement: the meter, the kilo, or the decibel.

But what if you were to ask, *Who's the smartest person in class?* You could answer this more complex question quantitatively too, using IQ tests or college entrance examinations that report results numerically. In fact, almost all college-bound students in the United States submit to this kind of evaluation, taking either the SAT or ACT to demonstrate their verbal and mathematical prowess. Such measures are widely accepted by educators and institutions, but they are also vigorously challenged. What do they actually measure? They predict likely success in college, which isn't the same thing as intelligence.

Like any standards of evaluation, quantitative criteria must be scrutinized carefully to make sure that what they measure relates to what's being evaluated. For example, in evaluating a car, you might use 0–60 mph times as a measure of acceleration, 60–0 mph distances as a measure of braking capability, skidpad numbers (0.85) as a measure of handling ability, and coefficient of drag (0.29) as a test of aerodynamic efficiency. But all these numbers are subject to error. And even when the numbers are gathered accurately and then compared, one vehicle with another, they may not tell the whole story because some cars generate great test numbers and yet still feel less competent than vehicles with lower scores. The same disparity between numbers and feel occurs with other items—compact disc recordings, for example. CDs can produce

Military Fatalities

Period	US	UK	Other*	Total	Avg	Days
5	159	5	0	164	1.82	90
4	715	13	18	746	2.35	318
3	579	25	27	631	2.92	216
2	718	27	58	803	1.89	424
1	140	33	0	173	4.02	43
Total	2311	103	103	2517	2.31	1091

Iraq Coalition Casuality Count

Time Periods:

Period 5: December 15, 2005 (the day after Iraq general elections) through today's date.

Period 4: January 31, 2005 (the day after Iraq Elections) through December 14, 2005.

Period 3: June 29, 2004 (the day after the official turnover of sovereignty to Iraq) through January 30, 2005 (Iraq Elections).

Period 2: May 2, 2003, through June 28, 2004 (the day of the official turnover of sovereignty to Iraq).

Period 1: March 20, 2003, through May 1, 2003 (the end of major combat).

Not Just Words

Even what looks like totally objective counting can make a powerful evaluative argument. Look at this simple chart kept by the group Iraq Coalition Casualty Count. It offers a measure of U.S. and British military fatalities in Iraq from March 20, 2003, when counting began, to March 15, 2006, when this chart was downloaded. What arguments of evaluation could be made based on these purely quantitative data?

awesome sonic accuracy numbers, but some listeners feel the music they produce may lack aural qualities important to listening pleasure. Educators, too, acknowledge that some students test better than others, which doesn't necessarily indicate greater intelligence.

We don't mean to belittle quantitative measures of evaluation, only to offer a caveat: even the most objective measures have limits. They've been devised by fallible people looking at the world from their own inevitably limited perspectives.

Qualitative Evaluations

Many issues of evaluation closest to people's hearts simply aren't subject to quantification. *What makes a movie great?* If you suggested a quantitative measure like length, your friends would probably hoot "Get serious!" But what about box office receipts, especially if they could be adjusted to reflect inflation? Would films that made the most money—an easily quantifiable measure—really be the "best pictures"? In that select group would be movies such as *Star Wars, The Sound of Music, Gone with the Wind, Titanic,* and *Harry Potter and the Sorcerer's Stone.* An interesting group of films—but the best?

Or you might go for the "quotability factor," determining which movies are the most quoted of all time. Based on a member survey, the American Film Institute lists the following as the top five most quotable movies:

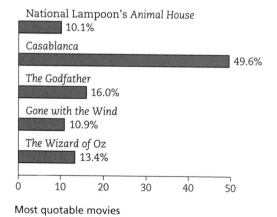

National Lampoon's *Animal House* 10.1%

Casablanca 49.6%

The Godfather 16.0%

Gone with the Wind 10.9%

The Wizard of Oz 13.4%

0   10   20   30   40   50

Most quotable movies

To argue for box office revenue and quotability as criteria of film greatness, though, you'd have to defend the criteria vigorously because many people in the audience would express serious doubts about them. More likely, then, in defining the criteria for "great movie," you'd look for standards to account for the merit of films widely respected among serious critics. You might consider the qualities common to such respected movies, exploring such elements as their societal impact, cinematic technique, dramatic structures, casting, and so on. Most of these markers of quality could be defined with some precision, but not measured or counted. Lacking hard numbers, you'd have to convince the audience to accept your standards and make your case rhetorically. As you might guess, a writer using qualitative measures could spend as much time defending criteria of evaluation as providing evidence that these standards are present in the film under scrutiny.

But establishing subtle criteria is what can make arguments of evaluation so interesting. They require you, time and again, to challenge conventional wisdom. Look at the way Nick Gillespie in Reasononline reviews the last *Star Wars* movie, *Revenge of the Sith*:

> **What might be called the continuing cultural hegemony of *Star Wars* is no small matter. With the possible exception of *The Lord of the Rings*,**

Star Wars may be "craptacular" when judged by the usual criteria, but it's also a cultural phenomenon. Here, a still from the first episode (1977).

no other franchise has maintained a similar hold on the public imagination for so long a period of time. In a curious way, the first two
installments in *The Godfather* saga did (as evidenced by the appropria-
tion of its themes and motifs in everything from countless lesser
mob movies to standup comedy to rap music). But it's undeniable that
Star Wars is in the warp and woof of American culture, ranging from
politics to toys to, of course, movies, novels, and comic books. It very
much provides a backdrop, a framework, a system of reference for
the ways we talk about things, whether we're talking about missile
defense systems, visions of the future and technology, good vs. evil,
you name it.

This is all the more stunning given the generally acknowledged
mediocrity of the *Star Wars* movies themselves. Indeed, it's a given that
if *Star Wars* didn't start to go downhill sometime during the "Cantina
Band" sequence in the very first flick, then the series actively started to
suck wind harder than Billy Dee Williams in an action sequence by the
start of the third release, *Return of the Jedi*, a film so bad that it may well
be the space opera equivalent of *The Day the Clown Cried*. (Personally, I
lay in with those who peg the beginning of the end, if not the actual
end of the end — or perhaps the high point — of the whole series to
1978's little-remembered yet still nightmare-inducing *The Star Wars
Holiday Special*, which comes as close to the death-inducing video in
The Ring as anything ever shown on non-premium cable.)

And yet, despite the craptacular nature of at least four out of six
Star Wars movies, there's little doubt that no film event has been more
anticipated than *Revenge of the Sith* (with the possible exception — and
in France only — of the next *Asterix et Obelix* extravaganza).
                                                   –Nick Gillespie, "Star Wars, Nothing but Star Wars"

As Gillespie acknowledges, the *Star Wars* saga is full of flaws, some of
them of a "craptacular" nature. And yet he goes on to make a much more
subtle argument:

> The enormous *Star Wars* industry — the movies, the cartoons, the toys,
> the pop-cult references — still generates interest, excitement, pleasure
> (this last is something that most critics, whether liberal or conserva-
> tive find absolutely terrifying), and, most important, a cultural conver-
> sation worth having. The series may well be crap — and a grave
> disappointment to critics who know so much better than the rest of
> us — but surely that's the least interesting thing about it.

Gillespie certainly knows that not everyone will agree with his
assessment of the *Star Wars* saga, but his lengthy review makes clear to
readers why he has come to the qualitative decision that the movies
have nurtured "a cultural conversation worth having."

Developing an Evaluative Argument

Developing an argument of evaluation can seem like a simple process, especially if you already know what your claim is likely to be:

Citizen Kane **is the finest film ever made by an American director.**

Having established a claim, you would then explore the implications of your belief, drawing out the reasons, warrants, and evidence that might support it:

Claim	*Citizen Kane* **is the finest film ever made by an American director . . .**
Reason	**. . . because it revolutionizes the way we see the world.**
Warrant	**Great films change viewers in fundamental ways.**
Evidence	**Shot after shot,** *Citizen Kane* **presents the life of its protagonist through cinematic images that viewers can never forget.**

The warrant here is, in effect, a statement of criteria—in this case, the quality that defines "great film" for the writer.

In developing an evaluative argument, you'll want to pay special attention to criteria, claims, and evidence.

Formulating Criteria

Most often neglected in evaluations is the discussion of criteria. Although even thoughtless evaluations (*The band stinks!*) might be traced to reasonable criteria, most people don't bother defending their positions until they are challenged (*Oh yeah?*). Yet when writers address audiences whom they understand well or with whom they share core values, they don't defend most of their criteria in detail. One wouldn't expect a film critic like Roger Ebert to restate all his principles every time he writes a movie review. Ebert assumes his readers will—over time—come to appreciate his standards.

Still, the criteria can make or break a piece. In an essay from *Salon.com*'s series of evaluative arguments called "Masterpieces," writer Stephanie Zacharek can barely contain her enthusiasm for the Chrysler Building in midtown Manhattan:

Architects, who have both intuition and training on their side, have some very good reasons for loving the Chrysler Building. The rest of

us love it beyond reason, for its streamlined majesty and its inherent sense of optimism and promise for the future, but mostly for its shimmery, welcoming beauty—a beauty that speaks of humor and elegance in equal measures, like a Noel Coward play.

How can a mere building make so many people so happy—particularly so many ornery New Yorkers, who often pretend, as part of their act, not to like anything? There may be New Yorkers who dislike the Chrysler Building, but they rarely step forward in public. To do so would only invite derision and disbelief.

—Stephanie Zacharek, "The Chrysler Building"

Why does this building make people happy?

Certainly, it may seem odd to suggest that one measure of a great building is that it makes people happy. And so the writer has a lot to prove. She's got to provide evidence that a building can, in fact, be delightful. And she seems to do precisely that later in the same essay when she gives life even to the windows in the skyscraper:

> Looking at the Chrysler Building now, though, it's hard to argue against its stylish ebullience, or its special brand of sophisticated cheerfulness. . . . Particularly at night, the crown's triangular windows—lit up, fanned out and stacked high into the sky—suggest a sense of movement that has more in common with dance than with architecture: Those rows of windows are as joyous and seductive as a chorus line of Jazz Age cuties, a bit of sexy night life rising up boldly from an otherwise businesslike skyline.

The criteria Zacharek uses lead to an inventive and memorable evaluation, one that perhaps teaches readers to look at buildings in a whole new way.

The Audiovox SMT 5600

So don't take criteria of evaluation for granted. If you offer vague, dull, or unsupportable principles, expect to be challenged. You're most likely to be vague about your beliefs when you haven't thought enough about your subject. So push yourself at least as far as you imagine the readers will. Imagine the readers looking over your shoulder, asking difficult questions. Say, for example, that you intend to argue that any person who wants to stay on the cutting edge of personal technology will obviously prefer Cingular's Audiovox SMT 5600. What standards would such people apply? That it's not only a great phone but a great PDA? But what does that mean? What makes it "great"? Perhaps that it gives access to email, the wireless Web, and PIM data and that it seamlessly integrates with Windows Media Player provide some criteria you could defend. But should you get more—or less—technical? Do you need to assert very sophisticated criteria to establish your authority to write about the subject? These are appropriate questions to ask.

Making Claims

Claims can be stated directly or, in rare instances, strongly implied. For most writers, the direct evaluative claim probably works better, with the statement carefully qualified. Consider the differences between the following claims and how much less the burden of proof would be for the second and third ones:

Jon Stewart is the most important entertainer of this decade.

Jon Stewart is one of the three or four most important TV entertainers of this decade.

Jon Stewart may come to be regarded as one of the three or four most important TV comedians of this decade.

The point of qualifying a statement isn't to make evaluative claims bland, but to make them responsible and manageable. Consider how sensitively Christopher Caldwell frames his claim in the eulogy he writes for former Beatle George Harrison (a eulogy is a very important kind of evaluative argument):

> Leaving aside the screaming Beatlemaniacs in thrall to the idiosyncrasies of sex appeal, there were never any George People or Ringo People. But George Harrison's death from cancer Thursday at the age of 58 reminds us that there ought to have been. If any of the four could be called "typical" of the group, the most Beatley Beatle, the heart of the Fab Four, the means of bridging Paul's appeal and John's, and thus the glue that held the band together, it was George.
> –Christopher Caldwell, "All Things Must Pass"

Caldwell will have to prove this claim, offering evidence that George contributed in important ways to a musical group dominated by John Lennon and Paul McCartney. But he doesn't have to show that George was the most important Beatle, just the group's binding element. And that's a much more manageable task.

Presenting Evidence

The more evidence the better in an evaluation, provided that the evidence is relevant. For example, in evaluating the performance of two computers, the speed of their processors would certainly be important, but the quality of their keyboards or the availability of service might be less crucial, perhaps irrelevant.

Just as important as relevance in selecting evidence is presentation. Not all pieces of evidence are equally convincing, nor should they be treated as such. Select evidence most likely to impress your readers, and arrange the argument to build toward your best material. In most cases, that best material will be evidence that's specific, detailed, and derived from credible sources. Look at the details in these paragraphs by David

Plotz evaluating rapper, producer, and entertainer P. Diddy—at the time still known as Sean "Puffy" Combs:

> Combs is a Renaissance man, but only by the standards of a P.T. Barnum world. Rarely has someone become so famous by being so mediocre at so many things—a boy wonder without any wonder. Puffy is a famous rapper who can't rap, and he's becoming a movie actor who can't act. He's a restaurateur who serves ho-hum food; a magazine publisher whose magazine was immediately forgettable (*Notorious*—see, you've forgotten already); a music producer whose only talents are stealing old songs and recycling the work of his dead friend the Notorious B.I.G.
>
> Combs can be seen as the inverse of the past century's great Renaissance man, Paul Robeson, a truly wonderful singer, actor, athlete, and political activist. Puffy has none of that talent, but unlike the Communist Robeson, he has a profound understanding of capitalism. Puffy has thrived because he has achieved his mediocrity with immense panache, with bling-bling hoopla and PR genius. Puffy is the Sam Glick of hip-hop—a man without wit, talent, charm, or convictions, but so full of drive that he made $230 million anyway.
>
> –David Plotz, "Sean Combs: Why Is Puffy Deflating?"

The details are rich enough to make the case that Sean Combs lacks the talent of a real artist or genius. But notice that Plotz admits what's obvious to anyone aware of the man's fame: he's a success by contemporary standards. Combs's income can't be ignored in this argument.

However, don't be afraid to concede such a point when evidence goes contrary to the overall claim you wish to make. If you're really skillful, you can even turn a problem into an argumentative asset, as Bob Costas does in acknowledging the flaws of baseball great Mickey Mantle in the process of praising him:

> None of us, Mickey included, would want to be held to account for every moment of our lives. But how many of us could say that our best moments were as magnificent as his?
>
> –Bob Costas, "Eulogy for Mickey Mantle"

Considering Design and Visuals

In thinking about how to present your evidence, don't forget to consider the visual aspects of doing so. Design features such as headings for the different criteria you're using or, in online evaluations, links to material related to your subject can enhance your authority and credibility and thus make your evaluation more persuasive. Think, too, about how you

might use visual evidence to good effect. For example, you might use a bar graph, as the American Film Institute did for the most quotable movies (see p. 259), to show how your subject measures up to a similar one. Or in the passage on Combs, Plotz could have included photos of both Combs and Robeson, choosing ones that drew a stark distinction between the two men. Here, for instance, is a photo of Combs, wearing a cut-off T-shirt and lots of bling; compare that photo to the one of Robeson as a serious and well-dressed young man.

If Everything's an Argument . . .

From your standpoint as a student, how would you evaluate this chapter on evaluations? How well does the chapter use examples, explanations, and visuals to establish what an evaluation argument does? How helpful is it in preparing you to write an evaluation argument? Finally, judged by the corresponding criteria, how does this chapter stack up against the two preceding chapters — on arguments of fact and arguments of definition? Think about these questions, and then write a one-page evaluation of this chapter.

Key Features of Evaluations

In drafting an evaluation, you should consider three basic elements:

- an evaluative claim that makes a judgment about a person, idea, or object
- the criterion or criteria by which you'll measure your subject
- evidence that the particular subject meets or falls short of the stated criteria

All these elements will be present in one way or another in arguments of evaluation, but they won't follow a specific order. In addition, you'll often need an opening paragraph to explain what you're evaluating and why. Tell readers why they should care about your subject and take your opinion seriously.

Nothing adds more depth to an opinion than letting others challenge it. When you can, use the resources of the Internet or more local online networks to get responses to your opinions. It can be eye-opening to realize how strongly people react to ideas or points of view that you regard as perfectly normal. When you're ready, share your draft with colleagues, asking them to identify places where your ideas need additional support, either in the discussion of criteria or in the presentation of evidence.

GUIDE to writing an evaluation

● **Finding a Topic**

You're entering an argument of evaluation when you:

- make a judgment about quality: Citizen Kane *is probably the finest film ever made by an American director.*

- challenge such a judgment: Citizen Kane *is vastly overrated by most film critics.*

- construct a ranking or comparison: Citizen Kane *is a more intellectually challenging movie than* Casablanca.

Issues of evaluation arise daily—in the judgments you make about public figures or policies; in the choices you make about instructors and courses; in the recommendations you make about books, films, or television programs; in the preferences you exercise in choosing products, activities, or charities. Be alert to evaluative arguments whenever you read or use terms that indicate value or rank: *good/bad, effective/ineffective, best/worst, competent/incompetent, successful/unsuccessful.* Finally, be aware of your own areas of expertise. Write about subjects or topics about which others regularly ask your opinion or advice.

● **Researching Your Topic**

You can research issues of evaluation by using the following sources:

- journals, reviews, and magazines (for current political and social issues)
- books (for assessing judgments about history, policy, etc.)
- biographies (for assessing people)
- research reports and scientific studies
- books, magazines, and Web sites for consumers
- periodicals and Web sites that cover entertainment and sports
- blogs for exploring current affairs

Surveys and polls can be useful in uncovering public attitudes: *What books are people reading? Who are the most admired people in the country? What activities or businesses are thriving or waning?* You'll discover that Web sites, newsgroups, and blogs thrive on evaluation. Browse these public forums for ideas, and, when possible, explore your own topic ideas there.

● Formulating a Claim

After exploring your subject, begin to formulate a full and specific claim, a thesis that lets readers know where you stand and on what criteria you'll base your judgments. Look for a thesis that's challenging enough to attract readers' attention, not one that merely repeats views already widely held. In moving toward this thesis, you might begin with questions of this kind:

- What exactly is my opinion? Where do I stand?
- Can I make my judgment more specific?
- Do I need to qualify my claim?
- According to what standards am I making my judgment?
- Will readers accept my criteria, or will I have to defend them, too?
- What major reasons can I offer in support of my evaluation?

Your thesis should be a complete statement. In one sentence, you need to make a claim of evaluation and state the reasons that support your claim. Be sure your claim is specific enough. Anticipate the questions readers might have: *Who? What? Where? Under what conditions? With what exceptions? In all cases?* Don't expect readers to guess where you stand.

● Examples of Evaluative Claims

- Though they may never receive Oscars for their work, Sandra Bullock and Keanu Reeves deserve credit as actors who have succeeded in a wider range of film roles than most of their contemporaries.
- Many computer users are discovering that Mac OS X is a more intuitive, stable, robust, and elegant operating system than anything currently available on PC platforms.
- Jimmy Carter has been highly praised for his work as a former president of the United States, but history may show that even his much-derided term in office laid the groundwork for the foreign policy and economic successes now attributed to later administrations.
- Because knowledge changes so quickly and people switch careers so often, an effective education today is one that trains people *how to learn* more than it teaches them *what to know.*

● **Preparing a Proposal**

If your instructor asks you to prepare a proposal for your project, here's a format that may help:

State your thesis completely. If you're having trouble doing so, try outlining it in Toulmin terms:

    Claim:

    Reason(s):

    Warrant(s):

- Explain why this issue deserves attention. What's at stake?
- Specify whom you hope to reach through your argument and why this group of readers would be interested in it.
- Briefly discuss the key challenges you anticipate: Defining criteria? Defending them? Finding quantitative evidence to support your claim? Developing qualitative arguments to bolster your judgment?
- Determine what research strategies you'll use. What sources do you expect to consult?
- Consider what format you expect to use for your project: A conventional research essay? A letter to the editor? A Web page?

● **Thinking about Organization**

Your evaluation may take various forms, but it's likely to include elements such as the following:

- a specific claim: *Most trucks are unsuitable for the kind of driving most Americans do.*
- an explanation or defense of the criteria (if necessary): *The overcrowding and pollution of American cities and suburbs might be relieved if more Americans drove small, fuel-efficient cars. Cars do less damage in accidents than heavy trucks and are also less likely to roll over.*
- an examination of the claim in terms of the stated criteria: *Most trucks are unsuitable for the kind of driving Americans do because they are not designed for contemporary urban driving conditions.*

- evidence for every part of the argument: *Trucks get very poor gas mileage; they are statistically more likely than cars to roll over in accidents; . . .*

- consideration of alternative views and counterarguments: *It is true, perhaps, that trucks make drivers feel safer on the roads and give them a better view of traffic conditions. . . .*

● Getting and Giving Response

All arguments benefit from the scrutiny of others. Your instructor may assign you to a peer group for the purpose of reading and responding to each other's drafts; if not, get some response on your own from some serious readers or consultants at a writing center. You can use the following questions to evaluate a draft. If you're evaluating someone else's draft, be sure to illustrate your points with examples. Specific comments are always more helpful than general observations.

The Claim

- Is the claim clearly an argument of evaluation? Does it make a judgment about something?

- Does the claim establish clearly what's being evaluated?

- Is the claim too sweeping? Does it need to be qualified?

- Will the criteria used in the evaluation be clear to readers? Do the criteria need to be defined more explicitly or precisely?

- Are the criteria appropriate ones to use for this evaluation? Are they controversial? Does evidence of their validity need to be added?

Evidence for the Claim

- Is enough evidence furnished to ensure that what's being evaluated meets the criteria established for the evaluation? If not, what kind of additional evidence is needed?

- Is the evidence in support of the claim simply announced, or are its significance and appropriateness analyzed? Is a more detailed discussion needed?

- Are any objections readers might have to the claim, criteria, or evidence adequately addressed?

- What kinds of sources, including visual sources, are cited? How credible and persuasive will they be to readers? What other kinds of sources might be more credible and persuasive?

- Are all quotations introduced with appropriate signal phrases (such as "As Will argues,") and blended smoothly into the writer's sentences?

Organization and Style

- How are the parts of the argument organized? Is this organization effective, or would some other structure work better?
- Will readers understand the relationships among the claims, supporting reasons, warrants, and evidence? If not, what could be done to make those connections clearer? Are more transitional words and phrases needed? Would headings or graphic devices help?
- Are the transitions or links from point to point, paragraph to paragraph, and sentence to sentence clear and effective? If not, how could they be improved?
- Are all visuals carefully integrated into the text? Is each visual introduced and commented on to point out its significance? Is each visual labeled as a figure or a table and given a caption as well as a citation?
- Is the style suited to the subject? Is it too formal? Too casual? Too technical? Too bland? How can it be improved?
- Which sentences seem particularly effective? Which ones seem weakest, and how could they be improved? Should some short sentences be combined, or should any long ones be separated into two or more sentences?
- How effective are the paragraphs? Do any seem too skimpy or too long? How can they be improved?
- Which words or phrases seem particularly effective, vivid, and memorable? Do any seem dull, vague, unclear, or inappropriate for the audience or the writer's purpose? Are definitions provided for technical or other terms that readers might not know?

Spelling, Punctuation, Mechanics, Documentation, Format

- Are there any errors in spelling, punctuation, capitalization, and the like?
- Is an appropriate and consistent style of documentation used for parenthetical citations and the list of works cited or references? (See Chapter 20.)
- Does the paper or project follow an appropriate format? Is it appropriately designed and attractively presented? How could it be improved? If it's a Web site, do all the links work?

RESPOND•

1. Choose one item from the following list that you understand well enough to evaluate. Develop several criteria of evaluation you could defend to distinguish excellence from mediocrity in the area. Then choose another item from the list, this time one you don't know much about at all, and explain the research you might do to discover reasonable criteria of evaluation for it.

   fashion designers

   Navajo rugs

   musicals

   spoken word poetry

   UN secretary generals

   NFL quarterbacks

   contemporary painters

   TV journalists

   TV sitcoms

   health food

   animated films

2. Review Kristin Cole's appeal for a pet-sitter for Baldrick (see pp. 251–252), and then write an email of your own in which you try to persuade friends to care for someone or something while you're away. Be sure that the argument includes strong elements of evaluation. Why should friends be eager to pamper your pit bull Killer, care for your fragile collection of tropical orchids, or babysit your ten-year-old twin siblings Bonnie and Clyde?

3. In the last ten years, there has been a proliferation of awards programs for movies, musicians, sports figures, and other categories. For example, before the Oscars are handed out, a half-dozen other organizations have given prizes to the annual crop of films. Write a short opinion piece assessing the merits of a particular awards show or a feature such as *People*'s annual "sexiest man" issue. What should a proper event of this kind accomplish? Does the event you're reviewing do so?

4. Local news-and-entertainment magazines often publish "best of" issues or articles that list readers' and editors' favorites in such categories as "best place to go on a first date," "best ice cream sundae," and "best dentist." Sometimes the categories are very specific: "best places to say 'I was retro before retro was cool'" or "best movie theater seats." Imagine that you're the editor of your own local magazine and

that you want to put out a "best of" issue tailored to your hometown. Develop ten categories for evaluation. For each category, list the evaluative criteria you would use to make your judgment. Next, consider that because your criteria are warrants, they're especially tied to audience. (The criteria for "best dentist," for example, might be tailored to people whose major concern is avoiding pain, to those whose children will be regular clients, or to those who want the cheapest possible dental care.) For several of the evaluative categories, imagine that you have to justify your judgments to a completely different audience. Write a new set of criteria for that audience.

5. Develop an argument using (or challenging) one of the criteria of evaluation presented in this chapter. Among the criteria you might explore are the following:

   A car should be a tool.

   Good TV quotes are those that impress themselves in people's memories.

   Great films change viewers in fundamental ways.

   Good pets need not have fur and four legs.

   Great veggie burgers need just the right shape and texture.

6. For examples of powerful evaluation arguments, search the Web or library for obituaries of famous, recently deceased individuals. Try to locate at least one such item, and analyze the types of claims it makes about the deceased. What criteria of evaluation are employed? What kinds of evidence does it present?

Why I Hate Britney

NISEY WILLIAMS

I'm afraid of having children. Not because of labor pains, but because of the odds that I may actually have a girl. Today, efficiently raising a daughter is almost impossible because of pop culture's persistent emphasis on sex. It's rare to watch MTV or BET and not be bombarded with images of women's bare midriffs, protruding cleavage, and round rumps. Bellies, breasts, and booties. I can't imagine how much more difficult it will be to protect my daughter from this in fifteen years when she'd be approaching puberty.

The thesis is stated clearly and emphatically.

And for my fear of motherhood, I blame Britney Spears.

Well, in all fairness, Britney's not the only one to influence our youth. There is a growing group of sexualized, so-called entertainers who seem to be multiplying like roaches: Britney Spears, Destiny's Child, Christina Aguilera, 3LW, Mariah Carey, Shakira, Jessica Simpson, Pink, J.Lo, etc.—hereafter known as Britney et al. Daily, these destructive divas serve young girls with an earful and eyeful of sex, tempting children to mimic their musical heroes. So much so that the media has coined such phrases as "Baby Britneys," "Teeny Christinees," and "Junior J.Los." Still, while there are other female artists who also discourage the healthy development of our

---

When she wrote this paper, Nisey Williams was a senior at the University of Texas, Austin, an African American Studies and Cultural Anthropology major who plans on teaching honors English to high school students. Although she enjoys all realms of creative writing, her passion is poetry. She hopes to publish poetry and short stories.

"Why I Hate Britney" is her response to an assignment that asked for an argument with a personal voice suitable for publication in a newspaper or magazine. Sources were to be documented in the paper itself, not through formal documentation.

youth—most recently J.Lo with her serial marrying/divorcing practices—Britney remains the most culpable.

A *Dallas Morning News* reporter claims it's "always convenient to blame the sinister influence of Britney" but it's much more than "convenient"—it's practical. Forbes magazine voted Britney as the most powerful celebrity of 2002, beating such influential personalities as Steven Spielberg and Oprah Winfrey. With such recognition comes responsibilities. It's undeniable that Britney is at the forefront of this sex-crazed phenomenon and I, like many others, hold her accountable. On a website called *Pax Vobiscum,* one concerned father of two teenage daughters refers to Britney as "the chief apostlette for the sexualization of our little girls" with her "revealing clothing and 'come-hither' image." This couldn't be more accurate.

Evidence suggests that Spears is responsible for influencing young women.

While she says she hopes to save her virginity for marriage, she also wears see-through outfits and dances like a stripper on the MTV Video Music Awards. Actions speak louder than words; her chastity claim falls short beside her sleazy image. Britney's marketing management is pimping her and she's without the dignity or strength to step off the street corner and hail a cab from Lolita Lane to Respectable Road.

Several other female artists don't sell their bodies in order to sell their music. Among them is Avril Lavigne, one of Arista's latest signers, who openly criticizes Britney for her confusing and contradictory image. In a recent interview with *Chart Attack,* Avril explains that: "The clothes I wear onstage are the clothes I would wear to school or to go shopping. Britney Spears goes up onstage and dresses like a showgirl. She's not being herself. I mean, the way she dresses . . . would you walk around the street in a bra? It's definitely not what I'm going to do." And so far, Avril hasn't had to compromise herself to be a success. Her first album, Let Go, debuted at No. 8 on the Billboard charts and has since gone double platinum. She was also awarded Best New Artist at the 2002 MTV Video Music Awards. Avril

An alternative to Spears's approach to success is offered.

is known as the "Anti-Britney" because, as AskMen.com explained, she "stands out in the current sea of female teen vocalists as a distinctly unmanufactured artist whose success can be directly linked to her musical talent." Can't say the same for Miss Spears.

It's amazing how Britney ignores her influence on children. In *Rolling Stone,* her response to critics judging her clothing style was a reference to her younger days of playing dress-up in her mother's closet—within the confines of her home. She explained: "We put on our mom's clothes and we dressed up. It was our time to daydream and fantasize." Does she seriously think wearing Mom's clothes is the same as having your own and flaunting them at the mall or in the classroom?

Then in an *In Style* interview, she says she has no patience for those who criticize her skin-baring. In her words: "I mean, I'm a girl! Why not?" Great message for the kiddies, Brit: if you got it, flaunt it. And what about those girls who don't "got it"? Britney basically tells girls that body image is of primary importance—a difficult problem for many young females. Some girls who feel this constant pressure to attain unrealistic goals end up with destructive behaviors such as eating disorders and low self-esteem. Many girls who strive to be Britney look-alikes do not realize they lack her resources, such as makeup artists, silicone enhancements, and millions of dollars.

The main argument against those like me who bash Britney is that it's up to parents—not celebrities—to teach their children morals and appropriate behavior. While I agree with elements of that claim, there is only so much a parent can do. Sexual material is so intertwined in pop culture that even cautious parents have a hard time keeping their children away from it. In the *Milwaukee Journal Sentinel,* one psychiatrist explains that parents "often don't even think about it [keeping children away from pop culture] because it's an overwhelming task," while another equated "trying to insulate a child from sexual material" with "fighting a tornado."

Spears does not live up to criteria for responsible behavior—given her role as a model for young girls.

An alternative perspective is explored and rejected.

During the crucial years of adolescence, popular opinion sometimes overrides that of parents. In the same Milwaukee article, one mother reports that her daughter threw a fit in the department store when she refused to buy her thongs. The mother was completely baffled by her child's reaction until the twelve-year-old admitted that the other girls in the locker room teased her for wearing bikini underwear instead of thongs. Many kids will do anything to fit in because peer approval is so necessary to a child learning her place in school.

Experts are torn on the long-term effects our sex-heavy pop culture may have on children, but many agree that there are likely negative consequences. According to Diane Levin, an education professor who has studied the effects of media on children's development for over twenty years, our sex-saturated culture will rub off on children in the most undesired ways. On *ABCNews.com*, Levin explains that "the kind of increased sexual images that children are seeing parallel with when they get a little older. They start becoming sexually active earlier." Currently, the Alan Guttmacher Institute reports that two out of ten girls and three out of ten boys have had sexual intercourse by age fifteen, while there are also several widespread reports of increased sexual activity—including oral sex—among middle-school students. How much worse will these statistics be by the time my daughter reaches the age of fifteen?

Although there is no documented evidence of how pop culture's over-sexualization affects children, an August 14th taping of *Good Morning, America*, entitled "From Oshkosh to Oh My Gosh," revealed some startling reactions. The show divided the children by sex and then interviewed the two groups separately about issues surrounding pop culture. The result was a roomful of shocked parents who had no idea the word *sexy* was such a frequent and familiar part of their children's vocabulary. When the girls' group watched a Jennifer Lopez video, the relationship between the mature concept of sexiness and popular music became obvious. After one young girl

Numerous examples enforce the claim that children are being sexualized too early by "Britney et al."

predicted the video's ending was J.Lo removing her shirt, another girl explained that J.Lo did this "to look sexy."

Being sexy is the latest fad for girls of all ages and with the current fashions available, their dreams can become a reality. Clothing designers work side by side with the entertainment industry. There is at least a $90 billion market targeting "tweens"—children between the ages of eight and twelve who are in the in between stages of adolescence and teenagehood. It is this up-and-coming group who fuel pop culture. They listen to the music, worship the singers, and crave their clothing. From Wal-Mart to the Limited Too, stores are fully aware of what their young consumers want and promote their merchandise accordingly.

As a consequence of Spears's influence, parents are finding it more difficult to raise children, underscoring the initial claim in the argument.

Modest girls' clothing is hard to find among the racks of grown-up fashions like low-riding hip huggers, tight midriff-revealing shirts, high-heeled platforms, and miniskirts. One of my co-workers said she had such a difficult time school shopping for her thirteen-year-old daughter that she ended up taking her to Academy for wind suits, free-flowing T-shirts, and soccer shorts. Sporting stores will soon be the last option for frustrated parents, as more retailers prey on the tween market.

However, my beef is not with these merchants. The clothing is harmless by itself. It would sit untouched and undesired if it weren't for Britney et al. flaunting revealing fashions in music videos, posters, magazine covers, and award shows. As *FashionFollower.com* revealed: "Queen Britney single-handedly made the bare midriff a staple of 15-year-old wardrobes across the globe. Now that's something every mother should be proud of."

Pop culture seems to be in downward spiral, continually going from bad to worse. It's bad enough to have to endure countless images of exposed female bodies on every music channel, but it's so much worse to see those same "barely there" outfits on children. Hopefully, there will come a day when it's no longer trendy to be so overtly sexual and pop culture will replace Britney et al. with more respectable female icons.

The Case against Coldplay

JON PARELES

June 5, 2005

There's nothing wrong with self-pity. As a spur to songwriting, it's right up there with lust, anger and greed, and probably better than the remaining deadly sins. There's nothing wrong, either, with striving for musical grandeur, using every bit of skill and studio illusion to create a sound large enough to get lost in. Male sensitivity, a quality that's under siege in a pop culture full of unrepentant bullying and machismo, shouldn't be dismissed out of hand, no matter how risible it can be in practice. And building a sound on the lessons of past bands is virtually unavoidable.

But put them all together and they add up to Coldplay, the most insufferable band of the decade.

This week Coldplay releases its painstakingly recorded third album, "X&Y" (Capitol), a virtually surefire blockbuster that has corporate for-

---

Jon Pareles is the pop music critic of the *New York Times*.

tunes riding on it. (The stock price plunged for EMI Group, Capitol's parent company, when Coldplay announced that the album's release date would be moved from February to June, as it continued to rework the songs.)

"X&Y" is the work of a band that's acutely conscious of the worldwide popularity it cemented with its 2002 album, "A Rush of Blood to the Head," which has sold three million copies in the United States alone. Along with its 2000 debut album, "Parachutes," Coldplay claims sales of 20 million albums worldwide. "X&Y" makes no secret of grand ambition.

Clearly, Coldplay is beloved: by moony high school girls and their solace-seeking parents, by hip-hop producers who sample its rich instrumental sounds and by emo rockers who admire Chris Martin's heart-on-sleeve lyrics. The band emanates good intentions, from Mr. Martin's political statements to lyrics insisting on its own benevolence. Coldplay is admired by everyone—everyone except me.

It's not for lack of skill. The band proffers melodies as imposing as Romanesque architecture, solid and symmetrical. Mr. Martin on keyboards, Jonny Buckland on guitar, Guy Berryman on bass and Will Champion on drums have mastered all the mechanics of pop songwriting, from the instrumental hook that announces nearly every song they've recorded to the reassurance of a chorus to the revitalizing contrast of a bridge. Their arrangements ascend and surge, measuring out the song's yearning and tension, cresting and easing back and then moving toward a chiming resolution. Coldplay is meticulously unified, and its songs have been rigorously cleared of anything that distracts from the musical drama.

Unfortunately, all that sonic splendor orchestrates Mr. Martin's voice and lyrics. He places his melodies near the top of his range to sound more fragile, so the tunes straddle the break between his radiant tenor voice and his falsetto. As he hops between them—in what may be Coldplay's most annoying tic—he makes a sound somewhere between a yodel and a hiccup. And the lyrics can make me wish I didn't understand English. Coldplay's countless fans seem to take comfort when Mr. Martin sings lines like, "Is there anybody out there who / Is lost and hurt and lonely too," while a strummed acoustic guitar telegraphs his aching sincerity. Me, I hear a passive-aggressive blowhard, immoderately proud as he flaunts humility. "I feel low," he announces in the chorus of "Low," belied by the peak of a crescendo that couldn't be more triumphant about it.

In its early days, Coldplay could easily be summed up as Radiohead minus Radiohead's beat, dissonance or arty subterfuge. Both bands looked to the overarching melodies of 1970's British rock and to the guitar dynamics of U2, and Mr. Martin had clearly heard both Bono's delivery and the way Radiohead's Thom Yorke stretched his voice to the creaking point.

Unlike Radiohead, though, Coldplay had no interest in being oblique or barbed. From the beginning, Coldplay's songs topped majesty with moping: "We're sinking like stones," Mr. Martin proclaimed. Hardly alone among British rock bands as the 1990's ended, Coldplay could have been singing not only about private sorrows but also about the final sunset on the British empire: the old opulence meeting newly shrunken horizons. Coldplay's songs wallowed happily in their unhappiness.

"Am I a part of the cure / Or am I part of the disease," Mr. Martin pondered in "Clocks" on "A Rush of Blood to the Head." Actually, he's contagious. Particularly in its native England, Coldplay has spawned a generation of one-word bands—Athlete, Embrace, Keane, Starsailor, Travis and Aqualung among them—that are more than eager to follow through on Coldplay's tremulous, ringing anthems of insecurity. The emulation is spreading overseas to bands like the Perishers from Sweden and the American band Blue Merle, which tries to be Coldplay unplugged.

A band shouldn't necessarily be blamed for its imitators—ask the Cure or the Grateful Dead. But Coldplay follow-throughs are redundant; from the beginning, Coldplay has verged on self-parody. When he moans his verses, Mr. Martin can sound so sorry for himself that there's hardly room to sympathize for him, and when he's not mixing metaphors, he fearlessly slings clichés. "Are you lost or incomplete," Mr. Martin sings in "Talk," which won't be cited in any rhyming dictionaries. "Do you feel like a puzzle / you can't find your missing piece."

Coldplay reached its musical zenith with the widely sampled piano arpeggios that open "Clocks": a passage that rings gladly and, as it descends the scale and switches from major to minor chords, turns incipiently mournful. Of course, it's followed by plaints: "Tides that I tried to swim against / Brought me down upon my knees."

On "X&Y," Coldplay strives to carry the beauty of "Clocks" across an entire album—not least in its first single, "Speed of Sound," which isn't the only song on the album to borrow the "Clocks" drumbeat. The album is faultless to a fault, with instrumental tracks purged of any glimmer of human frailty. There is not an unconsidered or misplaced note on "X&Y," and every song (except the obligatory acoustic "hidden track" at the end, which is still by no means casual) takes place on a monumental soundstage.

As Coldplay's recording budgets have grown, so have its reverberation times. On "X&Y," it plays as if it can already hear the songs echoing across the world. "Square One," which opens the album, actually begins with guitar notes hinting at the cosmic fanfare of "Also Sprach Zarathustra" (and "2001: A Space Odyssey"). Then Mr. Martin, never someone to evade the obvious, sings about "the space in which we're traveling."

As a blockbuster band, Coldplay is now looking over its shoulder at titanic predecessors like U2, Pink Floyd and the Beatles, pilfering freely from all of them. It also looks to an older legacy; in many songs, organ chords resonate in the spaces around Mr. Martin's voice, insisting on churchly reverence.

As Coldplay's music has grown more colossal, its lyrics have quietly made a shift on "X&Y." On previous albums, Mr. Martin sang mostly in the first person, confessing to private vulnerabilities. This time, he sings a lot about "you": a lover, a brother, a random acquaintance. He has a lot of pronouncements and advice for all of them: "You just want somebody listening to what you say," and "Every step that you take could be your biggest mistake," and "Maybe you'll get what you wanted, maybe you'll stumble upon it" and "You don't have to be alone." It's supposed to be compassionate, empathetic, magnanimous, inspirational. But when the music swells up once more with tremolo guitars and chiming keyboards, and Mr. Martin's voice breaks for the umpteenth time, it sounds like hokum to me.

10
Causal Arguments

Concerned that middle-school students are consuming too much junk food and soda pop at lunch, a principal considers banning vending machines on her campus. But then she discovers how much revenue those machines generate for her school, and she quickly has second thoughts.

A scientist questions the widespread assumption that glaciers are receding largely because of global warming caused by human behavior. He offers controversial evidence that glaciers have grown and receded in the Alps and elsewhere several times during the last ten thousand years—even before humans were capable of changing the climate.

Researchers in Marin County, California, discover that the occurrence of breast cancer cases is significantly higher there than in any other urban area in California. They immediately begin work to investigate possible causes.

A large clothing manufacturer wants to increase its worldwide market share among teenage buyers of blue jeans. Its executives know that another company has been the overwhelming market leader for years—and they set out to learn exactly why.

Convinced that there is a strong and compelling causal link between secondhand smoke and lung cancer, the City of New York institutes a total ban of smoking in public indoor spaces.

A state legislator notes that gasoline prices are consistently between twenty-five and fifty cents higher in one large city in the state than elsewhere. After some preliminary investigation, the legislator decides to bring a class action lawsuit on behalf of the people of this city, arguing that price fixing and insider deals are responsible for the price difference.

● ● ●

The eye-catching title image of a *National Geographic* story from August 2004 poses a simple question: "Why Are We So Fat?" You're probably smart enough to suspect that simple questions like this rarely have simple answers. But in this case the author, Cathy Newman, argues that there are no real surprises:

> . . . in one sense, the obesity crisis is the result of simple math. It's a calories in, calories out calculation. The First Law of Fat says that anything you eat beyond your immediate need for energy, from avocados to ziti, converts to fat. . . . The Second Law of Fat: The line between being in and out of energy balance is slight. Suppose you consume a mere 5 percent over a 2,000-calorie-a-day average. "That's just one hundred calories; it's a glass of apple juice," says Rudolph Leibel, head of molecular genetics at Columbia University College of Physicians and Surgeons. "But those few extra calories can mean a

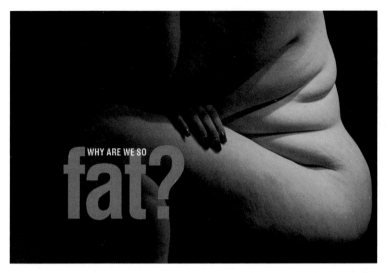

WHY ARE WE SO

And the answer is . . .?

huge weight gain." Since one pound of body weight is roughly equivalent to 3,500 calories, that glass of juice adds up to an extra 10
pounds over a year.

–Cathy Newman, "Why Are We So Fat?"

And yet you know that there's more to it than that—as Newman's
full story reveals. "Calories in, calories out" may explain the physics of
weight gain. But why in recent years have we so drastically shifted the
equation from *out* to *in?* Because food is more readily available and
cheaper, and humans instinctually crave fatty foods? Because we've
grown addicted to fast food? Because we walk less? Because we've
become Internet (or GameBoy) addicts? Whatever the reasons for our
increased tonnage, the consequences can be measured by everything
from the width of airliner seats to the rise of diabetes in the general population. Many explanations will be offered by scientists, social critics,
and health gurus, and just as many will likely be refuted. Figuring out
what's going on will be an importance exercise in cause-and-effect argument for years to come.

Understanding Causal Arguments

Causal arguments are at the heart of many major policy decisions, both national and international—from the consequences of poverty in Africa to the causes of terrorism around the globe. But arguments about causes and effects also inform many choices people make every day. Suppose that you need to petition for a grade change because you were unable to turn in a final project on time. You'd probably enumerate the reasons for your failure—the death of your cat, followed by an attack of the hives, followed by a crash of your computer—hoping that a committee reading the petition might see these explanations as tragic enough to change your grade. In identifying the *causes* of the situation, you're implicitly arguing that the *effect*—your failure to submit the project on time—should be considered in a new light. Unfortunately, the committee might accuse you of *faulty causality* (see pp. 506–508), judging that your failure to complete the project is really due more to procrastination and partying than to the reasons you offer.

Causal arguments exist in many forms and frequently appear as part of other arguments (such as evaluations or proposals).

It may help focus your work on causal arguments to separate them into three major categories:

- arguments that state a cause and then examine its effect(s)

- arguments that state an effect and then trace the effect back to its cause(s)

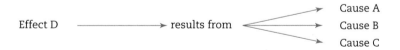

- arguments that move through a series of links: A causes B, which leads to C and perhaps to D

Cause A → leads to Cause B → leads to Cause C → leads to Effect D

ARGUMENTS THAT STATE A CAUSE AND THEN EXAMINE
ONE OR MORE OF ITS EFFECTS

What would happen if openly homosexual men and women were allowed to join (or stay in) the American military? That would be a "cause" whose possible effects could be examined in detail and argued powerfully. You could imagine the very different cases (and consequences) presented by people on contrary sides of this hot button issue. In such an argument, you'd be successful if you could show compellingly that the cause would indeed lead to the effects you describe. Or you could challenge the causal assumptions made by people you don't agree with. Take a look at the opening of an article from the Reuters news service reporting on the Live 8 concerts held in July 2005. One might have expected an event such as Live 8 to move the consciences of world leaders or heighten people's awareness about conditions in regions of Africa. But there was another consequence as well:

> LONDON (Reuters)—They came out of charity. They left with booming record sales.
>
> The galaxy of rock stars who took part in Live 8 concerts on Saturday to help beat the curse of poverty have seen their discs fly off the shelves in British music stores—a case of bank balances as well as consciences winning out.
>
> –Mike Collett-White, "Stars See Album Sales Soar after Live 8 Gigs"

But were audiences, in fact, rewarding the artists not so much for their good deeds as for their good performances? One detail in the story suggests the latter—and suggests how absorbing the details of causal arguments can be:

> The only Live 8 performer to have clocked a drop in sales was Pete Doherty. His former group the Libertines saw sales of their "Up the Bracket" album drop by 35 percent.
>
> Doherty's performance was singled out by the British media as one of the worst of the nine-hour Hyde Park music marathon. . . . people at the gig said he struggled with the words of "Children of the Revolution" and looked unsteady on his feet.

ARGUMENTS THAT BEGIN WITH AN EFFECT AND THEN TRACE
THE EFFECT BACK TO ONE OR MORE CAUSES

This type of argument might begin with a certain effect—for example, Hollywood experiencing a record-breaking slump in movie-going in 2005—and then trace the effect (or set of effects) to the most likely

Cartoonist Mark Alan Stamaty portrays an effect and three of its causes.

causes: a rise in DVD sales; the growing popularity of large-screen home theaters and HDTV; noisy, cell phone–using audiences; lousy movies; unimaginative remakes; red-state backlash against liberal Hollywood films or activism in the 2004 elections. Or you might examine the reasons Hollywood executives offer for their industry's dip and decide whether their causal analyses pass muster.

Like other kinds of causal arguments, those tracing effects to a cause can have far-reaching significance. For example, in 1962 the scientist Rachel Carson seized the attention of millions with a famous causal argument about the effects that the overuse of chemical pesticides might have on the environment. Here's an excerpt from the beginning of her book-length study of this subject. Note how she begins with the *effects* before saying she'll go on to explore the causes:

[A] strange blight crept over the area and everything began to change. Some evil spell had settled on the community: mysterious maladies swept the flocks of chickens; the cattle and sheep sickened and died. Everywhere was a shadow of death. The farmers spoke of much illness among their families. . . . There had been several sudden and unexplained deaths, not only among adults but even among children, who would be stricken suddenly while at play and die within a few hours. . . . The roadsides, once so attractive, were now lined with browned and withered vegetation as though swept by fire. These, too, were silent, deserted by all living things. Even the streams were now lifeless. Anglers no longer visited them, for all the fish had died.

In the gutters under the eaves and between the shingles of the roofs, a white granular powder still showed a few patches; some weeks before it had fallen like snow upon the roofs and the lawns, the fields and streams. No witchcraft, no enemy action had silenced the rebirth of new life in this stricken world. The people had done it themselves. . . . What has already silenced the voices of spring in countless towns in America? This book is an attempt to explain.

–Rachel Carson, *Silent Spring*

Today, one could easily write a casual argument of the first type about *Silent Spring* and the environmental movement it spawned.

ARGUMENTS THAT MOVE THROUGH A SERIES OF LINKS: CAUSE A LEADS TO B, WHICH LEADS TO C AND POSSIBLY TO D

In an environmental science class, for example, you might decide to argue that a national law regulating smokestack emissions from utility plants is needed because of the following reasons:

1. emissions from utility plants in the Midwest cause acid rain,
2. acid rain causes the death of trees and other vegetation in eastern forests,
3. powerful lobbyists have prevented midwestern states from passing strict laws to control emissions from these plants, and
4. as a result, acid rain will destroy most eastern forests by 2020.

In this case, the first link is that emissions cause acid rain; the second, that acid rain causes destruction in eastern forests; and the third, that states have not acted to break the cause-effect relationship established by the first two points. These links set the scene for the fourth link, which ties the previous points together to argue from effect: unless X, then Y.

Characterizing Causal Arguments

Causal arguments tend to share several characteristics.

THEY ARE OFTEN PART OF OTHER ARGUMENTS.

Many causal arguments do stand alone and address questions fundamental to our well-being: *Why are juvenile asthma and diabetes increasing so dramatically in the United States? What are the causes of global warming, and can we do anything to counter them? What will happen to Europe if its birth rate continues to decline?* But causal analyses often work to further other arguments—especially proposals. For example, a proposal to limit the time children spend playing video games might first draw on a causal analysis to establish that playing video games can have bad results—such as violent behavior, short attention spans, and decreased social skills. The causal analysis provides a rationale that motivates the proposal. In this way, causal analyses can be useful in establishing good reasons for arguments in general.

THEY ARE ALMOST ALWAYS COMPLEX.

The complexity of most causal relationships makes establishing causes and effects extremely difficult. For example, scientists and politicians continue to disagree over the extent to which acid rain is actually responsible for the so-called dieback of many eastern forests. Or consider the complexity of analyzing election results. If you compare articles explaining why George W. Bush *won* the presidency in 2004 with those that ask why John Kerry *lost,* you might as well be in different universes.

But when you can show that X *definitely* causes Y, you'll have a powerful argument at your disposal if for no other reason than that causal arguments must take into account an enormous number of factors, conditions, and alternative possibilities. That's why, for example, so much effort went into establishing an indisputable link between smoking and lung cancer. Once proven, decisive legal action could finally be taken to protect—or at least warn—smokers.

THEY ARE OFTEN DEFINITION BASED.

One reason causal arguments are so complex is that they often depend on extremely careful definitions. Recent figures from the U.S. Department of Education, for example, show that the number of high school dropouts is rising and that this rise has caused an increase in youth unemployment. But exactly how does the study define *dropout?* A closer look may suggest that some students (perhaps a lot) who drop out actually "drop back in" later and go on to complete high school. Further, how does the study define *employment?* Until you can provide explicit definitions that answer such questions, you should proceed cautiously with a causal argument like this one.

THEY USUALLY YIELD PROBABLE RATHER THAN ABSOLUTE CONCLUSIONS.

Because causal relationships are almost always extremely complex, they seldom yield more than a high degree of probability and are almost always subject to critique or charges of false causality. (We all know smokers who defy the odds to live long, cancer-free lives.) Scientists in particular are wary of making causal claims—that environmental factors cause infertility, for example, because it's highly unlikely that a condition as variable as infertility could be linked to any one cause.

Even *after* an event, proving what caused it can be hard. No one would disagree that the Japanese bombing of Pearl Harbor took place on December 7, 1941, or that the United States entered World War II shortly thereafter. But what are the causal connections? Did the bombing "cause" the U.S. entry into the war? Even if you're convinced that the bombing was the most immediate cause, what about other related causes: the unstable and often hostile relationship between the U.S. and Japanese governments in the years leading up to the bombing; Japanese imperial ambitions; common U.S. stereotypes of "Oriental" peoples; U.S. objections to the Japanese invasion of China; and so on?

As another example, during the campus riots of the late 1960s, a special commission was charged with determining the "causes" of riots on a particular campus. After two years of work—and almost a thousand pages of evidence and reports—the commission was unable to pinpoint anything but a broad network of contributing causes and related conditions. Thus to demonstrate that A caused B, you must find the strongest possible evidence and subject it to the toughest scrutiny. But understand that a causal argument doesn't fail just because you can't find a single compelling cause. In fact, causal arguments are often most effective when they help readers appreciate how tangled our lives and landscapes really are.

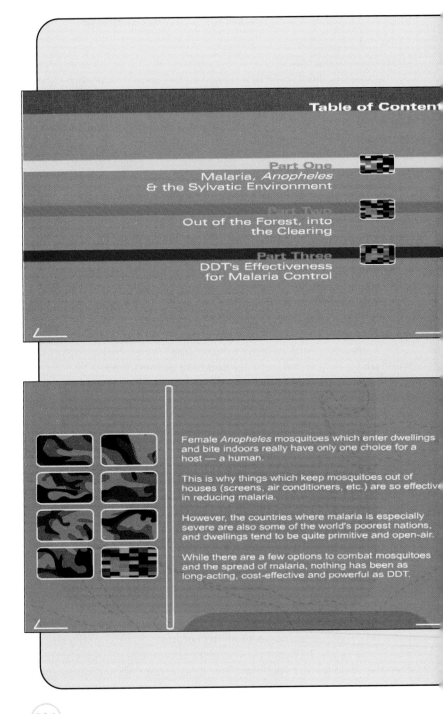
Female *Anopheles* mosquitoes which enter dwellings and bite indoors really have only one choice for a host — a human.

This is why things which keep mosquitoes out of houses (screens, air conditioners, etc.) are so effective in reducing malaria.

However, the countries where malaria is especially severe are also some of the world's poorest nations, and dwellings tend to be quite primitive and open-air.

While there are a few options to combat mosquitoes and the spread of malaria, nothing has been as long-acting, cost-effective and powerful as DDT.

Not Just Words

When Rachel Carson wrote *Silent Spring* to warn of the environmental dangers of pesticides (see p. 290), one of her targets was the widespread use of DDT in American agriculture. DDT was an effective pesticide, but used indiscriminately it had long-term side effects and harmed animals, especially birds. Environmentalists succeeded in virtually banning the use of DDT in the rich industrialized countries. But now there's an interest in some third world nations in restoring its use. Why? Because DDT kills or repels the mosquitoes responsible for malaria, one of the most insidious diseases in some African and Asian countries. One group called Africa Fighting Malaria <http://fightingmalaria.org/> makes a case for "the limited use of DDT for spraying homes and hospitals" in a

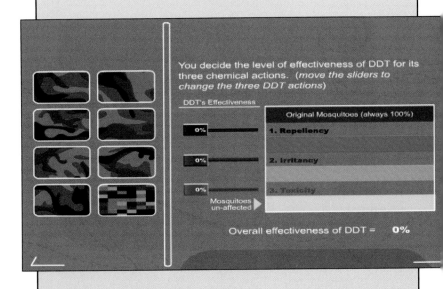

Flash presentation on its Web site. One screen, for example, uses clickable numbers to explain how mosquitoes cause malaria. Another demonstrates how selective spraying of DDT reduces the risk of getting infected by disease-carrying insects. We reproduce several of the screens here. Study them, or check to see if the full Flash presentation is available on the Web site. Then discuss either in class or in a short paper how well a complex causal argument might be made in multimedia environments like the Web and for which audiences they might prove most effective.

Developing Causal Arguments

Formulating a Claim

Of course, you might decide to write a wildly exaggerated or parodic causal argument for humorous purposes. Humorist Dave Barry does precisely this when he tries to explain the causes of El Niño and other weather phenomena: "So we see that the true cause of bad weather, contrary to what they have been claiming all these years, is TV weather forecasters, who have also single-handedly destroyed the ozone layer via overuse of hair spray." Most of the causal reasoning you do, however, will take a more serious approach to subjects you, your family, and friends care about. To begin creating a strong causal claim, try listing some of the effects—events or phenomena—you'd like to know the causes of:

- *What are the biological causes of aging in animals and humans?*
- *What's really responsible for the latest tuition hike?*
- *What has led to warnings of "contamination" along your favorite creek?*
- *Why has the divorce rate leveled off in recent decades?*
- *Why do so few Americans vote, even in major elections?*

For more than a century, mysterious lights have been observed in the night skies near the small west Texas town of Marfa. Numerous *causes* have been advanced, from Indian campfires to swamp gas, some more probable than others. Such unexplained phenomena often have the *effect* of attracting tourists.

Or try moving in the opposite direction, listing some phenomena or causes you're interested in and then hypothesizing what kinds of effects they may produce:

- *What will happen if your campus institutes (or abolishes) an honor code?*
- *What will be the effects of a total crackdown on peer-to-peer file sharing?*
- *What will happen if more conservative (or liberal) judges are appointed to the Supreme Court?*
- *What will happen when China and India become thriving first-world nations?*

Read a little about the causal issues that interest you most, and then try them out on friends and colleagues. Can they suggest ways to refocus or clarify what you want to do? Can they offer leads to finding information about your subject? If you've already asserted some cause-and-effect relationships, can they offer counterexamples or refutations? Finally, map out a rough statement about the causal relationship you want to explore:

A might cause (or might be caused by) B for the following reasons:

1.

2.

3.

Such a statement should be tentative because writing a causal argument will often be a research exercise in which you uncover the facts, not assume them to be true. Often, your early assumptions (*Tuition was raised to renovate the stadium*) might be undermined by the facts you later discover (*Tuition doesn't fund the construction or maintenance of campus buildings*).

Developing the Argument

Once you've drafted a claim, you can explore the cause-effect relationship(s), drawing out the reasons, warrants, and evidence that can support the claim most effectively:

Claim	Losing seasons caused the football coach to lose his job.
Reason	The team lost more than half its games for three seasons in a row.
Warrant	Winning is the key to success for major-team college coaches.
Evidence	For the last ten years, coaches with more than two losing seasons in a row have lost their jobs.

Claim	Certain career patterns cause women to be paid less than men.
Reason	Women's career patterns differ from men's, and in spite of changes in the relative pay of other groups, women's pay still lags behind that of men.
Warrant	Successful careers are made during the period between ages twenty-five and thirty-five.
Evidence	Women often drop out of or reduce work during the decade between ages twenty-five and thirty-five in order to raise families.

In further developing a causal argument, you can draw on many strategies we've already touched on. In the article the following passage is excerpted from, for instance, Stephen King uses dozens of examples—from *The Texas Chainsaw Massacre, The Gory Ones,* and *Invasion of the Body Snatchers* to *Night of the Living Dead, Psycho, The Amityville Horror,* and *The Thing*—in answering a causal question: Why do people love horror movies?

The mythic horror movie, like the sick joke, has a dirty job to do. It deliberately appeals to all that is worst in us. It is morbidity unchained, our most base instincts let free, our nastiest fantasies realized . . . and it all happens, fittingly enough, in the dark. For those reasons, good liberals often shy away from horror films. For myself, I like to see the most aggressive of them—*Dawn of the Dead,* for instance—as lifting a trap door in the civilized forebrain and throwing a basket of raw meat to the hungry alligators swimming around in that subterranean river beneath.

THEY WON'T STAY DEAD!

Why bother? Because it keeps them from getting out, man. It keeps them down there and me up here. It was Lennon and McCartney who said that all you need is love, and I would agree with that.

As long as you keep the gators fed.

–Stephen King, "Why We Crave Horror Movies"

Night of the Living Dead—satisfying uncivilized cravings since 1968

Another way to support (or undermine) a causal argument is through the use of analogies. In such an argument, the strength will lie in how closely you can relate the two phenomena being compared. In exploring why women consistently earn less pay than men even when they're performing the same jobs, Sarah Banda Purvis draws an analogy between working women and sports:

> An analogy I use when describing my experiences as a female manager in corporate America is that I was allowed to sit on the bench but never given a chance to get on the field and play in the game.
>
> —Sarah Banda Purvis, "What Do Working Women Want in the 21st Century?"

She goes on to trace the effects that constantly being relegated to the "bench" has on earning power. If you find this analogy unsatisfactory, you might suggest that it falsely portrays the causal relationship of women and promotion. After all, benchwarmers are usually players who don't perform as well as those on the field. Surely Purvis doesn't want to suggest that women aren't moving up in the business world because they don't play the game as well as men.

Establishing causes for physical effects—like diseases—often calls for another means of support: testing hypotheses, or theories about possible causes. This kind of reasoning, often highly technical, helped to identify a mystery disease that, years ago, struck some fifty people in Quebec City. Puzzled by cases all involving the same effects (nausea, shortness of breath, cough, stomach pain, weight loss, and a marked blue-gray coloration), doctors at first hypothesized that the common cause was severe vitamin deficiency. But too many cases in too short a time made this explanation unlikely; after all, sudden epidemics of vitamin deficiency are rare. In addition, postmortem examinations of the twenty people who died revealed severe damage to the heart muscle and the liver, features inconsistent with the vitamin-deficiency hypothesis. So the doctors sought a clue to the mysterious disease in something the victims shared: all fifty had been beer lovers and had, in fact, drunk a particular brew.

It seemed possible that the illness was somehow connected to that brand, brewed in both Quebec City and Montreal. But Montreal had no outbreak of the disease. The hypothesis, then, was further refined: Could the brewing processes be different in the two cities? Bingo. The Quebec brewery had added a cobalt compound to its product to enhance the beer's foaminess; the Montreal brewery had not. Furthermore, the compound had been added only a month before the first victims became ill.

Yet doctors in this case were still cautious about the causal connection because the cobalt hadn't been present in sufficient quantities to kill a normal person. Yet twenty had died. After persistent scientific analysis, the doctors decided that this fact must be related to the victims' drinking habits, which in some way reduced their resistance to the chemical. For those twenty people, a normally nonlethal dose of cobalt had, unfortunately, proven fatal.

Not all the evidence in compelling causal arguments needs to be so strictly scientific. Many causal arguments rely on ethnographic observations—that is, on the systematic study of ordinary people in their daily routines. How would you explain, for example, why, when people meet head-on, some step aside and some do not? In an argument that attempts to account for such behavior, investigators Frank Willis, Joseph Gier, and David Smith observed "1,038 displacements involving 3,141 persons" at a Kansas City shopping mall. In results that surprised the investigators, "gallantry" seemed to play a significant role in causing people to step aside for one another—more so than other causes the investigators had anticipated (such as deferring to someone who's physically stronger or higher in status). Doubtless you've read of other such studies—perhaps in psychology courses.

Yet another method of supporting a causal argument is to provide evidence for significant correlations. In such an argument, you try to show that if A occurs, B is also likely to occur—for example, if students come from families with high incomes, they're also likely to do well on standardized tests. (That's a correlation that has been repeatedly established.) And as we noted in an earlier chapter, there also seems to be a positive correlation between the attractiveness of college instructors and the teaching evaluations they receive. You may be most familiar with correlations from statistical procedures that enable you to predict, within a degree of certainty, how likely it is that two elements or events will occur together. Recent advances in the human genome project, for example, have identified "clusters" of genes that, when found in correlation with one another, strongly predict the occurrence of certain cancers.

Using a correlation as evidence of causation can be an especially complex task, though. In many cases, B proves to be the cause of A rather than the other way around, or the correlation turns out to be a coincidence, or A and B are both found to be effects of some other cause, rather than one of them causing the other. For example, it was once thought that when an elderly woman falls and her leg or hip is found to be broken, the break is caused by the fall, whereas medical experts now believe that the causal relationship usually runs the other way: the snapping of bones thinned by osteoporosis causes the fall. As you might guess, arguments about correlations keep researchers busy.

Finally, you may want to consider using personal experience in support of a causal argument. Indeed, people's experiences generally lead them to seek out or to avoid various causes and effects. If you're consistently praised for your writing ability, chances are that you'll look for opportunities to produce that pleasant effect. If three times in a row you get sick after eating shrimp, you'll almost certainly identify the shellfish as the cause of your difficulties and stop eating it. Personal experience can also help build your credibility as a writer, gain the empathy of your listeners, and thus support your causal claim. Although one person's experiences cannot ordinarily be universalized, they can still argue eloquently for causal relationships. Leslie Marmon Silko uses personal experience to explain her shift from studying to become a lawyer to becoming a writer/photographer/activist, arguing that the best way to seek justice isn't through the law but through the power of stories:

> When I was a sophomore in high school I decided law school was the place to seek justice. . . . I should have paid more attention to the lesson of the Laguna Pueblo land claims lawsuit from my childhood: The lawsuit was not settled until I was in law school. The U.S. Court of Indian Claims found in favor of the Pueblo of Laguna, but the Indian Claims Court never gives back land wrongfully taken; the court only pays tribes for the land. . . . The Laguna people wanted the land they cherished; instead, they got twenty-five cents for each of the six million acres stolen by the state. The lawsuit had lasted twenty years, so the lawyers' fees amounted to nearly $2 million.
>
> I completed three semesters in the American Indian Law School Fellowship Program before I realized that injustice is built into the Anglo-American legal system. . . . But I continued in law school until our criminal law class read an appeal to the U.S. Supreme Court to stop the execution of a retarded black man convicted of strangling a white librarian in Washington, D.C., in 1949. The majority on the Court refused to stop the execution, though it was clear that the man was so retarded that he had no comprehension of his crime. That case was the breaking point for me. I wanted nothing to do with such a barbaric legal system.
>
> My time in law school was not wasted: I had gained invaluable insights into the power structure of mainstream society, and I continue

to follow developments in the law to calculate prevailing political winds. It seems to me there is no better way to uncover the deepest values of a culture than to observe the operation of that culture's system of justice.

[But] I decided the only way to seek justice was through the power of stories.

—Leslie Marmon Silko, *Yellow Woman and a Beauty of Spirit:*
Essays on Native American Life Today

All these strategies—the use of examples, analogies, testing hypotheses, experimental evidence, correlations, and personal experience—can help you support a causal argument or undermine a causal claim you regard as faulty. However, you may still have to convince readers that the reasons you offer are indeed compelling. In terms of causal arguments, that may mean distinguishing among *immediate, necessary,* and *sufficient* reasons. In the case of the mysterious illness in Quebec City, the immediate reasons for illness were the symptoms themselves: nausea, shortness of breath, and so on. But they weren't the root causes of the disease. Drinking the particular beer in question served as a necessary reason: without the tainted beer, the illness wouldn't have occurred. However, the researchers had to search much harder for the sufficient reason—the reason that will cause the effect (the illness) if it's present. In the case of the Quebec City beer, that reason turned out to be the addition of cobalt.

If Everything's an Argument . . .

Choose any one or two of the examples or figures in this chapter, and make a stab at explaining why it might have been chosen for the book—over and above the obvious fact that it illustrates a point about causal arguments. For example, do you suspect that the "Why Are We So Fat?" figure leads off the chapter mainly because it would get your attention? Wasn't there a risk that it might repel or offend you? What other considerations might have been behind the decision to use it? Did the fact that the image originally appeared in *National Geographic* make it a plausible choice for a college text? Write at least a paragraph of causal analysis on the item(s) you've selected.

Even everyday causal analysis can draw on this distinction among reasons as well. What caused you, for instance, to pursue a college education? Immediate reasons might be that you needed to prepare for a career of some kind or that you had planned to do so for years. But what are the necessary reasons, the ones without which your pursuit of higher education couldn't occur? Adequate funds? Good test scores and academic record? The expectations of your family? You might even explore possible sufficient reasons, those that—if present—will guarantee the effect of your pursuing higher education. In such a case, you may be the only person with enough information to determine what the sufficient reasons might be.

Considering Design and Visuals

Don't forget the importance of design decisions—fonts, headings, links in online arguments—when composing causal arguments. Not infrequently, you may find that the best way to illustrate a causal relation-

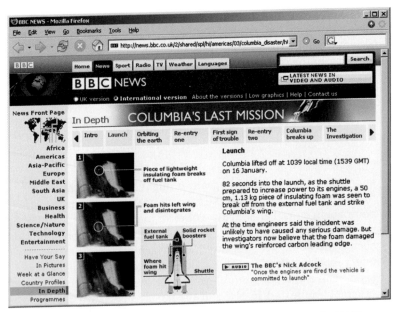

The BBC News provided this graphic to supplement its coverage of a NASA report detailing the cause of the breakup of the Space Shuttle *Columbia* in 2003. Note how the simple words and illustrations make a complex chain of events comprehensible to the general public.

Why have programs of financial aid failed to bring relief to many impoverished countries? Cartoonists Cox & Forkum offer one explanation.

ship is to present it visually. Consider the way even a simple graphic—one that combines words and images—helps readers grasp how or why something happened (see the figure on the facing page).

Or you might study the intriguing ways that editorial cartoonists embed causal relationships in some of their pieces, inviting readers to find causal connections as they interpret the images. You could write a book—and some scholars have—on the political relationships and historical circumstances summarized in the causal argument in the figure above.

Key Features of Causal Arguments

In drafting your own causal argument, you'll need to do the following:

- Thoroughly question every cause-and-effect relationship in the argument, both those you suggest yourself and others already in play.

- Show that the causes and effects you've suggested are highly probable and backed by evidence, or show what's wrong with faulty causal reasoning you may be critiquing.

- Assess any links between causal relationships (*what* leads to, or follows from, *what*).
- Show that your explanations of any causal chains are accurate, or show where links in a causal chain break down.
- Show that plausible cause-effect explanations haven't been ignored or that the possibility of multiple causes or effects has been given due consideration.

In developing a causal argument fully, you'll address many of these items, though their order may vary. You may want to open an essay dramatically by describing an effect and then "flash back" to its multiple causes. Or you might decide to open with a well-known phenomenon, identify it as a cause, and then trace its effects. Or you might begin by suggesting what plausible explanations for an event have been ignored, for one reason or another. In any case, you should sketch an organizational plan and get reactions to it from your instructor, writing center consultants, and colleagues before proceeding to a full draft. When the draft is complete, you should again look for critical readers willing to test the strength of your causal argument.

GUIDE to writing a causal argument

● Finding a Topic

Chances are that a little time spent brainstorming—either with friends or other students, or on paper—will turn up some good possibilities for causal arguments of several kinds, including those that grow out of your personal experience. *Just exactly what did lead to my much higher GPA last term?* Beyond your own personal concerns, you may find a good number of public issues that lend themselves to causal analysis and argument: *What factors have led to the near bankruptcy of the nation's major airlines? What will happen if the United States continues to refuse to sign the Kyoto Protocol aimed at reducing greenhouse gas emissions? What effects have been caused by the move to pay professional athletes astronomical sums of money?* As you're brainstorming possibilities for a causal argument of your own, don't ignore important current campus issues: *What have been the effects of recent increases in tuition* (or *What factors caused the increases)? What are the likely outcomes of shifting the academic calendar from a quarter to a semester system? If, as some argue, there has been a significant increase of racism and homophobia on campus, what has caused that increase? What are its consequences?*

Finally, remember that it's fair game to question existing assumptions about causality for being inaccurate or not probing deeply enough into the reasons for a phenomenon. You can raise doubts about the facts or assumptions that others have made and, perhaps, offer a better causal connection. For example, some writers have argued that violent video games will lead the teenagers obsessed with them into antisocial behavior. Others, however, have challenged that causal argument, pointing out that juvenile delinquency is, in fact, declining. Why? Maybe teens are too busy playing Resident Evil 4.

● Researching Your Topic

Causal arguments will lead you to many different resources:

- current news media—especially magazines and newspapers (online or in print)
- online databases
- scholarly journals

- books written on your subject (here you can do a keyword search, either in your library or online)
- blogs, Web sites, listservs, or newsgroups devoted to your subject

In addition, why not carry out some field research of your own? Conduct interviews with appropriate authorities on your subject, or create a questionnaire aimed at establishing a range of opinion on your subject. The information you get from interviews or from analyzing responses to a questionnaire can provide evidence to back up your claim(s).

● Formulating a Claim

First, identify the kind of causal argument you expect to make—one moving from cause(s) to effect(s); one moving from effect(s) to cause(s); or one involving a series of links, with Cause A leading to B, which then leads to C. (See pp. 288–291 for a review of these kinds of arguments.) Or it may be that you'll be debunking an existing cause-effect claim.

Your next move may be to explore your own relationship to your subject. What do you know about the subject and its causes and effects? Why do you favor (or disagree with) the claim? What significant reasons can you offer in support of your position? In short, you should end this process of exploration by formulating a brief claim or thesis about a particular causal relationship. It should include *a statement that says, in effect, A causes (or does not cause, or is caused by) B, and a summary of the reasons supporting this causal relationship.* Remember to make sure that your thesis is as specific as possible and that it's sufficiently controversial or interesting to hold your readers' interest. Recognize, too, than any such claim is tentative—subject to change as your project develops and you learn more about your subject.

● Examples of Causal Claims

- Right-to-carry gun laws are, in part, responsible for decreased rates of violent crimes in states that have approved such legislation.
- Newer Web-based techniques for campaign fund-raising will ultimately weaken the power of the national political parties and increase the clout of small, special interest groups.
- The proliferation of images in film, television, and computer-generated texts is changing literacy.
- The many extensions to the copyright terms have led to a serious imbalance between the necessary incentive to creators and the right of the

public to information, thereby closing off the public commons; doing away, in effect, with the fair use doctrine; and adding billions of dollars to the coffers of Disney and other huge entertainment conglomerates.

- Removing pluses and minuses from our school's grading system will have no effect on student grade point averages or grade inflation.

● Preparing a Proposal

If your instructor asks you to prepare a proposal for your project, here's a format that may help:

State the thesis of your argument completely. If you're having trouble doing so, try outlining it in Toulmin terms:

Claim:

Reason(s):

Warrant(s):

- Explain why this argument deserves attention. Why is it important for your readers to consider?
- Specify whom you hope to reach through your argument and why this group of readers is an appropriate audience. What interest or investment do they have in the issue? Why will they (or should they) be concerned?
- Briefly identify and explore the major challenges you expect to face in supporting your argument. Will demonstrating a clear causal link between A and B be particularly difficult? Will the data you need to support the claim be hard to obtain?
- List the strategies you expect to use in researching your argument. Will you be interviewing? Surveying opinion? Conducting library and online searches? Other?
- Briefly identify and explore the major counterarguments you might expect in response to your argument.
- Consider what format, genre, or media will work best for your argument. Will you be preparing a Web site? A press release? An editorial for the local newspaper? A report for an organization you belong to?

● Thinking about Organization

Whatever genre or format you decide to use, your causal argument should address the following elements:

- a specific causal claim somewhere in the paper: *Devastating flash floods associated with El Niño were responsible for the dramatic loss of homes in central California in early 2003.*

- an explanation of the claim's significance or importance: *Claims for damage from flooding put some big insurance companies out of business; as a result, homeowners couldn't get coverage and many who lost their homes had to declare bankruptcy.*

- supporting evidence sufficient to support each cause or effect—or, in an argument based on a series of causal links, evidence to support the relationships among the links: *The amount of rain that fell in central California in early 2003 was 50 percent above normal, leading inexorably to rapidly rising rivers and creeks.*

- consideration of alternative causes and effects, and evidence that you understand these alternatives and have thought carefully about them before rejecting them: *Although some say that excessive and sloppy logging and poor building codes were responsible for the loss of homes, the evidence supporting these alternative causes is not convincing.*

● Getting and Giving Response

All arguments can benefit from the scrutiny of others. Your instructor may assign you to a peer group for the purpose of reading and responding to each other's drafts; if not, get some response on your own from some serious readers or consultants at a writing center. You can use the following questions to evaluate a draft. If you're evaluating someone else's draft, be sure to illustrate your points with examples. Specific comments are always more helpful than general observations.

The Claim

- What's most effective about the claim? What are its strengths?

- Is the claim sufficiently qualified?

- Is the claim specific enough to be clear? How could it be narrowed and focused?

- How strong is the relationship between the claim and the reasons given to support it? How could that relationship be made more explicit?

- Is it immediately evident why the claim is important? How could it be rephrased in a way that more forcefully and clearly suggests its significance?

- Does the claim reveal a causal connection? How could it be revised to make the causal links clearer?

Evidence for the Claim

- What's the strongest evidence offered for the claim? What, if any, evidence needs to be strengthened?

- Is enough evidence offered that these particular causes are responsible for the effect that has been identified, that these particular effects result from the identified cause, or that a series of causes and effects are linked? If not, what kind of additional evidence is needed? What kinds of sources might provide this evidence?

- How credible and persuasive will the sources likely be to potential readers? What other kinds of sources might be more credible and persuasive?

- Is the evidence in support of the claim simply announced, or are its appropriateness and significance analyzed? Is a more detailed discussion needed?

- Have all the major alternative causes and effects as well as objections to the claim been considered? What support is offered for rejecting these alternatives? Where is additional support needed?

Organization and Style

- How are the parts of the argument organized? Is this organization effective, or would some other structure work better?

- Will readers understand the relationships among the claims, supporting reasons, warrants, and evidence? If not, what could be done to make those connections clearer? Are more transitional words and phrases needed? Would headings or graphic devices (diagrams, flowcharts, illustrations) help?

- Are the transitions or links from point to point, paragraph to paragraph, and sentence to sentence clear and effective? If not, how could they be improved?

- Is the style suited to the subject? Is it too formal? Too casual? Too technical? Too bland? Too geeky? How can it be improved?

- Which sentences seem particularly effective? Which ones seem weakest, and how could they be improved? Should some short sentences be combined, or should any long ones be separated into two or more sentences?

- How effective are the paragraphs? Do any seem too skimpy or too long? How can they be improved?

- Which words or phrases seem particularly effective, vivid, and memorable? Do any seem dull, unclear, or inappropriate for the audience or the writer's purpose? Are definitions provided for technical or other terms that readers might not know?

Spelling, Punctuation, Mechanics, Documentation, Format

- Are there any errors in spelling, punctuation, capitalization, and the like?

- Is an appropriate and consistent style of documentation used for parenthetical citations and the list of works cited or references? (See Chapter 20.)

- Does the paper or project follow an appropriate format? Is it appropriately designed and attractively presented? How could it be improved? If it's a Web site, do all the links work?

RESPOND •

1. The causes of some of the following events and phenomena are quite well known and frequently discussed. But do you understand them well enough yourself to spell out the causes to someone else? Working in a group, see how well (and in how much detail) you can explain each of the following events or phenomena. Which explanations are relatively clear-cut, and which seem more open to debate?

   tornadoes

   the Burning Man festival

   the collapse of communism in Eastern Europe in 1989

   earthquakes

   the common cold

   the popularity of the *Harry Potter* films

   the itching caused by a mosquito bite

   the economic recovery of 2004–2005

   a skid in your car on a slippery road

   the destruction of the Space Shuttle *Columbia*

   the rise in cases of autism

2. One of the fallacies of argument discussed in Chapter 17 is the *post hoc, ergo propter hoc* fallacy: "after this, therefore because of this." Causal arguments are particularly prone to this kind of fallacious reasoning, in which a writer asserts a causal relationship between two entirely unconnected events. After Elvis Presley's death, for instance, oil prices in the United States rose precipitously—but it would be a real stretch to argue that the King's passing caused gas prices to skyrocket.

   Because causal arguments can easily fall prey to this fallacy, you might find it useful to try your hand at creating and defending an absurd connection of this kind. Begin by asserting a causal link between two events or phenomena that likely have no relationship: *The enormous popularity of the iPod is partially due to global warming.* Then spend a page or so spinning out an imaginative argument to defend the claim: *A generation terrified by the prospects of drastic weather change try to drown out their fears in earsplitting music.* . . . It's OK to have fun with this exercise, but see how convincing you can be at generating plausible arguments.

3. Working with a group, write a big "Why?" on a sheet of paper or computer screen, and then generate a list of *why* questions. Don't be too critical of the initial list:

   Why?
   — *do people grow old?*
   — *do dogs and cats live such short lives?*
   — *do college students binge drink?*
   — *do teenage boys drive so fast?*
   — *do people cry?*

   Generate as long a list as you can in fifteen minutes or so. Then decide which of the questions might make plausible starting points for intriguing causal arguments.

4. Here's a schematic causal analysis of one event, exploring the difference among immediate, necessary, and sufficient causes. Critique and revise the analysis as you see fit. Then create another of your own, beginning with a different event, phenomenon, incident, fad, or effect.

   Event: Traffic fatality at an intersection

   Immediate Cause: SUV runs a red light and totals a Miata, killing its driver

   Necessary Cause: Two drivers navigating Friday rush-hour traffic (if no driving, then no accident)

   Sufficient Cause: SUV driver distracted by a cell phone conversation

What Makes a Serial Killer?

LA DONNA BEATY

Jeffrey Dahmer, John Wayne Gacy, Mark Allen Smith, Richard Chase, Ted Bundy—the list goes on and on. These five men alone have been responsible for at least ninety deaths, and many suspect that their victims may total twice that number. They are serial killers, the most feared and hated of criminals. What deep, hidden secret makes them lust for blood? What can possibly motivate a person to kill over and over again with no guilt, no remorse, no hint of human compassion? What makes a serial killer?

Serial killings are not a new phenomenon. In 1798, for example, Micajah and Wiley Harpe traveled the back-woods of Kentucky and Tennessee in a violent, year-long killing spree that left at least twenty—and possibly as many as thirty-eight—men, women, and children dead. Their crimes were especially chilling as they seemed particularly to enjoy grabbing small children by the ankles and smashing their heads against trees (Holmes and DeBurger 28). In modern society, however, serial killings have grown to near epidemic proportions. Ann Rule, a respected author and expert on serial murders, stated in a seminar at the University of Louisville on serial murder that between 3,500 and 5,000 people become victims of serial murder each year in the United States alone (qtd. in Holmes and DeBurger 21). Many others estimate that there are close to 350 serial killers currently at large in our society (Holmes and DeBurger 22).

The cause-effect relationship is raised in a question: What (the causes) makes a serial killer (the effect)?

An important term *(serial killer)* is defined through examples.

Authority is cited to emphasize the importance of the causal question.

La Donna Beaty wrote this essay while she was a student at Sinclair Community College in Dayton, Ohio. In the essay, she explores the complex web of possible causes—cultural, psychological, genetic, and others—that may help to produce a serial killer. The essay follows MLA style.

Fascination with murder and murderers is not new, but researchers in recent years have made great strides in determining the characteristics of criminals. Looking back, we can see how naive early experts were in their evaluations: in 1911, for example, Italian criminologist Cesare Lombrosco concluded that "murderers as a group [are] biologically degenerate [with] bloodshot eyes, aquiline noses, curly black hair, strong jaws, big ears, thin lips, and menacing grins" (qtd. in Lunde 84). Today, however, we don't expect killers to have fangs that drip human blood, and many realize that the boy-next-door may be doing more than woodworking in his basement. While there are no specific physical characteristics shared by all serial killers, they are almost always male and 92 percent are white. Most are between the ages of twenty-five and thirty-five and often physically attractive. While they may hold a job, many switch employment frequently as they become easily frustrated when advancement does not come as quickly as expected. They tend to believe that they are entitled to whatever they desire but feel that they should have to exert no effort to attain their goals (Samenow 88, 96). What could possibly turn attractive, ambitious human beings into cold-blooded monsters?

One popular theory suggests that many murderers are the product of our violent society. Our culture tends to approve of violence and find it acceptable, even preferable, in many circumstances (Holmes and DeBurger 27). According to research done in 1970, one out of every four men and one out of every six women believed that it was appropriate for a husband to hit his wife under certain conditions (Holmes and DeBurger 33). This emphasis on violence is especially prevalent in television programs. Violence occurs in 80 percent of all prime-time shows, while cartoons, presumably made for children, average eighteen violent acts per hour. It is estimated that by the age of eighteen, the average child will have viewed more than 16,000 television murders (Holmes and

[margin note] Evidence about general characteristics of serial killers is presented.

[margin note] One possible cause is explored: violence in society.

[margin note] Evidence, including statistics and authority, is offered to support the first cause.

DeBurger 34). Some experts feel that children demonstrate increasingly aggressive behavior with each violent act they view (Lunde 15) and become so accustomed to violence that these acts seem normal (35). In fact, most serial killers do begin to show patterns of aggressive behavior at a young age. It is, therefore, possible that after viewing increasing amounts of violence, such children determine that this is acceptable behavior; when they are then punished for similar actions, they may become confused and angry and eventually lash out by committing horrible, violent acts.

Another theory concentrates on the family atmosphere into which the serial killer is born. Most killers state that they experienced psychological abuse as children and never established good relationships with the male figures in their lives (Ressler, Burgess, and Douglas 19). As children, they were often rejected by their parents and received little nurturing (Lunde 94; Holmes and DeBurger 64–70). It has also been established that the families of serial killers often move repeatedly, never allowing the child to feel a sense of stability; in many cases, they are also forced to live outside the family home before reaching the age of eighteen (Ressler, Burgess, and Douglas 19–20). Our culture's tolerance for violence may overlap with such family dynamics: with 79 percent of the population believing that slapping a twelve-year-old is either necessary, normal, or good, it is no wonder that serial killers relate tales of physical abuse (Holmes and DeBurger 30; Ressler, Burgess, and Douglas 19–20) and view themselves as the "black sheep" of the family. They may even, perhaps unconsciously, assume this same role in society.

While the foregoing analysis portrays the serial killer as a lost, lonely, abused, little child, another theory, based on the same information, gives an entirely different view. In this analysis, the killer is indeed rejected by his family but only after being repeatedly defiant, sneaky, and threatening. As verbal lies and destructiveness

A second possible cause is introduced: family context.

Evidence is offered in support of the second cause.

An alternative analysis of the evidence in support of the second cause is explored.

increase, the parents give the child the distance he seems to want in order to maintain a small amount of domestic peace (Samenow 13). This interpretation suggests that the killer shapes his parents much more than his parents shape him. It also denies that the media can influence a child's mind and turn him into something that he doesn't already long to be. Since most children view similar amounts of violence, the argument goes, a responsible child filters what he sees and will not resort to criminal activity no matter how acceptable it seems to be (Samenow 15–18). In 1930, the noted psychologist Alfred Adler seemed to find this true of any criminal. As he put it, "With criminals it is different: they have a private logic, a private intelligence. They are suffering from a wrong outlook upon the world, a wrong estimate of their own importance and the importance of other people" (qtd. in Samenow 20).

A third possible cause is introduced: mental instability.

Most people agree that Jeffrey Dahmer or Ted Bundy had to be "crazy" to commit horrendous multiple murders, and scientists have long maintained that serial killers are indeed mentally disturbed (Lunde 48). While the percentage of murders committed by mental hospital patients is much lower than that among the general population (35), it cannot be ignored that the rise in serial killings happened at almost the same time as the deinstitutionalization movement in the mental health care system during the 1960s (Markman and Bosco 266).

Evidence in support of the third cause, including a series of examples, is offered.

While reform was greatly needed in the mental health care system, it has now become nearly impossible to hospitalize those with severe problems. In the United States, people have a constitutional right to remain mentally ill. Involuntary commitment can only be accomplished if the person is deemed dangerous to self, dangerous to others, or gravely disabled. However, in the words of Ronald Markman, "According to the way that the law is interpreted, if you can go to the mailbox to pick up your Social Security check, you're not gravely disabled even if you think you're living on Mars"; even if a patient is thought to be dangerous, he or she cannot be held longer than ninety days unless it can be proved that the patient actually committed dangerous acts while in the hospital (Markman and Bosco 267). Many of the most heinous criminals have had long histories of mental illness but could not be hospitalized due to these stringent requirements. Richard Chase, the notorious Vampire of Sacramento, believed that he needed blood in order to survive, and while in the care of a psychiatric hospital, he often killed birds and other small animals in order to quench this desire. When he was released, he went on to kill eight people, one of them an eighteen-month-old baby (Biondi and Hecox 206). Edmund Kemper was equally insane. At the age of fifteen, he killed both of his grandparents and spent five years in a psychiatric facility. Doctors determined that he was "cured" and released him into an unsuspecting society. He killed eight women, including his own mother (Lunde 53–56). In another case, the world was soon to be disturbed by a cataclysmic earthquake, and Herbert Mullin knew that he had been appointed by God to prevent the catastrophe. The fervor of his religious delusion resulted in a death toll of thirteen (Lunde 63–81). All of these men had been treated for their mental disorders, and all were released by doctors who did not have enough proof to hold them against their will.

Recently, studies have given increasing consideration to the genetic makeup of serial killers. The connection between biology and behavior is strengthened by research in which scientists have been able to develop a violently aggressive strain of mice simply through selective inbreeding (Taylor 23). These studies have caused scientists to become increasingly interested in the limbic system of the brain, which houses the amygdala, an almond-shaped structure located in the front of the temporal lobe. It has long been known that surgically altering that portion of the brain, in an operation known as a lobotomy, is one way of controlling behavior. This

A fourth possible cause is introduced: genetic makeup.

surgery was used frequently in the 1960s but has since been discontinued as it also erases most of a person's personality. More recent developments, however, have shown that temporal lobe epilepsy causes electrical impulses to be discharged directly into the amygdala. When this electronic stimulation is re-created in the laboratory, it causes violent behavior in lab animals. Additionally, other forms of epilepsy do not cause abnormalities in behavior, except during seizure activity. Temporal lobe epilepsy is linked with a wide range of antisocial behavior, including anger, paranoia, and aggression. It is also interesting to note that this form of epilepsy produces extremely unusual brain waves. These waves have been found in only 10 to 15 percent of the general population, but over 79 percent of known serial killers test positive for these waves (Taylor 28–33).

Statistical evidence in support of the fourth cause is offered.

The look at biological factors that control human behavior is by no means limited to brain waves or other brain abnormalities. Much work is also being done with neurotransmitters, levels of testosterone, and patterns of trace minerals. While none of these studies is conclusive, they all show a high correlation between antisocial behavior and chemical interactions within the body (Taylor 63–69).

A fifth possible cause—heavy use of alcohol—is introduced and immediately qualified.

One of the most common traits that all researchers have noted among serial killers is heavy use of alcohol. Whether this correlation is brought about by external factors or whether alcohol is an actual stimulus that causes certain behavior is still unclear, but the idea deserves consideration. Lunde found that the majority of those who commit murder had been drinking beforehand and commonly had a urine alcohol level of between .20 and .29, nearly twice the legal level of intoxication (31–32). Additionally, 70 percent of the families that reared serial killers had verifiable records of alcohol abuse (Ressler, Burgess, and Douglas 17). Jeffrey

Dahmer had been arrested in 1981 on charges of drunkenness and, before his release from prison on sexual assault charges, his father had written a heartbreaking letter which pleaded that Jeffrey be forced to undergo treatment for alcoholism, a plea that, if heeded, might have changed the course of future events (Davis 70, 103). Whether alcoholism is a learned behavior or an inherited predisposition is still hotly debated, but a 1979 report issued by Harvard Medical School stated that "[a]lcoholism in the biological parent appears to be a more reliable predictor of alcoholism in the children than any other environmental factor examined" (qtd. in Taylor 117). While alcohol was once thought to alleviate anxiety and depression, we now know that it can aggravate and intensify such moods (Taylor 110), which may lead to irrational feelings of powerlessness that are brought under control only when the killer proves he has the ultimate power to control life and death.

The complexity of causal relationships is emphasized: one cannot say with certainty what produces a particular serial killer.

"Man's inhumanity to man" began when Cain killed Abel, but this legacy has grown to frightening proportions, as evidenced by the vast number of books that line the shelves of modern bookstores—row after row of titles dealing with death, anger, and blood. We may never know what causes a serial killer to exact his revenge on an unsuspecting society. But we need to continue to probe the interior of the human brain to discover the delicate balance of chemicals that controls behavior. We need to be able to fix what goes wrong. We must also work harder to protect our children. Their cries must not go unheard. Their pain must not become so intense that it demands bloody revenge. As today becomes tomorrow, we must remember the words of Ted Bundy, one of the most ruthless serial killers of our time: "Most serial killers are people who kill for the pure pleasure of killing and cannot be rehabilitated. Some of the killers themselves would even say so" (qtd. in Holmes and DeBurger 150).

The conclusion looks toward the future: the web of causes examined here suggests that much more work needs to be done to understand, predict, and ultimately control the behavior of potential serial killers.

WORKS CITED

Biondi, Ray, and Walt Hecox. <u>The Dracula Killer</u>. New York: Simon, 1992.

Davis, Ron. <u>The Milwaukee Murders</u>. New York: St. Martin's, 1991.

Holmes, Ronald M., and James DeBurger. <u>Serial Murder</u>. Newbury Park, CA: Sage, 1988.

Lunde, Donald T. <u>Murder and Madness</u>. San Francisco: San Francisco Book, 1976.

Markman, Ronald, and Dominick Bosco. <u>Alone with the Devil</u>. New York: Doubleday, 1989.

Ressler, Robert K., Ann W. Burgess, and John E. Douglas. <u>Sexual Homicide—Patterns and Motives</u>. Lexington, MA: Heath, 1988.

Samenow, Stanton E. <u>Inside the Criminal Mind</u>. New York: Times, 1984.

Taylor, Lawrence. <u>Born to Crime</u>. Westport, CT: Greenwood, 1984.

Why Literature Matters

DANA GIOIA

April 10, 2005

In 1780, Massachusetts patriot John Adams wrote to his wife, Abigail, outlining his vision of how American culture might evolve. "I must study politics and war," he prophesied, so "that our sons may have liberty to study mathematics and philosophy." They will add to their studies geography, navigation, commerce, and agriculture, he continued, so that their children may enjoy the "right to study painting, poetry, music."

Adams's bold prophecy proved correct. By the mid 20th century, America boasted internationally preeminent traditions in literature, art, music, dance, theater, and cinema.

But a strange thing has happened in the American arts during the past quarter century. While income rose to unforeseen levels, college attendance ballooned, and access to information increased enormously, the interest young Americans showed in the arts—and especially literature—actually diminished.

According to the 2002 Survey of Public Participation in the Arts, a population study designed and commissioned by the National Endowment for the Arts (and executed by the US Bureau of the Census), arts participation by Americans has declined for eight of the nine major forms that are measured. (Only jazz has shown a tiny increase—thank you, Ken Burns.) The declines have been most severe among younger adults (ages 18–24). The most worrisome finding in the 2002 study, however, is the declining percentage of Americans, especially young adults, reading literature.

That individuals at a time of crucial intellectual and emotional development bypass the joys and challenges of literature is a troubling trend. If it were true that they substituted histories, biographies, or political works for literature, one might not worry. But book reading of any kind is falling as well.

That such a longstanding and fundamental cultural activity should slip so swiftly, especially among young adults, signifies deep transformation in

---

Dana Gioia, a poet and businessman, is chair of the National Endowment for the Arts.

contemporary life. To call attention to the trend, the Arts Endowment issued the reading portion of the Survey as a separate report, "Reading at Risk: A Survey of Literary Reading in America."

The decline in reading has consequences that go beyond literature. The significance of reading has become a persistent theme in the business world. The February issue of *Wired* magazine, for example, sketches a new set of mental skills and habits proper to the 21st century, aptitudes decidedly literary in character: not "linear, logical, analytical talents," author Daniel Pink states, but "the ability to create artistic and emotional beauty, to detect patterns and opportunities, to craft a satisfying narrative." When asked what kind of talents they like to see in management positions, business leaders consistently set imagination, creativity, and higher-order thinking at the top.

Ironically, the value of reading and the intellectual faculties that it inculcates appear most clearly as active and engaged literacy declines. There is now a growing awareness of the consequences of nonreading to the workplace. In 2001 the National Association of Manufacturers polled its members on skill deficiencies among employees. Among hourly workers, poor reading skills ranked second, and 38 percent of employers complained that local schools inadequately taught reading comprehension.

Corporate America makes similar complaints about a skill intimately related to reading—writing. Last year, the College Board reported that corporations spend some $3.1 billion a year on remedial writing instruction for employees, adding that they "express a fair degree of dissatisfaction with the writing of recent college graduates." If the 21st-century American economy requires innovation and creativity, solid reading skills and the imaginative growth fostered by literary reading are central elements in that program.

The decline of reading is also taking its toll in the civic sphere. In a 2000 survey of college seniors from the top 55 colleges, the Roper Organization found that 81 percent could not earn a grade of C on a high school–level history test. A 2003 study of 15- to 26-year-olds' civic knowledge by the National Conference of State Legislatures concluded, "Young people do not understand the ideals of citizenship . . . and their appreciation and support of American democracy is limited."

It is probably no surprise that declining rates of literary reading coincide with declining levels of historical and political awareness among young people. One of the surprising findings of "Reading at Risk" was that literary readers are markedly more civically engaged than nonreaders, scoring two to four times more likely to perform charity work, visit a museum, or attend a sporting event. One reason for their higher social and cultural interactions may lie in the kind of civic and historical knowledge that comes with literary reading.

Unlike the passive activities of watching television and DVDs or surfing the Web, reading is actually a highly active enterprise. Reading requires sustained and focused attention as well as active use of memory and imagination. Literary reading also enhances and enlarges our humility by helping us imagine and understand lives quite different from our own.

Indeed, we sometimes underestimate how large a role literature has played in the evolution of our national identity, especially in that literature often has served to introduce young people to events from the past and principles of civil society and governance. Just as more ancient Greeks learned about moral and political conduct from the epics of Homer than from the dialogues of Plato, so the most important work in the abolitionist movement was the novel "Uncle Tom's Cabin."

Likewise our notions of American populism come more from Walt Whitman's poetic vision than from any political tracts. Today when people recall the Depression, the images that most come to mind are of the travails of John Steinbeck's Joad family from "The Grapes of Wrath." Without a literary inheritance, the historical past is impoverished.

In focusing on the social advantages of a literary education, however, we should not overlook the personal impact. Every day authors receive letters from readers that say, "Your book changed my life." History reveals case after case of famous people whose lives were transformed by literature. When the great Victorian thinker John Stuart Mill suffered a crippling depression in late-adolescence, the poetry of Wordsworth restored his optimism and self-confidence — a "medicine for my state of mind," he called it.

A few decades later, W.E.B. DuBois found a different tonic in literature, an escape from the indignities of Jim Crow into a world of equality. "I sit with Shakespeare and he winces not," DuBois observed. "Across the color line I move arm in arm with Balzac and Dumas, where smiling men and welcoming women glide in gilded halls." Literature is a catalyst for education and culture.

The evidence of literature's importance to civic, personal, and economic health is too strong to ignore. The decline of literary reading foreshadows serious long-term social and economic problems, and it is time to bring literature and the other arts into discussions of public policy. Libraries, schools, and public agencies do noble work, but addressing the reading issue will require the leadership of politicians and the business community as well.

Literature now competes with an enormous array of electronic media. While no single activity is responsible for the decline in reading, the cumulative presence and availability of electronic alternatives increasingly have drawn Americans away from reading.

Reading is not a timeless, universal capability. Advanced literacy is a specific intellectual skill and social habit that depends on a great many educational, cultural, and economic factors. As more Americans lose this capability, our nation becomes less informed, active, and independent-minded. These are not the qualities that a free, innovative, or productive society can afford to lose.

11
Proposals

A student looking forward to a much-needed vacation emails three friends proposing that they pool their resources and rent a cottage at a nearby surfing beach since, working together, they can afford better digs closer to the surf.

The members of a club for business majors begin to talk about their common need to create informative, appealing—and easily scannable—résumés. After much talk, three members suggest that the club develop a Web site that will guide members in building such résumés and provide links to other resources.

A project team at a large architectural firm works for three months developing a proposal in response to an RFP (request for proposal) to convert a university library into a digital learning center.

Members of a youth activist organization propose to start an after-school program for neighborhood kids, using the organization's meeting place and volunteering their time as tutors and mentors.

The undergraduate student organization at a large state university asks the administration for information about how long it takes to complete a degree in each academic major. After analyzing this information, the group recommends a reduction in the number of hours needed to graduate.

● ● ●

Understanding and Categorizing Proposals

Think big and be patient. You might be amazed by what you accomplish. Executive director of the Sierra Club Foundation and renowned environmentalist David Brower (1912–2000) had long blamed himself for not standing firm against the Glen Canyon Dam project in northern Arizona—which in 1963 began holding back the waters of the Colorado River, flooding some of the most wild and beautiful canyons in the world to create a reservoir more than 100 miles long, Lake Powell. "I have worn sackcloth and ashes ever since, convinced that I could have saved the place if I had simply got off my duff," he wrote.

But he did more than penance. In a 1997 article entitled "Let the River Run through It," Brower made a blunt proposal:

> But as surely as we made a mistake years ago, we can reverse it now. We can drain Lake Powell and let the Colorado River run through the dam that created it, bringing Glen Canyon and the wonder of its side canyons back to life. We can let the river do what it needs to do downstream in the Grand Canyon itself.
>
> We don't need to tear the dam down, however much some people would like to see it go. Together the dam's two diversion tunnels can send 200,000 cubic feet of water per second downstream, twice as much as the Colorado's highest flows. Once again Grand Canyon would make its own sounds and, if you listened carefully, you would hear it sighing with relief. The dam itself would be left as a tourist attraction, like the Pyramids, with passers-by wondering how humanity ever built it, and why.
>
> –David Brower, "Let the River Run through It"

Three photos showing the Glen Canyon Dam and the landscapes it inundated—newly revealed as Lake Powell has receded during a recent prolonged drought.

Though drought in the West has shrunk Lake Powell dramatically in the past decade, the concrete arch of Glen Canyon Dam still holds fast against the Colorado River. But in that time, the logic of Brower's proposal and the notion of dam removal in general have gained remarkable traction. Hundreds of smaller dams have already been removed across rivers throughout the country in response to environmental concerns, allowing rivers to return to their natural state, restoring native landscapes, and enabling endangered species of fish to thrive once again. What once may have seemed unthinkable now seems plausible, thanks to Brower's audacious proposal and others like it—buttressed by carefully reasoned arguments showing that some dams did more harm than good, not only environmentally but economically too. Here's Brower, for example, explaining how much water is lost due to the dam and the lake it creates:

> In 1996, the Bureau [of Reclamation] found that almost a million acre-feet, or 8 percent of the river's flow, disappeared between the stations recording the reservoir's inflow and outflow. Almost 600,000 acre-feet were presumed lost to evaporation. Nobody knows for sure about the rest. The Bureau said some of the loss was a gain being stored in the banks of the reservoir but it has no idea how much of that gain it will ever get back. Some bank storage is recoverable, but all too likely the region's downward-slanting geological strata are leading some of Powell's waters into the dark unknown. It takes only one drain to empty a bathtub, and we don't know where, when, or how the Powell tub leaks.

Brower waxes poetic, too, in asking readers to imagine a better future—which is what proposals are all about:

> The sooner we begin, the sooner lost paradises will begin to recover Cathedral in the Desert, Music Temple, Hidden Passage, Dove Canyon, Little Arch, Dungeon, and a hundred others. Glen Canyon itself can probably lose its ugly white sidewalls in two or three decades. The tapestries can re-emerge, along with the desert varnish, the exiled species of plants and animals, the pictographs and other mementos of people long gone. The canyon's music will be known again, and "the sudden poetry of springs," Wallace Stegner's beautiful phrase, will be revealed again below the sculptured walls of Navajo sandstone. The phrase, "as long as the rivers shall run and the grasses grow," will regain its meaning.

Not all proposals are as dramatic as Brower's, but such arguments, whether casual or formal, are important in all of our lives. How many proposals do you make or respond to just in one day? Chances are, more than a few: Your roommate suggests you both skip breakfast in order to get in an extra hour of exercise; you and a colleague decide to collaborate on a project rather than go it alone; you call your best friend to propose checking out a new movie; you decide to approach your boss about implementing an idea you've just had. In each case, the proposal implies that some action should take place and suggests that there are sound reasons why it should.

In their simplest form, proposal arguments look something like this:

A should do B because of C.

┌──────── A ────────┐┌──────────── B ────────────┐
Our student government should endorse the Academic Bill of Rights
┌──────────────────── C ────────────────────┐
because students should not be punished in their courses for their reasonable political views.

Because proposals come at us so routinely, it's no surprise that they cover a dizzyingly wide range of possibilities, from very local and concrete practices (*A student should switch dorms immediately; A company should switch from one supplier of paper to another*) to very broad matters of policy (*The U.S. Congress should repeal the Homeland Security Act*). So it may help to think of proposal arguments as divided roughly into two kinds—those that focus on practices, and those that focus on policies.

Here are several examples:

Proposals about Practices

- The city should use brighter light bulbs in employee parking garages.
- The college should allow students to pay tuition on a month-by-month basis.
- The NCAA should implement a playoff system to determine its Division I football champion.

Proposals about Policies

- The college should adopt a policy guaranteeing a "living wage" to all campus workers.
- The state should repeal all English Only legislation.
- The Supreme Court should pay greater attention to the Tenth Amendment, which restricts the role of the federal government to powers enumerated in the Constitution.

Characterizing Proposals

Proposals have three main characteristics:

- They call for action or response, often in response to a problem.
- They focus on the future.
- They center on the audience.

Proposals always call for some kind of action. They aim at getting something done—understanding that sometimes what needs to be done is nothing. Proposals marshal evidence and arguments to persuade people to choose a course of action: *Let's build a stadium; Let's oppose the latest Supreme Court ruling; Let's create a campus organization for transfer students.* But you know the old saying, "You can lead a horse to water, but you can't make it drink." It's usually easier to *convince* audiences what a good course of action is than to *persuade* them to take it (or pay for it). You can present a proposal as cogently as possible—but most of the time you can't *make* any audience take the action you propose.

Thus proposal arguments must appeal to more than good sense—as David Brower does. Imagination and a little poetry might sometimes carry the day. Ethos matters too. It helps if a writer carries a certain *gravitas*—as Brower did as one of the grand old men of the environmental movement. (He was in his mid-eighties when he made his appeal to drain Lake Powell.) If your word, experience, and judgment are all credible, an audience is more likely to carry out the action you propose.

In addition, proposal arguments focus on the future: what people, institutions, or governments should do over the upcoming weeks, months, or even decades. This orientation toward the future presents special challenges, since few of us have crystal balls. Proposal arguments must therefore offer the best evidence available to suggest that actions we recommend will achieve what they promise.

Finally, proposals have to focus on particular audiences, especially on people who can get something done. Sometimes, proposal arguments are written to general audiences. You can find these arguments, for example, in newspaper editorials and letters to the editor. And such appeals to a broad group make sense when a proposal—say, to finance new toll roads or build an art museum—must surf on waves of community support and financing. But even such grand proposals also need to influence individuals with the power to make change actually happen,

THERE'S NOT ENOUGH ART IN OUR SCHOOLS.

NO WONDER PEOPLE THINK

CARAVAGGIO

IS A GUY ON THE SOPRANOS.

ART. ASK FOR MORE.

This advertisement by Americans for the Arts makes a clear proposal that targets parents or concerned citizens.

such as financiers, developers, public officials, and legislators. On your own campus, for example, a plan to alter admissions policies might be directed both to students in general and (perhaps in a different form) to the university president, members of the faculty council, and admissions officers. Identifying who all your potential audiences might be is critical to the success of any proposal.

For example, in 2005, many citizens were angered by a Supreme Court decision allowing communities to use the power of eminent domain to seize private property for projects that contributed not, as had been traditional, to the public good (such as roads or schools) but to private economic development (such as hotels and commercial ventures). To send a clear oppositional message, Logan Darrow Clements, a political figure in California, proposed that investors support the development of the "Lost Liberty Hotel" on the 4.8 acres of land in Weare, New Hampshire, that Justice David Souter calls home. Justice Souter is one of the judges who supported this broadening of government authority over personal property. Clements claimed (in a press release) that "This is not a prank. . . . The Towne of Weare has five people on the Board of Selectmen. If three of them vote to use the power of eminent domain to take this land from Mr. Souter we can begin our hotel development." Clements clearly had two audiences in mind: the general public aroused by the expanded scope of eminent domain, as well as the members of Weare's Board of Selectmen. It's unlikely that Souter will ever lose his property, but this proposal argument suggests that he could.

An alternative to open season?

An effective proposal also has to be compatible with the values of the audience. Some ideas may make good sense but cannot be enacted. For example, many American towns and cities have a problem with expanding deer populations. Without natural predators, the animals are moving closer to human homes, dining on gardens and shrubbery, and endangering traffic. Yet one obvious and entirely feasible solution to the problem—culling the herds through hunting or shooting—is usually not acceptable to the communities most plagued by the problem. Too many people still remember *Bambi*.

Developing Proposals

How do you develop an effective proposal? Start by showing that there's a problem that needs a solution or that there's some need that's not being met. Then make a proposal that addresses the problem or meets the need. Explain in detail why adopting your proposal will address the need or problem better than other solutions; finally, show that the proposal is both feasible and acceptable. Sounds easy, but you'll discover that writing a proposal argument can be a process of discovery: at the outset, you think you know exactly what ought to be done; by the end, you may see (and even recommend) other options.

Defining a Need or Problem

You typically make a proposal to solve a problem or prevent one. Thus establishing that a need or problem exists is job one for the writer of a proposal argument.

You'll typically describe the problem you intend to address at the beginning of your project—as a way of leading up to a specific claim. But in some cases you could put the need or problem right *after* your claim as the major reason for adopting the proposal: *Let's ban cell phones on campus now. Why? Because we've become a school of walking zombies. No one speaks or even acknowledges the people they meet or pass on campus. Half of our students are too busy chattering to people they can't see to participate in the community around them.*

Regardless of the practical choices about organization, the task of establishing a need or problem calls on you to:

- paint a picture of the need or problem in concrete and memorable ways
- show how the need or problem affects the audience for the argument as well as the larger society
- explain why the need or problem is significant
- explain why other attempts to address the issue may have failed

In proposing that a state board of higher education require community service from students enrolled in state colleges, for example, you might begin by painting a picture of a self-absorbed "me first and only" society that values instant gratification. After evoking such a dismal scene, you might trace the consequences of such behavior for your campus and community, arguing, for instance, that it fosters hyper-competition, leaves many of society's most vulnerable members without helping hands, and puts the responsibility of assisting people solely in the hands of government—thereby adding to its size and cost, raising taxes for all. You might have to cite some authorities and statistics to prove that the problem you're diagnosing is real and that it touches everyone likely to read your argument. Once you do, readers will be ready to hear your proposal.

Look at how Craig R. Dean, a lawyer and executive director of the Equal Marriage Rights Fund, prepares his claim—that the United States should legalize same sex marriage—by explaining the significant problems that the existing ban on gay marriages creates:

> In November 1990, my lover, Patrick Gill, and I were denied a marriage license because we are gay. In a memorandum explaining the District's decision, the clerk of the court wrote that "the sections of the District of Columbia code governing marriage do not authorize marriage between persons of the same sex." By refusing to give us the same legal recognition that is given to heterosexual couples, the District has degraded our relationship as well as that of every other gay and lesbian couple.
>
> At one time, interracial couples were not allowed to marry. Gays and lesbians are still denied this basic civil right in the U.S.—and around the world. Can you imagine the outcry if any other minority group was denied the right to legally marry today? Marriage is more than a piece of paper. It gives societal recognition and legal protection to a relationship. It confers numerous benefits to spouses; in the District alone, there are more than 100 automatic marriage-based rights. In every state in the nation, married couples have the right to be on each other's health, disability, life insurance and pension plans. Married couples receive special tax exemptions, deductions and refunds. Spouses may automatically inherit property and have rights of survivorship that avoid inheritance tax. Though unmarried couples—both gay and heterosexual—are entitled to some of these rights, they are by no means guaranteed.
>
> For married couples, the spouse is legally the next of kin in case of death, medical emergency or mental incapacity. In stark contrast, the family is generally the next of kin for same-sex couples. In the shadow of AIDS, the denial of marriage rights can be even more ominous....

Some argue that gay marriage is too radical for society. We disagree. According to a 1989 study by the American Bar Association, eight to 10 million children are currently being reared in three million gay households. Therefore, approximately 6 percent of the U.S. population is made up of gay and lesbian families with children. Why should these families be denied the protection granted to other families? Allowing gay marriage would strengthen society by increasing tolerance. It is paradoxical that mainstream America perceives gays and lesbians as unable to maintain long-term relationships while at the same time denying them the very institutions that stabilize such relationships.

–Craig R. Dean, "Legalize Gay Marriage"

Notice, too, that Dean makes it clear that the problems facing gays seeking to marry have consequences for all members of the potential audience—who might face problems of their own stemming from intolerance. Though homosexuals might benefit most directly from solving the problem he describes, ultimately everyone in society gains.

Personalizing an abstract problem—such as the legal benefits of marriage that are unavailable to gay and lesbian partners—can help make an argument for a solution. Dying of lung cancer, police lieutenant Laurel Hester (center) spent the last year of her life fighting to persuade Ocean County, New Jersey, officials to transfer her pension benefits to her partner, Stacie Andree (right), after Hester's death.

In describing the problem your proposal argument intends to solve, you may also need to review other earlier and failed attempts to address it. Many issues have a long history you can't afford to ignore. For example, were you to argue for a college football playoff, you might point out that the current Bowl Championship series itself represents an attempt—largely unsuccessful—to crown a more widely recognized national champion. Then there are those problems that seem to grow worse every time someone tinkers with them. Considering how the current system of financing political campaigns in federal elections developed might give you pause about proposing any additional attempt at reform—since every previous reform, one might argue, has resulted in more bureaucracy, more restrictions on political expression, and more unregulated money flowing into the system. *Enough is enough* is a potent argument in light of such a mess.

Making a Strong and Clear Claim

Once you've described and analyzed a problem or state of affairs, you're prepared to make a claim. Begin with your *claim* (a proposal of what X or Y should do) followed by the *reason(s)* why X or Y should act and the *effects* of adopting the proposal:

Claim	**Communities should encourage the development of charter schools.**
Reason	**Charter schools are not burdened by the bureaucracy associated with most public schooling.**
Effects	**Instituting such schools will bring more effective educational progress to communities and offer an incentive to the public schools to improve their programs as well.**

Having established a claim, you can explore its implications by drawing out the reasons, warrants, and evidence that can support it most effectively:

Claim	**In light of a recent Supreme Court decision upholding federal drug laws, Congress should immediately pass a bill allowing states to legalize the use of marijuana for medical purposes.**
Reason	**Medical marijuana relieves nausea for millions of patients being treated for cancer and AIDS.**
Warrant	**The relief of nausea is desirable.**

Evidence   Nine states have already approved the use of cannabis
for medical purposes, and referendums are planned in
other states. Evidence gathered in large double-blind
studies demonstrates that marijuana relieves nausea
associated with cancer and AIDS treatments.

In this proposal argument, the *reason* sets up the need for the proposal,
whereas the *warrant* and *evidence* demonstrate that the proposal is just
and could meet its objective. Your actual argument, of course, would develop each point in more detail.

Showing That the Proposal Addresses the Need or Problem

An important but tricky part of making a successful proposal lies in relating the claim to the need or problem it addresses. Everyone you know may
agree that rising tuition costs at your college constitute a major problem.
But will your spur-of-the-moment letter to the college newspaper proposing to reduce the size of the faculty and eliminate all campus bus services
really address the problem? Would anyone even take such a proposal seriously? Chances are, you would have a tough time making this connection.
On the other hand, proposing that the student government—aided by
students in accounting and financing—examine the school's use of its
discretionary funds just might kick-start some action on tuition, especially if you can suggest areas where the institution has been notably
wasteful. It makes sense that students shouldn't have to pay more to support activities or projects not directly related to their educations.

Of course, sometimes you have to ask audiences to dream a little, explaining to them how a proposal you're making fulfills a need or solves
a problem they might not immediately recognize. That's a strategy taken
by President John F. Kennedy in a famous speech given on September 12,
1962, explaining his proposal that the United States land a man on the
moon by the end of the 1960s. Here are two paragraphs from his speech
at Rice University, explaining why:

We set sail on this new sea because there is new knowledge to be
gained, and new rights to be won, and they must be won and used for
the progress of all people. For space science, like nuclear science and
all technology, has no conscience of its own. Whether it will become a
force for good or ill depends on man, and only if the United States
occupies a position of pre-eminence can we help decide whether this
new ocean will be a sea of peace or a new terrifying theater of war. I
do not say that we should or will go unprotected against the hostile

misuse of space any more that we go unprotected against the hostile use of land or sea, but I do say that space can be explored and mastered without feeding the fires of war, without repeating the mistakes that man has made in extending his writ around this globe of ours.

There is no strife, no prejudice, no national conflict in outer space as yet. Its hazards are hostile to us all. Its conquest deserves the best of all mankind, and its opportunity for peaceful cooperation may never come again. But why, some say, the moon? Why choose this as our goal? And they may well ask why climb the highest mountain? Why, 35 years ago, fly the Atlantic? Why does Rice play Texas?

We choose to go to the moon. We choose to go to the moon in this decade and do the other things, not because they are easy, but because they are hard, because that goal will serve to organize and measure the best of our energies and skills, because that challenge is one that we are willing to accept, one we are unwilling to postpone, and one which we intend to win, and the others, too.

–John F. Kennedy

Showing That the Proposal Is Feasible

To be effective, proposals must be *feasible*: that is, the action proposed can be carried out in a reasonable way. Demonstrating feasibility calls on you to present evidence—from similar cases, from personal experience, from observational data, from interview or survey data, from Internet research, or from any other sources—showing that what you propose can indeed be done with the resources available. "Resources available" is key: if the proposal calls for funds, personnel, or skills beyond reach or reason, your audience is unlikely to accept it. When that's

If Everything's an Argument . . .

This chapter proposes implicitly that you should follow its advice in order to learn how to write effective proposals. How persuasive do you find this argument? Write your own proposal about how this chapter could be improved for its intended audience of college students, considering such elements as the topics covered, the examples, the visuals, and the organization. What, if anything, strikes you as confusing, outdated, skimpy, overemphasized, biased, unnecessary, or missing? How could these problems be addressed? Consider the authors and editors your audience.

the case, it's time to reassess and modify your proposal, and to test any new ideas against these same criteria. This is also the point to reconsider proposals that others might suggest are better, more effective, or more workable than yours. There's no shame in admitting you may have been wrong. When drafting a proposal, it even makes sense to ask friends to think of counterproposals. If your own proposal can stand up to such challenges, it's likely a strong one.

Using Personal Experience

If your own experience demonstrates the need or problem your proposal aims to address, or backs up your claim, consider using it to develop your proposal (as Craig R. Dean does in the opening of his proposal to legalize gay marriage). Consider the following questions in deciding when to include your own experiences in making a proposal:

- Is your experience directly related to the need or problem you seek to address, or to your proposal about it?
- Will your experience be appropriate and speak convincingly to the audience? Will the audience immediately understand its significance, or will it require explanation?
- Does your personal experience fit logically with the other reasons you're using to support your claim?

Be careful. If a proposal seems crafted to serve mainly your own interests, you won't get far.

Considering Design and Visuals

Because proposals often address very specific audiences, they can take any number of forms: a letter or memo, a Web page, a feasibility report, a brochure, a prospectus. Each form has different design requirements; indeed, the design may add powerfully to—or detract significantly from—the effectiveness of the proposal. Even in a college essay written on a computer, the use of white space and margins, headings and subheadings, and variations in type (such as boldface or italics) can guide readers through the proposal and enhance its persuasiveness. So before you produce a final copy of any proposal, make a careful plan for its design.

A related issue to consider is whether a graphic might help readers understand key elements of the proposal—what the challenge is, why it demands action, what exactly you're suggesting—and help make the

Not Just Words

Enterprises, both private and public, frequently offer proposals for the approval of the citizens or investors who, one way or another, will wind up paying for them. Such proposals are typically packaged to give substance to what may be little more than a dream.

Examine the proposals below, which we've annotated to highlight just a few persuasive strategies. Look for similar examples online or, perhaps, in a magazine or newspaper. (Is your school or community considering a new museum, auditorium, or park, or maybe a local developer plans to turn a warehouse district into a shopping mall? Collect the brochures, ads, or public relations materials for these projects.)

After studying the techniques in such presentations, particularly their visual elements, create a mock-up for a proposal you—and perhaps several of your classmates—might like to offer to your school or community. Choose the medium you think would

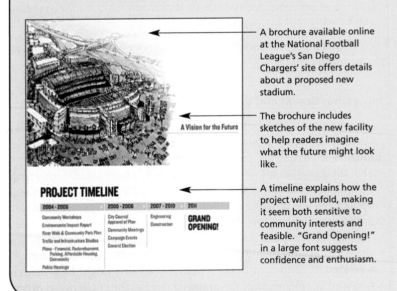

A brochure available online at the National Football League's San Diego Chargers' site offers details about a proposed new stadium.

The brochure includes sketches of the new facility to help readers imagine what the future might look like.

A timeline explains how the project will unfold, making it seem both sensitive to community interests and feasible. "Grand Opening!" in a large font suggests confidence and enthusiasm.

best reach your intended audience: pamphlet, brochure, poster, Web site, position paper, and so on. Be creative in your graphics, remembering that design involves more than just images and photos.

Alternatively, use your project to raise questions about an existing proposal. For instance, does an enhanced public transit system with a costly light-rail line really make sense in your town? How might you raise questions about its potential problems and costs in a pamphlet or print ad?

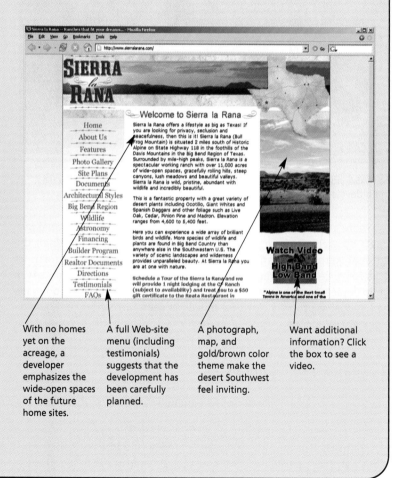

With no homes yet on the acreage, a developer emphasizes the wide-open spaces of the future home sites.

A full Web-site menu (including testimonials) suggests that the development has been carefully planned.

A photograph, map, and gold/brown color theme make the desert Southwest feel inviting.

Want additional information? Click the box to see a video.

The NASA video used high-quality animation to display the new hardware it would develop to once again explore the moon. See <http://nasa.gov>.

idea more attractive. That's a strategy routinely used in professional proposals by architects, engineers, and government agencies. When the National Aeronautics and Space Administration (NASA) put forth its plans for once again going to the moon, it presented a video on its Web site to depict what those flights might be like. The brief animation made the expensive proposal for new missions seem attractive and, just as important, plausible.

Key Features of Proposals

In drafting a proposal, make sure you include:

- a description of a problem in need of a solution
- a claim that proposes a practice or policy to address a problem or need and that's oriented toward action, directed at the future, and appropriate to your audience

- statements that clearly relate the claim to the problem or need
- evidence that the proposal will effectively address the need or solve the problem, and that it's workable

Fully developing your proposal will call for addressing all these elements, though you may choose to arrange them in several ways. A proposal might open with a vivid description of a problem—even an actual image that represents it (such as photographs of beautiful canyons destroyed by the Glen Canyon Dam). Or it might open with your proposal itself, perhaps stunning or unexpected in its directness.

In any case, organize your proposal carefully and get responses to your organizational plan from your instructor and classmates.

GUIDE to writing a proposal

● Finding a Topic/Identifying a Problem

Your everyday experience calls on you to consider problems and to make proposals all the time: for example, to change your academic major for some very important reasons, to add to the family income by starting a home-based business, or to oppose new scholarships restricted to specific student groups. In addition, your work or your job may require you to solve problems or make proposals—to a boss, a board of directors, the local school board, someone you want to impress—the list could go on and on. Of course, you also have many opportunities to make proposals to online groups; with email one click away, the whole world could be the audience for your proposal. In all these cases, you'll be aiming to call for action or to critique action, so why not make an informal list of proposals you'd like to explore in a number of different areas? Or do some freewriting on a subject of great interest to you and see if it leads to a proposal? Either method of exploration is likely to turn up several possibilities for a good proposal argument.

● Researching Your Topic

Proposals often call for some research. Even a simple one like *Let's all paint the house this weekend* would raise questions that require some investigation: *Who has the time for the job? What sort of paint will be the best? How much will the job cost?* A proposal that your school board adopt block scheduling would call for careful research into evidence supporting the use of such a system. *Where has it been effective, and why?* And for proposals about social issues (for example, that information on the Internet be freely accessible to everyone, even youngsters), extensive research would be necessary to provide adequate support.

For many proposals, you can begin your research by consulting the following types of sources:

- newspapers, magazines, reviews, and journals (online and print)
- online databases
- government documents and reports
- Web sites, blogs, and listservs or newsgroups
- books
- experts in the field, some of whom might be right on your campus

In addition, you might decide to carry out some field research: a survey of student opinion on Internet accessibility, for example, or interviews with people who are well informed about your subject.

● Formulating a Claim

As you think about and explore your topic, begin formulating a claim about it. To do so, come up with a clear and complete thesis that makes a proposal and states the reasons why this proposal should be followed. To get started on formulating a claim, explore and respond to the following questions:

- What do I know about the proposal I'm making?
- What reasons can I offer to support my proposal?
- What evidence do I have that implementing my proposal will lead to the results I want?

● Examples of Proposal Claims

- Because Condoleezza Rice is highly principled, is a proven leader, and has a powerful political story to tell, the Republican Party should consider choosing her as its first woman presidential nominee.
- Hospitals, state and local security agencies, and even citizens should stockpile surgical masks that could help prevent the rapid spread of plague pneumonia.
- Congress should repeal the Copyright Extension Act, since it disrupts the balance between incentives for creators and the right of the public to information set forth in the U.S. Constitution.
- The Environmental Protection Agency must move to approve additional oil drilling in Alaska to lessen American dependence on foreign supplies of fuel.

● Preparing a Proposal

If your instructor asks you to prepare a proposal for your project, here's a format that may help:

State the thesis of your proposal completely. If you're having trouble doing so, try outlining it in Toulmin terms:

Claim:

Reason(s):

Warrant(s):

- Explain the problem you intend to address and why your proposal is important. What's at stake in taking, or not taking, the action you propose?
- Identify and describe those readers you most hope to reach with your proposal. Why is this group of readers most appropriate for your proposal? What are their interests in the subject?
- Briefly discuss the major difficulties you foresee in preparing your argument: Demonstrating that the action you propose is necessary? Demonstrating that it's workable? Moving the audience beyond agreement to action? Something else?
- List the research you need to do. What kinds of sources do you need to consult?
- Note down the format or genre you expect to use: An academic essay? A formal report? A Web site?

● Thinking about Organization

Proposals, which can take many different forms, generally include the following elements:

- a description of the problem you intend to address or the state of affairs that leads you to propose the action: *Our neighborhood has recently experienced a rash of break-ins and burglaries. Neighbors feel like captives in their homes, and property values are threatened.*
- a clear and strong proposal, including the reasons for taking the action proposed and the effects that taking this action will have: *Our neighborhood should establish a Block Watch program that will help reduce break-ins and vandalism, and involve our kids in building neighborhood pride.*
- a clear connection between the proposal and a significant need or problem: *Break-ins and vandalism have been on the rise in our neighborhood for the last three years in part because neighbors have lost contact with each other.*
- a demonstration of ways in which the proposal addresses the need: *A Block Watch program establishes a rotating monitor system for the streets in a neighborhood and a voluntary plan to watch out for others' homes.*
- evidence that the proposal will achieve the desired outcome: *Block Watch programs in three other local areas have significantly reduced break-ins and vandalism.*
- consideration of alternative ways to achieve the desired outcome, and a discussion of why these are not preferable: *We could ask for additional police presence, but funding would be hard to get.*

- a demonstration that the proposal is workable and practical: *Because Block Watch is voluntary, our own determination and commitment are all we need to make it work.*

Getting and Giving Response

All arguments can benefit from the scrutiny of others. Your instructor may assign you to a peer group for the purpose of reading and responding to each other's drafts; if not, get some response on your own from some serious readers or consultants at a writing center. You can use the following questions to evaluate a draft. If you're evaluating someone else's draft, be sure to illustrate your points with examples. Specific comments are always more helpful than general observations.

The Claim

- Does the claim clearly call for action? Is the proposal as clear and specific as possible?
- Is the proposal too sweeping? Does it need to be qualified? If so, how?
- Does the proposal clearly address the problem it intends to solve? If not, how could the connection be strengthened?
- Is the claim likely to get the audience to act rather than just to agree? If not, how could it be revised to do so?

Evidence for the Claim

- Is enough evidence furnished to get the audience to support the proposal? If not, what kind of additional evidence is needed? Does any of the evidence provided seem inappropriate or otherwise ineffective? Why?
- Is the evidence in support of the claim simply announced, or are its significance and appropriateness analyzed? Is a more detailed discussion needed?
- Are any objections readers might have to the claim or evidence adequately addressed?
- What kinds of sources are cited? How credible and persuasive will they be to readers? What other kinds of sources might be more credible and persuasive?
- Are all quotations introduced with appropriate signal phrases (such as "As Ehrenreich argues,") and blended smoothly into the writer's sentences?
- Are all visuals titled and labeled appropriately? Have you introduced them and commented on their significance?

Organization and Style

- How are the parts of the argument organized? Is this organization effective, or would some other structure work better?

- Will readers understand the relationships among the claims, supporting reasons, warrants, and evidence? If not, what could be done to make those connections clearer? Are more transitional words and phrases needed? Would headings or graphic devices help?

- How have you used visual design elements to make your proposal more effective?

- Are the transitions or links from point to point, paragraph to paragraph, and sentence to sentence clear and effective? If not, how could they be improved?

- Is the style suited to the subject? Is it too formal? Too casual? Too technical? Too bland? How can it be improved?

- Which sentences seem particularly effective? Which ones seem weakest, and how could they be improved? Should some short sentences be combined, or should any long ones be separated into two or more sentences?

- How effective are the paragraphs? Do any seem too skimpy or too long? How can they be improved?

- Which words or phrases seem particularly effective, vivid, and memorable? Do any seem dull, vague, unclear, or inappropriate for the audience or the writer's purpose? Are definitions provided for technical or other terms that readers might not know?

Spelling, Punctuation, Mechanics, Documentation, Format

- Are there any errors in spelling, punctuation, capitalization, and the like?

- Is an appropriate and consistent style of documentation used for parenthetical citations and the list of works cited or references? (See Chapter 20.)

- Does the paper or project follow an appropriate format? Is it appropriately designed and attractively presented? How could it be improved? If it's a Web site, do all the links work?

RESPOND.

1. For each problem and solution, make a list of readers' likely objections to the off-the-wall solution offered. Then propose a more defensible solution of your own, and explain why you think it's more workable.

   Problem   Future bankruptcy of the Social Security system
   Solution   Raise the age of retirement to eighty.

   Problem   Traffic gridlock in major cities
   Solution   Allow only men to drive on Mondays, Wednesdays, and Fridays and only women on Tuesdays, Thursdays, and Saturdays. Everyone can drive on Sunday.

   Problem   Increasing rates of obesity in the general population
   Solution   Ban the sale of high-fat items in fast food restaurants

   Problem   Increasing school violence
   Solution   Authorize teachers and students to carry handguns.

   Problem   Excessive drinking on campus
   Solution   Establish an 8:00 P.M. curfew on weekends.

2. People write proposal arguments to solve problems, to change the way things are. But problems aren't always obvious; what troubles some people might be no big deal to others. To get an idea of the range of problems people face on your campus—some of which you may not even have thought of as problems—divide into groups and brainstorm about things that annoy you on and around campus, including everything from bad food in the cafeterias to 8:00 A.M. classes to long lines for football or concert tickets. Ask each group to aim for at least twenty gripes. Then choose one problem and, as a group, discuss how you'd go about writing a proposal to deal with it. Remember that you'll need to (a) make a strong and clear claim, (b) show that the proposal meets a clear need or solves a significant problem, (c) present good reasons why adopting the proposal will effectively address the need or problem, and (d) show that the proposal is workable and should be adopted.

3. In the essay "Mass Transit Hysteria" (see p. 364), P. J. O'Rourke playfully proposes turning public transportation systems into thrill rides to increase their use by the public. Using the Toulmin model discussed in Chapter 6, analyze the proposal's structure. What claim(s) does O'Rourke make, and what reasons does he give to support the claim? What warrants connect the reasons to the claim? What evidence does he provide? Alternatively, make up a rough outline of O'Rourke's proposal and track the good reasons he presents to support his claim.

A Call to Improve Campus Accessibility for the Mobility Impaired

MANASI DESHPANDE

INTRODUCTION

Wes Holloway, a sophomore at the University of Texas at Austin, never considered the issue of campus accessibility during his first year on campus. But when an injury his freshman year left him wheelchair-bound, he was astonished to realize that he faced an unexpected challenge: maneuvering around the UT campus. Hills that he had effortlessly traversed became mountains; doors that he had easily opened became anvils; and streets that he had mindlessly crossed became treacherous terrain. Says Wes: "I didn't think about accessibility until I had to deal with it, and I think most people are the same way."

> The paper opens with a personal example and dramatizes the issue of campus accessibility.

For the ambulatory individual, access for the mobility impaired on the UT campus is easy to overlook. Automatic door entrances and bathrooms with the universal handicapped symbol make the campus seem sufficiently accessible. But for many students and faculty at UT, including me, maneuvering the UT campus in a wheelchair is a daily experience of stress and frustration. Although the University has made a concerted and continuing effort to improve access, students and faculty with physical disabilities still suffer from discriminatory hardship, unequal opportunity to succeed, and lack of independence. The

---

Manasi Deshpande wrote this formidable essay for a course preparing her to work as a consultant in the Writing Center at the University of Texas at Austin. Note in particular how she reaches out to a general audience to make an argument that might seem to have a narrower constituency. She also makes good use of headings to guide readers through the complexities of her proposal. This essay is documented using MLA style.

University must make campus accessibility a higher priority and take more seriously the hardship that the campus at present imposes on people with mobility impairments. Administrators should devote more resources to creating a user-friendly campus rather than simply conforming to legal requirements for accessibility. The University should also enhance the transparency and approachability of its services for members with mobility impairments. Individuals with permanent physical disabilities would undoubtedly benefit from a stronger resolve to improve campus accessibility. Better accessibility would also benefit the more numerous students and faculty with temporary disabilities and help the University recruit a more diverse body of students and faculty.

Both problem and solution are previewed here, with more details to come in subsequent sections of the paper.

Assessment of Current Efforts

The current state of campus accessibility leaves substantial room for improvement. There are approximately 150 academic and administrative buildings on campus (Grant). Eduardo Gardea, intern architect at the Physical Plant, estimates that only about nineteen buildings fully comply with the Americans with Disabilities Act (ADA). According to Penny Seay, Ph.D., director of the Center for Disability Studies at UT Austin, the ADA in theory "requires every building on campus to be accessible." However, as Bill Throop, associate director of the Physical Plant, explains, there is "no legal deadline to make the entire campus accessible"; neither the ADA nor any other law mandates that certain buildings be made compliant by a certain time. Though not bound by specific legal obligation, the University should strive to fulfill the spirit of the law and recognize campus accessibility as a pressing moral obligation.

This section examines the bureaucratic dimensions of the campus accessibility problem. The author's fieldwork (mainly interviews) enhances her authority and credibility.

While the University has made substantial progress in accessibility improvements, it has failed to make campus accessibility a priority. For example, the Campus Master Plan, published in 1999 by the University, does not include improvements in campus accessibility as one of its major goals for the design and architecture of the University. It mentions accessibility only once to recommend that signs for wayfinding comply with the ADA. The signs should provide "direction to accessible building entrances and routes" and "clear identification of special facilities" (Gleeson et al. 90). Nowhere does the Master Plan discuss the need to design these accessible building entrances, routes, and special facilities or how to fit accessibility improvements into the larger renovation of the campus.

THE BENEFITS OF CHANGE

Benefits for People with Permanent Mobility Impairments

The paper uses several layers of headings to organize its diverse materials.

Improving campus accessibility would significantly enhance the quality of life of students and faculty with mobility impairments. The campus at present poses discriminatory hardship on these individuals by making daily activities such as getting to class and using the bathroom unreasonably difficult. Before Wes Holloway leaves home, he must plan his route carefully so as to avoid hills, use ramps that are easy to maneuver, and enter the side of the building with the accessible entrance. As he goes to class, Wes must go out of his way to avoid poorly paved sidewalks and roads. Sometimes he cannot avoid them and must take an uncomfortable and bumpy ride across potholes and uneven pavement. If his destination does not have an automatic door, he must wait for someone to open the door for him because it is too heavy for him to open himself. To get into Burdine Hall, he has to ask a stranger to push him through the heavy narrow doors because his fingers would get crushed if he pushed himself. Once in the classroom, Wes must find a suitable place to sit, often far away from his classmates because stairs block him from the center of the room.

The author outlines the challenges faced by a student with mobility impairment.

Other members of the UT community with mobility impairments suffer the same daily hardships as Wes.

According to Mike Gerhardt, student affairs administrator of Services for Students with Disabilities (SSD), approximately eighty students with physical disabilities, including twenty to twenty-five students using wheelchairs, are registered with SSD. However, the actual number of students with mobility impairments is probably higher because some students choose not to seek services from SSD. The current state of campus accessibility discriminates against all individuals with physical disabilities in the unnecessary hardship it imposes.

Beyond inflicting daily stress on people with mobility impairments, the poor accessibility on campus denies these individuals their independence. Students with physical disabilities must often ask for help from others, especially in opening doors without functional automatic door entrances. Bathrooms without access also deny these individuals their independence. Once when I needed to use a bathroom in Burdine Hall, I found that none of the stalls was accessible. To be able to use the bathroom in privacy, I had to ask a stranger to stand outside the bathroom and make sure no one entered.

Accessibility problems are given a human face in a section providing numerous examples of the problems mobility-impaired people face on campus.

The state of campus accessibility also denies people with physical disabilities an equal opportunity to succeed. In the summer of 2004, I registered for CH 204, a chemistry lab, because I planned to be a Human Biology major. The major requires students to take four labs. When I got to the lab on the first day of class, I found that I could not perform any tasks independently. The supposedly accessible lab bench was just as high as the other benches, so I could not write, take proper measurements, or handle equipment on the bench. I could not reach the sink. The lab was so cramped that I could hardly fit through the aisles, and I wheeled around in fear of bumping into someone carrying glass equipment. Services for Students with Disabilities informed me that it would not be able to provide me with an assistant. Though I was fully capable of performing the labs myself, the lack of accessibility made me unable to complete even the simplest tasks.

The author offers her personal perspective on the subject, a factual appeal with an emotional dimension.

Even with an assistant, I would have lacked independence and felt unequal to my classmates. After this experience, I dropped both the class and the major.

Benefits for People with Temporary Mobility Impairments

In addition to helping the few members of the UT campus with permanent mobility impairments, a faster rate of accessibility improvement would also benefit the much larger population of people with temporary physical disabilities. Many students and faculty will become temporarily disabled from injury at some point during their time at the University. Sprained ankles, torn ACLs, and fractured legs all require use of crutches or a wheelchair. Judy Lu, a second-year Business Honors Program/Plan II/Pre-med major, used crutches for two weeks when she sprained her ankle playing volleyball. She encountered difficulties similar to those facing people with permanent disabilities, including finding accessible entrances, opening doors without automatic entrances, and finding convenient classroom seating. Getting around campus on crutches "was not convenient at all," and her temporary disability required her to "plan ahead a whole lot more" to find accessible routes and entrances.

All members of the UT community face the risk of enduring an injury that could leave them with a temporary physical disability. According to Dr. Jennifer Maedgen, assistant dean of students and director of SSD, about 5 to 10% of the approximately 1,000 students registered with SSD at any given time have temporary disabilities. The number of students with temporary physical disabilities is largely underreported because many students do not know about SSD or do not feel the need for temporary academic accommodations. By improving campus accessibility, the University would reach out not only to its few members with permanent physical disabilities but in fact to all of its members, even those who have never considered the possibility of mobility impairment or the state of campus accessibility.

The author broadens the appeal of her proposal by showing how improved accessibility will benefit everyone on campus.

Numbers provide hard evidence for an important claim.

Benefits for the University

Better accessibility would also benefit the University as a whole by increasing recruitment of handicapped individuals and thus promoting a more diverse campus. When prospective students and faculty with disabilities visit the University, they might decide not to join the UT community because of poor access. On average, about 1,000 students, or 2% of the student population, are registered with SSD. Mike Gerhardt reports that SSD would have about 1,500 to 3,000 registered students if the University reflected the community at large with respect to disability. These numbers suggest that the University can recruit more students with disabilities by taking steps to ensure that they have an equal opportunity to succeed. Improving accessibility is one way to achieve a more diverse campus.

The author offers a new but related argument: enhanced accessibility could bolster recruitment efforts.

COUNTERARGUMENTS

Arguments against devoting more effort and resources to campus accessibility have some validity but ultimately prove inadequate. Some argue that accelerating the rate of accessibility improvements and creating more efficient services require too much spending on too few people. However, this spending actually enhances the expected quality of life of all UT community members rather than just the few with permanent physical disabilities. Unforeseen injury can leave anyone with a permanent or temporary disability at any time. In making decisions about campus accessibility, administrators must realize that having a disability is not a choice and that bad luck does not discriminate well. They should consider how their decisions would affect their campus experience if they became disabled. Despite the additional cost, the University should make accessibility a priority and accommodate more accessibility projects in its budget.

Others argue that more money would not accelerate change because the physical constraints of the campus

The paper examines and refutes two specific objections to the proposal.

limit the amount of construction that can take place. Mr. Gerhardt, for example, argues that "more money wouldn't make a difference" because ADA projects must be spaced over the long term so as to minimize disruption from construction. Other administrators, architects, and engineers, however, feel that money does play a significant role in the rate of ADA improvements. Although Mr. Throop of the Physical Plant acknowledges that the campus only has the capacity to absorb a certain amount of construction, he nonetheless feels that the Physical Plant "could do more if [it] had more monetary resources" and argues that the University "should fund [the Plant] more." Dr. Maedgen of SSD agrees, saying that the main constraint to making the campus more accessible more quickly is "mostly money." Even though there is "a real desire to do it," the problem "tends to be fiscally oriented in nature."

RECOMMENDATIONS

Foster Empathy and Understanding for Long-Term Planning

Having established a case for enhanced campus accessibility, the author offers several suggestions for action.

The University should make campus accessibility a higher priority and work toward a campus that not only fulfills legal requirements but also provides a user-friendly environment for the mobility impaired. Increased effort and resources must be accompanied by a sincere desire to understand and improve the campus experience of people with mobility impairments. It is difficult for the ambulatory person to empathize with the difficulties faced by these individuals. Recognizing this problem, the University should require the administrators who allocate money to ADA projects to use wheelchairs around the campus once a year. This program would help them understand the needs of people using wheelchairs. It would also allow them to assess the progress of campus accessibility as afforded by their allocation of resources. Administrators must realize that people with physical disabilities are not a small, distant, irrelevant group; anyone can join their ranks at any time. Administrators should ask themselves if they would find he current state of campus accessibility acceptable if an injury forced them to use a wheelchair on a permanent basis.

In addition, the University should actively seek student input for long-term improvements to accessibility. The University is in the process of creating the ADA Accessibility Committee, which, according to the Dean of Students' Web site, will "address institution-wide, systemic issues that fall under the scope of the Americans with Disabilities Act." This committee will replace the larger President's Committee on Students with Disabilities. Linda Millstone, the University's ADA coordinator, reports that the three student representatives on the President's Committee "were not engaged" and that even now she is "not hearing a groundswell of interest from students." The University should not take this apparent lack of interest to mean that its members with mobility impairments face no problems. According to Ms. Millstone, a survey done about two years ago indicated that students were "clueless" that the President's Committee even existed. This ignorance is not the fault of students but rather a failure of the University to make its accessibility efforts open and transparent. Students should play a prominent and powerful role in the new ADA Accessibility Committee. Since students with mobility impairments traverse the campus more frequently than most administrators, they understand the structural problems of the campus. The Committee should select its student representatives carefully to make sure that they are driven individuals committed to working for progress and representing the interests of students with disabilities. The University should consider making Committee positions paid so that student representatives can devote sufficient time to their responsibilities.

Improve Services for the Mobility Impaired

The University should also work toward creating more useful, transparent, and approachable services for its members with physical disabilities by making better use of online technology and helping students take control of their own experiences. Usefulness of services would decrease the dependence of people with physical disabilities on others and mitigate the stress of using a wheelchair on campus. Approachability would help these individuals take control of their campus experience by allowing more freedom of expression and encouraging self-advocacy. Transparency would allow people with mobility impairments to understand and appreciate the University's efforts at improving campus accessibility.

First, SSD can make its Web site more useful by updating it frequently with detailed information on construction sites that will affect accessible routes. The site should delineate alternative accessible routes and approximate the extra time required to use the detour. This information would help people with mobility impairments to plan ahead and avoid delays, mitigating the stress of maneuvering around construction sites.

The detail in these proposals makes them seem plausible and feasible.

The University should also develop software for an interactive campus map. The software would work like Mapquest or Google Maps but would provide detailed descriptions of accessible routes on campus from one building to another. It would be updated frequently with new ADA improvements and information on construction sites that impede accessible routes. In addition, the interactive map would rate building features such as entrances, bathrooms, and elevators on their level of accessibility. It would also report complaints received by SSD and the Physical Plant regarding access around and inside buildings. The software would undoubtedly ease the frustration of finding accessible routes to and from buildings.

Since usefulness and approachability of services are most important for students during their first encounters with the campus, SSD should hold formal one-on-one orientations for new students with mobility impairments. SSD should inform students in both oral and written format of their rights and responsibilities and make them aware of problems that they will encounter on the campus. For example, counselors should advise students to look at their classrooms well in advance and assess potential problems such as poor building access, the need for an elevator key, and the design of the classroom. Beyond making services more useful, these orientations would give students the impression of University services as open and responsive, encouraging students to report problems that they encounter and assume the responsibility of self-advocacy.

As a continuing resource for people with physical disabilities, the SSD Web site should include an anonymous forum for both general questions and specific complaints and needs. The forum should be restricted by the University of Texas Electronic Identification (UTEID) to students registered with SSD. Obviously, if a student has an urgent problem, he or she should visit or call SSD as soon as possible. However, for less pressing problems such as a nonfunctional automatic door button or the need for a curb cut, an anonymous forum would allow for an easy way to let administrators know of a problem. By looking at the forum, administrators and the Physical Plant can get a good idea of the most pressing accessibility issues on campus and notify students of when they will fix the reported problems. Many times, students notice problems but do not report them because they find visiting or calling SSD time-consuming or because they do not wish to be a burden. The anonymity and immediate feedback provided by the forum would allow for more freedom of expression and provide students an easier way to solve the problems they face.

Services for the mobility impaired should also increase their transparency by actively advertising current accessibility projects on their Web sites. My research has given me the strong impression that the administrators, architects, and engineers on the front lines of ADA improvements are devoted and hard-working. To a person

The level of detail bolsters the author's personal ethos: she has given careful thought to these ideas and has earned a serious hearing.

with a mobility impairment, however, improvements to campus accessibility seem sluggish at best. In addition to actually devoting more resources to accessibility, then, the University should give its members with mobility impairments a clearer idea of its ongoing efforts to improve campus accessibility. Detailed online descriptions of ADA projects, including the cost of each project, would affirm its resolve to create a better environment for its members with physical disabilities.

Conclusion

Although the University has made good progress in accessibility improvements on an old campus, it must take bold steps to improve the experience of its members with mobility impairments. At present, people with permanent mobility impairments face unreasonable hardship, unequal opportunity to succeed, and lack of independence. The larger number of people with temporary disabilities faces similar hardships, and the University as a whole suffers from lack of diversity with respect to disability. To enhance the quality of life of all of its members and increase recruitment of disabled individuals, the University should focus its resources on increasing the rate of accessibility improvements and improving the quality of its services for the mobility impaired. Administrators must learn not to view people with disabilities as a "them" distinct from "us," instead recognizing that the threat of mobility impairment faces everyone. As a public institution, the University has an obligation to make the campus more inclusive and serve as an example for disability rights. With careful planning and a genuine desire to respond to special needs, practical and cost-effective changes to the University campus can significantly improve the quality of life of many of its members and prove beneficial to the future of the University as a whole.

The conclusion summarizes the argument and rallies support for its proposals.

WORKS CITED

"ADA Student Forum." Office of the Dean of Students. 6 Apr. 2005. 23 Apr. 2005 <http://deanofstudents.utexas.edu/events/ssd_forum.php>.

Gardea, Eduardo. Personal interview. 24 Mar. 2005.

Gerhardt, Michael. Personal interview. 8 Apr. 2005.

Gleeson, Austin, et al. The University of Texas at Austin Campus Master Plan. Austin: U of Texas, 1999.

Grant, Angela. "Making Campus More Accessible." Daily Texan Online. 14 Oct. 2003. 1 Mar. 2005 <http://www.dailytexanonline.com/news/2003/10/14/TopStories/Making.Campus.More.Accessible-527606.shtml>.

Holloway, Wesley Reed. Personal interview. 5 Mar. 2005.

Lu, Judy Yien. Personal interview. 5 Mar. 2005.

Maedgen, Jennifer. Personal interview. 25 Mar. 2005.

Seay, Penny. Personal interview. 11 Mar. 2005.

Throop, William. Personal interview. 6 Apr. 2005.

Mass Transit Hysteria

P. J. O'ROURKE

Wednesday, March 16, 2005

The new transportation bill, currently working its way through Congress, will provide more than $52 billion for mass transit. Mass transit is a wonderful thing, all right-thinking people agree. It stops pollution "in its tracks" (a little ecology-conscious light-rail advocacy joke). Mass transit doesn't burn climate-warming, Iraq-war-causing hydrocarbons. Mass transit can operate with nonpolluting sustainable energy sources such as electricity. Electricity can be produced by solar panels, and geothermal generators. Electricity can be produced by right-thinking people themselves, if they talk about it enough near wind farms.

Mass transit helps preserve nature in places like Yellowstone Park, the Everglades and the Arctic wilderness, because mass transit doesn't go there. Mass transit curtails urban sprawl. When you get to the end of the trolley tracks, you may want to move farther out into the suburbs, but you're going to need a lot of rails and ties and Irishmen with pickaxes. Plus there's something romantic about mass transit. Think Tony Bennett singing "Where little cable cars / Climb halfway to the stars." (And people say mass transit doesn't provide flexibility in travel plans!) Or the Kingston Trio and their impassioned protest of the five-cent Boston "T" fare increase, "The Man Who Never Returned." No doubt some lovely songs will be written about the Washington County, Ore., Wilsonville-to-Beaverton commuter rail line to be funded by the new transportation bill.

There are just two problems with mass transit. Nobody uses it, and it costs like hell. Only 4% of Americans take public transportation to work. Even in cities they don't do it. Less than 25% of commuters in the New York metropolitan area use public transportation. Elsewhere it's far less— 9.5% in San Francisco–Oakland–San Jose, 1.8% in Dallas–Fort Worth. As for total travel in urban parts of America—all the comings and goings for work, school, shopping, etc.—1.7% of those trips are made on mass transit.

P. J. O'Rourke is a humorist whose books include *Eat the Rich* (1999) and *Peace Kills* (2005).

Then there is the cost, which is—obviously—$52 billion. Less obviously, there's all the money spent locally keeping local mass transit systems operating. The Heritage Foundation says, "There isn't a single light rail transit system in America in which fares paid by the passengers cover the cost of their own rides." Heritage cites the Minneapolis "Hiawatha" light rail line, soon to be completed with $107 million from the transportation bill. Heritage estimates that the total expense for each ride on the Hiawatha will be $19. Commuting to work will cost $8,550 a year. If the commuter is earning minimum wage, this leaves about $1,000 a year for food, shelter and clothing. Or, if the city picks up the tab, it could have leased a BMW X-5 SUV for the commuter at about the same price.

We don't want minimum-wage workers driving BMW X-5s. That's unfair. They're already poor, and now they're enemies of the environment? So we must find a way to save mass transit—get people to ride it, be eager to pay for it, no matter what the cold-blooded free-market types at Heritage say. We must do it for the sake of future generations, for our children.

That's it! The children. The solution to the problems of mass transit is staring us in the face. Or, in the case of my rather short children, staring us in the sternum. All over America men and women, at the behest of their children, are getting on board various light-rail systems that don't even go anywhere. And these trips—if you factor in the price of cotton candy, snow cones and trademarked plush toys—cost considerably more than $19. Yet we're willing to stand in line for ages to utilize this type of mass transit. All we have to do is equip Hiawatha with a slow climb, a steep, sudden plunge, several sharply banked curves, and maybe a loop-the-loop over by St. Paul.

The new mass transit can harness clean, renewable resources. "Unplug the Prius, honey! I'm taking the waterslide to work!" And it need not be expensive. In fact, we might be able to make certain advantageous cuts in transportation spending. A few reductions in Amtrak's already minimal maintenance budget would turn the evening Metroliner into a reeling, lurching journey through the pitch dark equal to anything Space Mountain has to offer. And here is a perfect opportunity for public/private partnership. The Disney Co. is looking for new profit centers. The New York subway can become a hair-raising thrill ride by means of a simple return to NYPD 1970s policing practices.

Not all of the new mass transit has to be frenetic. Bringing groceries home on the tilt-o-whirl presents difficulties. We can take a cue from the lucrative cruise ship industry—every commute a mini-luxury vacation. Perhaps this wouldn't be suitable in areas without navigable water. But don't be too sure. Many "riverboat casinos" are completely stationary, and a lot of commuters don't want to go to work anyway. Slot machines could be put on all forms of mass transit. Put slot machines on city buses and people will abandon their cars, or abandon their car payments, which comes to the same thing.

This is a revolutionary approach to mass transit. It can save the planet. And it can save me from taking the kids to Orlando. Now I can stay home in D.C. and send them for a ride on Washington's new, improved Metro of Horrors, where scary things jump out at you from nowhere—things like $52 billion appropriations for mass transit.

PART 3

STYLE AND PRESENTATION IN arguments

12
Style in Arguments

A person you know only slightly objects strenuously to your characterization of her in-class comments as being laced with sarcasm, saying, "Sorry, you're wrong again: sarcasm's not my style." Since you'd meant this as a compliment, you decide to apologize and ask her how *she* would describe her style.

An architectural team working to design a new fast food restaurant studies the most successful franchises of the last twenty-five years. What they find suggests that each franchise has a distinctive architectural style, so they go to work seeking something new and distinctive—and something as *unlike* McDonald's style as possible.

A photographer looking to land the cover photo on *Vogue* takes a tour of college campuses. At each school, he sits patiently in the student union, watching as students pass by. What he's looking for is a face with "fresh new style."

A researcher trying to describe teen style crafted a questionnaire and distributed it to 500 teens in three different cities. Why was she not surprised when the style mentioned most often as being desirable was "hip-hop style"?

● ● ●

Arguments, of course, have their own styles. One classical orator and statesman outlined three basic styles of communication, identifying them as "high" (formal or even ornate), "middle" (understated and very clear), and "low" (everyday or humorous). Even choice of font can help to convey such a style: think of 𝒻rench 𝒮cript, for example, as ornate or high, Garamond as understated or middle, and Comic Sans as everyday or low. High style in argument is generally formal, serious, even high-minded—an argument wearing its best tuxedo. Middle style marks most ordinary arguments, from the commonplace to the professional—these arguments have sturdy work clothes on. And low style is informal, colloquial, humorous—an argument with its shoes off and feet propped up.

Such broad characterizations can give only a very general sense of an argument's style, however. To think more carefully about style in argument, consider the relationship among style and word choice, sentence structure, punctuation, and what we'll call special effects.

Style and Word Choice

The vocabulary of an argument helps to create its style; most important, choice of words should match the tone the writer wants to establish as well as the purpose and topic of the argument. For most academic arguments, formal language is appropriate. In an argument urging every member of society to care about energy issues, Chevron CEO Dave

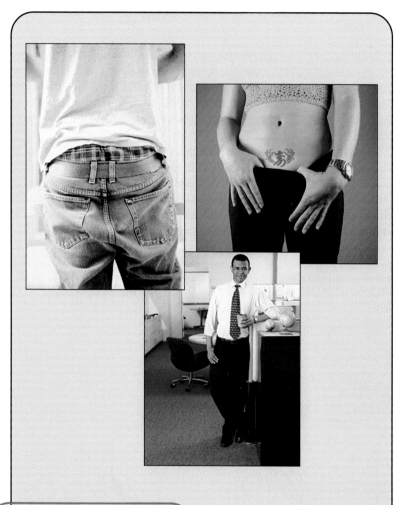

Not Just Words

Choose one of the images above and study it for a few minutes. How would you describe the style of the person depicted—just by thinking about the choice of pants, the stance, and so on? How does the photograph help to convey that style? Consider the composition, the use of color, and so on.

O'Reilly writes, "We call upon scientists and educators, politicians and policy-makers, environmentalists, leaders of industry, and each one of you to be part of reshaping the next era of energy." Note the formal and serious tone that O'Reilly's choice of words creates; writing "How 'bout everybody rallyin' round to mix up a new energy plan" would have had a very different effect.

While slang and colloquial language can sometimes add liveliness to an argument, they also can confuse readers. In an article for a general audience about tense arms-control negotiations, using the term *nukes* to refer to nuclear missiles might confuse some readers and irritate others since the shorthand term could indicate a frivolous reference to a deadly serious subject. Be alert, too, to the use of jargon in arguments: while

Or perhaps he'd better call them "freedom fries," as members of the House of Representatives did in 2003 after France threatened to use its veto power in the UN Security Council to block the Iraq war. A fuss over words can be silly, or significant. Or both.

"Your Honor, please ask the defendant to stop using the word 'fries' where 'French-fried potatoes' is implied."

jargon (the special vocabulary of members of a profession, trade, or field) is very useful for expert or technical audiences, serving as a kind of shorthand, it can also alienate readers who don't understand the terms being used.

Another key to an argument's style is the use of connotation, the associations that accompany many words. Note, for example, the differences in connotation among the following three statements:

> Students from the Labor Action Committee (LAC) carried out a hunger strike aimed at calling attention to the below-minimum wages being paid to campus temporary workers, saying, "the university must pay a living wage to all its workers."

> Left-wing agitators and radicals tried to use self-induced starvation to stampede the university into caving in to their demands.

> Supporters of human rights for all put their bodies on the line to protest the university's thinly veiled racist policies of scandalously low pay for immigrant temporary workers.

Here the first sentence is the most neutral, presenting the facts and offering a quotation from one of the students. The second sentence uses loaded terms like "agitators" and "radicals" and "stampede" to create a negative image of this event, while the final sentence uses other loaded words to create a positive view. As these examples demonstrate, words matter!

Finally, arguments that use more concrete and specific words rather than more abstract and general ones will make a more vivid impact on readers and listeners. In a review of Steven Bochco's TV series about the Iraq War, *Over There,* the reviewer says:

> The soldiers are pinned down; with their legs splayed in order to get as close to the ground as possible, they look like frogs in a dissecting tray. There's no cover around them, nowhere to hide, and viewers can feel this, too—a sense of loss of control and of danger everywhere.
> —Nancy Franklin, "The Yanks Are Coming"

The reviewer could have been more general, saying, "The soldiers have no hiding places and are completely vulnerable," but the concrete language ("pinned down," "legs splayed," "like frogs in a dissecting tray") makes this depiction much more memorable and hence helps to create an effective style.

Sentence Structure and Argument

Choices about sentence structure also play an important part in establishing the style of an argument. As with most writing, variety may be the key to constructing a strong series of sentences. Writers of effective arguments take this maxim to heart, working to vary such things as sentence pattern and length.

Varying sentence length can be especially effective. Here's George Orwell moving from a long, complicated sentence to a short, punchy one at the end:

> The fire of, I think, five machine guns was pouring upon us, and there was a series of heavy crashes caused by the Fascists flinging bombs over their parapet in the most idiotic manner. It was intensely dark.
>
> –George Orwell, *Homage to Catalonia*

Paying attention to the way sentences begin can also help to build an argument's effectiveness. In the letter from Chevron CEO O'Reilly mentioned on page 372, we find the following paragraph:

> Demand is soaring like never before. As populations grow and economies take off, millions in the developing world are enjoying the benefits of a lifestyle that requires increasing amounts of energy. In fact, some say that in 20 years the world will consume 40% more oil than it does today. At the same time, many of the world's oil and gas fields are maturing. And new energy discoveries are mainly occurring in places where resources are difficult to extract, physically, economically, and even politically. When growing demand meets tighter supplies, the result is more competition for the same resources.
>
> –Dave O'Reilly

Look at how much less effective this passage becomes when the sentences all begin in the same way—that is, with the subject first:

> Demand is soaring like never before. Millions in the rapidly developing world are enjoying the benefits of a lifestyle that requires increasing amounts of energy. Some say that in 20 years the world will consume 40% more oil than it does today. Many of the world's oil and gas fields are maturing. New energy discoveries are mainly occurring in places where resources are difficult to extract, physically, economically, and even politically. Growing demand and tighter supplies result in more competition for the same resources.

In the second version, taking out all the transitions ("In fact," "At the same time,") and the openings that vary the subject-first order ("As populations grow . . . ," "When growing demand meets tighter supplies,") makes the passage much less interesting to read and harder to understand, thus weakening its argument.

Effective arguments can also make good use of parallel structures in sentences. In a review of a new biography of writer Henry Roth, Jonathan Rosen includes the following description:

> His hands were warped by rheumatoid arthritis; the very touch of his computer keyboard was excruciating. But he still put in five hours a day, helped by Percocet, beer, a ferocious will, and the ministrations of several young assistants.
>
> –Jonathan Rosen, "Writer, Interrupted"

In the first sentence, Rosen chooses a coordinate structure, with the first clause about Roth's arthritic hands perfectly balanced by the following clause describing the results of putting those hands on a keyboard. In the second sentence, Rosen uses a series of parallel nouns and noun phrases ("Percocet," "beer," "the ministrations of . . . ," etc.) to build up a picture of Roth as extremely persistent.

Punctuation and Argument

In a memorable comment, actor and director Clint Eastwood says, "You can show a lot with a look. . . . It's punctuation." Eastwood is right about punctuation's effect, either in acting or in arguing. As you read and write arguments, consider choices of punctuation closely. Here are some ways in which punctuation helps to enhance style.

The semicolon is a handy punctuation mark since it signals a pause stronger than a comma but not as strong as a period. Here is Mary Gordon using a semicolon in an argument about "the ghosts of Ellis Island":

> Immigration acts were passed; newcomers had to prove, besides moral correctness and financial solvency, their ability to read.
>
> –Mary Gordon, "More than Just a Shrine"

Gordon could have put a period after *passed,* separating this passage into two sentences. But she chooses a semicolon instead, giving the sentence an abrupt rhythm that suits her topic: laws that imposed strict requirements on immigrants. Semicolons can also make passages easier

"You can show a lot with a look. . . . It's punctuation."

to read, as in the following example from an argument by William F. Buckley Jr.:

> Every year, whether the Republican or the Democratic party is in office, more and more power drains away from the individual to feed vast reservoirs in far-off places; and we have less and less say about the shape of events which shape our future.
>
> —William F. Buckley Jr., "Why Don't We Complain?"

Writers also use end punctuation to good effect. Though the exclamation point can be distracting and even irritating if overused (think of those email messages you get from friends that fairly bristle with them), it can be very helpful if used infrequently. Exclamation points are especially good for indicating a speaker's tone. For example, in an argument about the treatment of prisoners at Guantánamo, consider how Jane Mayer evokes the sense of desperation in some of the prisoners:

> As we reached the end of the cell-block, hysterical shouts, in broken English, erupted from a caged exercise area nearby. "Come here!" a man screamed. "See here! They are liars! . . . No sleep!" he yelled. "No food! No medicine! No doctor! Everybody sick here!"
>
> —Jane Mayer, "The Experiment"

The question mark is another handy mark of punctuation. In a fairly negative review of Steven Spielberg's *War of the Worlds*, David Denby uses a series of questions to drive home the point he's been making:

> As the scenes of destruction cease, one has to ponder the oddity of a science-fiction movie without science, or even routine curiosity. Who are the aliens? What is their chemical makeup and how might they be vulnerable? What does the attack mean? Nobody raises any of these issues.
>
> > –David Denby, "Stayin' Alive"

Two other punctuation marks are often important in establishing the style of an argument. While sometimes used interchangeably, the colon and the dash have very different effects. The colon introduces explanations or examples and separates elements from one another. Alison Lurie uses a colon in this way:

> The men may also wear the getup known as Sun Belt Cool: a pale beige suit, open-collared shirt (often in a darker shade than the suit), cream-colored loafers and aviator sunglasses.
>
> > –Alison Lurie, "The Language of Clothes"

A dash or a pair of dashes, on the other hand, is most often used to insert comments or highlight material within a sentence. Notice how columnist Maureen Dowd uses dashes to set off an important point she wants to make about the Bush administration's claim that it doesn't need search warrants to spy on individuals:

> Even when [Vice President Dick Cheney] can easily—and retroactively—get snooping warrants, he doesn't want their stinking warrants. Warrants are for sissies.
>
> > –Maureen Dowd, "Looking for a Democratic Tough Guy, or Girl"

In the following example, *New York Times Book Review* critic Joel Conarroe uses dashes to make fun of their overuse by sports writer Roger Angell and to show how they can slow down the pace of the prose:

> Mr. Angell is addicted to dashes and parentheses—small pauses or digressions in the narrative like those moments when the umpire dusts off home plate or a pitcher rubs up a new ball—that serve to slow an already deliberate movement almost to a standstill.
>
> > –Joel Conarroe, "Ode on a Rainbow Slider"

As these examples suggest, punctuation is often key to creating the rhythm of an argument. Take a look at how Maya Angelou uses a dash along with another punctuation mark—ellipsis points—to indicate a pause or hesitation, in this case one that builds anticipation:

> Then the voice, husky and familiar, came to wash over us—"The winnah, and still heavyweight champeen of the world . . . Joe Louis."
> –Maya Angelou, "Champion of the World"

Creating rhythms can be especially important in online communication, when writers are trying to invest their arguments with emotion or emphasis. Some writers still use asterisks in online communication to convey the sense that italic type creates in print texts: "You *must* respond to this email today!" Others use emoticons or new characters of all kinds (from the ubiquitous smiley face ☺ to combinations like g2g for "got to go") to establish the rhythm, tone, and style they want. The creativity available to writers online allows for great experimentation; but in an argument where the stakes are high, writers are careful not to go too far with such experiments—they don't want to alienate their audiences.

Special Effects: Figurative Language and Argument

Look at any magazine or Web site, and you'll see figurative language working on behalf of arguments. When the writer of a letter to the editor complains that "Donna Haraway's supposition that because we rely on cell phones and laptops we are cyborgs is [like] saying the Plains Indians were centaurs because they relied on horses," he's using an analogy to rebut (and perhaps ridicule) Haraway's claim. When another writer says that "the digital revolution is whipping through our lives like a Bengali typhoon," she's making an implicit argument about the speed and strength of the digital revolution. When still another writer calls Disney World a "smile factory," she begins a stinging critique of the way pleasure is "manufactured" there.

Just what is figurative language? Traditionally, the terms *figurative language* and *figures of speech* refer to language that differs from the ordinary—language that calls up, or "figures," something else. But, in fact, all language could be said to call up something else. The word *table*, for example, isn't itself a table; rather, it calls up a table in our imaginations. Thus just as all language is by nature argumentative, so are all figures of speech. Far from being mere decoration or embellishment (something like icing on the cake of thought), figures of speech are indispensable to language use.

More specifically, figurative language brings two major strengths to arguments. First, it aids understanding by likening something unknown to something known. For example, in arguing for the existence of DNA as they had identified and described it, scientists Watson and Crick used two familiar examples—a helix (spiral) and a zipper—to make their point. Today, arguments about new computer technologies are filled with similar uses of figurative language. Indeed, Microsoft's entire word processing system depends on likening items to those in an office (as in Microsoft Office) to make them more understandable and familiar to users. Second, figurative language is helpful in arguments because it is often extremely memorable. A person arguing that slang should be used in formal writing turns to this memorable definition for support: "Slang is language that takes off its coat, spits on its hands, and gets to work." In a brief poem that carries a powerful argument, Langston Hughes uses figurative language to explore the consequences of unfulfilled dreams:

What happens to a dream deferred?

Does it dry up
Like a raisin in the sun?
Or fester like a sore—
And then run?
Does it stink like rotten meat?
Or crust and sugar over—
Like a syrupy sweet?

Maybe it just sags
Like a heavy load.

Or does it explode?

–Langston Hughes, "Harlem—A Dream Deferred"

In 1963, Martin Luther King Jr. used figurative language to make his argument for civil rights unmistakably clear as well as memorable:

In a sense we have come to our nation's capital to cash a check. When the architects of our republic wrote the magnificent words of the Constitution and the Declaration of Independence, they were signing a promissory note to which every American was to fall heir. This note was a promise that all men would be guaranteed the unalienable rights of life, liberty, and the pursuit of happiness.

It is obvious today that America has defaulted on this promissory note insofar as her citizens of color are concerned. Instead of honoring this sacred obligation, America has given the Negro people a bad check; a check which has come back marked "insufficient funds." But we refuse to believe that the bank of justice is bankrupt. We refuse to believe that there are insufficient funds in the great vaults of opportunity in this nation. So we have come to cash this check—a check that will give us upon demand the riches of freedom and the security of justice.

–Martin Luther King Jr., "I Have a Dream"

The figures of the promissory note and the bad check are especially effective here because they suggest financial exploitation, which fits perfectly with the overall theme of King's speech.

You may be surprised to learn that during the European Renaissance, schoolchildren sometimes learned and practiced using as many as 180 figures of speech. Such practice seems more than a little excessive today, especially because figures of speech come so naturally to native speakers of the English language; you hear of "chilling out," "taking flak," "nipping a plot in the bud," "getting our act together," "blowing your cover," "marching to a different drummer," "seeing red," "smelling a rat," "being on cloud nine," "throwing in the towel," "tightening our belts," "rolling in the aisles," "turning the screws"—you get the picture. In fact, you and your friends no doubt have favorite figures of speech, ones you use every day. Why not take a quick inventory during one day—just listen to everything that's said around you, and jot down any figurative language you hear.

We can't aim for a complete catalog of figures of speech here, much less a thorough analysis of the power of the special effects they create. What we can offer, however, is a brief listing—with examples—of some of the most familiar kinds of figures, along with a reminder that they can be used to extremely good effect in the arguments you write.

Figures have traditionally been classified into two main types: *tropes,* which involve a change in the ordinary signification, or meaning, of a word or phrase; and *schemes,* which involve a special arrangement of words. Here are the most frequently used figures in each category, beginning with the familiar tropes of metaphor, simile, and analogy.

Tropes

METAPHOR

One of the most pervasive uses of figurative language, metaphor offers an implied comparison between two things and thereby clarifies and enlivens many arguments. In the following passage, bell hooks uses the metaphor of the hope chest to enhance her argument that autobiography involves a special kind of treasure hunt:

> Conceptually, the autobiography was framed in the manner of a hope chest. I remembered my mother's hope chest, with its wonderful odor of cedar, and thought about her taking the most precious items and placing them there for safekeeping. Certain memories were for me a similar treasure. I wanted to place them somewhere for safekeeping. An autobiographical narrative seemed an appropriate place.
>
> –bell hooks, *Bone Black*

In another example, a profile of conservative activist Grover Norquist quotes him using a metaphor in criticizing Republicans he thinks have gone in the wrong direction:

> "When you have a brand like Coca-Cola, and you find a rat head in the bottle, you create an outcry. . . . Republicans who raise taxes are rat heads in Coke bottles. They endanger the brand."
>
> –John Cassidy, "The Ringleader"

English language use is so filled with metaphors that these powerful, persuasive tools often zip by unnoticed, so be on the lookout for effective metaphors in everything you read. For example, when a reviewer of new software that promises complete filtering of advertisements on the World Wide Web refers to the product as "a weedwhacker for the Web," he's using a metaphor to advance an argument about the nature and function of that product.

SIMILE

A direct comparison between two things that uses *like* or *as*, simile is pervasive in both written and spoken language. Eminem's song "Like Toy Soldiers," for example, compares human beings to toy soldiers who "all fall down," are "torn apart," and "never win" but fight on anyway; a radio announcer says the UCLA men's basketball team are so eager for the NCAA playoffs that they're "like pit bulls on pork chops." One of our grandmothers used to say "prices are high as a cat's back" or, as a special compliment, "you look as pretty as red shoes." Here's a more formal written example from an article in the *New Yorker* magazine:

> You can tell the graphic-novels section in a bookstore from afar, by the young bodies sprawled around it like casualties of a localized disaster.
>
> –Peter Schjeldahl, "Words and Pictures: Graphic Novels Come of Age"

Similes play a major part in many arguments, as you can see in this excerpt from a brief *Wired* magazine review of a new magazine for women:

> Women's magazines occupy a special niche in the cluttered infoscape of modern media. Ask any *Vogue* junkie: no girl-themed Web site or CNN segment on women's health can replace the guilty pleasure of slipping a glossy fashion rag into your shopping cart. Smooth as a pint of chocolate Häagen-Dazs, feckless as a thousand-dollar slip dress, women's magazines wrap culture, trends, health, and trash in a single, decadent package. But like the diet dessert recipes they print, these slick publications can leave a bad taste in your mouth.
>
> – Tiffany Lee Brown, "En Vogue"

Here three similes are in prominent display: "smooth as a pint of chocolate Häagen-Dazs" and "feckless as a thousand-dollar slip dress" in the third sentence, and "like the diet dessert recipes" in the fourth. Together, the similes add to the image the writer is trying to create of mass-market women's magazines as a mishmash of "trash" and "trends."

ANALOGY

Analogies draw comparisons between two things, often point by point, in order to show similarity in certain respects (as in *Many are tempted to draw an analogy between the computer and the human brain*) or to argue that if two things are alike in one way they are probably alike in other ways as well. Often extended to several sentences, paragraphs, or even whole essays, analogies can clarify and emphasize points of comparison. In considering the movie *Hustle and Flow,* a reviewer draws an analogy between the character DJay and the late, great Duke Ellington:

> As [actor] Howard develops DJay's frustration and rue, he avoids the obvious, the overemphatic. His self-mocking performance is so ironically refined and allusive that one might think that Duke Ellington himself had slipped into an old undershirt and hit the fetid streets of Memphis.
>
> – David Denby, "Stayin' Alive"

And in an argument about the failures of the aircraft industry, another writer uses an analogy for potent contrast:

> If the aircraft industry had evolved as spectacularly as the computer industry over the past twenty-five years, a Boeing 767 would cost five hundred dollars today, and it would circle the globe in twenty minutes on five gallons of fuel.

CULTURAL CONTEXTS FOR ARGUMENT

Formality and Other Style Issues

Style is always affected by language, culture, and rhetorical tradition.
What constitutes effective style, therefore, varies broadly across
cultures and depends on the rhetorical situation—purpose, audience,
and so on. There's at least one important style question to consider
when arguing across cultures: what level of formality is most appropriate? In the United States, a fairly informal style is often acceptable,
even appreciated.

Many cultures, however, tend to value formality. If you're in doubt,
therefore, it's probably wise to err on the side of formality, especially in
communicating with elders or with those in authority:

- Take care to use proper titles as appropriate—*Ms., Mr., Dr.,* and
  so on.

- Don't use first names unless you've been invited to do so.

- Steer clear of slang. Especially when you're communicating with
  members of other cultures, slang may not be understood—or it
  may be seen as disrespectful.

Beyond formality, stylistic preferences vary widely. When arguing
across cultures, the most important stylistic issue might be clarity, especially when you're communicating with people whose native languages are different from your own. In such situations, analogies and
similes almost always aid in understanding. Likening something unknown to something familiar can help make your argument forceful—
and understandable.

Other Tropes

Several other tropes deserve special mention.

One distinctive trope found extensively in African American English
is **signifying,** in which a speaker cleverly and often humorously needles
the listener. In the following passage, two African American men (Grave
Digger and Coffin Ed) signify on their white supervisor (Anderson), who
has ordered them to discover the originators of a riot:

> "I take it you've discovered who started the riot," Anderson said.
> "We knew who he was all along," Grave Digger said.

> "It's just nothing we can do to him," Coffin Ed echoed.
>
> "Why not, for God's sake?"
>
> "He's dead," Coffin Ed said.
>
> "Who?"
>
> "Lincoln," Grave Digger said.
>
> "He hadn't ought to have freed us if he didn't want to make provisions to feed us," Coffin Ed said. "Anyone could have told him that."
>
> –Chester Himes, *Hot Day, Hot Night*

Coffin Ed and Grave Digger demonstrate the major characteristics of effective signifying: indirection, ironic humor, fluid rhythm — and a surprising twist at the end. Rather than insulting Anderson directly by pointing out that he's asked a dumb question, they criticize the question indirectly by ultimately blaming a white man (and not just any white man, but one they're all supposed to revere). This twist leaves the supervisor speechless, teaching him something and giving Grave Digger and Coffin Ed the last word — and the last laugh.

You'll find examples of signifying in the work of many African American writers. You may also hear signifying in NBA basketball, for it's an important element of trash talking; what Grave Digger and Coffin Ed do to Anderson, Allen Iverson regularly does to his opponents on the court.

Take a look at the example of signifying from a *Boondocks* cartoon (see the figure on p. 385). Note how Huey seems to be sympathizing with Jazmine and then, in not one but two surprising twists, reveals that he has been needling her all along.

Hyperbole is the use of overstatement for special effect, a kind of pyrotechnics in prose. The tabloid papers whose headlines scream at shoppers in the grocery checkout line probably qualify as the all-time champions of hyperbole (journalist Tom Wolfe once wrote a satirical review of a *National Enquirer* writers' convention that he titled "Keeps His Mom-in-Law in Chains Meets Kills Son and Feeds Corpse to Pigs"). Everyone has seen these overstated arguments and, perhaps, marveled at the way they seem to sell.

Hyperbole is also the trademark of more serious writers. In a column arguing that men's magazines fuel the same kind of neurotic anxieties about appearance that have plagued women for so long, Michelle Cottle uses hyperbole and humor to make her point:

> What self-respecting '90s woman could embrace a publication that runs such enlightened articles as "Turn Your Good Girl Bad" and "How to Wake Up Next to a One-Night Stand"? Or maybe you'll smile and

In these *Boondocks* strips, Huey signifies on Jazmine, using indirection, ironic humor, and two surprising twists.

wink knowingly: What red-blooded hetero chick wouldn't love all those glossy photo spreads of buff young beefcake in various states of undress, ripped abs and glutes flexed so tightly you could bounce a check on them? Either way you've got the wrong idea. My affection for *Men's Health* is driven by pure gender politics. . . . With page after page of bulging biceps and Gillette jaws, robust hairlines and silken skin, *Men's Health* is peddling a standard of male beauty as unforgiving and unrealistic as the female version sold by those dewy-eyed pre-teen waifs draped across covers of *Glamour* and *Elle*.

–Michelle Cottle, "Turning Boys into Girls"

As you can well imagine, hyperbole of this sort can easily backfire, so it pays to use it sparingly and for an audience whose reactions you can predict with confidence. American journalist H. L. Mencken ignored this advice in 1921 when he used relentless hyperbole to savage the literary style of President Warren Harding—and note that in doing so he says that he's offering a "small tribute," making the irony even more notable:

I rise to pay my small tribute to Dr. Harding. Setting aside a college professor or two and half a dozen dipsomaniacal newspaper reporters, he takes the first place in my Valhalla of literati. That is to say, he writes the worst English that I have ever encountered. It reminds me of a string of wet sponges; it reminds me of tattered washing on the line; it reminds me of stale bean-soup, of college yells, of dogs barking idiotically through endless nights. It is so bad that a sort of grandeur creeps into it. It drags itself out of the dark abysm (I was about to write abcess!) of pish, and crawls insanely up the topmost pinnacle of posh. It is rumble and bumble. It is flap and doodle. It is balder and dash.

–H. L. Mencken

Understatement, on the other hand, requires a quiet, muted message to make its point effectively. In her memoir, Rosa Parks—the civil rights activist who made history in 1955 by refusing to give up her bus seat to a white passenger—uses understatement so often that it might be said to be characteristic of her writing, a mark of her ethos. She refers to Martin Luther King Jr. simply as "a true leader," to Malcolm X as a person of "strong conviction," and to her own lifelong efforts as simply a small way of "carrying on."

Understatement can be particularly effective in arguments that would seem to call for its opposite. When Watson and Crick published their first article on the structure of DNA, they felt that they had done nothing less than discover the secret of life. (Imagine what the *National Enquirer* headlines might have been for this story!) Yet in an atmosphere of extreme scientific competitiveness they chose to close their article with a vast understatement, using it purposely to gain emphasis: "It has not escaped our notice," they wrote, "that the specific pairing we have postulated immediately suggests a possible copying mechanism for the genetic material." A half-century later, considering the profound developments that have taken place in genetics, including the cloning of animals, the power of this understatement resonates even more strongly.

Rhetorical questions don't really require answers. Rather, they help assert or deny something about an argument. Most of us use rhetorical questions frequently; think, for instance, of the times you've said "Who cares?" or "Why me?" or "How should I know?"—rhetorical questions all. Rhetorical questions also show up in written arguments. In a review of a book-length argument about the use and misuse of power in the Disney dynasty, Linda Watts uses a series of rhetorical questions to sketch in part of the book's argument:

If you have ever visited one of the Disney theme parks, though, you have likely wondered at the labor—both seen and unseen—necessary to maintain these fanciful environments. How and when are the grounds tended so painstakingly? How are the signs of high traffic erased from public facilities? What keeps employees so poised, meticulously groomed, and endlessly cheerful?

–Linda S. Watts, review of *Inside the Mouse*

And here's Debra Saunders, opening an argument for the legalization of medical marijuana with a rhetorical question:

> If the federal government were right that medical marijuana has no medicinal value, why have so many doctors risked their practices by recommending its use for patients with cancer or AIDS?
>
> –Debra Saunders

Antonomasia is probably most familiar to you from the sports pages: "His Airness" means Michael Jordan; "The Great One," Wayne Gretzky; "The Sultan of Swat," Babe Ruth; "The Swiss Miss," Martina Hingis. And in the 2006 Winter Olympics, snowboarder Shaun White became "The

Flying Tomato." Such shorthand substitutions of a descriptive word or phrase for a proper name can pack arguments into just one phrase. What does calling Jordan "His Airness" argue about him?

Irony, the use of words to convey a meaning in tension with or opposite to their literal meanings, also works powerfully in arguments. One of the most famous sustained uses of irony in literature occurs in Shakespeare's *Julius Caesar,* as Mark Antony punctuates his condemnation of Brutus with the repeated ironic phrase "But Brutus is an honourable man." You may be a reader of *The Onion,* noted for its ironic treatment of politics. Another journal, the online *Ironic Times,* devotes itself to irony. Take a

Sportscasters who dubbed snowboarder Shaun White "The Flying Tomato" probably didn't realize they were using the trope of antonomasia.

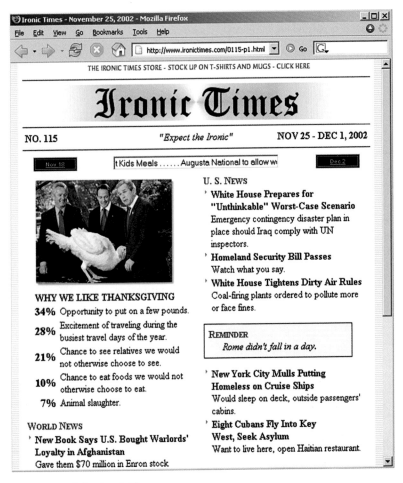

Front page of the *Ironic Times*

look at the front page above, whose lead story has taken on an additional layer of irony since it was published in 2002.

Schemes

Schemes, figures that depend on word order, can add quite a bit of syntactic "zing" to arguments. Here we present the ones you're likely to see most often.

Parallelism involves the use of grammatically similar phrases or clauses for special effect:

> Those who teach, and who think for a living about American history, need to be told: Keep the text, teach the text, and only then, if you must, deconstruct the text.
>
> –Peggy Noonan, "Patriots, Then and Now"

> Current government programs don't protect poor people very well against the cost of becoming sick. They do much better at protecting sick people against the risk of becoming poor.
>
> –Michael Kinsley, "To Your Health"

> The laws of our land are said to be "by the people, of the people, and for the people."

Antithesis is the use of parallel structures to mark contrast or opposition:

> That's one small step for a man, one giant leap for mankind.
>
> –Neil Armstrong

> Marriage has many pains, but celibacy has no pleasures.
>
> –Samuel Johnson

> Those who kill people are called murderers; those who kill animals, sportsmen.

Inverted word order, in which the parts of a sentence or clause are not in the usual subject-verb-object order, can help make arguments particularly memorable:

> Into this grey lake plopped the thought, I know this man, don't I?
>
> –Doris Lessing

> Hard to see, the dark side is.
>
> –Yoda

> Good looking he was not; wealthy he was not; but brilliant—he was.

As with anything else, however, too much of such a figure can quickly become, well, too much.

Anaphora, or effective repetition, can act like a drumbeat in an argument, bringing the point home. In an argument about the future of Chicago, Lerone Bennett Jr. uses repetition to link Chicago to innovation and creativity:

[Chicago]'s the place where organized Black history was born, where gospel music was born, where jazz and the blues were reborn, where the Beatles and the Rolling Stones went up to the mountaintop to get the new musical commandments from Chuck Berry and the rock'n'roll apostles.

–Lerone Bennett Jr., "Blacks in Chicago"

And speaking of the Rolling Stones, here's Dave Barry using repetition in his comments on their 2002 tour:

Recently I attended a Rolling Stones concert. This is something I do every two decades. I saw the Stones in the 1960s, and then again in the 1980s. I plan to see them next in the 2020s, then the 2040s, then the 2060s, at their 100th anniversary concert.

–Dave Barry, "OK, What Will Stones Do for 100th Anniversary?"

Reversed structures for special effect have been used widely in political argumentation since President John F. Kennedy's inaugural address in 1961 charged citizens, "Ask not what your country can do for you; ask what you can do for your country." Like the other figures we've listed here, this one can help make arguments memorable:

The Democrats won't get elected unless things get worse, and things won't get worse until the Democrats get elected.

–Jeane Kirkpatrick

Your manuscript is both good and original. But the part that is good is not original, and the part that is original is not good.

–Samuel Johnson

When the going gets tough, the tough get going.

If Everything's an Argument . . .

Choose a passage from this chapter (perhaps the description of high, middle, and low style on p. 370, or the introduction to figurative language on p. 378), and look carefully at the words the authors of this book have chosen to use. What tone do words in these passages create? Do you find the word choice effective—or not?

RESPOND●

1. Turn to something you read frequently—a Web log, a sports or news magazine, a zine—and look closely at the sentences. What seems distinctive about them? Do they vary in terms of their length and the way they begin? If so, how? Do they use parallel structures to good effect? How easy to read are they, and what accounts for that ease?

2. Try your hand at writing a brief movie review for your campus newspaper, experimenting with punctuation as one way to create an effective style. Consider whether a series of questions might have a strong effect, whether exclamation points would add or detract from the message you want to send, and so on. When you've finished the review, compare it to one written by a classmate and look for similarities and differences in your choices of punctuation.

3. In the following advertising slogans, identify the types of figurative language used: metaphor, simile, analogy, hyperbole, understatement, rhetorical question, antonomasia, irony, parallelism, antithesis, inverted word order, anaphora, or reversed structure.

   "Good to the last drop." (Maxwell House coffee)

   "It's the real thing." (Coca-Cola)

   "Melts in your mouth, not in your hands." (M&M's)

   "Be all that you can be." (U.S. Army)

   "Got Milk?" (America's Milk Processors)

   "Breakfast of champions." (Wheaties)

   "Double your pleasure; double your fun." (Doublemint gum)

   "Let your fingers do the walking." (the Yellow Pages)

   "Think small." (Volkswagen)

   "Like a Rock." (Chevy trucks)

   "Real bonding, real popcorn, real butter, real good times." (Pop-Secret Popcorn)

4. Some public speakers are well known for their use of tropes and schemes. (Jesse Jackson comes to mind, as does George W. Bush, who employs folksy sayings to achieve a certain effect.) Using the Internet, find the text of a recent speech by a speaker who uses figures liberally. Pick a paragraph that seems particularly rich in figures and rewrite it, eliminating every trace of figurative language. Then read the two paragraphs—the original and your revised version—aloud to your class. With your classmates' help, try to imagine rhetorical situations in which the figure-free version would be most appropriate.

Now find some prose that seems dry and pretty much nonfigurative. (A technical manual, instructions for operating appliances, or a legal document might serve.) Rewrite a part of the piece in the most figurative language you can muster. Then try to list rhetorical situations in which this newly figured language might be most appropriate.

13
Humor in Arguments

When the city council passes an ordinance requiring bicyclists to wear helmets to protect against head injuries, a cyclist responds by writing a letter to the editors of the local newspaper suggesting other requirements the council might impose to protect citizens—including wearing earplugs in dance clubs, water wings in city pools, and blinders in City Hall.

A distinguished professor at a prestigious school dashes off a column for the campus paper on a controversial issue, perhaps spending a little less time than she should backing up her claims. The op-ed piece gets picked up by a blogger who circulates it nationally, and responses flood in — including one from a student who grades the paper like a freshman essay. The professor doesn't get an "A."

An undergraduate who thinks his school's new sexual harassment policy amounts to Puritanism parodies it for the school humor magazine by describing in a short fictional drama what would happen if Romeo and Juliet strayed onto campus.

Tired of looking at the advertisements that cover every square inch of the campus sports arena walls, a student sends the college newspaper a satirical "news" article entitled "Sports Arena for Sale — to Advertisers!"

● ● ●

Breathes there a college student who doesn't read *The Onion* in its print or online versions? Sure, its humor can be sophomoric, yet that's just fine with many undergraduates. But it's not just four-letter words and bathroom jokes that make young people fans of *The Onion* today or that made their parents avid readers of *The National Lampoon* or even *Mad Magazine*. Nor has *Saturday Night Live* survived more than thirty years on TV because viewers (again, mainly young) want to hear Madonna sing "Fever" or watch the Rolling Stones creak through "Brown Sugar" one more time. No, we suspect that these productions — print and video — have attracted and held audiences so long because they use humor to argue passionately against all that's pompous, absurd, irritating, irrational, venal, hypocritical, and even evil in the adult world.

By its very nature, humor is risky. Sometimes playing fast and loose with good taste and sound reason, writers using humor turn what's comfortable and familiar inside out and hope readers get the joke. They play with words and situations, manipulating readers' sense of language, propriety, and normalcy until they react with that physiological explosion called laughter (or maybe just a smile or smirk). Here, for example, speaking to a gathering of the Republican Jewish Coalition, President George W. Bush uses a little religious humor to honor a rabbi who had aided victims of Hurricane Katrina:

Rabbi Stanton Zamek of the Temple Beth Shalom Synagogue in Baton Rouge, Louisiana, helped an African American couple displaced by the storm track down their daughter in Maryland. When Rabbi Zamek called the daughter, he told her, "We have your parents." She screamed out, "Thank you, Jesus!" (Laughter.) He didn't have the heart to tell her she was thanking the wrong rabbi. (Laughter and applause.)

If humorists play it too safe, they lose their audiences; if they step over an unseen line, people groan or hiss or act offended. Humor, especially satire, is a knife's edge that had better cut precisely or not at all.

Understanding Humor as Argument

To use humor in arguments, you must first understand the foibles of human nature. That's because humor often works best when it deals with ordinary life and day-to-day events, as well as controversies in the worlds of politics and entertainment. (You might be surprised how many Americans get their daily news from the monologues of late-night comedians or from programs like *The Colbert Report*.) Timeliness, too, makes comedians seem hip and smart: their sharp minds decide what many people will be chuckling and *thinking* about the next day. But for the same reason, a lot of humor doesn't have the shelf life of lettuce. And some humor doesn't easily cross canyons that divide ethnic groups, classes, or generations. Maybe Catholics still laugh hardest at jokes about Catholic schools. But comedians often use humor to demolish societal stereotypes while simultaneously exploring them: Chris Rock can poke fun at African Americans in ways that no white humorist would dare, while Margaret Cho uses her position as a bisexual Korean American to give political focus to her wickedly sharp humor.

Margaret Cho, a humorist with a political attitude.

Obviously, then, humor isn't simple, nor can it be learned quickly or easily. It often involves subtle strategies of exaggeration, amplification, repetition, understatement, and irony. But it's too powerful a tool to leave solely to comedians. For writers and speakers, humor can sharpen many different kinds of argument by giving heightened presence to logical, emotional, and — especially — ethical appeals. Occasionally, humor even dictates the structure of arguments — when, for example, you choose to make an argumentative point by writing a parody or satire. *The Onion*'s parody of news magazine graphics on p. 397, for example, may not offer an explicit thesis about the way the National Collegiate Athletic Association ranks college football teams, but it makes readers suspect that the current system doesn't work.

Humor can simply make people pay attention or feel good — or make them want to buy stuff or do what others ask. That's the rationale behind many "soft sell" commercials, from classic VW pitches of a generation ago ("Think small") to more recent ads for products such as insurance ("AFLAC!"). Advertisers use humor to capture your interest and make you feel good about their products. Who focused on AFLAC insurance prior to the duck, Geico before the gecko, or Energizer pre-bunny?

Humor has a darker side, too; it can make people feel superior to its targets of ridicule. And most of us don't want to associate with people who seem ridiculous. Bullies and cliques in secondary school often use humor to torment their innocent victims, behavior that's really nasty. In the political arena, however, politicians may be fairer game, given their resources and ambitions. So when *Saturday Night Live* set out after both George W. Bush and John Kerry during the presidential campaign season of 2004, the parodies of these men rang true. Voters were left to choose between a candidate who was portrayed as a moronic mangler of the English language or a pompous, preening windbag. Does such humor have an effect on voting? Maybe.

Humor plays a large role, too, in arguments of character. If you want audiences to like you, make them laugh. It's no accident that all but the most serious speeches begin with a few jokes or stories. The humor puts listeners at ease and helps them identify with the speaker. In fact, a little self-deprecation can endear writers or speakers to the toughest audiences. You'll listen to people confident enough to make fun of themselves because they seem clever and yet aware of their own limitations.

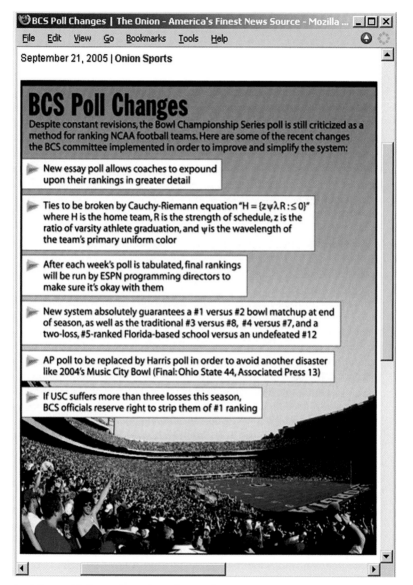

An infographic from *The Onion* takes on the way the NCAA determines its national champions in football.

Humor also works because a funny remark usually contains, at its core, an element of truth:

Clothes make the man. Naked people have little or no influence in society.

– Samuel Clemens

Fame changes a lot of things, but it can't change a light bulb.

–Gilda Radner

Some humor may even involve looking at a subject a little too logically. Dave Barry, for example, responds to Elizabeth Marshall Thomas's arguments in *The Hidden Life of Dogs* that Fido is a complex creature capable of highly refined cogitations, by doing a little tongue-in-cheek ethnographic study of his own pets:

Anyway, reading this book got me to thinking about my own dogs. Did they have a hidden life? If so, could I discover it, and—more important—write a best-selling book?

To find out, I removed my dogs from the confined, controlled environment of our house and put them outside, where they were free to reveal their hidden lives. I observed them closely for the better part of a day, and thus I am able to reveal here, for the first time anywhere, that what dogs do, when they are able to make their own decisions in accordance with their unfettered natural instincts, is: Try to get back inside the house. They spent most of the day pressing sad moony faces up against the glass patio door, taking only occasional breaks to see if it was a good idea to eat worms (Answer: No).

Of course, the dogs have important and complex socio-biological reasons for wanting to get back into the house. For one thing, the house contains the most wondrous thing in the world: the kitchen counter. One time a piece of turkey fell off of it. The dogs still regularly visit the spot where it landed, in case it shows up again. There's an invisible Dog Historic Marker there.

–Dave Barry, "The Hidden Life of Dogs"

Many forms of humor, especially satire and parody, get their power from just such twists of logic. When Jonathan Swift in the eighteenth century suggested in "A Modest Proposal" that Ireland's English rulers consider a diet of fricasseed Irish toddlers, he gambled on readers seeing the parallel between his outrageous proposal and the brutal policies of an oppressive English colonial government. The satire works precisely because it's perfectly logical, given the political facts of Swift's time— though some of his contemporaries missed the joke:

> I profess, in the sincerity of my heart, that I have not the least personal interest in endeavoring to promote this necessary work, having no other motive but the public good of my country, by advancing our trade, providing for infants, relieving the poor, and giving some pleasure to the rich.
>
> –Jonathan Swift, "A Modest Proposal"

In our own era, columnist Molly Ivins ridicules opponents of gun control by seeming to agree with them and then adding a logical twist that makes her real point:

> I think that's what we need: more people carrying weapons. I support the [concealed gun] legislation but I'd like to propose one small amendment. Everyone should be able to carry a concealed weapon. But everyone who carries a weapon should be required to wear one of those little beanies on their heads with a little propeller on it so the rest of us can see them coming.
>
> –Molly Ivins

Characterizing Kinds of Humor

It's possible to write whole books about comedy, exploring its many forms such as satire, parody, burlesque, travesty, pastiche, lampoon, caricature, farce, and more. Almost all types of humor involve some kind of argument because laughter can make people think, even while they're having a good time. As we've noted, not all such purposes are praiseworthy; schoolyard bullies and vicious editorial cartoonists may use their humor just to hurt or humiliate their targets. But laughter can also expose hypocrisy or break down barriers of prejudice and thereby help people see their worlds differently. When it's robust and honest, humor is a powerful rhetorical form.

Humor can contribute to almost any argument, but you have to know when to use it—especially in academic writing. You'll catch a reader's attention if you insert a little laughter to lighten the tone of a serious or dry piece. Here, for example, is the African American writer Zora Neale Hurston addressing the very real issue of discrimination, with a nod, a wink, and a rhetorical question:

> Sometimes I feel discriminated against, but it does not make me angry. It merely astonishes me. How can any deny themselves the pleasure of my company? It's beyond me.
>
> –Zora Neale Hurston, "How It Feels to Be Colored Me"

You might use a whole sequence of comic examples and anecdotes to keep readers interested in a serious point—a rhetorical device called

Not Just Words

Visual arguments that make their case through humor have a way of turning up unexpectedly. Consider the case of U.S. Senator Deborah Stabenow, who took to the floor of the Senate to denounce the Bush administration as "dangerously incompetent"—a theme set by the Democratic Party in spring 2006. Unfortunately, she made the mistake of being photographed next to a large yellow-on-red chart bearing that slogan. Her opponents had a field day, distributing her image across the Internet and even creating a "Dangerous Debbie" Web site. The visual image Stabenow herself had created suddenly became an argument humorously undermining her own competence.

Armed with a digital camera, look for unexpected visual arguments of this kind—preferably humorous ones—in your own environment. Your photograph may make a claim on its own or, if you have the skill, you may want to underscore your point by doctoring the image using PhotoShop or other software, cropping it strategically, or adding a caption. Here, for example, is a photograph taken in Death Valley National Park, which seems to poke fun at the National Park Service, the use of park fees, or perhaps, the competence of government in general.

amplification. How would you, for example, make the rather academic point that nurture and socialization alone can't account for certain differences between girls and boys? Here's how Prudence Mackintosh, mother of three sons, defends that claim:

> How can I explain why a little girl baby sits on a quilt in the park thoughtfully examining a blade of grass, while my baby William uproots grass by handfuls and eats it? Why does a mother of very bright and active daughters confide that until she went camping with another family of boys, she feared that my sons had a hyperactivity problem? I am sure there are plenty of noisy, rowdy little girls, but I'm not just talking about rowdiness and noise. I'm talking about some sort of primal physicalness that causes the walls of my house to pulsate on rainy days. I'm talking about something inexplicable that makes my sons fall into a mad, scrambling, pull-your-ears-off-kick-your-teeth-in heap just before bedtime, when they're not even mad at each other. I mean something that causes them to climb the doorjamb with honey and peanut butter on their hands while giving me a synopsis of *Star Wars* that contains only five unintelligible words. . . . When Jack and Drew are not kicking a soccer ball or each other, they are kicking the chair legs, the cat, the baby's silver rattle, and inadvertently, Baby William himself, whom they have affectionately dubbed "Tough Eddy."
>
> –Prudence Mackintosh, "Masculine/Feminine"

In reading this cascade of words, you can just about feel the angst of a mother who thought she could raise her boys to be different. Most readers will chuckle at little William eating grass, the house pulsating, doorjambs sticky with peanut butter—and appreciate Mackintosh's point, whether they agree with it or not. Her intention, however, isn't so much to be funny, as to give her opinion presence. And, of course, she exaggerates. But exaggeration is a basic technique of humor. We make a situation bigger than life so we can see it better.

Satire

Most of the humor college students create is either satire or parody, which is discussed in the next section. Type "college humor magazines" into the search engine Google, and you'll find Web sites that list dozens of journals such as the University of Michigan's *Gargoyle,* Penn State's *Phroth,* UC Berkeley's *The Heuristic Squelch,* and Ohio State's *The Shaft.* In these journals you'll find humor of all varieties, some pretty

Digital photography creates new opportunities for college humorists, such as the editors of Penn State's *Phroth.*

raunchy, but much of it aimed at the oddities of college life, ranging from unsympathetic administrations to crummy teachers and courses. There's lots of grousing, too, about women and men and campus parking. Much of this material is satire, a genre of writing that uses humor to unmask problems and then suggest (not always directly) how they might be fixed. The most famous piece of satire in English literature is probably Jonathan Swift's *Gulliver's Travels,* which pokes fun at all human shortcomings, targeting especially politics, religion, science, and sexuality. For page after page, Swift argues for change in human character and institutions. In a much different way, so do campus humor magazines.

You'll find social and political satire in television programs such as *The Simpsons* and *South Park* and movies such as *This Is Spinal Tap, Dr. Strangelove,* and *Election.* Most editorial cartoons are also satiric when they highlight a problem in society that the cartoonist feels needs to be both ridiculed *and* remedied (see the figure on p. 403).

Satire often involves a shift in perspective that asks readers to look at a situation in a new way. In *Gulliver's Travels,* for example, we see human society reduced in scale (in Lilliput), exaggerated in size (in Brobdingnag), even viewed through the eyes of a superior race of horses (the Houyhnhnms). In the land of the giants, Gulliver notices that, seen up close on a gargantuan scale, women aren't as alluring as they once seemed to him:

> Their skins appeared so coarse and uneven, so variously coloured, when I saw them near, with a mole here and there as broad as a trencher, and hairs hanging from it thicker than pack-threads, to say nothing further concerning the rest of their persons.
>
> –Jonathan Swift, *Gulliver's Travels*

www.CoxAndForkum.com

Was the Supreme Court right to support federal efforts to override state laws supporting the medical use of marijuana? Cartoonists Cox and Forkum don't think so.

So much for human beauty. You'll note that there's nothing especially funny in Gulliver's remarks. That's because satire is sometimes more thought-provoking than funny, the point of some satire being to open readers' eyes rather than to make them laugh out loud.

The key to writing effective satire may be finding a humorous or novel angle on a subject and then following through. In other words, you say "What if?" and then employ a kind of mad logic, outlining in great detail all that follows from the question. For example, to satirize groups that believe homosexuals are using the nation's public schools to recruit children to their lifestyle, *The Onion* asks its readers to consider that the charge might be true. For paragraph after paragraph, the satirists let the idea unfold using all the logic and apparatus of a news story happily reporting on the campaign, complete with a graph. You can see from just a few paragraphs how satire of this kind works by making the implausible seem comically real (see the figure on p. 404).

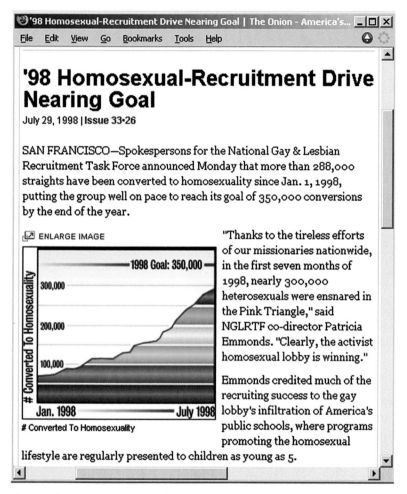

The complete story appears in *The Onion,* July 29, 1998.

Parody

Like satire, parody also offers an argument. What distinguishes the two forms is that parody makes its case by taking something familiar—be it songs, passages of prose, TV shows, poems, films, even people—and turning it into something new. The argument sparkles in the tension between the original work and its imitation. That's where the humor lies, too. The editors of *The Travesty*, for example, explain exactly how *The Onion* works (see the figure below) in their own parody of that humor publication: "ANYWHERE, US—Normally occurring incidents of every-day life—such as people eating cornflakes, going shopping for new tires and getting bad haircuts—are made humorous when they are written about as if they were serious news." The parody, of course, includes a full mockup of *The Onion*'s distinctive graphics, photographs, and headlines.

Needless to say, parodies work best when audiences make the connection with the object being imitated. For instance, you wouldn't entirely

The Travesty parodies a parody.

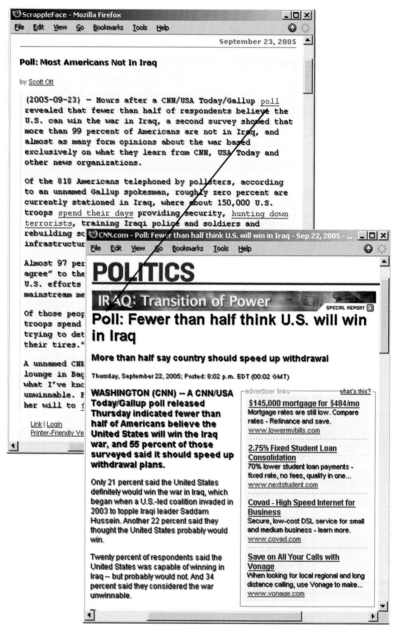

Clicking on a link in this parody by Scott Ott takes a reader to the source that inspires his humor.

appreciate the film *Galaxy Quest* unless you knew the *Star Trek* series. Blogger and humorist Scott Ott <http://ScrappleFace.com> makes sure his readers know whom he's targeting in his daily parodies simply by providing Web links (see the figure on p. 406). That enables readers to make their own judgments about Ott's criticism and humor.

If you write a parody, you need to be thoroughly knowledgeable about the work on which it's based, particularly its organization and distinctive features. In parodying a song, for example, you've got to be sure listeners recognize familiar lines or choruses. In parodying a longer piece, boil it down to essential elements—the most familiar actions in the plot, the most distinctive characters, the best-known passages of dialogue—and then arrange those elements within a compact and rapidly moving design. When a subject or work becomes the object of a successful parody, it's never seen in quite the same way again.

If Everything's an Argument . . .

Because of its subject matter, this chapter obviously can draw on examples of wit, satire, and parody that lighten the discussion and make it more appealing. But is there any larger and more general role for humor in textbooks? Have you noticed whether humor is used in other chapters of this book? If it's used, how successful did you find it? Why are textbooks generally so free of levity? What are the possible drawbacks of using humor, satire, or parody in such publications? Explore these issues in a brief essay, arguing for or against more humor in college textbooks and drawing on this book for support as appropriate.

Developing Humorous Arguments

It's doubtful anyone can offer a formula for being funny; some would suggest that humor is a gift. But at least the comic perspective is a trait widely distributed among the population. Most people can be funny, given the right circumstances. You can use humor in an argument to:

- point out flaws in a policy, proposal, or other kind of argument
- suggest a policy of your own

- put people in a favorable frame of mind
- acknowledge weaknesses or deflect criticism
- satirize or parody a position, point of view, or style

However, the stars may not always be aligned when you need them in composing an argument. And just working hard may not help: laughter arises from high-spirited, not labored, insights. Yet once you strike the spark, a blaze usually follows.

Look for humor in incongruity or in "What if?" situations, and then imagine the consequences. *What if reading caused flatulence? What if students hired special prosecutors to handle their grade complaints? What if broccoli tasted like chocolate? What if politicians always told the truth? What if the Pope wasn't Catholic?*

Don't look for humor in complicated ideas. You're more apt to find it in simple premises, such as a question Dave Barry once asked: "How come guys care so much about sports?" There are, of course, serious answers to the question. But the humor practically bubbles up on its own once you think about men and their favorite games. You can write a piece of your own just by listing details: *ESPN Football, sports bars, beer commercials, sagging couches, fantasy camps, 50-inch plasma-screen TVs, Little League, angry wives.* Push a little further, relate such items to your own personal insights and experiences, and you're likely to discover some of the incongruities and implausibilities at the heart of humor.

Let us stress detail. Abstract humor probably doesn't work for anyone except German philosophers and drunken graduate students. Look for humor in concrete and proper nouns, in people and places readers will recognize but not expect to find in your writing. Consider the technique Dave Barry uses in the following passage defending himself against those who might question his motives for attacking "sports guys":

> And before you accuse me of being some kind of sherry-sipping ascotwearing ballet-attending MacNeil-Lehrer-NewsHour-watching wussy, please note that I am a sports guy myself, having had a legendary athletic career consisting of nearly a third of the 1965 season on the track team at Pleasantville High School ("Where the Leaders of Tomorrow Are Leaving Wads of Gum on the Auditorium Seats of Today").
>
> —Dave Barry, "A Look at Sports Nuts—And We Do Mean Nuts"

Remove the lively details from the passage, and this is what's left:

And before you accuse me of being some kind of wussy, please note that I am a sports guy myself, having had an athletic career on the track team at Pleasantville High School.

Timeliness is a factor, too; you need to know whom or what your readers will recognize and how they might respond. Seek inspiration for humor in these sources:

- popular magazines, especially weekly journals (for current events)
- TV, including commercials (especially for material about people)
- classic books, music, films, artwork (as inspiration for parodies)
- comedians (to observe how they make a subject funny)

Humorous arguments can be structured exactly like more serious ones—with claims, supporting reasons, warrants, evidence, qualifiers, and rebuttals. In fact, humor has its own relentless logic. Once you set an argument going, you should press it home with the same vigor you apply in serious pieces.

Creating humor is, by nature, a robust, excessive, and egotistical activity. It requires assertiveness, courage, and often a (temporary) suspension of good judgment and taste. Whereas drafting more material than necessary usually makes good sense for writers, you can afford to be downright prodigal with humor. Pile on the examples and illustrations. Take all the risks you can with language. Indulge in puns. Leap into innuendo. Stretch your vocabulary. Play with words and have fun. Be clever, but not immaturely obscene.

Then, when you revise, recall that Polonius in Shakespeare's *Hamlet* is right about one thing: "Brevity is the soul of wit." Once you've written a humorous passage, whether a tooting horn or a full symphonic parody, you must pare your language to the bone. Think: less is more. Cut, then cut again.

That's all there is to it.

RESPOND●

1. For each of the following topics, list particular details that might contribute to a humorous look at the subject:

    overzealous environmentalists

    avaricious builders and developers

aggressive drivers

violent Hollywood films

anti-war or hemp activists

drivers of lumbering recreational vehicles

Britney Spears

high school coaches

college instructors

malls and the people who visit them

2. Spend some time listening to a friend who you think is funny. What kind of humor does he or she use? What sorts of details crop up in it? Once you've put in a few days of careful listening, try to write down some of the jokes and stories just as your friend told them. Writing humor may be excruciating at first, but you might find it easier with practice.

   After you've written a few humorous selections, think about how well they translate from the spoken word to the written. What's different? Do they work better in one medium than in another? Show your written efforts to your funny friend, and ask for comments. How would he or she revise your written efforts?

3. Using Internet search tools, find a transcript of a funny television or radio show. Read the transcript a few times, paying attention to the places where you laugh the most. Then analyze the humor, trying to understand what makes it funny. This chapter suggests several possible avenues for analysis, including normality, incongruity, simplicity, and details. How does the transcript reflect these principles? Or does it operate by a completely different set of principles? (Some of the best humor is funny because it breaks all the rules.)

14

Visual Arguments

You know you shouldn't buy camping gear just because you see it advertised on TV. But what's the harm in imagining yourself in Yosemite with the sun setting, the camp stove open, the tent up and ready? That could be you reminiscing about the rugged eight-mile climb that got you there, just like the tanned campers in the ad. Now what's that brand name again, and what's its URL?

A student government committee is meeting to talk about campus safety. One member has prepared a series of graphs showing the steady increase in the number of on-campus attacks over the last five years, along with several photographs that bring these crimes vividly to life.

It turns out that the governor and now presidential candidate who claims to be against taxes actually raised taxes in his home state—according to his opponent, who's running thirty-second TV spots to make that point. The ads feature a plainly dressed woman who sure looks credible; she's got to be a real person, not an actor, and she says he raised taxes. She wouldn't lie—would she?

You've never heard of the sponsoring time-share firm. But its letter, printed on thick bond with smart color graphics, is impressive—and hey, the company CEO is offering you a free weekend at its Palm Beach resort facility, just to consider investing in a time-share. In addition, the firm's Web site seems quite professional—quick-loading and easy to navigate. Somebody's on the ball. Perhaps you should take the firm up on its offer?

A shiny silver convertible passes you effortlessly on a steep slope along a curving mountain interstate. It's moving too fast for you to read the nameplate, but on the grill you see a three-pointed star. Hmmmm . . . Maybe after you graduate from law school and your student loans are paid off . . .

● ● ●

The Power of Visual Arguments

We don't need to be reminded that visual images have clout. Just think for a moment of where you were on September 11, 2001, and what you remember of the events of that day: almost everyone we know still reports being able to see the hijacked planes slamming into the World Trade Center Towers as though that image were forever etched in some inner eye.

What other potent images are engraved in your memory? Even in mundane moments, not memorable in the way an event like 9/11 is, visual images still surround us, from T-shirts to billboards to movie and computer screens. It seems everyone's trying to get our attention, and doing it with images as well as words. In fact, several recently published books argue that images today pack more punch than words. As tech-

A visual argument on wheels

nology makes it easier for people to create and transmit images, those images are more compelling than ever, brought to us via DVD and HDTV on our cell phones and computers, on our walls, in our pockets, even in our cars.

But let's put this in perspective. Visual arguments weren't invented by Steve Jobs, and they've always had power. The pharaohs of Egypt lined the Nile with statues of themselves to assert their authority, and Roman emperors had their portraits stamped on coins for the same reason. Some thirty thousand years ago people in the south of France created magnificent cave paintings, suggesting that people have indeed always used images to celebrate and to communicate (see the top figure on p. 414).

In our own era (speaking as authors of this book), two events marked turning points in the growing power of media images. The first occurred in 1960, when presidential candidates John F. Kennedy and Richard M. Nixon met in a nationally televised debate. Kennedy, robust and confident in a dark suit, faced a pale and haggard Nixon barely recovered from an illness. Kennedy looked cool and "presidential"; Nixon did not.

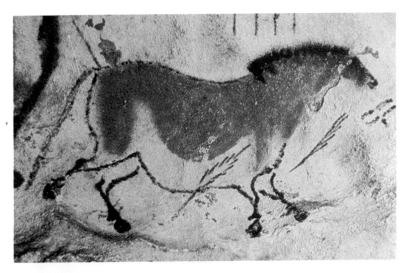

Ceiling of the Lascaux Caves, southern France

Richard Nixon and John Kennedy in a televised debate, 1960

Many viewers believe that the contrasting images Kennedy and Nixon presented on that evening radically changed the direction of the 1960 election campaign, leading to Kennedy's narrow victory. For better or worse, the debate also established television as the chief medium for political communication in the United States.

The second event is more recent—the introduction in the early 1980s of personal computers with graphic interfaces. These machines, which initially seemed strange and toylike, operated with icons and pictures rather than through arcane commands. Subtly at first, and then with the smack of a tsunami, graphic computers (the only kind people use now) moved our society away from an age of print into an era of electronic, image-saturated communications.

So that's where we are in the opening decade of a new millennium. People today are adjusting rapidly to a world of seamless, multichannel, multimedia communications. The prophet of this time is Marshall McLuhan, the guru of *Wired* magazine who proclaimed forty-some years ago that "the medium is the massage," with the play on words (*message/massage*) definitely intentional. Certainly images "massage" us all the time, and anyone reading and writing today has to be prepared to deal with arguments that shuffle more than words.

Shaping the Message

Images make arguments of their own. A photograph, for example, isn't a faithful representation of reality; it's reality shaped by the photographer's point of view. You can see photographic and video arguments at work everywhere, but perhaps particularly so during political campaigns. Staff photographers work to place candidates in settings that show them in the best possible light—shirtsleeves rolled up, surrounded by smiling children and red-white-and-blue bunting—whereas their opponents look for opportunities to present them in a bad light. Closer to home, you may well have chosen photographs that showed you at your best to include on <Myspace.com> or on a Facebook site.

Even if those who produce images shape the messages those images convey, those of us who "read" them are by no means passive. Human vision is selective: to some extent, we actively shape what we see. Much of what we see is laden with cultural meanings, too, and we must have "learned" to see things in certain ways. Consider a photograph of the Statue of Liberty welcoming immigrants to America's shores—and then

Not Just Words

One of the best-loved photographs appearing in the wake of the September 11, 2001, terrorist attacks was shot by Thomas Franklin: it shows three firefighters struggling to hoist the American flag in the wreckage of the World Trade Center as dust settles around them. In 2002, the image was used on a fund-raising "semipostal" stamp that sold for forty-five cents, with proceeds going to the Federal Emergency Management Agency. Part of the picture's appeal was its resemblance to another beloved American image: Joe Rosenthal's photo of U.S. Marines raising the flag on Iwo Jima in 1945. That image was made into a stamp as well, which became the best-selling U.S. stamp for many years. Take a look at the two images and consider how they're composed—what attracts your attention, how your eyes move over the images, what immediate impression they create. Also notice other features of the stamps—tinting, text placement, font, and wording. What argument do these stamps make about America?

In the cultural shorthand of Americans, the Statue of Liberty represents their country's promise of freedom and opportunity. When the Russian art group AES photoshopped Islamic visual elements onto images of the statue and other landmarks of Western countries (such as Big Ben and the Eiffel Tower), they capitalized on such connotations to draw out, in their words, "fears of Western society about Islam."

look at a version that shows her wearing a burka. In this moment, she's a very different kind of statue making a very different statement.

Of course, people don't always see things the same way, which is one reason eyewitnesses to the same event often report it differently. Or why even instant replays don't always solve disputed calls on football fields. Thus the visual images that surround us today—and that argue forcefully for our attention and often for our time and money—are constructed to invite, perhaps even coerce, us into seeing them in just one way. But each of us has our own powers of vision, our own frames of reference that influence how we see. So visual arguments might best be described as a give-and-take, a dialogue, or even a tussle.

Achieving Visual Literacy

Why take images so seriously? Because they matter. Images shape behavior and change lives. When advertisements for sneakers are powerful enough to lead some kids to kill for the coveted footwear, when five- and ten-second images and sound bites are deciding factors in presidential elections, or when a cultural icon like Oprah Winfrey can sell more books in one TV show than a hundred writers might do—or dramatically expose a best-selling author for presenting fiction as fact—it's high time to start paying careful attention to visual elements of argument.

How text is presented affects how it is read—whether it is set in fancy type, plain type, or handwritten; whether it has illustrations or not; whether it looks serious, fanciful, scholarly, or commercial. The figures on pp. 419–420 show information about a peer-tutoring service presented visually in three different ways—as an email message, as a flyer with a table, and as a flyer with a visual (which is how the information was actually presented to its intended audience). Look at the three different versions of this text, and consider in each case how the presentation affects the way you perceive the information. Do the photograph and the play on the movie title *The Usual Suspects,* for example, make you more or less likely to use this tutoring service? The point, of course, is that as you read any text, you need to consider its presentation—a highly crucial element.

Analyzing Visual Elements of Arguments

We've probably said enough to suggest that analyzing the visual elements of argument is a challenge, one that's even greater when you encounter multimedia appeals, especially on the Web. Here are some questions that can help you recognize—and analyze—visual and multimedia arguments. After you've read them, spend some time analyzing the flyer with the visual text on p. 420—in order to assess its effectiveness.

About the Creators/Authors

- Who created this visual text?
- What can you find out about this person(s), and what other work have they done?
- What does the creator's attitude seem to be toward the visual image?
- What does the creator intend its effects to be?

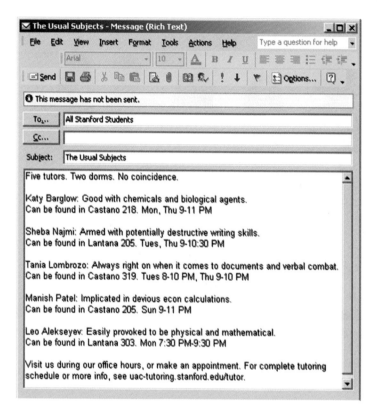

five tutors. two dorms. no coincidence

6'6"
6'0"
5'6"
5'0"
4'6"
4'
3

The Usual Subjects

Katy Barglow	Sheba Najmi	Tania Lombrozo	Manish Patel	Leo Alekseyev
Good with chemicals and biological agents.	Armed with potentially destructive writing skills.	Always right on when it comes to documents and verbal combat.	Implicated in devious econ calculations.	Easily provoked to be physical and mathematical.
Can be found in:	*Can be found in:*	*Can be found in:*	*Can be found in:*	*Can be found in:*
Castano 218	Lantana 205	Castano 319	Castano 205	Lantana 303
Mon, Thu	*Tue, Thu*	*Tue* 8 – 10 PM	*Sun* 9 – 11 PM	*Mon*
9 – 11 PM	9 – 10:30 PM	*Thu* 9 – 10 PM		7:30 – 9:30 PM

Visit us during our office hours, or make an appointment.
For complete tutoring schedule or more info, see

uac-tutoring. stanford.edu/tutor

About the Medium

- Which media are used for this visual text? Images only? Words and images? Sound, video, graphs, charts?
- What effect does the choice of medium have on the message of the visual text? How would the message be altered if different media were used?
- What's the role of words that may accompany the visual text? How do they clarify or reinforce (or blur or contradict) the message?

About Viewers/Readers

- What does the visual text assume about its viewers, and about what they know and agree with?
- What overall impression does the visual text create in you?
- What positive—or negative—feelings about individuals, scenes, or ideas does the visual intend to evoke in viewers?

About Content and Purpose

- What argumentative purpose does the visual text convey? What is it designed to convey?
- What cultural values or ideals does the visual evoke or suggest? The good life? Love and harmony? Sex appeal? Youth? Adventure? Economic power or dominance? Freedom? Does the visual reinforce these values or question them? What does the visual do to strengthen the argument?
- What emotions does the visual evoke? Which ones do you think it intends to evoke? Desire? Envy? Empathy? Shame or guilt? Pride? Nostalgia? Something else?

About Design

- How is the visual text composed? What's your eye drawn to first? Why?
- What's in the foreground? In the background? What's in or out of focus? What's moving? What's placed high, and what's placed low? What's to the left, in the center, and to the right? What effect do these placements have on the message?
- Is any particular information (such as a name, face, or scene) highlighted or stressed in some way to attract your attention?
- How are light and color used? What effect(s) are they intended to have on you? What about video? Sound?

- What details are included or emphasized? What details are omitted or deemphasized? To what effect? Is anything downplayed, ambiguous, confusing, distracting, or obviously omitted? To what ends?

- What, if anything, is surprising about the design of the visual text? What do you think is the purpose of that surprise?

- Is anything in the visual repeated, intensified, or exaggerated? Is anything presented as "supernormal" or idealistic? What effects are intended by these strategies, and what effects do they have on you as a viewer? How do they clarify or reinforce (or blur or contradict) the message?

- How are you directed to move within the argument? Are you encouraged to read further? Click on a link? Scroll down? Fill out a form? Provide your email address? Place an order?

Now take a look at the homepage of United Colors of Benetton, <www.http://benetton.com>, a company that sells sportswear, handbags, shoes, and more. You might expect a company that sells eighty million items of clothing and accessories annually to feature garments on its homepage or to make a pitch to sell you something, and indeed the company does all those things. But if you look closer, you'll find a section of the site that features Benetton's well-known campaigns for social and political causes. The 2004 campaign departed from Benetton's usual focus on improving the lives of people to extend its "reflection on diversity as a wealth of our planet, from the human races to our nearest cousins," the great apes.

If you check out this site, you'll find pictures not only of Pumbu (shown on p. 423) but of a number of other orphaned or rescued apes, along with information about them. As the site says, "[photographer] James Mollison has taken close-up pictures of the orphans, who were confiscated from illegal traders and form the population of at least seven sanctuaries in Africa and Asia. Many of them saw their mothers killed before their eyes. Together . . . they testify to the importance of saving the various species of great apes, because even if just one should become extinct, we would lose a significant part of the 'bridge' leading back to the origins of humankind" (see <http://benettongroup.com/apes/pressinfo/press/index.html>). The site goes on to say that this Benetton campaign includes not only the Web-site images and billboard ads (billboards in major cities around the world carried these images during 2004) but also a book, *James and Other Apes*, published in fall 2004. Finally,

Benetton makes use of design elements like color and composition to draw viewers into "James and Other Apes," one of a number of the company's campaigns for social and political causes.

the Natural History Museum in London hosted an exhibit of the photographs and the entire project in 2005.

Even this brief investigation of the Benetton site reveals that this manufacturer of clothing and accessories promotes its wares through an involvement in social activism. So its images challenge viewers to join in—or at least to consider doing so. What effect does Pumbu's page have on you?

Using Visuals in Your Own Arguments

You too can, and perhaps must, use visuals in your writing. Many college classes now call for projects to be posted on the Web, which almost always involves the use of images. Many courses also invite or require students to make multimedia presentations using software such as PowerPoint, or even good old-fashioned overhead projectors with transparencies.

Here we sketch out some basic principles of visual rhetoric. To help you appreciate the argumentative character of visual texts, we examine them under some of the same categories we use for written and oral arguments earlier in this book (Chapters 2, 3, and 4), though in a different order. You may be surprised by some of the similarities you'll see between visual and verbal arguments.

Visual Arguments Based on Character

What does character have to do with visual argument? Consider two argumentative essays submitted to an instructor. One is scrawled in thick pencil on pages ripped from a spiral notebook, little curls of paper still dangling from the left margin. The other is neatly typed on bond paper and in a form the professor likely regards as "professional." Is there much doubt about which argument will (at least initially) get the more sympathetic reading? You might object that appearances shouldn't count for so much, and you would have a point. The argument scratched in pencil could be the stronger piece, but it faces an uphill battle because its author has sent the wrong signals. Visually, the writer seems to be saying, "I don't much care about this message or the people I'm sending it to." There may be times when you want to send exactly such a signal to an audience, but the point is that the visual rhetoric of any piece you create ought to be a deliberate choice, not an accident. Also keep control of your own visual image. In most cases, when you present an argument, you want to appear authoritative and credible.

LOOK FOR IMAGES THAT REINFORCE YOUR AUTHORITY AND CREDIBILITY

For a brochure about your new small business, for instance, you would need to consider images that prove your company has the resources to do its job. Consumers might feel reassured seeing pictures that show you have an actual office, state-of-the-art equipment, and a competent staff. Similarly, for a Web site about a company or organization you represent, you would consider including its logo or emblem. Such emblems have authority and weight. That's why university Web sites so often include the seal of the institution somewhere on the homepage, or why the president of the United States always travels with a presidential seal to hang upon the speaker's podium. The emblem or logo can convey a wealth of cultural and historical implications.

Three images used to convey authority and credibility: the U.S. presidential seal and corporate logos for McDonald's and Philip Morris

CONSIDER HOW DESIGN REFLECTS YOUR CHARACTER

Almost every design element sends signals about character and ethos, so be sure to think carefully about them. For example, the type fonts you select for a document can mark you as warm and inviting or efficient and contemporary. The warm and inviting fonts often belong to a family called *serif*. The serifs are those little flourishes at the ends of the strokes that make the fonts seem handcrafted and artful:

warm and inviting (Bookman Old Style)

warm and inviting (Times New Roman)

warm and inviting (Bookman)

Cleaner, modern fonts go without those little flourishes and are called *sans serif*. These fonts are cooler and simpler—and, some argue, more readable on a computer screen (depending on screen resolution):

efficient and contemporary (Helvetica)

efficient and contemporary (Arial Black)

efficient and contemporary (Arial)

You may also be able to use decorative fonts. These are appropriate for special uses, but not for extended texts:

decorative and special uses (Zapf Chancery)

decorative and special uses (Goudy Handtooled BT)

Other typographic elements shape your ethos as well. The size of type, for one, can make a difference. If your text or headings are boldfaced and too large, you'll seem to be shouting. Tiny type, on the other hand, might make you seem evasive:

Lose weight! Pay nothing!*

*Excludes the costs of enrollment and required meal purchases. Minimum contract: 12 months.

Similarly, your choice of color—especially for backgrounds—can make a statement about your taste, personality, and common sense. For instance, you'll create a bad impression with a Web page whose background colors or patterns make reading difficult. If you want to be noticed, you might use bright colors—the same sort that would make an impression in clothing or cars. But more subtle shades might be a better choice in most situations.

Don't ignore the impact of illustrations and photographs. Because they reveal what you visualize, images can send powerful signals about your preferences, sensitivities, and inclusiveness—and sending the right ones isn't always easy. Conference planners designing a program,

Catherine Harrell's Web site

for example, are careful to include pictures that represent all the participants who'll be attending; as a result, they double-check to make sure
that they don't show only women in the program photos, or only men,
or only members of one racial or ethnic group.

Even your choice of medium says something important about you. If
you decide to make an appeal on a Web site, you send signals about your
technical skills and contemporary orientation as well as about your personality. Take a look at the homepage of student Catherine Harrell's
Website on p. 426. What can you deduce about her from this page—her
personality, her values and interests, and so on?

A presentation that relies on an overhead projector gives a different
impression from one presented on an LCD projector with software—or
one presented with a poster and handouts. When reporting on a children's story you're writing, the most effective medium of presentation
might be old-fashioned cardboard and paper made into an oversized
book and illustrated by hand.

FOLLOW REQUIRED DESIGN CONVENTIONS

Many kinds of writing have required design conventions. When that's the
case, follow them to the letter. It's no accident that lab reports for science
courses are sober and unembellished. Visually, they reinforce the serious
character of scientific work. The same is true of a college research paper.
You might resent the tediousness of placing page numbers in the right
place or aligning long quotations just so, but these visual details help convey your competence. So whether you're composing a term paper, résumé,
screenplay, or Web site, look for authoritative models and follow them.
Student Erin Krampetz's résumé is shown on p. 428. Note that its look is
serious: The type is clear and easy to read; the black on white is simple and
no-nonsense; the headings call attention to Krampetz's accomplishments.

Visual Arguments Based on Facts and Reason

People tend to associate facts and reason with verbal arguments, but
here too visual elements play an essential role. Indeed, it's hard to imagine a compelling presentation these days that doesn't rely, to some degree, on visual elements to enhance or even make the argument.

Many readers and listeners now expect ideas to be represented
graphically. Not long ago, media critics ridiculed the colorful charts and

ERIN MCCLURE KRAMPETZ

PO Box 12782, Stanford, CA 94309 • (210) 643-7999 Mobile • krampetz@stanford.edu

---

EDUCATION

9/00 – 6/05   **Stanford University,** Stanford, CA
- BA, International Relations (Honors); Minor, Spanish Language and Culture Studies

RESEARCH EXPERIENCE

6/02 – Present   **Research Assistant,** Stanford Study of Writing, Stanford, CA
- Contributing author and researcher for study analyzing a large collection of college writing.
- Manage Oracle database; conduct statistical and qualitative analyses of data collected.
- Research presented at Conference on College Composition (2004, 2005).

4/03 – Present   **Teaching Assistant/Researcher,** Stanford Program in Writing and Rhetoric, Stanford, CA
- Co-designed, taught, and carried out research new course focusing on multimedia.
- Co-authored multimedia magazine under review: *Computers and Composition: An International Journal.*

7/03 – 9/03   **Researcher,** International Relations Senior Honors Thesis, Ayacucho, Peru
- Completed case study investigating international funding for girls' education.
- Designed and administered surveys to government, teachers, and students in Spanish.
- Presented findings at International Education Society Conference (2005).

BUSINESS/MANAGEMENT EXPERIENCE

9/03 – Present   **Development Manager,** MobileMedia, Stanford, CA
- Build relationships with partners IBM, Palm Inc., and the U.S. and Brazilian governments.
- Secured funding from the Kellogg Foundation for pilot project beginning winter 2005.

9/04 – Present   **Oral Communication Tutor,** Stanford Center for Teaching and Learning, Stanford, CA

6/04 – 8/04   **Eben Tisdale Fellow,** Hewlett-Packard Company, Washington, DC
- Authored position papers on national e-recycling legislation and state and local procurement reform.
- Collaborated with University Relations team to develop presentation for HP CEO.

6/02 – 9/02   **Program Department Intern,** World Affairs Council, San Francisco, CA
- Compiled outreach database and assisted in speaker selection.

LEADERSHIP EXPERIENCE

9/03 – Present   **President,** Future Social Innovators Network (FUSION), Stanford, CA
- Led student group on social entrepreneurship with 350+ members.
- Invited as a guest speaker to the First World Forum on Social Entrepreneurship.

9/03 – Present   **Peer Advisor,** Stanford International Relations Department, Stanford, CA
- Oversee program events and provide academic support to current and potential students.

9/03 – Present   **Board Member,** Social Entrepreneurship Advisory Board, Stanford, CA
- Developed proposal for minor in Social Innovation.

AWARDS/RECOGNITION

International Relations Summer Research Grant (2003)
Latin American Studies Department Research Fellowship (2003)
Stanford Athletic Director's Scholar Athlete (2001)

graphs in newspapers like *USA Today*. Today, comparable features appear in even the most traditional publications because they work: they convey information efficiently.

ORGANIZE INFORMATION VISUALLY

A design works well when readers can look at an item and understand what it does. A brilliant, much-copied example of such an intuitive design is a seat adjuster invented many years ago by Mercedes-Benz (see below). It's shaped like a tiny seat. Push any element of the control, and the real seat moves the same way—back and forth, up and down. No instructions are necessary.

Good visual design can work the same way in an argument, conveying information without elaborate instructions. Titles, headings, subheadings, blown-up quotations, running heads, boxes, and so on are some common visual signals. When you present parallel headings in a similar type font, size, and color, you make it clear that the information under these headings is in some way related. So in a conventional term paper, you should use headings and subheadings to group information that's connected or parallel. Similarly, on a Web site, you might create two or three types of headings for groups of related information.

Use headings when they'll help guide your readers through the document you're presenting. For more complex and longer pieces, you may choose to use both headings and subheadings.

You should also make comparable inferences about the way text should be arranged on a page: search for relationships among items that should look alike. In this book, for example, bulleted lists are used to offer specific guidelines, while boxes with colored backgrounds mark the sections on visual argument titled "Not Just Words." You might use a list or a box to set off information that should be treated differently from the rest of the presentation, or you might visually mark it in other ways—by shading, color, or typography.

An item presented in large type or under a larger headline should be more important than one that gets less visual attention. Place illustrations carefully: what you position front and center will

Mercedes-Benz's seat adjuster

The Service Employees International Union's Web site uses various headings to group different kinds of information.

appear more important than items in less conspicuous places. On a Web site, key headings should usually lead to subsequent pages on the site.

Needless to say, you take a risk if you violate the expectations of your audience or if you present a visual text without coherent signals. Particularly for Web-based materials that may be accessible to people around the world, you can't make many assumptions about what will count as "coherent" across cultures. So you need to think about the roadmap you're giving viewers whenever you present them with a visual text. Remember that design principles evolve and change from medium to medium. A printed text or an overhead slide, for example, ordinarily works best when its elements are easy to read, simply organized, and surrounded by restful white space. But some types of Web pages seem to thrive on visual clutter, attracting and holding audiences' attention through the variety of information they can pack onto a relatively limited screen. Check out the way the opening screens of most search engines assault a viewer with enticements. Yet look closely, and you may find the logic in these designs.

One group that regularly analyzes Web sites, the Stanford Persuasive Technology Lab, recently concluded that Google News may soon become the most credible Web site of all (see the figure on p. 432). Here are just a few of the Lab's points about what makes Google News credible: It's easy to navigate; it provides a diversity of viewpoints; it has a reputation for outstanding performance in other areas; it has no broken links, typos, and so on; it provides clear information about the site; it has an easy-to-understand structure; it discloses information about the organization; and it has no ads. Take a look at Google News yourself. Do you agree that it's a fairly credible site? Beyond the points listed here, what else makes it credible?

USE VISUALS TO CONVEY DATA EFFICIENTLY

Words are immensely powerful and capable of enormous precision and subtlety. But the simple fact is that some information is conveyed more efficiently by charts, graphs, drawings, maps, or photos. When making an argument, especially to a large group, consider what information should be delivered in nonverbal form.

A *pie chart* is an effective way of comparing parts to the whole. You might use a pie chart to illustrate the ethnic composition of your school, the percentage of taxes paid by people at different income levels, or the

Google News site

consumption of energy by different nations. Pie charts depict such information memorably, as those on p. 433 show.

A *graph* is an efficient device for comparing items over time or according to other variables. You could use a graph to trace the rise and fall of test scores over several decades, or to show college enrollment by sex, race, and Hispanic origin, as in the bar graph on p. 433.

Diagrams or drawings are useful for drawing attention to details. You can use drawings to illustrate complex physical processes or designs of all sorts. After the 2001 attack on the World Trade Center, for example, engineers used drawings and diagrams to help citizens understand precisely what led to the total collapse of the buildings.

You can use *maps* to illustrate location and spatial relationships — something as simple as the distribution of office space in your student union or as complex as the topography of Utah. Such information would probably be far more difficult to explain using words alone.

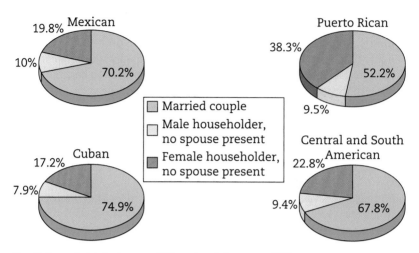

Family households by type and Hispanic origin group: 2002

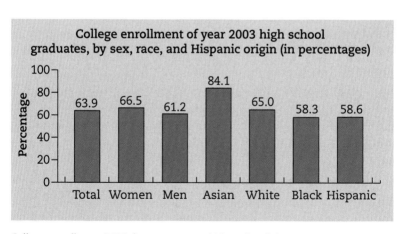

College enrollment 2003, by sex, race, and Hispanic origin

FOLLOW PROFESSIONAL GUIDELINES FOR PRESENTING VISUALS

Charts, graphs, tables, and illustrations play such an important role in many fields that professional groups have come up with specific guidelines for labeling and formatting these items. You need to become familiar with those conventions as you advance in a field. A guide such as the *Publication Manual of the American Psychological Association* (5th edition) or the *MLA Handbook for Writers of Research Papers* (6th edition) describes these rules in detail.

REMEMBER TO CHECK FOR COPYRIGHTED MATERIAL

You also must be careful to respect copyright rules when using visual items created by someone else. It's relatively easy these days to download visual texts of all kinds from the Web. Some of these items—such as clip art or government documents—may be in the public domain, meaning that you're free to use them without requesting permission or paying a royalty. But other visual texts may require permission, especially if you intend to publish your work or use the item commercially. And remember: anything you place on a Web site is considered "published." (See Chapter 18 for more on intellectual property.)

Visual Arguments That Appeal to Emotion

To some extent, people tend to be suspicious of arguments supported by visual and multimedia elements because they can seem to manipulate our senses. And many advertisements, political documentaries, rallies, marches, and even church services do in fact use visuals to trigger emotions. Who hasn't teared up at a funeral when members of a veteran's family are presented with the American flag, with a bugler blowing taps in the distance? Who doesn't remember being moved emotionally by a powerful film performance accompanied by a heart-wrenching musical score? But you might also have seen or heard about *Triumph of the Will,* a Nazi propaganda film from the 1930s that powerfully depicts Hitler as the benign savior of the German people, a hero of Wagnerian dimensions. It's a chilling reminder of how images can be manipulated and abused.

Yet you can't flip through a magazine without being cajoled or seduced by images of all kinds—most of them designed in some way to attract your eye and attention. Not all such seductions are illicit, nor should you avoid using them when emotions can support the legitimate claims you hope to advance. Emotions certainly ran high as Lance

Lance Armstrong wins again.

Armstrong won a record seventh Tour de France: what's the effect of the image presented above?

APPRECIATE THE EMOTIONAL POWER OF IMAGES

Images can bring a text or presentation to life. Sometimes the images have power in and of themselves to persuade. This was the case with images in the 1960s that showed civil rights demonstrators being assaulted by police dogs and water hoses, and with horrifying images in 2005 of victims of Hurricane Katrina, which led many people to contribute to relief campaigns.

Images you select for a presentation may be equally effective if the visual text works well with other components of the argument. Indeed,

A striking image, like this *Apollo 8* photograph of the earth shining over the moon, can support many different kinds of arguments.

a given image might support many different kinds of arguments. Consider the famous *Apollo 8* photograph of our planet as a big blue marble hanging above the horizon of the moon. You might use this image to introduce an argument about the need for additional investment in the space program. Or it might become part of an argument about the need to preserve our frail natural environment, or part of an argument against nationalism: *From space, we are one world.* You could, of course, make any of these claims without the image. But the photograph—like most images—might touch members of your audience more powerfully than words alone could.

APPRECIATE THE EMOTIONAL POWER OF COLOR

Consider the color red. It attracts hummingbirds—and cops. It excites the human eye in ways that other colors don't. You can make a powerful statement with a red dress or a red car—or red shoes. In short, red evokes emotions. But so do black, green, pink, and even brown. The fact that we respond to color is part of our biological and cultural makeup. So it makes sense to consider carefully what colors are compatible with the kind of argument you're making. You might find that the best choice is black on a white background.

In most situations, you can be guided in your selection of colors by your own good taste (guys — check your ties), by designs you admire, or by the advice of friends or helpful professionals. Some design and presentation software will even help you choose colors by offering dependable "default" shades or an array of preexisting designs and compatible colors — for example, of presentation slides.

The colors you choose for a design should follow certain common-sense principles. If you're using background colors on a poster, Web site, or slide, the contrast between words and background should be vivid enough to make reading easy. For example, white letters on a yellow background will likely prove illegible. Any bright background color should be avoided for a long document. Indeed, reading seems easiest with dark letters against a light or white background. Avoid complex patterns, even though they might look interesting and be easy to create. Quite often, they interfere with other, more important elements of a presentation.

As you use visuals in your college projects, test them on prospective readers. That's what professionals do because they appreciate how delicate the choices about visual and multimedia texts can be. These responses will help you analyze your own arguments as well as improve your success with them.

If Everything's an Argument . . .

Look back through this chapter, paying special attention to visual elements. What part has color played in getting across the message of this chapter — that visual arguments are all around us? What visual example in this chapter do you find most compelling or memorable, and why? Would it be possible to substitute words for that image, and, if so, what would the differences be?

RESPOND●

1. The December 2002 issue of *The Atlantic Monthly* included the following poem, along with the photograph that may have inspired it, shown on the following page. Look carefully at the image and then read the poem several times, at least once aloud. Working with another person in your class, discuss how the words of the poem and the image interact with one another. What difference would it make if the image hadn't accompanied this text? Write a brief report of your findings, and bring it to class for discussion.

> A waterfall of black chains
> looms behind the man in the stovepipe hat.
> Cigar. Wrinkled clothes. This is
> Isambard Kingdom Brunel.
> Who could not stop working. Slept
> and ate at the shipyard.
> The largest ship in the world.
> Driven to outdo himself.
> Fashioned from iron plate and
> powered by three separate means.
> Able to sail to Ceylon and back
> without refueling. Fated
> to lay the Atlantic cable, the India cable.
> Untouched in size for forty years.
> The Great Leviathan. The Little Giant,
> Isambard Kingdom Brunel.
> Builder of tunnels, ships, railroads, bridges.
> Engineer and Genius of England.
> He should have built churches, you know.
> Everything he prayed for came true.
>
> > –John Spaulding, "The Launching Chains of the *Great Eastern*"
> > (By Robert Howlett, 1857)

2. Find an advertisement with both verbal and visual elements. Analyze the ad's visual argument by answering some of the questions on pp. 418, 421, and 422, taking care to "reread" its visual elements just as carefully as you would its words. After you've answered each question as thoroughly as possible, switch ads with a classmate and analyze the new argument in the same way. Then compare your own and your classmate's responses to the two advertisements. If they're different—and there's every reason to expect they will be—how do you account for the differences? What's the effect of audience on the argu-

This photograph of Isambard Kingdom Brunel was taken by Robert Howlett and is included in the National Portrait Gallery's collection in London.

ment's reception? What are the differences between your own active reading and your classmate's?

3. You've no doubt noticed the relationships between visual design and textual material on the Web. In the best Web pages, the elements work together rather than simply competing for space. In fact, even if you'd never used the Web, you'd still know a great deal about graphic design: newspapers, magazines, and your own college papers make use of design principles to create effective texts.

Find three or four Web or magazine pages that you think exemplify good visual design — and then find just as many that don't. When you've picked the good and bad designs, draw a rough sketch of their physical layout. Where are the graphics? Where is the text? What are the size and position of text blocks relative to graphics? How is color used? Can you discern common design principles among the pages, or does each good page work well in its own way? Write a brief explanation of what you find, focusing on the way the visual arguments influence audiences.

4. Go to the Web page for the Pulitzer Prize archives at <http://pulitzer.org>. Pick a year to review, and then study the images of the winners in three categories: editorial cartooning, spot news photography, and feature photography. (Click on "Works" to see the images.) From among the images you review, choose one you believe makes a strong argument. Then, in a paragraph, describe that image and the argument it makes.

15
Presenting Arguments

In the wake of a devastating hurricane, local ministers search for just the right words to offer comfort and inspire hope in their congregations.

At a campus rally, a spoken word poet performs a piece against racism and homophobia.

To raise money for an AIDS awareness campaign, a group of students creates a poster advertising the local AIDS Walk, an informational brochure, and a Web site through which people can learn about the campaign and make a donation.

441

For a course in psychology, a student creates a multimedia presentation on the work of neuroscientist Constance Pert.

During their wedding, a couple exchanges the special vows they've worked together to create.

Sometimes the choice of how best to deliver an argument to a particular audience is made for you: the boss says "write a report" or an instructor says "build a Web site" or "make a 15-minute presentation that uses slides." But many times, you'll need to think carefully about what form of presentation is most appropriate and effective for your topic, your purpose, and your audience. Providing detailed advice about all available choices for presentation would take a book, not a brief chapter. But we can get you started thinking about issues of presentation in your own work.

● ● ●

Print Presentations

For many arguments you make in college, print is still the best system of delivery. Print texts, after all, are more permanent than most Web-based materials. Moreover, they're relatively cheap and increasingly easy to produce—and they offer an efficient way to convey abstract ideas or to provide complicated chains of reasoning. But in choosing a print presentation, writers face an embarrassment of riches: whereas print arguments used to come in standard formats—black print on 8½ × 11 white paper printed left to right, top to bottom—today's print texts come in a dizzying array of shapes, sizes, colors, and so on. As you think about presenting arguments in print, here are some issues to consider:

- What's the overall tone you want to create in this written argument? What's the purpose of your argument, and to whom is it addressed?

- What format will get your message across most effectively? A triple-fold brochure? A newsletter? A formal report with table of contents, executive summary, and so on?

- What fonts will make your argument most memorable and readable? Will you vary font or type size to guide readers through your text? To get attention or signal what's most important?

Not Just Words

The figures above illustrate three different modes of presentation—an oral/multimedia presentation for a live audience, a printed report, and an informative blog. Spend some time talking with a classmate about the choices involved in selecting each of these methods of presentation, and then report your findings to the class.

- Should you use colors other than black and white in presenting your argument? If so, what colors best evoke your tone and purpose? What colors will be most appealing to your audience?

- How will you use white or blank space in your argument? To give readers time to pause? To establish a sense of openness or orderliness?

- Will you use subheads as another guide to readers? If so, will you choose a different type size for them? Will you use all caps, boldface, or italics? In any case, be consistent in the type and the structure of subheads (all nouns, for example, or all questions).

- Will you use visuals in your print argument? If so, how will you integrate them smoothly into the text? (For more on the role of visuals in arguments, see Chapter 14.)

Take a look at the cover of one particular print document, the annual report for corporate giant IBM (below). Note the horizontal layout of the report's cover, which draws the reader's eye to the words at the center of the page announcing *IBM Annual Report 2004*. This band of text runs right

IBM's understated yet stylish design signals seriousness.

across the middle of the cover, within a band of color in a subtly different shade from the photograph of IBM headquarters on which it's superimposed. This superimposition gives the title a three-dimensional quality; the words seem to stand out from the cover. The pale shades of blue and green and grey are very cool and calm, and the building's image is one of light and glass and stability. The "look" of this cover says "I'm important" to its readers.

Oral/Multimedia Presentations

While most students are used to preparing arguments in print forms, you may be less familiar with making effective choices for a live presentation. In fact, students tell us that they're being assigned to make presentations more and more frequently in their classes—but that they're hardly ever given concrete instruction in how to do so. And students coming back from summer internship positions across a range of fields, from engineering to the arts, say that their employers simply expect them to be proficient at delivering arguments orally (and at accompanying such presentations with appropriate illustrative materials).

It's hard to generalize here, but we think it's fairly safe to say that successful oral/multimedia presenters credit several crucial elements in their success:

- They have thorough knowledge of their subjects.
- They pay very careful attention to the values, ideas, and needs of their listeners.
- They use structures and styles that make their spoken arguments easy to follow.
- They keep in mind the interactive nature of oral arguments (live audiences can argue back!).
- They realize that most oral presentations involve visuals of some sort, and they plan accordingly for the use of presentation software, illustrations, and so on.
- They practice, practice—and then practice some more.

Oral Arguments and Discussion

It's worth stopping for a moment to remember that the most common context for oral arguments you'll make in college may well take place in ordinary discussions, whether you're trying to persuade your parents that you need a new computer for your coursework, or to explore the meaning of a poem in class, or to argue against a textbook's interpretation of an economic phenomenon. In such everyday contexts, many people automatically choose the tone of voice, kind of evidence, and length of speaking time to suit the situation.

You can improve your own performance in such contexts by observing closely other speakers you find effective and by joining in on conversations whenever you possibly can; after all, the more you participate in lively discussions, the more comfortable you'll be doing so. To make sure your in-class comments count, follow these tips:

- Be well prepared so that your comments will be relevant to the class.
- Listen with a purpose, jotting down important points.
- Ask a key question — or offer a brief analysis or summary of the points that have already been made, to make sure you and other students (and the instructor) are "on the same page."
- Respond to questions or comments by others in specific rather than vague terms.
- Offer a brief analysis of an issue or text that invites others to join in and build on your comments.

Formal Oral/Multimedia Presentations

You've probably already been asked to make a formal presentation in some of your classes or on the job. In such cases, you need to consider the full context carefully. Note how much time you have to prepare and how long the presentation should be. You want to use the allotted time effectively, while not infringing on the time of others. Consider also what visual aids, handouts, or other materials might help make the

---

CULTURAL CONTEXTS FOR ARGUMENT

Speaking Up in Class

Speaking up in class is viewed as inappropriate or even rude in some cultures. In the United States, however, doing so is expected and encouraged. Some instructors even assign credit for such class participation.

presentation successful. Will you have to use an overhead projector? Can you use PowerPoint or other presentation software? Be aware that a statistical pie chart may carry a lot of weight in one argument, whereas photographs may make your point better in another. (See Chapter 14.)

Think about whether you're to make the presentation alone or as part of a group—and plan and practice accordingly. If you're going to be part of a group, turn-taking will need to be worked out carefully. Check out where your presentation will take place. In a classroom with fixed chairs? A lecture or assembly hall? An informal sitting area? Will you have a lectern? Other equipment? Will you sit or stand? Remain in one place or move around? What will the lighting be, and can you adjust it? Finally, note any criteria for evaluation: how will your live oral argument be assessed?

In addition to these logistical considerations, you need to consider several other key elements whenever you make a formal presentation:

Purpose

- Determine your major argumentative purpose. Is it to inform? To convince or persuade? To explore? To make a decision? To entertain? Something else?

Audience

- Who is your audience? An interested observer? A familiar face? A stranger? What will be the mix of age groups, men and women, and so on? Are you a peer of the audience members? Think carefully about what they'll already know about your topic and what opinions they're likely to hold.

Structure

- Structure your presentation so that it's easy to follow, and take special care to plan an introduction that gets the audience's attention and a conclusion that makes your argument memorable. You'll find more help with structure on p. 449.

Arguments to Be Heard

Even if you work from a print script in delivering a live presentation, that script must be written to be *heard* rather than read. Such a text—whether in the form of an overhead list, note cards, or a fully written-out text—should feature a strong introduction and conclusion, a clear organization with helpful structures and signposts, concrete diction, and straightforward syntax.

INTRODUCTIONS AND CONCLUSIONS

Like readers, listeners tend to remember beginnings and endings most readily. Work hard, therefore, to make these elements of your spoken argument especially memorable. Consider including a provocative or puzzling statement, opinion, or question; a memorable anecdote; a powerful quotation; or a vivid visual image. If you can refer to the interests or experiences of your listeners in the introduction or conclusion, do so.

Look at the introduction in Toni Morrison's acceptance speech to the Nobel Academy when she won the Nobel Prize for Literature:

> "Once upon a time there was an old woman. Blind but wise." Or was it an old man? A guru, perhaps. Or a griot soothing restless children. I have heard this story, or one exactly like it, in the lore of several cultures. "Once upon a time there was an old woman. Blind. Wise."
>
> – Toni Morrison

Here Morrison uses a storytelling strategy, calling on the traditional "Once upon a time" to signal to her audience that she's doing so. Note

Toni Morrison accepting the Nobel Prize for Literature in 1993

also the use of repetition and questioning. These strategies raise interest and anticipation in her audience: how will she use this story in accepting the Nobel Prize?

STRUCTURES AND SIGNPOSTS

For a spoken argument, you want your organizational structure to be crystal clear. Offer an overview of your main points toward the beginning of your presentation, and make sure that you have a clearly delineated beginning, middle, and end to the presentation. Throughout, remember to pause between major points and to use helpful signposts to mark your movement from one topic to the next. Such signposts act as explicit transitions in your spoken argument and thus should be clear and concrete: *The second crisis point in the breakup of the Soviet Union occurred hard on the heels of the first,* rather than *The breakup of the Soviet Union came to another crisis.* In addition to such explicit transitions as *next, on the contrary,* or *finally,* you can offer signposts to your listeners by repeating key words and ideas as well as by carefully introducing each new idea with concrete topic sentences.

DICTION AND SYNTAX

Avoid long, complicated sentences, and use straightforward syntax (subject-verb-object, for instance, rather than an inversion of that order) as much as possible. Remember, too, that listeners can hold onto concrete verbs and nouns more easily than they can grasp a steady stream of abstractions. So when you need to deal with abstract ideas, try to illustrate them with concrete examples.

Take a look at the following text that student Ben McCorkle wrote on *The Simpsons,* first as he prepared it for an essay and then as he adapted it for a live oral/multimedia presentation:

Print Version

The Simpson family has occasionally been described as a "nuclear" family, which obviously has a double meaning: first, the family consists of two parents and three children, and, second, Homer works at a nuclear power plant with very relaxed safety codes. The overused label *dysfunctional,* when applied to the Simpsons, suddenly takes on new meaning. Every episode seems to include a scene in which son Bart is being choked by his father, the baby is being neglected, or Homer is sitting in a drunken stupor transfixed by the television screen. The comedy in these scenes comes from the exaggeration of commonplace household events (although some talk shows and news programs would have us believe that these exaggerations are not confined to the madcap world of cartoons).

–Ben McCorkle, "The Simpsons: A Mirror of Society"

Oral Version (with a visual illustration)

What does it mean to describe the Simpsons as a *nuclear* family? Clearly, a double meaning is at work. First, the Simpsons fit the dictionary meaning—a family unit consisting of two parents and some children. The second meaning, however, packs more of a punch. You see, Homer works at a nuclear power plant [pause here] with *very* relaxed safety codes!

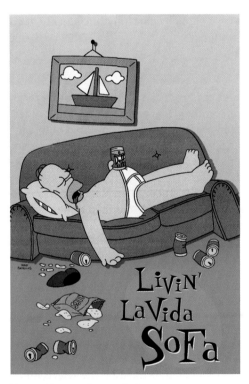

Homer Simpson in a typical pose

Still another overused family label describes the Simpsons. Did everyone guess I was going to say *dysfunctional?* And like "nuclear," when it comes to the Simpsons, "dysfunctional" takes on a whole new meaning.

Remember the scene when Bart is being choked by his father?

How about the many times the baby is being neglected?

Or the classic view—Homer sitting in a stupor transfixed by the TV screen!

My point here is that the comedy in these scenes often comes from double meanings—and from a lot of exaggeration of everyday household events.

Note that the revised version presents the same information as the original, but this time it's written to be *heard.* The revision uses helpful signposts, some repetition, a list, italicized words to prompt the speaker to give special emphasis, and simple syntax so that it's easy to listen to.

Arguments to Be Remembered

You can probably think of oral/multimedia arguments that still stick in your memory—a song like Bruce Springsteen's "Born in the USA," for instance, or Notorious B.I.G.'s "One More Chance." Such arguments are memorable in part because they call on the power of figures of speech and other devices of language. In addition, careful repetition can make spoken arguments memorable, especially when linked with parallelism and climactic order. (See Chapter 12 for more on using figurative language to make arguments more vivid and memorable.)

REPETITION, PARALLELISM, AND CLIMACTIC ORDER

Whether they're used alone or in combination, repetition, parallelism, and climactic order are especially appropriate for spoken arguments that sound a call to arms or that seek passionate engagement from the audience. Perhaps no person in the twentieth century used them more effectively than Martin Luther King Jr., whose sermons and speeches helped to spearhead the civil rights movement. Standing on the steps of the Lincoln Memorial in Washington, D.C., on August 23, 1963, with hundreds of thousands of marchers before him, King called on the nation to make good on the "promissory note" represented by the Emancipation Proclamation.

Look at the way King uses repetition, parallelism, and climactic order in the following paragraph to invoke a nation to action:

> It is obvious today that America has defaulted on this promissory note insofar as her citizens of color are concerned. Instead of honoring this sacred obligation, America has given the Negro people a bad check which has come back marked "insufficient funds." But *we refuse* to believe that the bank of justice is bankrupt. *We refuse* to believe that there are insufficient funds in the great vaults of opportunity of this nation. So *we have come* to cash this check—a check that will give us upon demand the riches of freedom and the security of justice. *We have also come* to this hallowed spot to remind America of the fierce urgency of now. This is *no time* to engage in the luxury of cooling off or to take the tranquilizing drug of gradualism. *Now is the time* to rise from the dark and desolate valley of segregation to the sunlit path of racial justice. *Now is the time* to open the doors of opportunity to all of God's children. *Now is the time* to lift our nation from the quicksands of racial injustice to the solid rock of brotherhood.
>
> –Martin Luther King Jr., "I Have a Dream" (emphasis added)

The italicized words highlight the way King uses repetition to drum home his theme. But along with that repetition, he sets up a powerful set of parallel verb phrases, calling on all "to rise" from the "dark and desolate valley of segregation" to the "sunlit path of racial justice" and "to open the doors of opportunity" for all. The final verb phrase ("to lift") leads to a strong climax, as King moves from what each individual should do to what the entire nation should do: "to lift our nation from the quicksands of racial injustice to the solid rock of brotherhood." These stylistic choices, together with the vivid image of the "bad check," help to make King's speech powerful, persuasive—and memorable.

Thank goodness you don't have to be as highly skilled as King to take advantage of the power of repetition and parallelism. Simply repeating a key word in your argument can impress it on your audience, as can arranging parts of sentences or items in a list in parallel order.

The Role of Visuals in Oral/Multimedia Arguments

Visuals often play an important part in oral arguments, and they should be prepared with great care. Don't think of them as add-ons but rather as a major means of getting across your message and supporting the claims you're making. In many cases, a picture can truly be worth a thousand words, helping your audience see examples or illustrations or other data that make your argument compelling.

Whatever visuals you use—charts, graphs, photographs, summary statements, sample quotations, lists—must be large enough to be readily seen by all members of your audience. If you use slides or overhead projections, be sure that the information on each frame is simple, clear, and easy to read and process. In order for audience members to read information on a transparency, this means using 36 point type for major headings, 24 point for subheadings, and at least 18 point for all other text. For slides, use 24 point for major headings, 18 point for subheadings, and at least 14 point for other text.

The same rule of clarity and simplicity holds true for posters, flip charts, or a chalkboard. And remember not to turn your back on your audience while you refer to these visuals. Finally, if you prepare supplementary materials for the audience—bibliographies or other handouts—wait to distribute them until the moment the audience will need them or until the end of the presentation so that they won't distract the audience from your spoken argument.

If you've seen many PowerPoint presentations, you're sure to have seen some really bad ones: the speaker just stands up and reads off what is on each slide. Nothing can be more deadly boring than that. So in your own use of PowerPoint or other presentation slides, make sure that they provide an overview and serve as visual signposts to guide listeners, but *never* read them word for word.

For an oral/multimedia presentation, one student used the PowerPoint slides shown on pp. 454, 456, and 458 to compare Frank Miller's graphic novel *Sin City* and its movie adaptation. Notice that the student uses text throughout, but in moderation. Next take a look at the written script—written to be heard—that the student developed for this presentation. The student does *not* read from the slides; rather, the slides illustrate the points being made. Their text sums up—and, occasionally, supplements—his oral presentation. This careful use of text makes the student's argument clear and easy to follow.

His choices in layout and font size also put a premium on clarity—but without sacrificing visual appeal. The choice of white and red text on a black background is an appropriate one for the topic—a stark black-and-white graphic novel and its shades-of-gray movie version. But be aware that light writing on a dark background can be hard to read. Dark writing on a white or light cream-colored background is a safer choice.

(Note that if your presentation shows or is based on source materials—either text or images—your instructor may want you to include a Works Cited slide listing the sources at the end of the presentation.)

From Frames to Film:
Graphic Novels on the Big Screen

Presentation by Sach Wickramasekara
PWR 2-06, Professor Lunsford
Wallenberg Hall Room 329
March 8, 2006

Introduction

A frame from the *Sin City* graphic novel.

"Instead of trying to make it [*Sin City*] into a movie which would be terrible, I wanted to take cinema and try and make it into this book."

- Robert Rodriguez, DVD Interview

The same scene from the *Sin City* movie.

[Opening Slide: Title]

Hi, my name is Sach.

[Change Slide: Introduction]

Take a look at this pair of scenes. Can you tell which one's from a movie and which one's from a graphic novel? How can two completely different media produce such similar results? Stay tuned; you're about to hear how.

[Pause]

Today I'll be analyzing *Sin City's* transition from a graphic novel to the big screen. The past decade has seen an increasing trend of comic books and graphic novels morphing into big-budget movies, with superhero flicks such as *Spiderman* and *X-men* headlining this list. However, until recently, movies borrowed from their comic book licenses but never stuck fully to their scripts. That all changed with *Sin City,* and I'll show you how dedication to preserving the look and feel of the graphic novel is what makes the screen version of *Sin City* neither a conventional graphic novel nor a conventional movie, but a new, innovative art form that's a combination of the two.

[Body]

[Change Slide—Technology]

Part of what makes *Sin City* so innovative is the technology powering it. The movie captures the look of the graphic novel so

Technology

Right: The original scene from the graphic novel.

Left: The scene is filmed with live actors on a green screen set.

Right: The final version of the scene, after the colors have been changed to shades of black and white. Notice the sapphire shade of the convertible, and how it stands out from the background.

Audio and Voice

"When I read the books, I felt that they were fantastic exactly as they were ... I loved that the dialogue didn't sound like movie dialogue." - Robert Rodriguez

JUST ONE HOUR TO GO. MY LAST DAY ON THE JOB. EARLY RETIREMENT. NOT MY IDEA. DOCTOR'S OR- DERS. HEART CONDITION. *ANGINA,* HE CALLS IT.

"Just one hour to go. My last day on the job. Early retirement. Not my idea. Doctor's orders. Heart condition. Angina, he calls it."

- Sin City movie

well by filming actors on a green screen and using digital imagery to put detailed backdrops behind them. Computer technology also turns the movie's visuals into shades of black and white with rare dashes of color splashed in, reproducing the noir feel of the original novels. Thus, scenes in The *Sin City* have a photorealistic yet stylized quality that differentiates them from both the plain black-and-white images of the comics and the real sets used in other movies.

[Change Slide—Audio and Voice]

Pretty pictures are all well and good, but everyone knows that voice is just as important in a movie, especially because the media of comics and film use words so differently. The *Sin City* movie reproduces many sections of the novel that have a first-person narrator as monologues, and the script is lifted word for word from Miller's originals. This gives the dialogue an exaggerated quality that is more fantastic than realistic, which is exactly what director Robert Rodriguez intended. Here is an example from the film. *"Just one hour to go. My last day on the job. Early retirement. Not my idea. Doctor's orders. Heart condition. Angina, he calls it."* A text box monologue fits perfectly in comics, where you read it and hear the character's voice in your head, but you wouldn't expect to hear it within an actual film. This contrast in narrative styles between the spoken word and how it is used is another factor that makes *Sin City* such an original work.

[Change Slide—Time and Structure]

Films are based on movement and sound, but comics divide movement into a series of "freeze-frame" images and represent

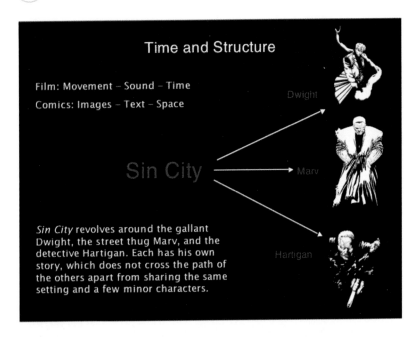

Time and Structure

Film: Movement – Sound – Time
Comics: Images – Text – Space

Dwight

Sin City →

Marv

Hartigan

Sin City revolves around the gallant Dwight, the street thug Marv, and the detective Hartigan. Each has his own story, which does not cross the path of the others apart from sharing the same setting and a few minor characters.

Works Consulted

Goldstein, Hillary. "Five Days of Sin." IGN.com. 1 Apr. 2006. IGN Entertainment. 12 Feb. 2006 <http://comics.ign.com/articles/600/600846p1.html>.

"The Making of Sin City." Sin City DVD preview page. Buena Vista Online Entertainment. 4 Feb. 2006 <http://video.movies.go.com/sincity/>.

Miller, Frank. That Yellow Bastard. Milwaukie: Dark Horse Books, 1996.

---. The Big Fat Kill. Milwaukie: Dark Horse Books, 1994.

---. The Hard Goodbye. Milwaukie: Dark Horse Books, 1991.

Otto, Jeff. "Sin City Review." IGN.com: Filmforce. 29 March 2005. IGN Entertainment. 10 Feb 2006 <http://filmforce.ign.com/articles/598/598322p1.html>.

Robertson, Barbara. "The Devil's in the Details." Computer Graphics World Apr. 2005: 18. Expanded Academic ASAP. Gale Group Databases. Stanford U Lib., Palo Alto, CA. 11 Feb. 2006 <http://www.galegroup.com/>.

Sin City. Dir. Robert Rodriguez. Perf. Bruce Willis, Jessica Alba, Mickey Rourke, and Clive Owen. DVD. Dimension, 2005.

sound as text. If you freeze the *Sin City* movie at certain frames, the scene might look identical to what is portrayed in the graphic novel. Press the play button again, and the characters appear to jump to life and begin moving within the frame. Thus, it's easy to view *Sin City* as a beautifully depicted, real-time graphic novel, where time is the factor that makes the story move forward, instead of space separating the different panels of the graphic novel.

[Pause]

Like the graphic novel by Frank Miller that it's based on, the *Sin City* movie is composed of a series of stories with different protagonists such as Marv, Dwight, and the detective Hartigan. These separate tales share only their settings and several secondary characters. Therefore, the movie feels episodic, rather than continuous like a feature-length film. Just as Miller's originals were a compilation of short stories linked by their setting, *Sin City* has the unique feel of being three short films linked by Miller's vision of an alternate universe.

[Change Slide—Works Consulted]

[Pause]

Sin City has opened the doors for future comic adaptations, none more anticipated than *Sin City 2* itself. There hasn't been a lot of info. on this movie, but apparently it'll be based on a brand new story that Frank Miller is writing. It'll be intriguing to see director Rodriguez adapt a graphic novel that hasn't even been written yet, so keep an eye out for this one. Any questions?

The best way to test the effectiveness of all your visuals is to try them out on friends, family members, classmates, or roommates. If they don't get the meaning of the visuals right away, revise and try again.

Finally, remember that visuals can help make your presentation accessible: some members of your audience may not be able to see your presentation or may have trouble hearing it. Here are a few key rules to remember:

- Don't rely on color or graphics alone to get across information; use words along with them.

- Consider providing a written overview of your presentation, or put the text on an overhead projector—for those who learn better by reading *and* listening.

- If you use video, take the time to label sounds that won't be audible to some audience members. (Be sure your equipment is caption capable.)

Some Oral/Multimedia Presentation Strategies

In spite of your best preparation, you may feel some anxiety before a live presentation. This is perfectly natural. (According to one Gallup poll, Americans often identify public speaking as a major fear, scarier than attacks from outer space!) Experienced speakers say they have strategies for dealing with anxiety—and even that a little anxiety (and accompanying adrenaline) can act to a speaker's advantage.

The most effective strategy seems to be knowing your topic and material through and through. Confidence in your own knowledge goes a long way toward making you a confident speaker. In addition to being well prepared, you may want to try some of the following strategies:

- Practice a number of times, and tape yourself (video if at all possible) at least once so that you can listen to your voice. Tone of voice and body language can dispose audiences for—or against—speakers. For most oral arguments, you want to develop a tone that conveys interest in and commitment to your position as well as respect for your audience.

- Time your presentation carefully to make sure you stay within the allotted time.

- Think carefully about how you'll dress for your presentation, remembering that audience members usually take careful note of how a speaker looks. Dressing for an effective presentation, of course, depends on what's appropriate for your topic, audience, and setting, but most experienced speakers like to wear clothes that are comfortable and that allow for easy movement—but that aren't overly casual. "Dressing up" a little indicates that you take pride in your appearance, that you have confidence in your argument, and that you respect your audience.

- Visualize your presentation. Go over the scene of the presentation in your mind, and think it through completely.

- Get some rest before the presentation, and avoid consuming too much caffeine.

- Concentrate on relaxing. Consider doing some deep-breathing exercises right before you begin.

- Pause before you begin, concentrating on your opening lines.

- Remember that most speakers make a stronger impression standing than sitting. Moving around a bit may help you make good eye contact with members throughout the audience.

- When using presentation slides, remember to stand to the side so that you don't block the view and to look at the audience rather than the slide.

- Remember to interact with the audience whenever possible; doing so will often help you relax and even have some fun.

Finally, remember to allow time for audience members to respond and ask questions. Try to keep your answers brief so that others may get in on the conversation. And at the very end of your presentation, thank the audience for attending so generously to your arguments.

A Note about Webcasts—Live Presentations over the Web

This discussion of live oral/multimedia presentations has assumed that you'll be speaking before an audience that's in the same room with you. Increasingly, though—especially in business, industry, and science—the presentations you make will be live, all right, but you won't actually be in the same physical space as the audience. Instead, you'll be in front of a camera that will capture your voice and image and relay them via the Web to attendees who might be anywhere in the world. Other Webcasts might show only your slides or some software you're demonstrating, using a screen capture relay without cameras. In this second model, you're not visible, but are still speaking live.

In either case, as you learn to adapt to Webcast environments, most of the strategies that work in oral/multimedia presentations for an audience that's actually present will continue to serve you well. But there are some significant differences:

- Practice is even more important in Webcasts, since you need to make sure that you can access everything you need online—a set of slides, for example, or a document or video clip, as well as any names, dates, or sources that you might be called on to provide during the Webcast.

- Because you can't make eye contact with audience members, it's important to remember to look into the camera, if you are using one, at least from time to time. If you're using a stationary Webcam, perhaps one mounted on your computer, practice standing or sitting still enough to stay in the frame without looking stiff.

- Even though your audience may not be visible to you, assume that if you're on camera, the Web-based audience can see you quite well; if you slouch, they'll notice. Also assume that your microphone is always live—don't mutter under your breath, for example, when someone else is speaking or asking a question.

Web-Based Presentations

Even without the interactivity of Webcasts, most students have enough access to the Web to use its powers for effective presentations, especially in Web sites and blogs.

Web Sites

Students we know are increasingly creating Web sites for themselves, working hard at their self-presentation, at showcasing their talents and accomplishments. Other students create Web sites for extracurricular organizations, for work, or for class assignments—or create sites for themselves on <Myspace.com> or as a Facebook.

Chapter 14 includes the homepage of student Catherine Harrell's Web site (see p. 426). Take a look at that example now to see how Harrell works with color and design to create an overall impression of who she is and what she does.

In planning any Web site, you'll need to pay careful attention to your rhetorical situation—to the purpose of your site, the intended audience, and the overall impression you want to make. To get started, you may want to visit several sites you admire, looking for effective design ideas and ways of organizing navigation and information. Creating a map or storyboard for your site will also help you to think through the links from page to page.

Experienced Web designers cite several important principles for Web-based presentations. The first of these is *contrast,* achieved through the use of color, icons, boldface, and so on; contrast helps guide readers through the site. The second principle, *proximity,* calls on you to keep together the parts of a page that are closely related, again for ease of reading. *Repetition* is another important principle: using the same consistent design throughout the site for elements such as headings, links, and so on will help readers move smoothly through the site. Finally, designers caution you to concentrate on *overall impression,* or mood, for the site. That means making sure that the colors and visuals you choose help to create that impression rather than challenge or undermine it.

Here are some additional tips that may help as you design your site:

- The homepage of your site should be eye-catching, inviting, and informative: use titles and illustrations to make clear what the site is about.

- Think carefully about two parts of every page: the navigation area (menus or links) and content areas. You want to make these two areas clearly distinct from one another. And make sure you *have* a navigation area for every page, including links to the key sections of the site and a link back to the homepage. Ease of navigation is one key to a successful Web site.

- Either choose a design template provided by Web-writing tools (like DreamWeaver), or create a template of your own so that the elements of each page will be consistent.

- Remember that some readers may not have the capacity to download heavy visuals or to access elements like Flash. If you want to reach a wide audience, stick with visuals that can be downloaded easily.

- Remember to include your name and contact information on every page.

Below is the homepage for a Web site that's part of a satiric anti-smoking campaign. The site introduces Shards O' Glass Freeze Pops with a straight face, saying that the company's goal is "to be the most responsible, effective, and respected developer of glass shard consumer products intended for adults." This deadpan tone is sustained throughout the site, from the "About Us" page, which informs readers that "We pride ourselves on responsible marketing," to a page on "Health Concerns" that announces, "Those who eat glass freeze pops are far more likely to develop shards-related ailments than those who don't eat them."

Take a close look at the homepage, and assess how well the designers of this site follow the principles of design noted above. How effective do you find the design? What might you suggest to improve it?

A satirical Web site sponsored by the anti-smoking campaign "The Truth" demonstrates that good design can help sell anything.

Blogs

Of all the kinds of Web texts we know, none has captured the public imagination more swiftly than Web logs, or blogs, which now number, by some estimates, up to 35 million. In essence, blogs take the idea of a personal Web page and give it the interactivity of a listserv, with readers able to make comments and respond both to the blogger and to one another. Many if not most blogs contain nothing more than personal self-expression by the blogger, but others have become prominent sources of news and opinion in politics, entertainment, and other fields.

As such, blogs create an ideal space for building communities, engaging in arguments, and giving voice to views and opinions of ordinary, everyday folks, those we seldom see writing or being written about in major print media (many of which now sponsor blogs themselves as part of their electronic versions). Proponents point to the democratizing function of blogs and to the corrective role they can play as bloggers run efficient and effective fact-checking projects. It was a blog, after all, that identified the many falsehoods disseminated by the Swift Boat Veterans group during the 2004 presidential election campaign, and it was a blog that led to the revelation that Dan Rather used less-than-factual information on a *60 Minutes* show and that led, eventually, to Rather's withdrawal from that show.

Of course, blogs have a downside (or several): they're idiosyncratic almost by nature and can sometimes be self-indulgent and egoistic. A more serious point is that they can distort issues by spreading misinformation very quickly.

Nevertheless, blogs appear to be changing the ways people communicate and perhaps redistributing power in ways we still don't fully

If Everything's an Argument . . .

Look at the layout and design of the first few pages of any chapter in this book. What choices have the editors and authors made about how to present this print text, and how effective or ineffective do you find those choices? How might this material have been treated differently if it were part of an oral/multimedia presentation or a Web site?

understand. If you're a reader of blogs, be sure to read very carefully indeed, understanding that the information on the blog hasn't been subjected to the rigorous kind of peer review that is expected from traditional print sources. If you're a blogger yourself, you know that the rules of etiquette for blogging and conventions for blogs are still evolving. In the meantime, you'll be wise to join the spirit of any blog you contribute to, to be respectful in your comments—even very critical ones, and to think carefully about the audience you want to reach in every entry you make.

RESPOND •

1. Take a brief passage—three or four paragraphs—from an essay you've recently written. Then, following the guidelines in this chapter, rewrite the passage to be *heard* by a live audience. Finally, make a list of every change you made.

2. Find a print presentation that you find particularly effective. Study it carefully, noting how its format, type sizes, and typefaces, its use of color, white space, and visuals, and its overall layout work to deliver its message. If you find a particularly ineffective print presentation, carry out the same analysis to figure out why it's so bad. Finally, prepare a five-minute presentation of your findings to deliver in class.

3. Attend a lecture or presentation on your campus, and observe the speaker's delivery very carefully. Note what strategies the speaker uses to capture and hold your attention (or not). What signpost language and other guides to listening can you detect? How well are any visuals integrated into the presentation? What aspects of the speaker's tone, dress, eye contact, and movement affect your understanding and appreciation (or lack of it)? What's most memorable about the presentation, and why? Finally, write up an analysis of this presentation's effectiveness.

4. Go to a Web site you admire or consult frequently. Then spend some time answering the following questions: Why is a Web site—a digital presentation—the best way to present this material? What advantages over a print text or a live oral/multimedia presentation does the Web site have? What would you have to do to "translate" the argument(s) of this site into print or live oral format? What might be gained, or lost, in the process?

PART 4

CONVENTIONS OF
argument

16
What Counts as Evidence

A downtown office worker who can never find a space in the company lot to park her motorcycle decides to argue for a designated motorcycle parking area. In building her argument, she conducts a survey to find out exactly how many employees drive cars to work and how many ride motorcycles.

A business consultant wants to identify characteristics of effective teamwork so that he can convince his partners to adopt these characteristics as part of their training program. To begin gathering evidence for this argument, the consultant decides to conduct on-site observations of three effective teams, followed by in-depth interviews with each member.

To support his contention that people are basically honest, an economist points to the detailed records kept by a vendor who sells bagels on the honor system in downtown offices. The merchant discovers that only a small percentage of people take advantage of him. The numbers also show that executives cheat more than middle-management employees.

For an argument aimed at showing that occupations are still often unconsciously thought of as either masculine or feminine, a student decides to carry out an experiment: she will ask fifty people chosen at random to draw pictures of a doctor, a police officer, a nurse, a CEO, a lawyer, and a secretary—and see which are depicted as men, which as women. The results of this experiment will become evidence for (or against) the argument.

Trying to convince her younger brother to invest in a PC laptop, a college student mentions her three years of personal experience using a similar computer for her college coursework.

In arguing that virtual reality technology may lead people to ignore or disregard the most serious of "real" world problems, a student writer provides evidence for this claim in part by citing sixteen library sources that review and critique cyberspace and virtual reality.

• • •

Evidence and the Rhetorical Situation

As the examples above demonstrate, people use all kinds of evidence in making and supporting claims. But this evidence doesn't exist in a vacuum; instead, the quality of evidence—how it was collected, by whom, and for what purposes—may become part of the argument itself. Evidence may be persuasive in one time and place but not in another; it may convince one kind of audience but not another; it may work with one type of argument but not the kind you are writing.

To be most persuasive, then, evidence should match the time and place in which you make your argument. For example, arguing that a Marine general should employ tactics of delay and strategic retreat because that very strategy worked effectively for George Washington is likely to fail if Washington's use of the tactic is the only evidence provided. After all, a military maneuver that was effective in 1776 for an outnumbered band of revolutionaries is more than likely an *irrelevant* one today for a much different fighting force. In the same way, a writer may achieve excellent results by citing her own experience as well as an extensive survey of local teenagers as evidence to support a new teen center for her small-town community, but she may have less success in arguing for the same thing in a distant, large inner-city area, where her personal authority may count for less.

College writers also need to consider in what fields or areas they're working. In disciplines such as experimental psychology or economics, empirical data — the sort that can be observed and counted — may be the best evidence, but the same kind of data may be less appropriate or persuasive, or even impossible to come by, in many historical or literary studies. As you become more familiar with a particular discipline, you'll gain a sense of just what it takes to prove a point or support a claim. The following questions will help you begin to understand the rhetorical situation of a particular discipline:

- How do other writers in the field use precedence — examples of actions or decisions that are very similar — and authority as evidence? What or who counts as an authority in this field? How are the credentials of authorities established?

- What kinds of data are preferred as evidence? How are such data gathered and presented?

- How are statistics or other numerical information used and presented as evidence? Are tables, charts, or graphs commonly used? How much weight do they carry?

- How are definitions, causal analyses, evaluations, analogies, and examples used as evidence?

- How does the field use firsthand and secondhand sources as evidence?

- Is personal experience allowed as evidence?

- How are quotations used as part of evidence?

- How are images used as part of evidence, and how closely are they related to the verbal parts of the argument being presented?

As these questions suggest, evidence may not always travel well from one field to another.

Firsthand Evidence and Research

Firsthand evidence comes from research you yourself have carried out or been closely involved with, and much of this kind of research requires you to collect and examine data. Here we'll discuss the kinds of firsthand research most commonly conducted by student writers.

Observations

"What," you may wonder, "could be any easier than observing something?" You just choose a subject, look at it closely, and record what you see and hear. If observing were so easy, eyewitnesses would all provide reliable accounts. Yet experience shows that several people who have observed the same phenomenon generally offer different, sometimes even contradictory, evidence on the basis of those observations. (When TWA Flight 800 exploded off the coast of New Jersey in 1996, eyewitnesses gave various accounts, some even claiming that they saw what might have been a missile streaking toward the passenger jet. The official report found that an internal short likely ignited vapors in a fuel tank.) Trained observers say that getting down a faithful record of an observation requires intense concentration and mental agility.

Before you begin an observation, then, decide exactly what you want to find out and anticipate what you're likely to see. Do you want to observe an action repeated by many people (such as pedestrians crossing a street, in relation to an argument for putting in a new stoplight)? A sequence of actions (such as the stages involved in student registration, which you want to argue is far too complicated)? The interactions of a group (such as meetings of the campus Young Republicans, which you want to see adhere to strict parliamentary procedures)? Once you have a clear sense of what you'll observe and what questions you'll wish to answer through the observation, use the following guidelines to achieve the best results:

- Make sure the observation relates directly to your claim.
- Brainstorm about what you're looking for, but don't be rigidly bound to your expectations.

- Develop an appropriate system for collecting data. Consider using a split notebook or page: on one side, record the minute details of your observations directly; on the other, record your thoughts or impressions.

- Be aware that the way you record data will affect the outcome, if only in respect to what you decide to include in your observational notes and what you leave out.

- Record the precise date, time, and place of the observation.

In the following excerpt, travel writer Pico Iyer uses information drawn from minute and prolonged observation in an argument about what the Los Angeles International Airport (LAX) symbolizes about America:

> LAX is, in fact, a surprisingly shabby and hollowed-out kind of place, certainly not adorned with the amenities one might expect of the

The LAX Web site offers a more glamorous view of the airport than Pico Iyer does on the basis of his direct observation.

world's strongest and richest power. When you come out into the Arrivals area in the International Terminal, you will find exactly one tiny snack bar, which serves nine items; of them, five are identified as Cheese Dog, Chili Dog, Chili Cheese Dog, Nachos with Cheese, and Chili Cheese Nachos. There is a large panel on the wall offering rental car services and hotels, and the newly deplaned American dreamer can choose between the Cadillac Hotel, the Banana Bungalow . . . and the Backpacker's Paradise.

–Pico Iyer, "Where Worlds Collide"

Another observer, however, might see and describe an entirely different LAX.

Interviews

Some evidence is best obtained through direct interviews. If you can talk with an expert—in person, on the phone, or online—you might get information you couldn't have obtained through any other type of research. In addition to getting expert opinion, you might ask for firsthand accounts, biographical information, or suggestions of other places to look or other people to consult. The following guidelines will help you conduct effective interviews:

- Determine the exact purpose of the interview, and be sure it's directly related to your claim.

- Set up the interview well in advance. Specify how long it'll take, and if you wish to tape-record the session, ask permission to do so.

- Prepare a written list of both factual and open-ended questions. (Brainstorming with friends can help you come up with good questions.) Leave plenty of space for notes after each question. If the interview proceeds in a direction that you hadn't expected but that seems promising, don't feel you have to cover every one of your questions.

- Record the subject's full name and title, as well as the date, time, and place of the interview.

- Be sure to thank those you interview, either in person or with a follow-up letter or email message.

In arguing that the Gay Games offer a truly inclusive alternative—rather than a parallel—to the Olympics, Caroline Symons uses data drawn from extensive interviews with organizers and participants in the Gay Games:

> Out of twenty-four in-depth interviews I conducted with gay men in-
> volved in the Gay Games as organizers, over half indicated that they
> had sufficiently alienating experiences with sport during childhood
> and adolescence to be put off participating until the advent of gay
> sports organizations and events. . . . Gay men in particular have found
> a safe and welcoming environment to engage in sport through the
> emergence of gay sports organizations and the Gay Games.
>
> –Caroline Symons, "Not the Gay Olympic Games"

Newspapers, too, often use interviews to add perspective to stories or
to check the authenticity of claims. Steve Fainuru, a reporter for the
Washington Post, uses that technique to weigh the validity of an internal
army report that found flaws in the Stryker, a military transport vehicle
used in Iraq:

> But in more than a dozen interviews, commanders, soldiers and me-
> chanics who use the Stryker fleet daily in one of Iraq's most danger-
> ous areas unanimously praised the vehicle. The defects outlined in
> the report were either wrong or relatively minor and did little to ham-
> per the Stryker's effectiveness, they said.

Do Stryker armored personnel carriers like the one shown here deserve praise
or criticism? Ask the man who drives one?

> "I would tell you that at least 100 soldiers' lives have been saved because of the Stryker," said Col. Robert B. Brown, commander of the 1st Brigade, 25th Infantry Division, Stryker Brigade Combat Team, which uses about 225 Strykers for combat operations throughout northern Iraq. "That's being conservative," he said.
>
> —Steve Fainuru, "Soldiers Defend Faulted Strykers"

Note how the story uses a dramatic quotation to represent the opinion expressed in the interviews. A more academic study, however, might include the full transcript of the interviews to give readers access to more data.

Surveys and Questionnaires

Surveys usually require the use of questionnaires. Any questions posed should be clear, easy to understand, and designed so that respondents' answers can be analyzed readily. Questions that ask respondents to say "yes" or "no" or to rank items on a scale (1 to 5, for example, or "most helpful" to "least helpful") are particularly easy to tabulate. Because tabulation can take time and effort, limit the number of questions you ask. Note also that people often resent being asked to answer more than about twenty questions, especially online.

Here are some other guidelines to help you prepare for and carry out a survey:

- Write out your purpose in conducting the survey, and make sure its results will be directly related to your claim.

- Brainstorm potential questions to include in the survey, and ask how each relates to your purpose and claim.

- Figure out how many people you want to contact, what the demographics of your sample should be (for example, men in their twenties, or an equal number of men and women), and how you plan to reach these people.

- Draft questions as free of bias as possible, making sure that each calls for a short, specific answer.

- Think about possible ways respondents could misunderstand you or your questions, and revise with these points in mind.

- Test the questions on several people, and revise those questions that are ambiguous, hard to answer, or too time-consuming to answer.

- If your questionnaire is to be sent by mail or email or posted on the Web, draft a cover letter explaining your purpose and giving a clear deadline. For mail, provide an addressed, stamped return envelope.

A key requirement of survey questions is that they be easy to understand.

"Next question: I believe that life is a constant striving for balance, requiring frequent tradeoffs between morality and necessity, within a cyclic pattern of joy and sadness, forging a trail of bittersweet memories until one slips, inevitably, into the jaws of death. Agree or disagree?"

- On the final draft of the questionnaire, leave plenty of space for answers.
- Proofread the final draft carefully; typos will make a bad impression on those whose help you're seeking.

After you've done your tabulations, set out your findings in clear and easily readable form, using a chart or spreadsheet if possible.

In an argument over whether the government should label geneti-
cally modified foods, analyst Gary Langer draws on data from an ABC
News Poll asking Americans what they thought about such food:

> Nearly everyone—93 percent—says the federal government should
> require labels on food saying whether it's been genetically modified,
> or "bio-engineered" (this poll used both phrases). Such near-
> unanimity in public opinion is rare.
>
> Fifty-seven percent also say they'd be less likely to buy foods la-
> beled as genetically modified. That puts the food industry in a
> quandary: By meeting consumer demand for labeling, it would be
> steering business away from its genetically modified products.
>
> —Gary Langer, "Behind the Label: Many Skeptical
> of Genetically Modified Foods"

Experiments

Some arguments may be supported by evidence gathered through experiments. In the sciences, data from experiments conducted under rigorously controlled conditions are highly valued. For other kinds of
writing, "looser" and more informal experiments may be acceptable, especially if they're intended to provide only part of the support for an argument. If you want to argue, for instance, that the recipes in *Gourmet*
magazine are impossibly tedious to follow and take far more time than
the average person wishes to spend preparing food, you might ask five
or six people to conduct a little experiment: following two recipes apiece
from a recent issue, and recording and timing every step. The evidence
you gather from this informal experiment could provide some concrete
support—by way of specific examples—for your contention. But such
experiments should be taken with a grain of salt; they may not be effective with certain audiences, and if they can easily be attacked as skewed
or sloppily done ("The people you asked to make these recipes couldn't
cook a poptart"), then they may do more harm than good.

In an essay about computer hackers and the threats they pose to various individuals and systems, Winn Schwartau reports on an experiment, performed by a former hacker he knows, that was aimed at
showing how easy it is to rob a bank. The experiment Schwartau describes makes his claim about bank security more believable:

> Jesse took his audience to a trash bin behind Pacific Bell, the Southern
> California Baby Bell service provider. Dumpster diving proved to be an
> effective means of social engineering because within minutes, an in-
> ternal telephone company employee list was dredged out of the

garbage. On it, predictably, were handwritten notes with computer passwords.

In the neighborhood was a bank, which shall go nameless. After some more dumpster diving, financial and personal profiles of wealthy bank customers surfaced. That was all Jesse said he needed to commit the crime.

At a nearby phone booth, Jesse used a portable computer with an acoustic modem to dial into the telephone company's computer. Jesse knew a lot about the telephone company's computers, so he made a few changes. He gave the pay phone a new number, that of one of the wealthy clients about whom he now knew almost everything. He also turned off the victim's phone with that same number. Jesse then called the bank and identified himself as Mr. Rich, an alias.

"How can we help you, Mr. Rich?"

"I would like to transfer $100,000 to this bank account number."

"I will need certain information."

"Of course."

"What is your balance?"

"About _____," he supplied the number accurately.

"What is your address?"

Jesse gave the address.

"Are you at home, Mr. Rich?"

"Yes."

"We'll need to call you back for positive identification."

"I understand. Thank you for providing such good security."

In less than a minute the phone rang.

"Hello, Rich here."

The money was transferred, then transferred back to Mr. Rich's account again, to the surprise and embarrassment of the bank. The money was returned and the point was made.

–Winn Schwartau, "Hackers: The First Information Warriors"

Personal Experience

Personal experience can serve as powerful evidence when it's appropriate to the subject, to your purpose, and to the audience. If it's your *only* evidence, however, personal experience probably won't be sufficient to carry the argument. Nevertheless, it can be especially effective for drawing in listeners or readers, as Gloria Naylor demonstrates early in an argument about language and racism:

I remember the first time I heard the word "nigger." In my third-grade class, our math tests were being passed down the rows, and as I handed the papers to a little boy in back of me, I remarked that once

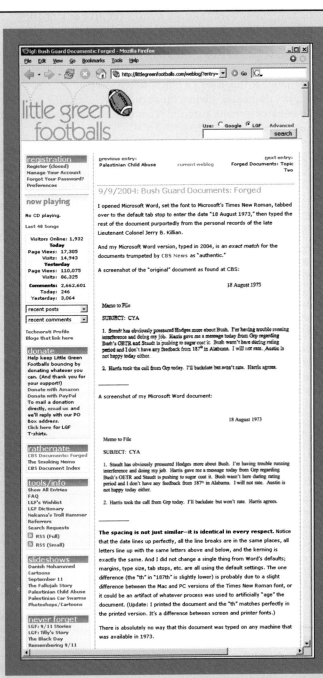

Not Just Words

Images often play a role in arguments. Charts, tables, and photographs are familiar types of visual evidence, but such arguments can also take unconventional forms. One of the more memorable examples of an argument supported visually occurred during the 2004 presidential election. In a segment aired on September 8, 2004, CBS's *60 Minutes II* claimed that newly discovered documents confirmed that George W. Bush had shirked military duties during his term in the National Guard. The photocopied memos, in official military form, seemed to be the smoking gun in a case that reporters had been pursuing for years. Here's what followed, according to political writer Michael Barone:

> . . . the network posted its 1972-dated documents on the Web. Within four hours, a blogger on freerepublic.com pointed out that they looked as though they had been created in Microsoft Word; the next morning, Scott Johnson of powerlineblog.com relayed the comment and asked for expert views. Charles Johnson oflittlegreenfootballs.com showed that the documents exactly matched one he produced in Word using default settings. CBS defended the documents for 11 days but finally confessed error and eased Rather out as anchor.
>
> –Michael Barone, "Blogosphere Politics"

Details of the documents' style and formatting had been questioned almost as soon as CBS made them available for online scrutiny. But Johnson's discovery brought focus and clarity to the discussion: since Microsoft Word hadn't existed when the CBS documents were supposedly written, documents mirroring its fonts, spacing, and defaults would have been difficult to create.

On the facing page is a screenshot of Johnson's experiment with the text of one of the questionable CBS documents. Examine the screenshot carefully, paying particular attention to the relationship between the two versions of the memo and Johnson's comments on them. Do you find Johnson's analysis convincing? Has he found a smoking gun, or would you want more data before agreeing that the case against the documents has reached a critical mass? Why or why not? What would be lost if Johnson had offered only a verbal description of his comparison of the documents?

again he had received a much lower mark than I did. He snatched his test from me and spit out that word. Had he called me a nymphomaniac or a necrophiliac, I couldn't have been more puzzled. I didn't know what a nigger was, but I knew that whatever it meant, it was something he shouldn't have called me. This was verified when I raised my hand, and in a loud voice repeated what he had said and watched the teacher scold him for using a "bad" word. I was later to go home and ask the inevitable question that every black parent must face—"Mommy, what does 'nigger' mean?"

–Gloria Naylor, "Mommy, What Does 'Nigger' Mean?"

Secondhand Evidence and Research

Secondhand evidence comes from sources beyond yourself—books, articles, films, online documents, photographs, and so on.

Library Sources

Your college library has not only printed materials (books, periodicals, reference works) but also computer terminals that provide access to electronic catalogs and indexes as well as to other libraries' catalogs via the Internet. Although this book isn't designed to give a complete overview of library resources, we can make some important distinctions and pose a few key questions that can help you use the library most efficiently.

CULTURAL CONTEXTS FOR ARGUMENT

Using Personal Experience

Personal experience counts in making academic arguments in some but not all cultures. Showing that you have personal experience with a topic can carry strong persuasive appeal with many English-speaking audiences, however, so it will probably be a useful way to argue a point in the United States. As with all evidence used to make a point, evidence based on your own experience must be pertinent to the topic, understandable to the audience, and clearly related to your purpose and claim.

Two Important Distinctions

- Remember the distinction between the *library databases* and the *Internet/Web*. Your library's computers hold important resources that either aren't available on the Web at all or aren't easily accessible to you except through the library's own system. The most important of these resources is the library's own catalog of its holdings (mostly books), but in addition college libraries usually pay to subscribe to a large number of scholarly databases — guides to journal and magazine articles, the Lexis/Nexis database of news stories and legal cases, and compilations of statistics, for example — that you can use for free. You'll be wise, then, to begin research using the electronic sources available to you through your college library before turning to the Web.

- Remember the distinction between *subject headings* and *keywords*. Library catalogs and databases usually index their contents by author, by title, by publication date, and by subject headings — a standardized set of words and phrases used to classify the subject matter of books and articles. When you do a subject search of the catalog, then, you're searching only one part of the electronic record of the library's books, and you need to use the exact wording of the *Library of Congress Subject Headings* (LCSH) classifications. This reference work is available in your library. On the other hand, searches using keywords make use of the computer's ability to look for any term in any field of the electronic record. So keyword searching is less restrictive than searching by subject headings, but it requires you to think carefully about your search terms in order to get good results. In addition, you need to learn to use the techniques for combining keywords with the terms *and, or,* and *not* and with parentheses and quotation marks (or using similar procedures built into the catalog's or database's search mechanism) to limit (or expand) your search.

Some Questions for Beginning Research

- What kinds of sources do you need to consult? Check your assignment to see whether you're required to consult different kinds of sources. If you'll use print sources, find out whether they're readily available in your library or whether you must make special arrangements (such as an interlibrary loan) to use them. If you need to locate nonprint sources (such as audiotapes or videotapes, artwork, photos), find out where those are kept and whether you need special permission to examine them.

- How current do your sources need to be? If you must investigate the very latest findings about, say, a new treatment for Alzheimer's, you'll probably want to check periodicals, medical journals, or the Web. If you want broader, more detailed coverage and background information, you may need to depend more on books. If your argument deals with a specific time period, you may need to examine newspapers, magazines, or books written during that period.

- How many sources should you consult? Expect to look over many more sources than you'll end up using, and be sure to cover all major perspectives on your subject. The best guideline is to make sure you have enough sources to support your claim.

- Do you know your way around the library? If not, ask a librarian for help in locating the following resources in the library: general and specialized encyclopedias; biographical resources; almanacs, yearbooks, and atlases; book and periodical indexes; specialized indexes and abstracts; the circulation computer or library catalog; special collections; audio, video, and art collections; the interlibrary loan office.

Online Sources

Many important resources for argument are now available in databases, either online or on CD-ROM, and many libraries now share the resources of their electronic catalogs through WorldCat. But the Internet has no overall index quite like the *Library of Congress Subject Headings* yet. However, like library catalogs and databases, the Internet and Web offer two ways to search for sources related to your argument: one using subject categories, and one using keywords.

A subject directory organized by categories—such as you might find at <http://dir.yahoo.com>—allows you to choose a broad category like "Entertainment" or "Science" and then click on increasingly narrow categories like "Movies" or "Astronomy" and then "Thrillers" or "The Solar System" until you reach a point where you're given a list of Web sites or the opportunity to do a keyword search.

With the second kind of Internet search option, a search engine, you start right off with a keyword search—filling in a blank, for example, on the opening page of <http://Google.com>. Because the Internet contains vastly more material than even the largest library catalog or database, exploring it with a search engine requires even more care in the choice and combination of keywords. For an argument about the fate of the hero in contemporary films, for example, you might find that *film* and

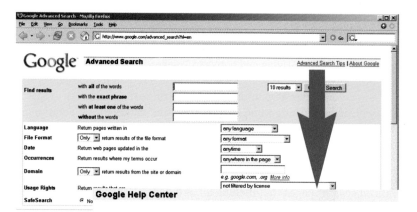

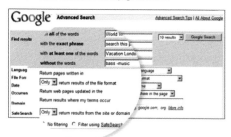

Google Help Center

Advanced Search Made Easy

Once you know the basics of Google search, you might want to try Advanced Search, which offers numerous options for making your searches more precise and getting more useful results.

You can reach this page by clicking (no surprise) the "Advanced Search" link on the Google home page.

Here's what the Advanced Search page looks like:

You can do a lot more with Google search than just typing in search terms. With Advanced Search, you can search only for pages:

- that contain ALL the search terms you type in
- that contain the exact phrase you type in
- that contain at least one of the words you type in
- that do NOT contain any of the words you type in
- written in a certain language
- created in a certain file format
- that have been updated within a certain period of time
- that contain numbers within a certain range
- within a certain domain, or website
- that don't contain "adult" material

To refine your online search techniques, use the resources provided by search engines. On Google, clicking on "Advanced Search Tips" takes you to a help center.

hero produce far too many possible matches, or hits. You might further narrow the search by adding a third keyword, say, *American* or *current*.

In doing such searches, you'll need to observe the search logic for a particular database. Using *and* between keywords (*movies and heroes*) usually indicates that both terms must appear in a file for it to be called up.

Using *or* between keywords usually instructs the computer to locate every file in which either one word or the other shows up, whereas using *not* tells the computer to exclude files containing a particular word from the search results (*movies not heroes*).

As you can see, searching has usually become just a matter of typing in a few strategic words. Tools such as Google or Yahoo! incorporate "advanced search" pages that include all of these options in an easy-to-use fill-in-the-blank format, while also allowing you to search for exact phrases or narrow your searches to particular dates, languages, parts of a Web site, domains on the Web (such as .edu, .org, or .gov), and more.

Using Evidence Effectively

You may gather an impressive amount of evidence on your topic—from firsthand interviews, from careful observations, and from intensive library and online research. But until that evidence is woven into the fabric of your own argument, it's just a pile of data. You still have to turn that data into information that will be persuasive to your intended audiences.

Considering Audiences

The ethos you bring to an argument (see Chapter 3) is crucial to your success in connecting with your audience. Of course, you want to present yourself as reliable and credible, but you also need to think carefully about the way your evidence relates to your audience. Is it appropriate to this particular group of readers or listeners? Does it speak to them in ways they'll understand and respond to? Does it acknowledge where they're coming from and speak in terms they'll understand? It's hard to give definite advice for making sure that your evidence fits an audience. But in general, timeliness is important to audiences: the more up-to-date your evidence, the better. In addition, evidence that represents typical rather than extreme circumstances usually is more convincing. For example, in arguing for a campus-wide security escort

Defining Evidence

How do you decide what evidence will best support your claims? The answer depends, in large part, on how you define *evidence*. Differing notions of what counts as evidence can lead to arguments that go nowhere fast. Journalists are often called on to interview those whose view of what constitutes effective evidence differs markedly from their own. For example, when in 1971 Italian journalist Oriana Fallaci interviewed the Ayatollah Khomeini, Iran's supreme leader, she argued in a way that's common in North American and Western European cultures: she presented what she considered to be claims adequately backed up with facts ("Iran denies freedom to people. . . . Many people have been put in prison and even executed, just for speaking out in opposition"). In response, Khomeini relied on very different kinds of evidence: analogies ("Just as a finger with gangrene should be cut off so that it will not destroy the whole body, so should people who corrupt others be pulled out like weeds so they will not infect the whole field") and, above all, the authority of the Qur'an. Partly because of these differing beliefs about what counts as evidence, the interview ended unsuccessfully.

People in Western nations tend to give great weight to factual evidence; but even in those countries, what constitutes evidence can differ radically, as it does, for example, in debates in the United States between proponents of evolutionary theory and supporters of the viewpoint on life's origins termed "intelligent design." In arguing across cultural divides, whether international or otherwise, you need to think carefully about how you're accustomed to using evidence — and to pay attention to what counts as evidence to other people *without simply surrendering your own intellectual principles*. Here are some questions to help you review the types of evidence on which you're building your argument:

- Do you rely on facts? Examples? Firsthand experience?
- Do you include testimony from experts? Which experts are valued most (and why)?
- Do you cite religious or philosophical texts? Proverbs or everyday wisdom?
- Do you use analogies and metaphors as evidence? How much do they count?

Once you've determined what counts as evidence in your own arguments, ask the same questions about the use of evidence by members of other cultures.

487

service after 10 P.M., a writer who cites actual numbers of students recently threatened or attacked on their way across campus after dark will be in a stronger position than one who cites only one sensational attack that occurred four years ago.

Building a Critical Mass

Throughout this chapter we've stressed the need to discover as much evidence as possible in support of your claim. If you can find only one or two pieces of evidence, only one or two reasons or illustrations to back up your contention, then you may be on weak ground. Although there's no magic quantity, no definite way of saying how much evidence is "enough," you should build toward a critical mass, with a number of pieces of evidence all pulling in the direction of your claim. If your evidence for a claim relies mainly on personal experience or on one major example, you should extend your search for additional sources and good reasons to back up your claim—or modify the claim. Your initial position may have been wrong.

If Everything's an Argument . . .

The authors of this book were trained primarily in the liberal arts. That means that they're more inclined to provide verbal and textual support for the claims they make rather than evidence that's numerical or graphical. Given that this is a textbook on writing, you probably aren't surprised to find many more passages of writing than pie charts, bar graphs, columns of figures, maps, or formulas. Yet how might this book have been different if the authors had backgrounds in, say, business, the natural sciences, the physical sciences, architecture, or some field outside of the traditional humanities (that is, English, philosophy, history, linguistics, foreign languages, and so on)? What if the authors were sports junkies? Do people in different fields instinctively draw upon distinctive kinds of examples or evidence? Explore this topic in a group that includes people with a variety of majors, backgrounds, or interests.

Arranging Evidence

Review your evidence, deciding which pieces support which points in the argument. In general, try to position your strongest pieces of evidence in key places — near the beginning of paragraphs, at the end of the introduction, or where you build toward a powerful conclusion. In addition, try to achieve a balance between, on the one hand, your own argument and your own words, and on the other hand, the sources you use or quote in support of the argument. The sources of evidence are important props in the structure, but they shouldn't overpower the structure (your argument) itself.

RESPOND ●

1. What counts as evidence depends in large part on the rhetorical situation. One audience might find personal testimony compelling in a given case, whereas another might require data that only experimental studies can provide.

    Imagine that you want to argue for a national educational campaign promoting the cutting of "pork" — that is, spending projects benefiting a particular state or congressional district that are added to the federal budget mainly to get incumbents reelected. Your campaign will be composed of television ads scheduled to air before and during the Super Bowl — and you want the Democratic and Republican national committees to pay for those ads. Make a list of reasons and evidence to support your claim, aimed simultaneously at political bigwigs *from both parties*. What kind of evidence would be most compelling to that mixed group? How would you rethink your use of evidence if you were writing for the newsletter of a community of retirees or for your student newspaper, urging political activism to cut out-of-control spending by politicians? This isn't an exercise in pulling the wool over anyone's eyes; your goal is simply to anticipate the kind of evidence that different audiences would find persuasive, given the same case.

2. Finding, evaluating, and arranging evidence in an argument is often a *discovery* process: sometimes you're concerned not only with digging up support for an already established claim but also with creating and revising tentative claims. Surveys and interviews can help you figure out what to argue, as well as provide evidence for a claim.

    Interview a classmate with the goal of writing a brief proposal argument about his or her career goals. The claim should be *My classmate should be doing X five years from now.* Limit yourself to ten questions; write them ahead of time, and don't deviate from them. Record the results of the interview (written notes are fine—you don't need a tape recorder).

Then interview another classmate, with the same goal in mind. Ask the same first question, but this time let the answer dictate the rest of the questions. You still get only ten questions.

Which interview gave you more information? Which one helped you learn more about your classmate's goals? Which one better helped you develop claims about his or her future?

3. Imagine that you're trying to decide whether to take a class with a particular professor, but you don't know if he or she is a good teacher. You might already have an opinion, based on some vaguely defined criteria and dormitory gossip, but you're not sure if that evidence is reliable. You decide to observe a class to inform your decision.

Visit a class in which you aren't currently enrolled, and make notes on your observations following the guidelines in this chapter (p. 472–473). You probably only need a single day's visit to get a sense of the note-taking process, though you would, of course, need much more time to write a thorough evaluation of the professor.

Write a short evaluation of the professor's teaching abilities on the basis of your observations. Then write an analysis of your evaluation. Is it honest? Fair? What other kinds of evidence might you need if you wanted to make an informed decision about the class and the teacher? What evidence is available to you in terms of local files of teaching evaluations, online teaching evaluation sites, and so on?

17
Fallacies of Argument

"Are you going to agree with what that racist pig is saying?"

"If I don't get an 'A' in this class, I won't get into medical school."

"Ask not what your country can do for you; ask what you can do for your country."

"No blood for oil!"

"All my friends have AOL. I'm the only one who can't get instant messages!"

"9/11 changed everything."

• • •

Certain types of argumentative moves are so controversial they've been traditionally classified as *fallacies,* a term we use in this chapter. But you might find it more interesting to think of them as *flashpoints* or *hotspots* because they instantly raise questions about the ethics of argument—that is, whether a particular strategy of argument is fair, accurate, or principled. Fallacies are arguments supposedly flawed by their very nature or structure; as such, you should avoid them in your own writing and challenge them in arguments you hear or read. That said, it's important to appreciate that one person's fallacy may well be another person's stroke of genius.

Consider, for example, the fallacy termed *ad hominem* argument—"to the man." It describes a strategy of attacking the character of people you disagree with rather than the substance of their arguments: *So you think Eminem is a homophobic racist? Well, you're just a thumb-sucking, white-bread elitist.* Many people have blurted out such insults at some time in their lives and later regretted them. Other *ad hominem* attacks are more consciously produced, such as Edward Klein's book-length attack on Hillary Clinton. Here's just one example of the use of *ad hominem* in that book:

> Gone was the left-wing Hillary, the gender feminist who sounded to many people like a radical bomb thrower. . . .
> —Edward Klein, *The Truth about Hillary*

Of course, there are situations when someone's character is central to an argument. If that weren't so, appeals based on character would be pointless. The problem arises in deciding when such arguments are legitimate and when they are flashpoints. You're much more likely to think of attacks on people you admire as *ad hominem* slurs, but personal attacks on those you disagree with as reasonable criticisms. Obviously, debates about character can become quite polarizing. Consider Anita Hill and Clarence Thomas, Eminem and Moby, Barry Bonds and those who accuse him of steroid use. (For more on arguments based on character, see Chapter 3.)

It might be wise to think of fallacies not in terms of errors you can detect and expose in someone else's work, but as strategies that hurt everyone (including the person using them) because they make productive argument more difficult. Fallacies muck up the frank but civil conversations people should be able to have—regardless of their differences.

To help you understand flashpoints of argument, we've classified them according to three rhetorical appeals discussed in earlier chapters: emotional arguments, ethical arguments, and logical arguments (see Chapters 2, 3, and 4).

Flashpoints of Emotional Argument

Emotional arguments can be both powerful and suitable in many circumstances, and most writers use them frequently. However, writers who pull on their readers' heartstrings or raise their blood pressure too often can violate the good faith on which legitimate argument depends. Readers won't trust a writer who can't make a point without frightening someone or provoking tears or stirring up hatred.

Scare Tactics

Corrupters of children, the New Testament warns, would be better off dropped into the sea with millstones around their necks. Would that politicians, advertisers, and public figures who peddle their ideas by scaring people and exaggerating possible dangers well beyond their statistical likelihood face similarly stern warnings. Yet scare tactics are remarkably common in everything ranging from ads for life insurance to threats of audits by the Internal Revenue Service. Such ploys work because it's usually easier to imagine something terrible happening than to appreciate its statistical rarity. That may be why so many people fear flying more than driving. Auto accidents occur much more frequently, but they don't have the same impact on our imaginations as air disasters do.

Scare tactics can also be used to stampede legitimate fears into panic or prejudice. People who genuinely fear losing their jobs can be persuaded, easily enough, to mistrust all immigrants as people who might work for less money; people living on fixed incomes can be convinced that even minor modifications of entitlement programs represent dire threats to their standard of living. Such tactics have the effect of closing off thinking because people who are scared seldom act rationally. Even well-intended fear campaigns—like those directed against the use of illegal drugs or HIV infection—can misfire if their warnings prove too shrill.

Either-Or Choices

A way to simplify arguments and give them power is to reduce the options for action to only two choices. The preferred option or the existing policy might be drawn in the warmest light, whereas the alternative is cast as an ominous shadow. That's the nature of the choices President George W. Bush offered in his August 20, 2005, radio address to the nation:

> Our troops know that they're fighting in Iraq, Afghanistan, and elsewhere to protect their fellow Americans from a savage enemy. They know that if we do not confront these evil men abroad, we will have to face them one day in our own cities and streets, and they know that the safety and security of every American is at stake in this war, and they know we will prevail.

Sometimes neither of the alternatives is pleasant: that's the nature of many "ultimatums." For instance, the allies in World War II offered the Axis powers only two choices as the conflict drew to a close: either continued war and destruction, or unconditional surrender. No third option was available.

Either-or arguments can be well-intentioned strategies to get something accomplished. Parents use them all the time, telling children that either they'll eat their broccoli or they won't get dessert. Such arguments become fallacious when they reduce a complicated issue to excessively simple terms or when they're designed to obscure legitimate alternatives.

For instance, to suggest that Social Security must be privatized or the system will go broke may have rhetorical power, but the choice is too simple. The financial problems of Social Security can be fixed in any number of ways, including privatization. But to defend privatization, falsely, as the *only* possible course of action is to risk losing the support of people who know better.

But then *either-or* arguments—like most scare tactics—are often purposefully designed to seduce those who don't know much about a subject. That's another reason the tactic violates principles of civil

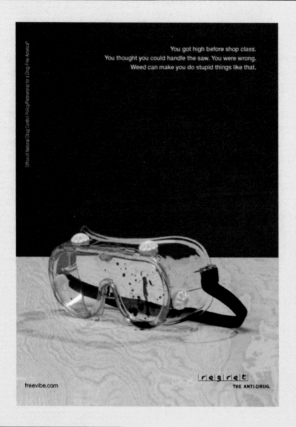

Not Just Words

Look at the advertisement above. Is it a scare tactic? A legitimate warning? Something in between? How effective do think this ad would be for college students, or for people you might know who use marijuana or might be tempted to? What effect does the text in the upper right-hand corner have on your answers to these questions? What about the text at the bottom? Do graphic images like this and sponsor labels like "Partnership for a Drug-Free America" make the campaign against marijuana and other illegal drugs more effective—or less so? How does this ad compare with the one about drunk driving on p. 111?

discourse. Argument should enlighten people, making them more knowledgeable and more capable of acting intelligently and independently. Very often, we don't have to choose one side over the other. Here are analysts from the Economic Policy Institute making just that point:

> The Social Security dilemma is typically framed as a false choice between caring for the nation's elderly at the expense of living standards and fiscal responsibility or reducing our commitment to retirees by cutting back on Social Security and Medicare. The two goals of improving living standards for workers and their families and caring for the elderly do not have to be mutually exclusive. They can be achieved through sensible, equitable economic policies that include productivity-boosting investments, the broad distribution of economic gains, and the fundamental restructuring of the public and private health care systems.
>
> –Edith Rasell, Max Sawicky, Dean Baker, "America's Golden Years"

The parental ultimatum: a classic form of the either-or argument

"They say we can go there for Thanksgiving or they can cut us out of the will. Our choice."

Although the previous discussion focuses on *either-or* arguments as scare tactics to justify proposed or current actions, they can also involve simple lapses of logic, less emotionally charged issues, or matters of fact, definition, evaluation, or causal analysis. For example, in a *New York Times* column about a sociologist's book describing how differently upper-middle-class parents and poor and working-class parents bring up their children, David Brooks concludes that "the core issue is that today's rich don't exploit the poor; they just outcompete them." But these two possibilities aren't mutually exclusive: the rich could be outcompeting the poor *and* exploiting them. (And, in fact, the column mentions the sociologist's finding that the poorer "[c]hildren, like their parents, were easily intimidated and pushed around by verbally dexterous teachers and doctors.") Similarly, a tomato could be considered both a vegetable and a fruit; a novel could be neither a literary masterpiece nor a worthless potboiler but something in between; and current global warming could be the result of both human activity and natural climate cycles.

Slippery Slope

The slippery slope flashpoint is well named, describing an argument that casts today's tiny misstep as tomorrow's slide into disaster. Of course, not all arguments aimed at preventing dire consequences are slippery slope fallacies; for example, the parent who corrects a child for misbehavior now is acting sensibly to prevent more serious problems as the child grows older. A slippery slope argument becomes a flashpoint when a writer exaggerates the likely consequences of an action, usually to frighten readers. As such, slippery slope arguments are also scare tactics. For instance, defenders of free speech often regard even mild attempts to regulate behavior as leading inexorably to Big Brother—charging, for example, that if school officials can require a student to cut his ponytail, they'll eventually be allowed to impose uniforms and crew cuts. Similarly, opponents of gun control warn that any legislation regulating firearms is just a first step toward the government knocking down citizens' doors and seizing weapons.

In recent years, the issue of same-sex marriage has brought out a number of slippery slope arguments:

> Anyone else bored to tears with the "slippery slope" arguments against gay marriage? Since few opponents of homosexual unions are brave enough to admit that gay weddings just freak them out, they hide behind the claim that it's an inexorable slide from legalizing gay

marriage to having sex with penguins outside JC Penney's. The problem is it's virtually impossible to debate against a slippery slope.
                                    –Dahlia Lithwick, "Slippery Slop"

Of course, ideas and actions do have consequences, but they aren't always as dire as writers fond of slippery slope tactics would have you believe.

Sentimental Appeals

Sentimental appeals are arguments that use tender emotions excessively to distract readers from facts. Quite often, such appeals are highly personal and individual—focusing attention on heart-warming or heart-wrenching situations that make readers feel guilty if they challenge an idea, policy, or proposal. Emotions become an impediment to civil discourse when they keep people from thinking clearly.

This calendar is designed to elicit sympathy for the giant pandas on its cover and inspire donations for the wildlife organization that protects them. But sentimental images of threatened species are sometimes attached to much less worthy sales pitches—for soda or camping gear, for example.

Yet sentimental appeals are a major vehicle of television news, where it's customary to convey ideas through personal tales that tug at viewers' heartstrings. For example, a camera might document the day-to-day life of a single mother on welfare whose on-screen generosity, kindness, and tears come to represent the spirit of an entire welfare clientele under attack by callous legislators; or the welfare recipient might be shown driving a new pickup and illegally trading food stamps for money while a lower-middle-class family struggles to meet its grocery budget. In either case, the conclusion the reporter wants you to reach is supported by powerful images that evoke emotions in support of that conclusion. But though the individual stories presented may be genuinely moving, they seldom give a complete picture of a complex social or economic issue.

Bandwagon Appeals

Bandwagon appeals are arguments that urge people to follow the same path everyone else is taking. Curiously, many American parents seem innately endowed with the ability to refute bandwagon appeals. When their kids whine, *Everyone else is going camping overnight without chaperones*, the parents reply instinctively, *And if everyone else jumps off a cliff (or a railroad bridge, or the Empire State Building), you will too?* The children stomp and groan—and then try a different line of argument.

Unfortunately, not all bandwagon approaches are so transparent. Though Americans like to imagine themselves as rugged individualists, they're easily seduced by ideas endorsed by the mass media and popular culture. Such trends are often little more than harmless fashion statements. At other times, however, Americans are encouraged to become obsessed by issues that politicians or the media select for their attention—such as the seemingly endless coverage of the controversy over removing life support systems from Terri Schiavo in 2005. In recent decades, bandwagon issues have included the war on drugs, the nuclear freeze movement, health care reform, AIDS prevention, gun control, drunk driving, tax reform, welfare reform, teen smoking, campaign finance reform, illegal immigration, Social Security reform, and the defense of traditional heterosexual marriage.

In the atmosphere of obsession, there's a feeling that everyone must be concerned by this issue-of-the-day, and something—*anything*—must be done! More often than not, enough people jump on the bandwagon to achieve a measure of change. And when changes occur because people have become sufficiently informed to exercise good judgment, then one can speak of "achieving consensus," a rational goal for civil argument.

But sometimes bandwagons run out of control—as they did in the 1950s when some careers were destroyed by "witch hunts" for suspected communists during the McCarthy era, and in the late 1980s when concerns over child abuse sometimes mushroomed into indiscriminate prosecutions of parents and child care workers. In a democratic society, the bandwagon appeal is among the most potentially serious and permanently damaging flashpoints of argument.

Flashpoints of Ethical Argument

Not surprisingly, readers give their closest attention to authors whom they respect or trust. So, writers usually want to present themselves as honest, well informed, likable, or sympathetic in some way. But *trust me*

When support for a bandwagon cause is just a fashion statement

"Grab some lederhosen, Sutfin. We're about to climb aboard the globalization bandwagon."

is a scary warrant. Not all the devices writers use to gain the attention and confidence of readers are admirable. (For more on appeals based on character, see Chapter 3.)

Appeals to False Authority

One of the effective strategies a writer can use to support an idea is to draw on the authority of widely respected people, institutions, and texts. In fact, many academic research papers are essentially exercises in finding and reflecting on the work of reputable authorities. Writers usually introduce these authorities into their arguments through direct quotations, citations (such as footnotes), or allusions. (For more on assessing the reliability of sources, see Chapter 19.) False authority occurs chiefly when writers offer themselves, or other authorities they cite, as sufficient warrant for believing a claim:

Claim	X is true because I say so.
Warrant	What I say must be true.
Claim	X is true because Y says so.
Warrant	What Y says must be true.

Rarely will you see authority asserted quite so baldly as in these formulas, because few readers would accept a claim stated in either of these ways. Nonetheless, claims of authority drive many persuasive campaigns. American pundits and politicians are fond of citing the U.S. Constitution or Bill of Rights as ultimate authorities, a reasonable practice when the documents are interpreted respectfully. However, as often as not, the constitutional rights claimed aren't in the texts themselves or don't mean what the speakers think they do. And most constitutional matters are quite debatable—as centuries of court records could prove.

Likewise, religious believers often base arguments on books or traditions that wield great authority within a particular religious community. However, the power of these texts or ways of thinking is usually somewhat limited outside, or even inside, that group and, hence, less capable of persuading others solely on the grounds of their authority alone—though arguments of faith often have power on other grounds.

Institutions can be cited as authorities too. Certainly, serious attention should be paid to claims supported by authorities one respects or recognizes—the Centers for Disease Control, the National Science Foundation, the *New York Times*, the *Wall Street Journal*, and so on. But one ought not to accept information or opinions simply because they have

An argument based on the Bible has limited power among nonbelievers. Nor will all believers find such an argument convincing, since there are often many interpretations of a single biblical passage.

the imprimatur of such offices and agencies. To quote a Russian proverb made famous by Ronald Reagan, "Trust, but verify."

Dogmatism

A writer who attempts to persuade by asserting or assuming that a particular position is the only one conceivably acceptable within a community is trying to enforce dogmatism. Indeed, dogmatism is a flashpoint of character because the tactic undermines the trust that must exist between those who make arguments and those to whom they make them. In effect, people who speak or write dogmatically imply that there are no arguments to be made: the truth is self-evident to those who know better. You can usually be sure you're listening to a dogmatic opinion when someone begins a sentence with *No rational person would disagree that . . .* or *It's clear to anyone who has thought about it that . . .*

Of course, there are some arguments beyond the pale of civil discourse—positions and claims so outrageous or absurd that they're unworthy of serious attention. For example, attacks on the historical reality of the Holocaust fall into this category. But relatively few subjects in a free society ought to be off the table from the start—certainly, none that can be defended with facts, testimony, and good reasons. In general, therefore, when someone suggests that merely raising an issue for debate is somehow "unacceptable" or "inappropriate" or "outrageous"— whether on the grounds that it's racist, sexist, unpatriotic, blasphemous, or insensitive or offensive in some other way—you should be suspicious.

Moral Equivalence

A fallacy of argument perhaps more common today than in earlier decades is moral equivalence—that is, suggesting that serious wrong-doings don't differ in kind from minor offenses. A warning sign that this fallacy may be coming into play is the retort of the politician or bureaucrat accused of wrongdoing: *But everyone else does it too!* Richard Nixon insisted that the crimes that led to his resignation were no worse than the actions of previous presidents; Bill Clinton made similar responses to charges about the fund-raising practices of his administration. Regardless of the validity of these particular defenses, there's a point at which such comparisons become highly questionable if not absurd.

For example, political blogger Andrew Sullivan charged that Daniel P. Moloney reached such a point when Moloney suggested in an article in the conservative magazine *National Review* that what he considers inadequate attention to sin by "Western liberal Christians" makes contemporary Western society little better than Nazi Germany:

> In this regard, the consumerism and relativism of the West can be just as dangerous as the totalitarianism of the East: It's just as easy to forget about God while dancing to an iPod as while marching in a Hitler Youth rally. There's a difference, to be sure, but hardly anyone would contest the observation that in elite Western society, as in totalitarian Germany, the moral vocabulary has been purged of the idea of sin. And if there's no sense of sin, then there's no need for a Redeemer, or for the Church.
>
> – Daniel P. Moloney, "Sin's the Thing"

As this example shows, moral equivalence can work both ways, with relatively innocuous activities or situations raised to the level of major crimes or catastrophes. Some would say that the national campaign against smoking falls into this category—a common and legally sanctioned

In "American as Apple Pie," cartoonist Sage Stossel equates the common and widely accepted use of prescription drugs with the use of steroids among baseball players.

behavior now given the social stigma of serious drug abuse. And if smoking is almost criminal, shouldn't one be equally concerned with people who use and abuse chocolate—a sweet and fatty food responsible for a host of health problems? You can see how easy it is to make an equivalence argument. Yet suggesting that all behaviors of a particular kind—in this case, abuses of substances—are equally wrong (whether they involve cigarettes, alcohol, drugs, or fatty foods) blurs the distinctions people need to make in weighing claims.

Ad Hominem Arguments

Ad hominem (from the Latin for "to the man") arguments are attacks directed at the character of a person rather than at the claims he or she makes. The theory is simple: Destroy the credibility of your opponents, and either you destroy their ability to present reasonable appeals or you distract from the successful arguments they may be offering. Here, for example, is Christopher Hitchens questioning whether former secretary of state Henry Kissinger should be appointed to head an important government commission in 2002:

> **But can Congress and the media be expected to swallow the appointment of a proven coverup artist, a discredited historian, a busted liar, and a man who is wanted in many jurisdictions for the vilest of offenses?**
>
> –Christopher Hitchens, "The Case against Henry Kissinger"

Not much doubt where Hitchens stands. Critics of Rush Limbaugh's conservative politics rarely fail to note his weight (even after he had lost most of it); critics of Michael Brown, former director of the Federal Emergency Management Agency, just as reliably note his earlier job as commissioner of the Arabian Horse Association.

In such cases, *ad hominem* tactics turn arguments into two-sided affairs with good guys and bad guys, and that's unfortunate, since character often does matter in argument. People expect the proponent of peace to be civil, the advocate of ecology to respect the environment, the champion of justice to be fair even in private dealings. But it's fallacious to attack an idea by uncovering the foibles of its advocates or attacking their motives, backgrounds, or unchangeable traits.

Flashpoints of Logical Argument

You'll encounter a flashpoint in any argument when the claims, warrants, and/or evidence in it are invalid, insufficient, or disconnected. In the abstract, such problems seem easy enough to spot; in practice, they can be camouflaged by a skillful use of words or images. Indeed, logical fallacies pose a challenge to civil argument because they often seem quite reasonable and natural, especially when they appeal to people's self-interests. Whole industries (such as phone-in psychic networks) depend on one or more of the logical fallacies for their existence; political campaigns, too, rely on them to prop up that current staple of democratic interchange—the fifteen-second TV spot.

Hasty Generalization

Among logical fallacies, only faulty causality might be able to challenge hasty generalization for the crown of most prevalent. A hasty generalization is an inference drawn from insufficient evidence: *Because my*

Honda broke down, all Hondas must be junk. It also forms the basis for most stereotypes about people or institutions: because a few people in a large group are observed to act in a certain way, one infers that all members of that group will behave similarly. The resulting conclusions are usually sweeping claims of little merit: *Women are bad drivers; men are boors; Scots are stingy; Italians are romantic; English teachers are nit-picking; scientists are nerds.* You could, no doubt, expand this roster of stereotypes by the hundreds.

To draw valid inferences, you must always have sufficient evidence: a random sample of a population, a selection large enough to represent fully the subjects of your study, an objective methodology for sampling the population or evidence, and so on (see Chapter 16). And you must qualify your claims appropriately. After all, people do need generalizations to help make reasonable decisions in life; such claims can be offered legitimately if placed in context and tagged with appropriate qualifiers: *some, a few, many, most, occasionally, rarely, possibly, in some cases, under certain circumstances, in my experience.*

You should be especially alert to the fallacy of hasty generalization when you read reports and studies of any kind, especially case studies based on carefully selected populations. Be alert for the fallacy, too, in the interpretation of poll numbers. Everything from the number of people selected to the time the poll was taken to the exact wording of the questions may affect its outcome.

Faulty Causality

In Latin, the fallacy of faulty causality is described by the expression *post hoc, ergo propter hoc,* which translates word-for-word as "after this, therefore because of this." Odd as the translation may sound, it accurately describes what faulty causality is — the fallacious assumption that because

If Everything's an Argument. . .

Consider the title of this textbook, *Everything's an Argument.* What fallacies could this title carry with it? Take some time to look at the introduction to one of the fallacies in this chapter. Can you detect any fallacious reasoning at work?

one event or action follows another, the first necessarily causes the second. Consider a lawsuit commented on in the *Wall Street Journal* in which a writer sued Coors (unsuccessfully), claiming that drinking copious amounts of the company's beer had kept him from writing a novel.

Some actions, of course, do produce reactions. Step on the brake pedal in your car, and you move hydraulic fluid that pushes calipers against disks to create friction that stops the vehicle. Or, if you happen to be chair of the Federal Reserve Board, you raise interest rates to increase the cost of borrowing to slow the growth of the economy in order to curb inflation — you hope. Causal relationships of this kind are reasonably convincing because one can provide evidence of relationships between the events sufficient to convince most people that an initial action did, indeed, cause subsequent actions.

In other cases, however, a supposed connection between cause and effect turns out to be completely wrong. For example, doctors now believe that when an elderly person falls and is found to have a broken leg or hip, the break usually caused the fall rather than the other way around. And as the Federal Reserve example suggests, causality can be especially difficult to control or determine when economic, political, or social relationships are involved.

Did drinking too much Coors cause a writer's literary paralysis? A court said no.

That's why suspiciously simple or politically convenient causal claims should always be subject to scrutiny. In the 1990s, for example, crime rates in New York City fell sharply. Then-mayor Rudolph Giuliani and his supporters claimed that the credit was largely due to the Giuliani administration's innovative policing strategies, such as a crackdown on petty crimes to prevent the commission of more serious offenses. But some of these policies had actually begun under Giuliani's predecessor; moreover, during the same period crime fell just as much in many other American cities—including ones whose police operated very differently from New York's. Giuliani's strategies may well have contributed to the drop, but analysts can—and do—disagree strongly about how much.

Begging the Question

There's probably not a teacher in the country who hasn't heard the following argument: *You can't give me a "C" in this course; I'm an "A" student.* For a member of Congress accused of taking bribes, a press secretary makes a version of the same argument: *Congressman X can't be guilty of accepting bribes; he's an honest person.* In both cases, the problem with the claim is that it's made on grounds that cannot be accepted as true because those grounds are in doubt. How can the student claim to be an "A" student when she just earned a "C"? How can the accused bribe-taker defend himself on the grounds of honesty when that honesty is now suspect? Setting such arguments in Toulmin terms helps to expose the fallacy:

Claim + Reason	You can't give me a "C" in this course because I'm an "A" student.
Warrant	An "A" student is someone who can't receive "C"s.
Claim + Reason	Congressman X can't be guilty of accepting bribes because he's an honest person.
Warrant	An honest person cannot be guilty of accepting bribes.

With the warrants stated, you can see why begging the question—that is, assuming as true the very claim that's disputed—is a form of circular argument, divorced from reality. If you assume that an "A" student can't receive "C"s, then the first argument stands. But no one is an "A" student *by definition;* that standing has to be earned by performance in individual courses. Likewise, even though someone with a record of honesty is unlikely to accept bribes, a claim of honesty isn't an adequate defense against specific charges. An honest person won't accept bribes, but merely claiming someone is honest doesn't make him so. (For more on Toulmin argument, see Chapter 6.)

Equivocation

Both the finest definition and the most famous literary examples of equivocation come from Shakespeare's tragedy *Macbeth*. In the drama three witches, representing the fates, make prophecies that favor the ambitious Macbeth but that prove disastrous when understood more fully. He's told, for example, that he has nothing to fear from his enemies "till Birnam wood / Do come to Dunsinane" (*Mac.* 5.5.44–45); although it seems impossible that a forest could move, these woods do indeed move when enemy soldiers cut down branches from the forest of Birnam for camouflage and march on Macbeth's fortress. Catching on to the game, Macbeth starts "[t]o doubt the equivocation of the fiend / That *lies like truth*" (5.5.43–44, emphasis added). An equivocation, then, is an argument that gives a lie an honest appearance; it's a half-truth.

Equivocations are usually juvenile tricks of language. Consider the plagiarist who copies a paper word-for-word from a source and then declares — honestly, she thinks — that "I wrote the entire paper myself," meaning that she physically copied the piece on her own. But the plagiarist is using "wrote" equivocally — that is, in a limited sense, knowing that most people would understand "writing" as something more than the mere copying of words. Many public figures are fond of parsing their words carefully so that no certain meaning emerges. In the 1990s, Bill Clinton's "I never had sex with that woman" claim became notorious; in the first decade of the twenty-first century, critics of the Bush administration said its many attempts to deny that "torture" was being used on U.S. prisoners abroad amounted to a long series of equivocations.

Non Sequitur

A *non sequitur* is an argument in which claims, reasons, or warrants fail to connect logically; one point doesn't follow from another. As with other fallacies, children are notably adept at framing *non sequiturs*. Consider this familiar form: *You don't love me or you'd buy me that bicycle!*

Baseball great Barry Bonds admitted to a grand jury that he had taken undetectable steroids during the 2003 season, but claimed he didn't know the substances—a cream and a clear liquid—were steroids. Some observers think that's an equivocation—a dishonest play on the word "know." As Olympic skier Bode Miller opined in a *Rolling Stone* profile, referring to Bonds and other athletes, "Yeah, they're not knowingly taking any substance, they don't . . . ask what it is, but they are sure . . . taking it."

It might be more evident to harassed parents that no connection exists between love and Huffys if they were to consider the implied warrant:

Claim	You must not love me . . .
Reason	. . . because you haven't bought me that bicycle.
Warrant	Buying bicycles for children is essential to loving them.

A five-year-old might endorse that warrant, but no responsible adult would because love doesn't depend on buying things, at least not a particular bicycle. Activities more logically related to love might include feeding and clothing children, taking care of them when they're sick, providing shelter and education, and so on.

In effect, *non sequiturs* occur when writers omit a step in an otherwise logical chain of reasoning, assuming that readers agree with what may be a highly contestable claim. For example, it's a *non sequitur* simply to argue that the comparatively poor performance of American students on international mathematics examinations means the country should spend more money on math education. Such a conclusion might be justified if a correlation were known or found to exist between mathematical ability and money spent on education. But the students' performance might be poor for reasons other than education funding, so a writer should first establish the nature of the problem before offering a solution.

The Straw Man

Those who resort to the "straw man" fallacy attack an argument that isn't really there, one that's much weaker or more extreme than the one the opponent is actually making. By "setting up a straw man" in this way, the speaker or writer has an argument that's easy to knock down and proceeds to do so, then claiming victory over the opponent—whose real argument was quite different.

A lot of "straw man" arguments have been advanced in the recent debate over evolution and intelligent design. Those arguing against intelligent design may say that *intelligent design advocates claim that life was created by some white-haired figure in the sky,* while those arguing against evolution sometimes say that *evolutionists claim that evolution is all random chance, so the human eye just came into existence randomly.* In both instances, these speakers are choosing to refute arguments that go beyond the claims their opponents have actually made. At least in their public political or legal statements, supporters of intelligent design don't make any claims about who or what the "intelligent designer" is. And supporters of evolution contend that the process is random only in the sense that it's driven by random mutations in genes; organisms "evolve" only if such mutations make them better adapted to their environment (such as by increasing their ability to detect light) and thus more likely to reproduce. Both sides are attacking weak arguments their opponents aren't actually making; as a result, both sides are ignoring the tougher issues.

Faulty Analogy

Comparisons give ideas greater presence or help clarify concepts. Consider the comparisons in this comment on Britney Spears's album *In the Zone:*

> [R]egardless of how hard she tries, Britney's not Madonna. To be fair, Madonna wasn't Madonna at first either, but emulating someone else—even if they're as successful as Madonna—usually doesn't work in the end.
>
> –Erik J. Barzeski

When comparisons are extended, they become analogies—ways of understanding unfamiliar ideas by comparing them with something that's already known. It's true that people understand the world around them largely through comparisons, metaphors, and analogies. But useful as such comparisons are, they may prove quite false either on their own or when pushed too far or taken too seriously. At this point they become faulty analogies, inaccurate or inconsequential comparisons between objects or concepts. The *Wikipedia* cites the following example of such a questionable analogy:

The universe is like an intricate watch.

A watch must have been designed by a watchmaker.

Therefore, the universe must have been designed by some kind of creator.

RESPOND●

1. Following is a list of political slogans or phrases that may be examples of logical fallacies. Discuss each item to determine what you may know about the slogan; then decide which, if any, fallacy might be used to describe it.

   "Leave no child behind." (George Bush policy and slogan)

   "It's the economy, stupid." (sign on the wall at Bill Clinton's campaign headquarters)

   "Nixon's the one." (campaign slogan)

   "Remember the Alamo."

   "Make love, not war." (antiwar slogan during the Vietnam War)

   "A chicken in every pot."

   "No taxation without representation."

   "There's no free lunch."

   "Loose lips sink ships."

   "Guns don't kill, people do." (NRA slogan)

   "If you can't stand the heat, get out of the kitchen."

2. We don't want you to argue fallaciously, but it's fun and good practice to frame argumentative fallacies in your own language. Pick an argumentative topic—maybe even one that you've used for a paper in this class—and write a few paragraphs making nothing but fallacious arguments in each sentence. Try to include all the fallacies of emotional, ethical, and logical argument that are discussed in this chapter.

3. Choose a paper you've written for this or another class, and analyze it carefully for signs of fallacious reasoning. Once you've tried analyzing your own prose, find an editorial, a syndicated column, and a political speech and look for the fallacies in them. Which fallacies are most common in the four arguments? How do you account for their prevalence? Which are the least common? How do you account for their absence? What seems to be the role of audience in determining what's a fallacy and what isn't?

4. Arguments on the Web are no more likely to contain fallacies than are arguments in any other text, but the fallacies can take on different forms. The hypertextual nature of Web arguments and the ease of including visuals along with text make certain fallacies more likely to occur there. Find a Web site sponsored by an organization (the Future of Music Coalition, perhaps), business (Coca-Cola, perhaps), or other group (the Democratic or Republican National Committee, perhaps), and analyze the site for fallacious reasoning. Among other considerations, look at the relationship between text and graphics, and between individual pages and the pages that surround or are linked to them. How does the technique of separating information into discrete pages affect the argument? Then send an email message to the site's creators, explaining what you found and proposing ways the arguments in the site could be improved.

5. Political blogs such as <wonkette.com>, <andrewsullivan.com>, <DailyKos>, and <InstaPundit.com> typically provide quick responses to daily events and detailed critiques of material in other media sites, including national newspapers. Study one active political blog for a few days to determine whether and how the blogger critiques the material he or she links to. Does the blogger point to flashpoints and fallacies in arguments? If so, does he or she explain them or just assume readers understand them or will figure them out? Summarize your findings in an oral report to your class.

18
Intellectual Property, Academic Integrity, and Avoiding Plagiarism

On a college campus, a student receives a warning: she has been detected using peer-to-peer music file-sharing software. Has she been practicing fair use, or is she guilty of copyright infringement?

A student writing an essay about Title IX's effect on college athletic programs finds some powerful supporting evidence for his argument on a Web site. Can he use this information without gaining permission?

Day care centers around the country receive letters arguing that they'll be liable to lawsuit if they use

Thanks to protests from GM, this car will not be called a "Chery" in the United States.

representations of Disney characters without explicit permission or show Disney films "outside the home."

The importer of a line of low-cost Chinese automobiles agrees not to market the cars under the brand name "Chery" after General Motors threatens to sue, claiming the name looks and sounds too much like "Chevy."

Musicians argue against other musicians, saying that the popular use of "sampling" in songs amounts to a form of musical plagiarism.

In cyberspace, the development of digital "watermarks" and other forms of tracking systems have made it possible to trace not only documents printed out but those read online as well; as a result, some lawyers argue that public access to information is being limited in ways that are unconstitutional.

● ● ●

In agricultural and industrial eras, products that could provide a livelihood were likely to be concrete things: crops, tools, machines. But in an age of information such as the current one, ideas, which we consider as intellectual property, are arguably society's most important products.

Hence the growing importance of—and growing controversies surrounding—what counts as "property" in an information age.

Perhaps the framers of the Constitution foresaw such a shift in the bases of the nation's economy. At any rate, they expressed in the Constitution a delicate balance between the public's need for information and the incentives necessary to encourage people to produce work—both material and intellectual. Thus the Constitution empowers Congress "[t]o promote the progress of Science and useful Arts, by securing for limited Times to Authors and Inventors the exclusive Right to their respective Writings and Discoveries" (Article 1, Section 8, Clause 8). This passage allows for limited protection (copyright) of the expression of ideas ("Writings and Discoveries"), and through the years that time limit has been extended to up to lifetime plus seventy years.

Why is this historical information important to student writers? First, because writers need to know that ideas themselves cannot be copyrighted—only the expression of those ideas. Second, this information explains why some works fall out of copyright and are available for students to use without paying a fee (as you must for copyright-protected material in a coursepack, for instance). Third, this information is crucial

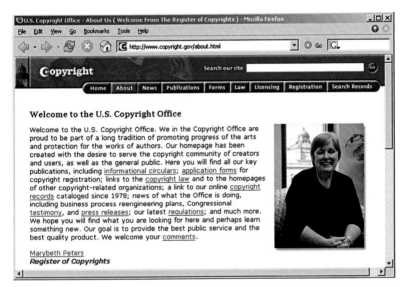

As a unit within the Library of Congress, the U.S. Copyright Office works to uphold copyright laws.

to the current debates over who owns online materials—materials that may never take any form of concrete expression. The debate will certainly be raging during and after the publication of this book—and the way in which it's resolved will have many direct effects on students and teachers. For up-to-date information about copyright law, see the U.S. Copyright Office site at <http://copyright.gov>.

Crediting Sources in Arguments

Acknowledging your sources and giving full credit is especially important in argumentative writing because doing so helps establish your ethos as a writer. In the first place, saying "thank you" to those who've helped you suggests gratitude and openness, qualities that audiences generally respond to well. Second, acknowledging your sources demonstrates that you've "done your homework," that you know the conversation surrounding your topic and understand what others have written about it, and that you want to help readers find other contributions to the conversation and perhaps join it themselves. Finally, acknowledging sources reminds you to think critically about your own stance in an argument and about how well you've used your sources. Are they timely and reliable? Have you used them in a biased or overly selective way? Have you used them accurately, double-checking all quotations and paraphrases? Thinking through these questions will improve your overall argument.

Citing Sources and Recognizing Plagiarism

In many ways, "nothing new under the sun" is more than just a cliché. Most of what you think or write or say draws on what you've previously heard or read or experienced. And trying to recall every influence or source of information you've drawn on, even on just one day, would take so long that you would have little time left to say anything. Luckily, you'll seldom, if ever, be called on to list every single influence on your life. But you do have responsibilities in academic situations to acknowledge the intellectual property you've used to create your own argumentative writing. If you don't, you may be accused of plagiarism—claiming for your own the words or intellectual work of others.

Not Just Words

Like words, images and designs can also be claimed as intellectual property. As we explain in this chapter, you can download a photograph you find on the Web and use it, with appropriate documentation, in an academic paper. But you'd probably need permission from the copyright holder to use it online, even for an academic Web project.

Logos and other visual designs are similarly protected. The T-shirt or ball cap you buy bearing your school's symbol and colors likely has a royalty cost built in, with the money going back to the institution. For commercial and artistic reasons, both institutions and corporations fiercely protect their designs, logos, symbols, and signs.

How then can *The Onion, Saturday Night Live,* or <Adbusters.org> take familiar designs and logos and use them in their publications, shows, or Web sites? For instance, it's unlikely that McDonalds approved a spoof showing a chubby youngster decked out in the company's trademarked golden arches. Yet there it is on <Adbusters.org>, along with dozens of other like-minded parodies.

The answer is in the word *parody*: the Supreme Court has decided that parody falls within fair use provisions of copyright law and that satire is protected by the First Amendment's protection of free speech, at least when such a lampoon targets public figures. You can explore these decisions easily on the Web (by googling "Parody" and "Supreme Court").

Working in a small group, try your hand at creating a parody of some familiar visual item or advertising campaign, perhaps beginning with an image from the Web. Be sure to take advantage of any skills people in your group may have with software such as Photoshop—which will enable you to change or manipulate images. Or use paper: cutting and pasting still works. Design a parody that makes a thoughtful point.

DOONESBURY   BY GARRY TRUDEAU

A *Doonesbury* cartoon on intellectual property

Avoiding plagiarism is very important, for in Western culture the use of someone else's language and ideas without acknowledgment is an act of dishonesty that can bring devastating results—especially, though not only, in school. Moreover, as we noted above, taking care to cite your sources works to your advantage in an academic setting: it builds your credibility, showing that you've done your homework as a researcher.

Inaccurate or Incomplete Citation of Sources

If you use a paraphrase that's too close to the original wording or sentence structure (even if you cite the source), if you leave out the parenthetical reference for a quotation (even if you include the quotation marks themselves), or if you don't indicate clearly the source of an idea you obviously didn't come up with on your own, you may be accused of plagiarism—even if that wasn't your intent. This kind of inaccurate or incomplete citation of sources often results either from carelessness or from not learning how to use citations accurately and fully.

Here, for example, is the first paragraph from an essay by Russell Platt published in *The Nation* and read in its online version at <http://thenation.com/doc/20051003/platt>:

> **Classical music in America, we are frequently told, is in its death throes: its orchestras bled dry by expensive guest soloists and greedy musicians' unions, its media presence shrinking, its prestige diminished, its educational role ignored, its big record labels dying out or merging into faceless corporate entities. We seem to have too many well-trained musicians in need of work, too many good composers going without commissions, too many concerts to offer an already satiated public.**
>
> –Russell Platt, "New World Symphony"

To cite this passage correctly in MLA style, you could quote directly from it, using both quotation marks and some form of attribution. Either of the following versions would be acceptable:

> Russell Platt has doubts about claims that classical music is "in its death throes: its orchestras bled dry by expensive guest soloists and greedy musicians' unions" ("New World").

> But is classical music in the United States really "in its death throes," as some critics of the music scene suggest (Platt)?

You might also paraphrase Platt's paragraph, putting his ideas entirely in your own words but giving him due credit:

> A familiar story told by critics is that classical music faces a bleak future in the United States, with grasping soloists and unions bankrupting orchestras and classical works vanishing from radio and television, school curricula, and the labels of recording conglomerates. The public may not be able or willing to support all the talented musicians and composers we have today (Platt).

All of these sentences with citations would be keyed to a Works Cited entry at the end of the paper that would look like the following in MLA style:

> Platt, Russell. "New World Symphony." The Nation 3 Oct. 2005. 15 Oct. 2005 <http://www.thenation.com/doc/20051003/platt>.

How might a citation go wrong? As we indicated, omitting either the quotation marks around a borrowed passage or the acknowledgment of the source are grounds for complaint. Neither of the following sentences provides enough information for a correct citation:

> But is classical music in the United States really in its death throes, as some critics of the music scene suggest (Platt)?

> But is classical music in the United States really "in its death throes," as some critics of the music scene suggest?

Just as faulty is a paraphrase such as the following, which borrows the words or ideas of the source too closely. It represents plagiarism, though it identifies the source from which almost all the ideas — and a good many words — are borrowed:

> In "New World Symphony," Russell Platt observes that classical music is thought by many to be in bad shape in America. Its orchestras are being sucked dry by costly guest artists and insatiable unionized musicians, its place on TV and radio is shrinking, its stature is diminished, its role in education is largely ignored, and its big record contracts are declining too. The problem may also be that we have too many well-trained musicians who need employment, too many good composers going without jobs, too many concerts for a public that prefers Desperate Housewives.

Even the original observation at the end of the paragraph isn't enough to change the fact that the paraphrase is just Platt's original, lightly stirred.

Precisely because the consequences of even unintentional plagiarism can be severe, it's important to understand how it can happen and how you can guard against it. In a January 2002 article published in *Time* magazine, historian Doris Kearns Goodwin explains how someone else's writing wound up unacknowledged in her book. The book in question, nine hundred pages long and with thirty-five hundred footnotes, took Goodwin ten years to write. During these ten years, she says, she took most of her notes by hand, organized the notes into boxes, and — once the draft was complete — went back to her sources to check that all the material from them was correctly cited. "Somehow in this process," Goodwin claims, "a few books were not fully rechecked," and so she omitted some necessary quotation marks in material she didn't acknowledge. Reflecting back on this experience, Goodwin says that discovering such carelessness in her own work was very troubling — so troubling that in the storm of criticism that ensued over the discovery of these failures to cite properly, she resigned from her position as a member of the Pulitzer Prize Committee.

Acknowledging Your Use of Sources

The safest way to avoid charges of plagiarism is to acknowledge as many of your sources as possible, with the following three exceptions:

- common knowledge, a specific piece of information most readers will know (that George W. Bush won the 2004 presidential election, for instance)
- facts available from a wide variety of sources (that the Japanese bombed Pearl Harbor on December 7, 1941, for example)
- your own findings from field research (observations, interviews, experiments, or surveys you have conducted), which should simply be presented as your own.

For all other source material you should give credit as fully as possible, placing quotation marks around any quoted material, citing your sources according to the documentation style you're using, and including them in a list of references or works cited. Material to be credited includes all of the following:

- direct quotations
- facts not widely known or arguable statements
- judgments, opinions, and claims made by others
- images, statistics, charts, tables, graphs, or other illustrations from any source
- collaboration — that is, the help provided by friends, colleagues, instructors, supervisors, or others

For more on using and documenting sources, see Chapters 19 and 20.

Using Copyrighted Internet Sources

If you've done any surfing on the Net, you already know that it opens the doors to worldwide collaborations: as you can contact individuals and groups around the globe and have access to whole libraries of information.

CULTURAL CONTEXTS FOR ARGUMENT

Understanding Plagiarism

Not all cultures accept Western notions of plagiarism, which rest on a belief that language can be owned by writers. Indeed, in many countries, and in some communities within the United States, using the words of others is considered a sign of deep respect and an indication of knowledge — and attribution is not expected or required. In writing arguments in the United States, however, you should credit all materials except those that are common knowledge, that are available in a wide variety of sources, or that are your own findings from field research.

As a result, writing (most especially, online writing) seems increasingly to be made up of a huge patchwork of materials that you and many others weave. (For a fascinating discussion of just how complicated charges and countercharges of plagiarism can be on the Internet, see <http://ombuds.org/narrative1.html>, where you can read a description of a mediation involving a Web site that included summaries of other people's work.) But when you use information gathered from Internet sources in your own work, it's subject to the same rules that govern information gathered from other types of sources.

Thus whether or not the material includes a copyright notice or symbol ("© 2007 by John J. Ruszkiewicz and Andrea A. Lunsford," for example), it's more than likely copyrighted — and you may need to request permission to use part or all of it. Although they're currently in danger, "fair use" laws still allow writers to quote brief passages from published works without permission from the copyright holder if the use is for educational or personal, noncommercial reasons and full credit is given to the source. For personal communication such as email or for listserv postings, however, you should ask permission of the writer before you include any of his or her material in your own argument. For graphics, photos, or other images you wish to reproduce in your text, you should also request permission from the creator or owner if the text is going to be disseminated beyond your classroom — especially if it's going to be published online.

Here are some examples of student requests for permission:

To: litman@mindspring.com
CC: lunsford.2@stanford.edu
Subject: Request for permission

Dear Professor Litman:

I am writing to request permission to quote from your essay "Copyright, Owners' Rights and Users' Privileges on the Internet: Implied Licences, Caching, Linking, Fair Use, and Sign-on Licences." I want to quote some of your work as part of an essay I am writing for my composition class at Stanford University to explain the complex debates over ownership on the Internet and to argue that students in my class should be participating in these debates. I will give full credit to you and will cite the URL where I first found your work: <msen.com/~litman/dayton/htm>.

Thank you very much for considering my request.

Raul Sanchez <sanchez.32@stanford.edu>

To: fridanet@aol.com
CC: lunsford.2@stanford.edu
Subject: Request for permission

Dear Kimberley Masters:

I am a student at Stanford University writing to request your permission to download and use a photograph of Frida Kahlo in a three-piece suit <fridanet/suit.htm#top> as an illustration in a project about Kahlo that I and two other students are working on in our composition class. In the report on our project, we will cite <members.aol.com/fridanet/kahlo.htm> as the URL, unless you wish for us to use a different source.

Thank you very much for considering our request.

Jennifer Fox <fox.360@stanford.edu>

Acknowledging Collaboration

We've already noted the importance of acknowledging the inspirations and ideas you derive from talking with others. Such help counts as one form of collaboration, and you may also be involved in more formal kinds

If Everything's an Argument . . .

This chapter concludes with a discussion of how to acknowledge the contributions of various hands when a project is produced collaboratively. *Everything's an Argument* is obviously such a collaboration; like most books, it uses a title page and an acknowledgments section in the Preface to give credit to the authors, editors, designers, reviewers, graduate students, and undergraduates who had a hand in its creation. But who did what exactly? As a reader, would you like to know more specifically who wrote a particular chapter, who edited it, who deserves credit for a particularly good image or bright idea in the book, and so on? When might such information matter to you—if ever?

of collaborative work—preparing for a group presentation to a class, for example, or writing a group report. Writers generally acknowledge all participants in collaborative projects at the beginning of the presentation, report, or essay—in print texts, often in a footnote or brief prefatory note.

The sixth edition of the *MLA Handbook for Writers of Research Papers* (2003) calls attention to the growing importance of collaborative work and gives the following advice on how to deal with issues of assigning fair credit all around:

> Joint participation in research and writing is common and, in fact, encouraged in many courses and in many professions. It does not constitute plagiarism provided that credit is given for all contributions. One way to give credit, if roles were clearly demarcated or were unequal, is to state exactly who did what. Another way, especially if roles and contributions were merged and shared, is to acknowledge all concerned equally. Ask your instructor for advice if you are not certain how to acknowledge collaboration.

RESPOND ●

1. Not everyone agrees with the concept of intellectual material as property, as something to be protected. Lately the slogan "information wants to be free" has been showing up in popular magazines and on the Internet, often along with a call to readers to take action against

forms of protection such as data encryption and further extension of copyright.

Using a Web search engine, look for pages where the phrase "free information" appears. Find several sites that make arguments in favor of free information, and analyze them in terms of their rhetorical appeals. What claims do the authors make? How do they appeal to their audience? What's the site's ethos, and how is it created? Once you've read some arguments in favor of free information, return to this chapter's arguments about intellectual property. Which arguments do you find more persuasive? Why?

2. Although this text is principally concerned with ideas and their written expression, there are other forms of protection available for intellectual property. For example, scientific and technological developments are protectable under patent law, which differs in some significant ways from copyright law.

Find the standards for protection under U.S. copyright law and U.S. patent law. You might begin by visiting the U.S. copyright Web site at <http://copyright.gov>. Then imagine that you're the president of a small, high-tech corporation and are trying to inform your employees of the legal protections available to them and their work. Write a paragraph or two explaining the differences between copyright and patent, and suggesting a policy that balances employees' rights to intellectual property with the business's needs to develop new products.

3. Define plagiarism in your own terms, making your definition as clear and explicit as possible. Then compare your definition with those of two or three other classmates, and write a brief report on the similarities and differences you noted in the definitions. You might research terms such as *plagiarism, academic honesty,* and *academic integrity* on the Web.

4. Spend fifteen or twenty minutes jotting down your ideas about intellectual property and plagiarism. Where do you stand, for example, on the issue of music file-sharing? On downloading movies free of charge? Do you think these forms of intellectual property should be protected under copyright law? How do you define your own intellectual property, and in what ways and under what conditions are you willing to share it? Finally, come up with your own definition of *academic integrity.*

19
Evaluating and Using Sources

As many examples in this text have shown, the quality of an argument often depends on the quality of the sources used to support or prove it. As a result, careful evaluation and assessment of all your sources is important, including those you gather in libraries or from other print sources, in online searches, or in field research you conduct yourself. Remember, though, that sources can contribute in different ways to your work. In most cases, you'll be looking for reliable sources that provide accurate and unbiased information or clearly and persuasively expressed opinionsthat might serve as evidence for a case you're making. At other times, you may be looking for material that expresses ideas or attitudes—how people are thinking and feeling at a given time. You might need to use a graphic image, a sample of avant-garde music, or a controversial video clip that won't fit neatly into categories such as reliable, accurate, or unbiased, yet is central to an argument you're making or refuting. With any and all such sources and evidence, you want to be as knowledgeable as possible about them and as responsible in their use as you can be, sharing honestly what you learn about them with readers.

● ● ●

Indeed, you don't want to be naïve in your use of any source material, even material from influential and well-known sources. The fact is that most of what constitutes the evidence used in arguments on public issues comes with considerable baggage. Scientists and humanists alike have axes to grind, corporations have products to sell, bureaucracies have power to maintain, politicians have policies and candidacies to promote, journalists have reputations to make, media owners and editors have readers, listeners, viewers, and advertisers to attract—and to avoid offending. All of these groups produce and use information to their benefit. It's not (usually) a bad thing that they do so; you just have to be aware that when you take information from a given source, it may carry with it the enthusiasms, assumptions, and biases, conscious or not, of the people who produce and disseminate it. Teachers and librarians are not exempted from this caution.

The way to correct for the biases is always to draw on as many reliable sources as you can manage when you're preparing to write. You shouldn't assume that all arguments are equally good or that all the sides in a controversy can be supported by the same weight of evidence and good reasons. But what you want to avoid is treading so narrowly among sources that you miss essential issues and perspectives. That's especially easy to do when you read only sources that agree with you or when the sources you tend to read all seem to carry the same message. Especially when writing on political subjects, you should be aware that the sources you're reading or viewing will almost always have an agenda to push. That fact has become much more apparent in recent years thanks to the work of a diverse group of bloggers on the Web—from all

CNN's Nancy Grace, a former prosecutor, has been accused of allowing her pro-prosecution bias to influence her commentary.

parts of the political spectrum—who have put the traditional news media under daily scrutiny, exposing stunning errors, biases, and omissions. Of course, political bloggers (mostly amateurs in the realms of journalism, though many are professionals in their own fields) have their own prejudices; but unlike most writers in mainstream news outlets, they admit their biases openly and frankly. How should researchers react when reading the *New York Times,* the *Wall Street Journal,* or the *Washington Post* or watching PBS, NBC, CBS, CNN, or FOX? Trust, but verify.

Evaluating Sources

Print Sources

Since you want the information you glean from sources to be reliable and persuasive, it pays to evaluate each potential source thoroughly. The following principles can help you in conducting such an evaluation for print sources:

- *Relevance.* Begin by asking what a particular source will add to your argument and how closely related to your argumentative claim it is. For a book, the table of contents and the index may help you decide. For an article, check to see if there's an abstract that summarizes the contents. And if you can't think of a good reason for using the source, set it aside; you can almost certainly find something better.

- *Credentials of the author.* You may find the author's credentials set forth in an article, book, or Web site, so be sure to look for a description of the author. Is the author an expert on the topic? To find out, you can also go to the Internet to gather information: just open a search tool such as Yahoo!, and type in the name of the person you're looking for. Still another way to learn about the credibility of an author is to search Google Groups for postings that mention the author or to check the Citation Index to find out how others refer to this author. And if you see your source cited by other sources you're using, look at how they cite it and what they say about it that could provide clues to the author's credibility.

- *Stance of the author.* What's the author's position on the issue(s) involved, and how does this stance influence the information in the source? Does the author's stance support or challenge your own views?

- *Credentials of the publisher or sponsor.* If your source is from a newspaper, is it a major one (such as the *Wall Street Journal* or the *New York Times*) that has historical credentials in reporting, or is it a tabloid? Is it a popular magazine like *People* or a journal sponsored by a professional group, such as the *Journal of the American Medical Association?* If your source is a book, is the publisher one you recognize or can find described on its own Web site?

- *Stance of the publisher or sponsor.* Sometimes this stance will be absolutely obvious: a magazine called *Mother Earth* will clearly take a pro-environmental stance, whereas one called *America First!* will

Note the differences between the *Vanity Fair* cover and that of a literary journal.

Source Map: Evaluating Articles

Determine the relevance of the source.

1 Look for an abstract, which provides a summary of the entire article. Is this source directly related to your research? Does it provide useful information and insights? Will your readers consider it persuasive support for your thesis?

Determine the credibility of the publication.

2 Consider the publication's title. Words in the title such as *Journal, Review,* and *Quarterly* may indicate that the periodical is a scholarly source. Most research essays rely on authorities in a particular field, whose work usually appears in scholarly journals.

3 Try to determine the publisher or sponsor. This journal is published by Johns Hopkins University Press. Academic presses such as this one generally review articles carefully before publishing them and bear the authority of their academic sponsors.

Determine the credibility of the author.

4 Evaluate the author's credentials. In this case, they are given in a note, which indicates that the author is a college professor and has written at least two books on related topics.

Determine the currency of the article.

5 Look at the publication date and think about whether your topic and your credibility depend on your use of very current sources.

Determine the accuracy of the article.

6 Look at the sources cited by the author of the article. Here, they are documented in footnotes. Ask yourself whether the works the author has cited seem credible and current. Are any of these works cited in other articles you've considered?

certainly take a conservative stance. But other times, you need to read carefully between the lines to identify particular positions, so you can see how the stance affects the message the source presents. Start by asking what the source's goals are: what does the publisher or sponsoring group want to make happen?

- *Currency.* Check the date of publication of any book or article. Recent sources are often more useful than older ones, particularly in the sciences. However, in some fields such as history or literature, the most authoritative works are often the older ones.

- *Level of specialization.* General sources can be helpful as you begin your research, but later in the project you may need the authority or currency of more specialized sources. However, keep in mind that extremely specialized works on your topic may be too difficult for your audience to understand easily.

- *Audience.* Was the source written for a general readership? For specialists? For advocates or opponents?

- *Length.* Is the source long enough to provide adequate detail in support of your claim?

- *Availability.* Do you have access to the source? If it isn't readily accessible, your time might be better spent looking elsewhere.

- *Omissions.* What's missing or omitted from the source? Might such exclusions affect whether or how you can use the source as evidence?

If Everything's an Argument . . .

Have you ever checked out the credentials of a textbook publisher or author? Is the publisher of this book, Bedford/St. Martin's, for example, a fly-by-night operation run by the authors using Photoshop in their basements? Or is it a company with real assets and real editors? Spend a few moments on the Web discovering how much you can find out about the company, its reputation, and its track record. You might do the same with one of the authors. They claim to be at Stanford University (Andrea Lunsford) and the University of Texas at Austin (John Ruszkiewicz). How might you quickly and unobtrusively confirm their credentials—and that they do indeed work at the real Stanford and Texas?

Electronic Sources

You'll probably find working on the Internet and the World Wide Web both exciting and frustrating, for even though these tools have great potential, the Web will always contain information of widely varying quality. That's the nature of a source as open and generally unregulated as the Web. As a result, careful researchers look for corroboration before accepting evidence they find online, especially if it comes from a site whose sponsor's identity is less than clear. In such an environment, you must be the judge of how accurate and trustworthy particular electronic sources are. In making these judgments, you should rely on the same kinds of criteria and of careful thinking you would use to assess print sources. In addition, you may find some of the following questions helpful in evaluating online sources:

- Who has posted the document or message or created the site? An individual? An interest group? A company? A government agency? Does the URL offer any clues? Note especially the final suffix in a domain name: .com (commercial); .org (nonprofit organization); .edu (educational institution); .gov (government agency); .mil (military); .net (network)—or the geographical domains that indicate country of origin, as in .ca (Canada) or .ar (Argentina). The homepage or first page of a site should tell you something about the sponsorship of the source, letting you know who can be held accountable for its information. (You may need to click on an "About Us" button.) Finally, links may help you learn how credible and useful the source is. Click on some of them to see if they lead to legitimate and helpful sites.

- What can you determine about the credibility of the author or sponsor? Can the information in the document or site be verified in other sources? How accurate and complete is it? On a blog, for example, look for a link that identifies the creator of the site—some blogs are managed by multiple authors. Also review the links the blog offers; they'll often help you understand both the perspective of the site and its purposes.

- Who can be held accountable for the information in the document or site? How well and thoroughly does it credit its own sources?

- How current is the document or site? Be especially cautious of undated materials. Most reliable will be those that are updated regularly.

- What perspectives are represented? If only one perspective is represented, how can you balance or expand this point of view?

SOURCE MAP: Evaluating Web Sources

Determine the credibility of the sponsoring organization.

1 Consider the URL, specifically the top-level domain name. (For example, *.edu* may indicate that the sponsor is an accredited college or university; *.org* may indicate it's a nonprofit organization.) Ask yourself whether such a sponsor might be biased about the topic you're researching.

2 Look for an *About* page or a link to the homepage for background information on the sponsor, including a mission statement. What is the sponsoring organization's stance or point of view? Does the mission statement seem biased or balanced? Does the sponsor seem to take other points of view into account? What is the intended purpose of the site? Is this site meant to inform? Or is it trying to persuade, advertise, or accomplish something else?

Determine the credibility of the author.

3 Evaluate the author's credentials. On this Web page, the authors' professional affiliations are listed, but other information about them isn't provided. You will often have to look elsewhere — such as at other sites on the Web — to find out more about an author. When you do, ask yourself if the author seems qualified to write about the topic.

Determine the currency of the Web source.

4 Look for the date that indicates when the information was posted or last updated. Here, the date is given at the beginning of the press release.

5 Check to see if the sources referred to are also up-to-date. These authors cite sources from September and October 2003. Ask yourself if, given your topic, an older source is acceptable or if only the most recent information will do.

Determine the accuracy of the information.

6 How complete is the information in the source? Examine the works cited by the author. Are sources for statistics included? Do the sources cited seem credible? Is a list of additional resources provided? Here, the authors cite the U.S. Navy and the U.S. Air Force, but they do not give enough information to track down these sources. Ask yourself whether you can find a way to corroborate what a source is saying.

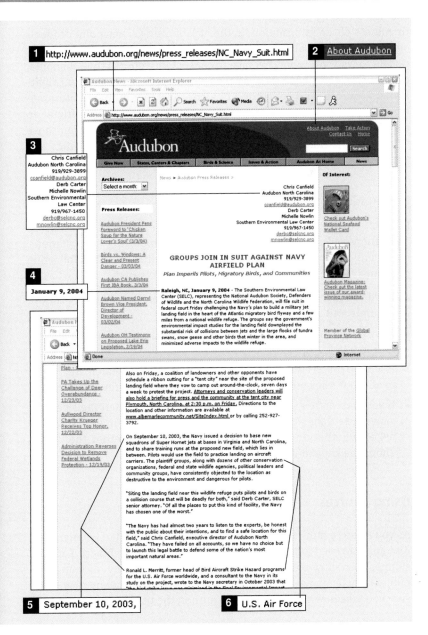

1 http://www.audubon.org/news/press_releases/NC_Navy_Suit.html

2 About Audubon

3
Chris Canfield
Audubon North Carolina
919/929-3899
ccanfield@audubon.org
Derb Carter
Michelle Nowlin
Southern Environmental
Law Center
919/967-1450
derbc@selcnc.org
mnowlin@selcnc.org

4 January 9, 2004

5 September 10, 2003,

6 U.S. Air Force

Several years ago, the Stanford Persuasive Technology Lab argued that Google News might become the "most credible Web site of them all." The Lab listed twenty-five reasons in support of this conclusion, from the timeliness of the information, to the lack of a single viewpoint or ideology, to the ad-free policy. Since then, however, liberals have charged that Google News gives more coverage to conservative stories than it should, and conservatives have claimed that it excludes some important right-leaning sources. And yet computer algorithms, not human editors, select the stories in Google News. Clearly, it's increasingly difficult to satisfy readers sensitive to media perspectives and biases, even those attributable to machines. But, then, humans create the machines and the algorithms.

Field Research

If you've conducted experiments, surveys, interviews, observations, or any other field research in developing and supporting an argument, make sure to review your own results with a critical eye. The following questions can help you evaluate your own field research:

- Have you rechecked all data and all conclusions to make sure they're accurate and warranted?
- Have you identified the exact time, place, and participants in all field research?
- Have you made clear what part you played in the research and how, if at all, your role could have influenced the results or findings?
- If your research involved other people, have you gotten their permission to use their words or other material in your argument? Have you asked whether you could use their names or whether the names should be kept confidential?

Using Sources

As you locate, examine, and evaluate sources in support of an argument, remember to keep a careful record of where you've found them. For print sources, you may want to keep a working bibliography on your computer—or a list in a notebook you can carry with you. In any case, make sure you take down the name of the author; the title of the book or periodical; the title of the article, or the publisher and city of publication of the book; the date of publication; relevant volume, issue, and exact page numbers; and any other information you may later need in preparing a Works Cited list or References list. In addition, for a book, note where you found it—the section of the library, for example, along with the call number for the book.

For electronic sources, keep a careful record of the information you'll need in a Works Cited list or References list—particularly the name of the database or other online site where you found the source; the full electronic address (URL); the date the document was first produced; the date the document was published on the Web or most recently updated; and the date you accessed and examined the document. The simplest way to ensure that you have this information is to get a printout of the source, highlighting source information and writing down any other pertinent information.

Signal Words and Introductions

Because your sources are crucial to the success of your arguments, you need to introduce them carefully to your readers. Doing so usually calls for using a signal phrase of some kind in the sentence to introduce the source. Typically, the signal phrase precedes the quotation, though that's not a hard-and-fast rule by any means:

> According to noted child psychiatrist Robert Coles, children develop complex ethical systems at extremely young ages.

> Children develop complex ethical systems at extremely young ages, according to noted child psychiatrist Robert Coles.

> Most children, observes noted child psychiatrist Robert Coles, develop complex ethical systems at extremely young ages.

In these sentences, the signal phrases all tell readers that you're drawing on the work of a person named Robert Coles and that this person is a "noted child psychiatrist." Now look at an example that uses a quotation from a source in more than one sentence:

> In Job Shift, consultant William Bridges worries about "dejobbing and about what a future shaped by it is going to be like." Even more worrisome, Bridges argues, is the possibility that "the sense of craft and of professional vocation . . . will break down under the need to earn a fee" (228).

Not Just Words

What's wrong with this picture? the editors of the *New York Times* might have asked before posting it on the paper's Web site following a strike by an American Predator drone on a village in Pakistan. Intelligence had suggested that Al Qaeda's second-in-command, Ayman al-Zawahiri, was in one of the buildings targeted by the missile. But al-Zawahiri was not there, and eighteen villagers died. The compelling photograph purportedly shows the aftermath. Its original caption had read: "Pakistani men with the remains of a missile fired at a house in the Bajaur tribal zone near the Afghan border." But it didn't take long for bloggers to point out that the missile part was actually an artillery shell—and maybe not even of American origin. Here's the correction that the newspaper subsequently ran:

> Correction appended Jan. 17, 2006: A caption Saturday on NYTimes.com with a photograph of damage from a U.S. airstrike in Pakistan misidentified an item in the photograph. Agence France-Presse, the agency that provided the photograph, later changed the caption to report that the item appears to be an unexploded artillery shell, not a piece of a missile from Friday's attack.

What issues do the image, the caption, and the correction raise about evaluating and using sources? For instance, who was responsible for the original photograph? Who was responsible for the error in captioning it? How is your perception of the image (particularly its pose) changed by the correction? Is the correction adequate? What gaps in editorial knowledge does the original caption suggest? To what degree, if any, does such an error undermine the authority of a source?

The signal verbs "worries" and "argues" add a sense of urgency to the message Bridges offers and suggest that the writer either agrees with—or is neutral about—Bridges's points. Other signal verbs have a more negative slant, indicating that the point being introduced in the quotation is open to debate and that others (including the writer) might disagree with it. If the writer of the passage above had said, for instance, that Bridges "unreasonably contends" or that he "fantasizes," these signal verbs would carry quite different connotations from those associated with "argues." In some cases, a signal verb may require more complex phrasing to get the writer's full meaning across:

> Bridges recognizes the dangers of changes in work yet refuses to be overcome by them: "The real issue is not how to stop the change but how to provide the necessary knowledge and skills to equip people to operate successfully in this New World" (229).

As these examples illustrate, the signal verb is important because it allows you to characterize the author's or source's viewpoint as well as your own—so choose these verbs with care.

Some Frequently Used Signal Verbs

acknowledges	claims	emphasizes	remarks
admits	concludes	expresses	replies
advises	concurs	hypothesizes	reports
agrees	confirms	interprets	responds
allows	criticizes	lists	reveals
argues	declares	objects	states
asserts	disagrees	observes	suggests
believes	discusses	offers	thinks
charges	disputes	opposes	writes

Quotations

For supporting argumentative claims, you'll want to quote—that is, to reproduce an author's precise words—in at least three kinds of situations: when the wording is so memorable or expresses a point so well that you cannot improve it or shorten it without weakening it; when the author is a respected authority whose opinion supports your own ideas particularly well; and when an author challenges or disagrees profoundly with others in the field.

Direct quotations can be effective in capturing your readers' attention—for example, through quoting a memorable phrase in your introduction or quoting an eyewitness account in arresting detail. In an argument, quotations from respected authorities can help build your ethos as someone who has sought out experts in the field. Finally, carefully chosen quotations can broaden the appeal of your argument by drawing on emotion as well as logic, appealing to the reader's mind and heart. A student writing on the ethical issues of bullfighting, for example, might introduce an argument that bullfighting is not a sport by quoting Ernest Hemingway's comment that "the formal bull-fight is a tragedy, not a sport, and the bull is certain to be killed," and might accompany the quotation with an image such as the one below.

The following guidelines can help you make sure that you quote accurately:

- If the quotation extends over more than one page in the original source, note the placement of page breaks in case you decide to use only part of the quotation in your argument.

A tragedy, not a sport?

- Label the quotation with a note that tells you where and/or how you think you'll use it.

- Make sure you have all the information necessary to create an in-text citation as well as an item in your Works Cited list or References list.

- When using a quotation in your argument, make sure you've introduced the author(s) of the quotation and that you follow the quotation with some commentary of your own that points out the significance of the quotation.

- Copy quotations carefully, being sure that punctuation, capitalization, and spelling are exactly as they are in the original.

- Enclose the quotation in quotation marks; don't rely on your memory to distinguish your own words from those of your source. If in doubt, recheck all quotations for accuracy.

- Use square brackets if you introduce words of your own into the quotation or make changes to it. ("And [more] brain research isn't going to define further the matter of 'mind.'")

- Use ellipsis marks if you omit material. ("And brain research isn't going to define . . . the matter of 'mind.'")

- If you're quoting a short passage (four lines or less, MLA style; forty words or less, APA style), it should be worked into your text, enclosed by quotation marks. Longer quotations should be set off from the regular text. Begin such a quotation on a new line, indenting every line one inch or ten spaces (MLA) or five to seven spaces (APA). Set-off quotations do not need to be enclosed in quotation marks.

CULTURAL CONTEXTS FOR ARGUMENT

Identifying Sources

Although some language communities and cultures expect audiences to recognize the sources of important documents and texts, thereby eliminating the need to cite them directly, conventions for writing in North America call for careful attribution of any quoted, paraphrased, or summarized material. When in doubt, explicitly identify your sources.

Paraphrases

Paraphrases involve putting an author's material (including major and minor points, usually in the order they're presented in the original) into your own words and sentence structures. Here are guidelines that can help you paraphrase accurately:

- When using a paraphrase in your argument, make sure that you identify the source of the paraphrase and that you comment on its significance.

- Make sure you have all the information necessary to create an in-text citation as well as an item in your Works Cited list or References list. For online sources without page numbers, record the paragraph, screen, or other section number(s) if indicated.

- If you're paraphrasing material that extends over more than one page in the original source, note the placement of page breaks in case you decide to use only part of the paraphrase in your argument.

- Label the paraphrase with a note suggesting where and/or how you intend to use it in your argument.

- Include all main points and any important details from the original source, in the same order in which the author presents them.

- Leave out your own comments, elaborations, or reactions.

- State the meaning in your own words and sentence structures. If you want to include especially memorable or powerful language from the original source, enclose it in quotation marks.

- Recheck to make sure that the words and sentence structures are your own and that they express the author's meaning accurately.

Summaries

A summary is a significantly shortened version of a passage—or even a whole chapter of a work—that captures the main ideas in your own words. Unlike a paraphrase, a summary uses just enough information to record the points you want to emphasize. Summaries can be extremely valuable in supporting arguments. Here are some guidelines to help you prepare accurate and helpful summaries:

- When using a summary in an argument, be sure to identify the source and add your own comments about why the material in the summary is significant for the argument you're making.

- Make sure you have all the information necessary to create an in-text citation as well as an item in your Works Cited list or References list. For online sources without page numbers, record the paragraph, screen, or other section number(s) if available.

- If you're summarizing material that extends over more than one page, indicate page breaks in case you decide to use only part of the summary in your argument.

- Label the summary with a note that suggests where and/or how you intend to use it in your argument.

- Include just enough information to recount the main points you want to cite. A summary is usually much shorter than the original.

- Use your own words. If you include any language from the original, enclose it in quotation marks.

- Recheck to make sure that you've captured the author's meaning accurately and that the wording is entirely your own.

Visuals

If a picture is worth a thousand words, then using pictures calls for caution: one picture might overwhelm or undermine the message you're trying to send in your argument. However, as you've seen in Chapter 14, visuals can have a powerful impact on audiences and can help bring them to understand or accept your arguments. In choosing visuals to include in your argument, make sure that each one makes a strong contribution to your message and that each is appropriate and fair to your subject or topic and your audience.

When you use visuals in your written arguments, treat them as you would any other sources you integrate into your text. Like quotations, paraphrases, and summaries, visuals need to be introduced and commented on in some way. In addition, label (as figures or as tables) and number (Figure 1, Figure 2, and so on) all visuals, provide a caption that includes source information and describes the visual, and cite the source in your bibliography or Works Cited list. Keep in mind that even if you create a visual (such as a bar graph) by using information from a source (the results, say, of a Gallup Poll), you must cite the source. If you use a photograph you took yourself, cite it as a personal photograph.

On the facing page is a visual that accompanied the introduction to an argument about bankruptcy that appeared on the front page of the December 15, 2002, *New York Times* Business section. Note that the source

A lawyer with a binder of paperwork involving the US Airways bankruptcy
filing. Companies can lose considerable value during the Chapter 11 process.
(Source: Bloomberg News)

of the visual is listed (Bloomberg News) and that the caption indicates in
what way the visual is related to the argument (in this case, the visual
depicts bankruptcy papers). If you were going to use this as the first visual in an essay of your own, you would need to include the source, describe the image in relationship to your topic, and head it Figure 1. As
long as this image will appear only in a print text for your instructor and
classmates, you're allowed fair use of it. If you intend to post your argument on the Web, however, or otherwise publish it for a wider audience,
you would need to request permission from the copyright owner (see
Chapter 18, p. 524).

RESPOND ●

1. Select one of the essays at the end of Chapters 7 to 11. Write a brief
   summary of the essay that includes both direct quotations and paraphrases. Be careful to attribute the ideas properly, even when you paraphrase, and to use signal phrases to introduce quotations. Then trade
   summaries with a partner, comparing the passages you selected to
   quote and paraphrase, and the signal phrases you used to introduce

them. How do your choices create an ethos for the original author that differs from the one your partner has created? How do the signal phrases shape a reader's sense of the author's position? Which summary best represents the author's argument? Why?

2. Return to the Internet sites you found in exercise 1 of Chapter 18 (p. 526–527) that discuss free information. Using the criteria in this chapter for evaluating electronic sources, judge each of those sites. Select three that you think are most trustworthy, and write a paragraph summarizing their arguments and recommending them to an audience unfamiliar with the debate.

3. Choose a Web site that you visit frequently. Then, using the guidelines discussed in this chapter, spend some time evaluating its credibility. You might begin by comparing it with Google News or another site that has a reputation for being extremely reliable.

20
Documenting Sources

What does documenting sources have to do with argument? First, the sources themselves form part of the argument, showing that a writer has done some homework, knows what others have said about the topic, and understands how to use these sources as support for a claim. The list of works cited or references makes an argument, saying, perhaps, "Look at how thoroughly this essay has been researched" or "Note how up-to-date I am!" Second, even the style of documentation makes an argument, though in a very subtle way. You'll note in the instructions that follow, for example, that for a print source the Modern Language Association (MLA) style requires putting the date of publication at or near the end of an entry, whereas the American Psychological Association (APA) style involves putting the date near the beginning. (An exercise at the end of this chapter asks you to consider what argument this difference represents.) Third, when a documentation style calls for listing only the first author followed by "et al." in citing works by multiple authors, it's subtly arguing that only the first author really matters—or at least that acknowledging the others is less important than keeping citations brief. Pay attention to the fine points of documentation and documentation style, always asking what these elements add (or don't add) to your arguments.

If Everything's an Argument . . .

You may have noticed that this book doesn't document its sources in any formal academic way. Instead, authors, titles, and sometimes information such as magazine names and publication dates are cited informally in the text, and the copyright holders who granted permission for their words or images to be used in the book are acknowledged in a list starting on the copyright page. Why do you think the authors, editors, and publishers of most textbooks don't follow a formal documentation style? What would be gained or lost if they did so?

MLA Style

Documentation styles vary from discipline to discipline, with different formats favored in the social sciences and the natural sciences, for example. Widely used in the humanities, the MLA style is fully described in the *MLA Handbook for Writers of Research Papers* (6th edition, 2003). In this discussion, we provide guidelines drawn from the *MLA Handbook* for in-text citations, notes, and entries in the list of works cited.

MLA Handbook for Writers of Research Papers

SIXTH EDITION

Joseph Gibaldi

The 6th edition of the *MLA Handbook for Writers of Research Papers*

In-Text Citations

MLA style calls for in-text citations in the body of an argument to document sources of quotations, paraphrases, summaries, and so on. For in-text citations, use a signal phrase to introduce the material, often with the author's name (As *LaDoris Cordell explains* . . .). Keep an in-text citation short, but include enough information for readers to locate the source in the list of works cited. Place the parenthetical citation as near to the relevant material as possible without disrupting the flow of the sentence, as in the following examples. Finally, note that MLA encourages (but does not require) the use of underlining to indicate italics.

1. Author Named in a Signal Phrase

Ordinarily, use the author's name in a signal phrase — to introduce the material — and cite the page number(s) in parentheses.

> Loomba argues that Caliban's "political colour" is black, given his stage representations, which have varied from animalistic to a kind of missing link (143).

2. Author Named in Parentheses

When you don't mention the author in a signal phrase, include the author's last name before the page number(s) in the parentheses.

> Renaissance visions of "other" worlds, particularly in plays and travel narratives, often accentuated the differences of the Other even when striking similarities to the English existed (Bartels 434).

3. Two or Three Authors

Use all authors' last names.

Gortner, Hebrun, and Nicolson maintain that "opinion leaders" influence other people in an organization because they are respected, not because they hold high positions (175).

4. Four or More Authors

The MLA allows you to use all authors' last names, or to use only the first author's name with *et al.* (in regular type, not underlined or italicized). Although either format is acceptable when applied consistently throughout a paper, in an argument it is better to name all authors who contributed to the work.

Similarly, as Goldberger, Tarule, Clinchy, and Belenky note, their new book builds on their collaborative experiences (xii).

5. Organization as Author

Give the full name of a corporate author if it's brief or a shortened form if it's long.

In fact, one of the leading foundations in the field of higher education supports the recent proposals for community-run public schools (Carnegie Corporation 45).

6. Unknown Author

Use the full title of the work if it's brief or a shortened form if it's long.

"Hype," by one analysis, is "an artificially engendered atmosphere of hysteria" ("Today's Marketplace" 51).

7. Author of Two or More Works

When you use two or more works by the same author, include the title of the work or a shortened version of it in the citation.

Gardner presents readers with their own silliness through his description of a "pointless, ridiculous monster, crouched in the shadows, stinking of dead men, murdered children, and martyred cows" (Grendel 2).

8. Authors with the Same Last Name

When you use works by two or more authors with the same last name, include each author's first initial in the in-text citation.

Father Divine's teachings focused on eternal life, salvation, and socioeconomic progress (R. Washington 17).

9. Multivolume Work

Note the volume number first and then the page number(s), with a colon and one space between them.

> Aristotle's "On Plants" is now available in a new translation, edited by Barnes (2: 1252).

10. Literary Work

Because literary works are often available in many different editions, you need to include enough information for readers to locate the passage in any edition. For a prose work such as a novel or play, first cite the page number from the edition you used, followed by a semicolon; then indicate the part or chapter number (114; ch. 3) or act or scene in a play (42; sc. 2).

> In The Madonnas of Leningrad, Marina says "she could see into the future" (7; ch. 1).

For a poem, cite the stanza and line numbers. If the poem has only line numbers, use the word line(s) in the first reference (lines 33-34).

> On dying, Whitman speculates "All that goes onward and outward, nothing collapses, / And to die is different from what any one supposed, and luckier" (6.129-30).

For a verse play, omit the page number, and give only the act, scene, and line numbers, separated by periods.

> Before he takes his own life, Othello says he is "one that loved not wisely but too well" (5.2.348).

> As Macbeth begins, the witches greet Banquo as "Lesser than Macbeth, and greater" (1.3.65).

11. Works in an Anthology

For an essay, short story, or other short work within an anthology, use the name of the author of the work, not the editor of the anthology; but use the page number(s) from the anthology.

> In the end, if the black artist accepts any duties at all, that duty is to express the beauty of blackness (Hughes 1271).

12. Sacred Text

To cite a sacred text, such as the Qur'an or the Bible, give the title of the edition you used, the book, and the chapter and verse (or their equivalent), separated by a period. In your text, spell out the names of books. In a parenthetical reference, use an abbreviation for books with names of five or more letters (for example, *Gen.* for Genesis).

He ignored the admonition "Pride goes before destruction, and a haughty spirit before a fall" (New Oxford Annotated Bible, Prov. 16.18).

13. Indirect Source

Use the abbreviation *qtd. in* to indicate that what you're quoting or paraphrasing is quoted (as part of a conversation, interview, letter, or excerpt) in the source you're using.

As Catherine Belsey states, "to speak is to have access to the language which defines, delimits and locates power" (qtd. in Bartels 453).

14. Two or More Sources in the Same Citation

Separate the information for each source with a semicolon.

Adefunmi was able to patch up the subsequent holes left in worship by substituting various Yoruba, Dahomean, or Fon customs made available to him through research (Brandon 115-17; Hunt 27).

15. Entire Work or One-Page Article

Include the citation in the text without any page numbers or parentheses.

The relationship between revolutionary innocence and the preservation of an oppressive post-revolutionary regime is one theme Milan Kundera explores in The Book of Laughter and Forgetting.

16. Work without Page Numbers

If the work isn't paginated but has another kind of numbered section, such as parts or paragraphs, include the name and number(s) of the section(s) you're citing. (For paragraphs, use the abbreviation *par.* or *pars.*; for section, use *sec.*; for part, use *pt.*)

Zora Neale Hurston is one of the great anthropologists of the twentieth century, according to Kip Hinton (par. 2).

17. Electronic or Nonprint Source

Give enough information in a signal phrase or parenthetical citation for readers to locate the source in the list of works cited. Usually give the author or title under which you list the source.

> In his film version of Hamlet, Zeffirelli highlights the sexual tension between the prince and his mother.

> Describing children's language acquisition, Pinker explains that "what's innate about language is just a way of paying attention to parental speech" (Johnson, sec. 1).

Explanatory and Bibliographic Notes

The MLA recommends using explanatory notes for information or commentary that doesn't readily fit into your text but is needed for clarification, further explanation, or justification. In addition, the MLA allows bibliographic notes for citing several sources for one point and for offering thanks to, information about, or evaluation of a source. Use superscript numbers in your text at the end of a sentence to refer readers to the notes, which usually appear as endnotes (with the heading *Notes*, not underlined or italicized) on a separate page before the list of works cited. Indent the first line of each note five spaces, and double-space all entries.

TEXT WITH SUPERSCRIPT INDICATING A NOTE

> Stewart emphasizes the existence of social contacts in Hawthorne's life so that the audience will accept a different Hawthorne, one more attuned to modern times than the figure in Woodberry.[3]

NOTE

> [3] Woodberry does, however, show that Hawthorne was often unsociable. He emphasizes the seclusion of Hawthorne's mother, who separated herself from her family after the death of her husband, often even taking meals alone (28). Woodberry seems to imply that Mrs. Hawthorne's isolation rubbed off on her son.

List of Works Cited

A list of works cited is an alphabetical listing of the sources you cite in your essay. The list appears on a separate page at the end of your argument, after any notes, with the heading *Works Cited* centered an inch from the top of the page; don't underline or italicize it or enclose it in quotation marks. Double-space between the heading and the first entry, and double-space the entire list. (If you're asked to list everything you've read as background—not just the sources you cite—call the list *Works Consulted*.) The first line of each entry should align on the left; subsequent lines indent one-half inch or five spaces. See p. 568 for a sample Works Cited page.

BOOKS

The basic information for a book includes three elements, each followed by a period:

- the author's name, last name first
- the title and subtitle, underlined
- the publication information, including the city, a shortened form of the publisher's name (such as Harvard UP), and the date

For a book with multiple authors, only the first author's name is inverted.

1. One Author

Castle, Terry. Boss Ladies, Watch Out: Essays on Women, Sex, and Writing. New York: Routledge, 2002.

2. Two or More Authors

Appleby, Joyce, Lynn Hunt, and Margaret Jacob. Telling the Truth about History. New York: Norton, 1994.

3. Organization as Author

American Horticultural Society. The Fully Illustrated Plant-by-Plant Manual of Practical Techniques. New York: American Horticultural Society and DK Publishing, 1999.

4. Unknown Author

National Geographic Atlas of the World. New York: National Geographic, 1999.

5. Two or More Books by the Same Author

List the works alphabetically by title.

Lorde, Audre. A Burst of Light. Ithaca: Firebrand, 1988.

---. Sister Outsider. Trumansburg: Crossing, 1984.

6. Editor

Rorty, Amelie Oksenberg, ed. Essays on Aristotle's Poetics. Princeton: Princeton UP, 1992.

7. Author and Editor

Shakespeare, William. The Tempest. Ed. Frank Kermode. London: Routledge, 1994.

8. Selection in an Anthology or Chapter in an Edited Book

Brown, Paul. "'This thing of darkness I acknowledge mine': The Tempest and the Discourse of Colonialism." Political Shakespeare: Essays in Cultural Materialism. Ed. Jonathan Dillimore and Alan Sinfield. Ithaca: Cornell UP, 1985. 48-71.

9. Two or More Works from the Same Anthology

Gates, Henry Louis, Jr., and Nellie McKay, eds. The Norton Anthology of African American Literature. New York: Norton, 1997.

Neal, Larry. "The Black Arts Movement." Gates and McKay 1960-72.

Karenga, Maulana. "Black Art: Mute Matter Given Force and Function." Gates and McKay 1973-77.

10. Translation

Hietamies, Laila. Red Moon over White Sea. Trans. Borje Vahamaki. Beaverton, ON: Aspasia, 2000.

11. Edition Other Than the First

Lunsford, Andrea A., John J. Ruszkiewicz, and Keith Walters. Everything's an Argument. 4th ed. Boston: Bedford, 2007.

12. One Volume of a Multivolume Work

Byron, Lord George. Byron's Letters and Journals. Ed. Leslie A. Marchand. Vol. 2. London: J. Murray, 1973-82.

13. Two or More Volumes of a Multivolume Work

Byron, Lord George. Byron's Letters and Journals. Ed. Leslie A. Marchand. 12 vols.
London: J. Murray, 1973-82.

14. Preface, Foreword, Introduction, or Afterword

Hymes, Dell. Foreword. Beyond Ebonics: Linguistic Pride and Racial Prejudice. By
John Baugh. New York: Oxford, 2000. vii-viii.

15. Article in a Reference Work

Kettering, Alison McNeil. "Art Nouveau." World Book Encyclopedia. 2002 ed.

16. Book That Is Part of a Series

Moss, Beverly J. A Community Text Arises. Language and Social Processes Ser. 8.
Cresskill: Hampton, 2003.

17. Republication

Scott, Walter. Kenilworth. 1821. New York: Dodd, 1996.

18. Government Document

United States. Cong. House Committee on the Judiciary. Impeachment of the
President. 40th Cong., 1st sess. H. Rept. 7. Washington: GPO, 1867.

19. Pamphlet

An Answer to the President's Message to the Fiftieth Congress. Philadelphia:
Manufacturer's Club of Philadelphia, 1887.

20. Published Proceedings of a Conference

Edwards, Ron, ed. Proceedings of the Third National Folklore Conference. Canberra,
Austral.: Australian Folk Trust, 1988.

21. Title within a Title

Tauernier-Courbin, Jacqueline. Ernest Hemingway's A Moveable Feast: The Making
of a Myth. Boston: Northeastern UP, 1991.

PERIODICALS

The basic entry for a periodical includes the following three elements, separated by periods:

- the author's name, last name first
- the article title, in quotation marks
- the publication information, including the periodical title (under-lined), the volume and issue numbers (if any), the date of publication, and the page number(s)

For works with multiple authors, only the first author's name is inverted. Note that the period following the article title goes inside the closing quotation mark. Finally, note that the MLA omits *the* in titles such as *The New Yorker*.

22. Article in a Journal Paginated by Volume

Anderson, Virginia. "'The Perfect Enemy': Clinton, the Contradictions of Capitalism, and Slaying the Sin Within." Rhetoric Review 21 (2002): 384-400.

23. Article in a Journal Paginated by Issue

Radavich, David. "Man among Men: David Mamet's Homosocial Order." American Drama 1.1 (1991): 46-66.

24. Article That Skips Pages

Seabrook, John. "Renaissance Pears." New Yorker 5 Sept. 2005: 102+.

25. Article in a Monthly Magazine

Wallraff, Barbara. "Word Count." Atlantic Nov. 2002: 144-45.

26. Article in a Weekly Magazine

Reed, Julia. "Hope in the Ruins." Newsweek 12 Sept. 2005: 58-59.

27. Article in a Newspaper

Friend, Tim. "Scientists Map the Mouse Genome." USA Today 2 Dec. 2002: A1.

28. Editorial or Letter to Editor

Posner, Alan. "Colin Powell's Regret." Editorial. New York Times 9 Sept. 2005: A20.

29. Unsigned Article

"Court Rejects the Sale of Medical Marijuana." New York Times 26 Feb. 1998, late
ed.: A21.

30. Review

Ali, Lorraine. "The Rap on Kanye." Rev. of Late Registration, by Kanye West.
Newsweek 5 Sept. 2005: 72-73.

ELECTRONIC SOURCES

Most of the following models are based on the MLA's guidelines for citing electronic sources in the *MLA Handbook* (6th edition, 2003), as well as
on up-to-date information available at <http://mla.org/>. The MLA requires that URLs be enclosed in angle brackets. Also, if a URL won't all fit
on one line, it should be broken only after a slash. If a particular URL is
extremely complicated, you can instead give the URL for the site's search
page, if it exists, or for the site's homepage. The basic MLA entry for most
electronic sources should include the following elements:

- name of the author, editor, or compiler
- title of the work, document, or posting
- information for print publication, if any
- information for electronic publication
- date of access
- URL in angle brackets

31. CD-ROM, Diskette, or Magnetic Tape, Single Issue

McPherson, James M., ed. The American Heritage New History of the Civil War.
CD-ROM. New York: Viking, 1996.

32. Periodically Revised CD-ROM

Include the author's name; publication information for the print version of the text (including its title and date of publication); the title of
the database; the medium (CD-ROM); the name of the company producing it; and the electronic publication date (month and year, if possible).

Heyman, Steven. "The Dangerously Exciting Client." Psychotherapy Patient 9.1
(1994): 37-46. PsycLIT. CD-ROM. SilverPlatter. Nov. 2006.

33. Multidisc CD-ROM

The 1998 Grolier Multimedia Encyclopedia. CD-ROM. 2 discs. Danbury: Grolier
      Interactive, 1998.

34. Article from Online Database or Subscription Service

"Bolivia: Elecciones Presidenciales de 2002." Political Database of the Americas.
      1999. Georgetown U and Organization of Amer. States. 12 Nov. 2006
      <http://www.georgetown.edu/pdba/Elecdta/Bolivia/pres02B.html>.

35. Document from a Professional Web Site

When possible, include the author's name; title of the document;
print publication information; electronic publication information; date
of access; and the URL.

"A History of Women's Writing." The Orlando Project: An Integrated History
      of Women's Writing in the British Isles. 2000. U of Alberta. 14 Mar. 2006
      <http://www.ualberta.ca/ORLANDO/>.

36. Entire Web Site

Include the name of the person or group who created the site, if relevant; the title of the site (underlined) or (if there is no title) a description
such as *Home page* (neither underlined nor italicized); the electronic publication date or last update, if available; the name of any institution or
organization associated with the site; the date of access; and the URL.

Bowman, Laurel. Classical Myth: The Ancient Source. Dept. of Greek and Roman
      Studies, U of Victoria. 7 Mar. 2006 <http://web.uvic.ca/grs/bowman/myth>.

Mitten, Lisa. The Mascot Issue. 8 Apr. 2006. American Indian Library Assn. 12 Sept.
      2002 <http://www.nativeculture.com/lisamitten/mascots.html>.

37. Course, Department, or Personal Web Site

Include the Web site's author; name of the site; description of site (such
as *Course home page, Dept. home page,* or *Home page*—neither underlined
nor italicized); dates for the course; date of publication or last update;
name of academic department, if relevant; date of access; and the URL.

Lunsford, Andrea A. "Memory and Media." Course home page. Sept.-Dec. 2002.
      Dept. of English, Stanford U. 13 Mar. 2006 <http://www.stanford.edu/class/
      english12sc>.

Lunsford, Andrea A. Home page. 15 Mar. 2006 <http://www.stanford.edu/
~lunsfor1/>.

38. Online Book

Begin with the name of the author—or, if only an editor, a compiler, or a translator is identified, the name of that person followed by *ed.*, *comp.*, or *trans.* (neither underlined nor italicized). Then give the title and the name of any editor, compiler, or translator not listed earlier, preceded by *Ed.*, *Comp.*, or *Trans.* (again, neither underlined nor italicized). If the online version of the text hasn't been published before, give the date of electronic publication and the name of any sponsoring institution or organization. Then give any publication information (city, publisher, and/or year) for the original print version that's given in the source; the date of access; and the URL.

Riis, Jacob A. How the Other Half Lives: Studies among the Tenements of New
York. Ed. David Phillips. New York: Scribner's, 1890. 26 Mar. 1998 <http://
www.cis.yale.edu/amstud/Inforev/riis/title.html>.

For a poem, essay, or other short work within an online book, include its title after the author's name. Give the URL of the short work, not of the book, if they differ.

Dickinson, Emily. "The Grass." Poems: Emily Dickinson. Boston: Roberts
Brothers, 1891. Humanities Text Initiative American Verse Collection.
Ed. Nancy Kushigian. 1995. U of Michigan. 9 Oct. 1997 <http://
www.planet.net/pkrisxle/emily/poemsOnline.html>.

39. Article in an Online Periodical

Follow the formats for citing articles in print periodicals, but adapt them as necessary to the online medium. Include the page numbers of the article or the total number of pages, paragraphs, parts, or other numbered sections, if any; the date of access; and the URL.

Johnson, Eric. "The 10,000-Word Question: Using Images on the World-Wide Web."
Kairos 4.1 (1999). 20 Mar. 2003 <http://english.ttu.edu/kairos/4.1/>.

Walsh, Joan. "The Ugly Truth about Republican Racial Politics." Salon 15 Dec.
2002. 3 Jan. 2003 <http://www.salon.com/politics/feature/2002/12/14/
race/index_np.html>.

40. Posting to a Discussion Group

Begin with the author's name, the title of the posting, the description *Online posting* (neither underlined nor italicized), and the date of the posting. For a listserv posting, give the name of the listserv, the date of access, and either the URL of the listserv or (preferably) the URL of an archival version of the posting. If a URL is unavailable, give the email address of the list moderator. For a newsgroup posting, end with the date of access and the name of the newsgroup, in angle brackets.

> "Web Publishing and Censorship." Online posting. 2 Feb. 1997. ACW: Alliance for Computers and Writing Discussion List. 10 Oct. 1997 <http://english.ttu.edu/acw-1/archive.htm>.

> Martin, Jerry. "The IRA & Sinn Fein." Online posting. 31 Mar. 1998. 31 Mar. 1998 <news:soc.culture.irish>.

41. Work from an Online Subscription Service

For a work from an online service to which your library subscribes, list the information about the work, followed by the name of the service, the library, the date of access, and the URL.

> "Breaking the Dieting Habit: Drug Therapy for Eating Disorders." Psychology Today Mar. 1995: 12+. Electric Lib. Green Lib., Stanford, CA. 30 Nov. 2002 <http://www.elibrary.com/>.

If you're citing an article from a subscription service to which you subscribe (such as AOL), use the following model:

> Weeks, W. William. "Beyond the Ark." Nature Conservancy. Mar.-Apr. 1999. America Online. 30 Nov. 2002. Keyword: Ecology.

42. Email Message

Include the writer's name, the subject line, the description *E-mail to the author* or *E-mail to [the recipient's name]* (neither underlined nor italicized), and the date of the message.

> Moller, Marilyn. "Seeing Crowns." E-mail to Beverly Moss. 3 Jan. 2003.

43. Synchronous Communication (MOO, MUD, or IRC)

Include the name of any specific speaker(s) you're citing; a description of the event; its date; the name of the forum; the date of access; and the URL of the posting (with the prefix *telnet:*) or (preferably) of an archival version.

Patuto, Jeremy, Simon Fennel, and James Goss. The Mytilene debate. 9 May 1996.
    MiamiMOO. 28 Mar. 1998 <http://moo.cas.muohio.edu>.

44. Online Interview, Work of Art, Radio Program, or Film

Follow the general guidelines for the print version of the source, but
also include information on the electronic medium, such as publication
information for a CD-ROM or the date of electronic publication, the date
of access, and the URL for a Web site.

McGray, Douglas. Interview with Andrew Marshall. Wired. Feb. 2003. 17 Mar. 2003
    <http://www.wired.com/wired/archive/11.02/marshall.html>.

Aleni, Giulio. K'un-yu t'u-shu. ca. 1620. Vatican, Rome. 28 Mar. 1998
    <http://www.ncsa.uiuc.edu/SDG/Experimental/vatican.exhibit/exhibit/
    full-images/i-rome-to-china/china02.gif>.

Columbus, Chris, dir. Harry Potter and the Chamber of Secrets.
    16 Dec. 2002 <http://movies.go.com/movies/H/
    harrypotterandthechamberofsecrets_2002/>.

45. FTP (File Transfer Protocol), Telnet, or Gopher Site

Substitute FTP, *telnet*, or *gopher* for *http* at the beginning of the URL.

Korn, Peter. "How Much Does Breast Cancer Really Cost?" Self Oct. 1994. 5 May
    1997 <gopher://nysernet.org:70/00/BCTC/Sources/SELF/94/how-much>.

46. Computer Software or Video Game

The Sims 2. Redwood City: Electronic Arts, 2004.

Web Cache Illuminator. Vers. 4.02. 12 Nov. 2003 <http://www.tucows.com/
    adnload/332309_126245.html>.

OTHER SOURCES

47. Unpublished Dissertation

Fishman, Jenn. "'The Active Republic of Literature': Performance and Literary
    Culture in Britain, 1656-1790." Diss. Stanford U, 2003.

48. Published Dissertation

Baum, Bernard. Decentralization of Authority in a Bureaucracy. Diss. U of Chicago.
    Englewood Cliffs: Prentice, 1961.

49. Article from a Microform

Sharpe, Lora. "A Quilter's Tribute." <u>Boston Globe</u> 25 Mar. 1989: 13. <u>NewsBank:
Social Relations</u> 12 (1989): fiche 6, grids B4-6.

50. Personal and Published Interview

Royster, Jacqueline Jones. Personal interview. 2 Feb. 2003.

Schorr, Daniel. Interview. <u>Weekend Edition</u>. Natl. Public Radio. KQED, San
Francisco. 23 Dec. 2002.

51. Letter

Jacobs, Harriet. "Letter to Amy Post." 4 Apr. 1853. <u>Incidents in the Life of a Slave
Girl</u>. Ed. Jean Fagan Yellin. Cambridge: Harvard UP, 1987. 234-35.

52. Film

<u>The Lord of the Rings: The Two Towers</u>. Dir. Peter Jackson. Perf. Elijah Wood, Ian
McKellen. New Line Cinema, 2002.

53. Television or Radio Program

<u>Box Office Bombshell: Marilyn Monroe</u>. Narr. Peter Graves. Writ. Andy Thomas, Jeff
Schefel, and Kevin Burns. Dir. Bill Harris. A&E Biography. Arts and
Entertainment Network. 23 Oct. 2002.

54. Sound Recording

Black Rebel Motorcycle Club. "Howl." <u>Red Int / Red Ink</u>. 2005.

Massive Attack. "Future Proof." <u>100th Window</u>. Virgin, 2003.

55. Work of Art or Photograph

Kahlo, Frida. <u>Self-Portrait with Cropped Hair</u>. 1940. Museum of Modern Art, New York.

56. Lecture or Speech

Steve Jobs. Baccalaureate Address. Stanford University. 18 June 2005.

57. Performance

<u>Anything Goes</u>. By Cole Porter. Perf. Klea Blackhurst. Shubert Theatre, New Haven.
7 Oct. 2003.

58. Map or Chart

The Political and Physical World. Map. Washington: Natl. Geographic, 1975.

59. Cartoon

Brodner, Steve. Cartoon. Nation 31 Mar. 2003: 2.

60. Advertisement

Chevy Avalanche. Advertisement. Time 14 Oct. 2002: 104.

On p. 567, note the formatting of the first page of a sample essay written in MLA style. On p. 568, you'll find a sample Works Cited page written for the same student essay.

Sample First Page for an Essay in MLA Style

Lesk 1

Emily Lesk

Professor Arraéz

Electric Rhetoric

15 November 2005

Red, White, and Everywhere

America, I have a confession to make: I don't drink Coke. But don't call me a hypocrite just because I am still the proud owner of a bright red shirt that advertises it. Just call me an American. Even before setting foot in Israel three years ago, I knew exactly where I could find one. The tiny T-shirt shop in the central block of Jerusalem's Ben Yehuda Street did offer other designs, but the one with a bright white "Drink Coca-Cola Classic" written in Hebrew cursive across the chest was what drew in most of the dollar-carrying tourists. While waiting almost twenty minutes for my shirt (depicted in Fig. 1), I watched nearly every customer ahead of me ask for "the Coke shirt, todah rabah [thank you very much]."

Fig. 1. Hebrew Coca-Cola T-shirt. Personal photograph. Despite my dislike for the beverage, I bought this Coca-Cola T-shirt in Israel.

At the time, I never thought it strange that I wanted one, too. After having absorbed sixteen years of Coca-Cola propaganda through everything from NBC's Saturday morning cartoon lineup to the concession stand at Camden Yards (the Baltimore Orioles' ballpark), I associated the shirt with singing along to the "Just for the Taste of It" jingle and with America's favorite pastime, not with a brown fizzy beverage I refused to consume. When I later realized the immensity of Coke's

Sample List of Works Cited for an Essay In MLA Style

Lesk 7

Works Cited

Coca-Cola Santa pin. Personal photograph by author. 9 Nov. 2002.

"The Fabulous Fifties." Beverage Industry 87.6 (1996): 16. 2 Nov. 2002
    <http://memory.loc/gov.ammem/ccmphtml/indshst.html>.

"Haddon Sundblom." Coca-Cola and Christmas 1999. 2 Nov. 2002 <http://
    www.coca-cola.com.ar/Coca-colaweb/paginas_ingles/christmas
    .html>.

Hebrew Coca-Cola T-shirt. Personal photograph by author. 8 Nov. 2002.

Ikuta, Yasutoshi, ed. '50s American Magazine Ads. Tokyo: Graphic-Sha,
    1987.

Library of Congress. Motion Picture, Broadcasting and Recorded Sound
    Division. 5 Nov. 2002 <http://memory.loc.gov/ammem/ccmphtml/
    index.html>.

Pendergrast, Mark. For God, Country, and Coca-Cola: The Unauthorized
    History of the Great American Soft Drink and the Company That
    Makes It. New York: Macmillan, 1993.

jurisprudence

How Do You Solve the Problem of Scalia?

The razor-thin line between obscenity and bad judgment.

By Dahlia Lithwick

Posted Thursday, March 30, 2006, at 6:21 PM ET

Leave it to Justice Antonin Scalia to trigger a nationwide debate about the hermeneutics of chin flips.

But first, a brief glance at the procedural history: It's undisputed that a newspaper reporter approached Scalia as he left a special Red Mass for lawyers and politicians at Boston's Cathedral of the Holy Cross. It's also not disputed that when the reporter, Laurel Sweet, asked what Scalia had to say to critics who question his impartiality in light of his Roman Catholic beliefs, he offered a familiar hand gesture, adding, "You know what I say to those people?" and, evidently by way of explanation, "That's Sicilian."

Where the parties differ is regarding the meaning of the gesture in question. The _Boston Herald_ initially characterized it as "obscene." Supreme Court spokeswoman Kathy Arberg carefully described it, by contrast, as "a hand off the chin gesture that was meant to be dismissive," but not obscene.

The lower courts immediately issued conflicting opinions: Evidently in some jurisdictions, the chin flick "is a gesture of contempt, somewhat less rude than giving a person 'the finger.' When used in the United States, it usually means 'Bug off, I've had enough of you.' Not a polite gesture, but not a particularly hostile one, either," according to one blog. A concurrence by Wonkette (complete with an illustrated appendix) reached a similarly benign conclusion: "Justice Scalia's gesture wasn't a full-fledged flipping of the proverbial bird. But it still wasn't exactly the most polite of actions; in some quarters, it could be interpreted as pretty darn close to giving someone the middle finger." Dissenters disagreed, finding that the gesture, whether chin flip, finger, or otherwise, is improper. The "thought of flipping somebody off in church, minutes after receiving the Eucharist, is just, well, beyond shocking, insulting, infuriating."

Not Just Words

Like the article from _Slate.com_ shown above, many online texts acknowledge their sources not with parenthetical citations or lists of references but with direct electronic links to the sources themselves. What are the implications of documenting sources in this nonverbal way? Links obviously make it much easier to check what a source actually says and the context in which it occurs. But is there a downside for the writer or the reader in not having the source's name appear within the text and a list of sources at the end? Might the colors and underlining used to indicate links distract the reader from the writer's point, or give unintended emphasis to the source relative to the writer's own ideas?

APA Style

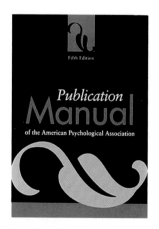

The 5th edition of the *Publication Manual of the American Psychological Association*

The Publication Manual of the American Psychological Association (5th edition, 2001) provides comprehensive advice to student and professional writers in the social sciences. Here we draw on the *Publication Manual*'s guidelines to provide an overview of APA style for in-text citations, content notes, and entries in the list of references.

In-Text Citations

APA style calls for in-text citations in the body of an argument to document sources of quotations, paraphrases, summaries, and so on. These in-text citations correspond to full bibliographic entries in the list of references at the end of the text.

1. Author Named in a Signal Phrase

Generally, use the author's name in a signal phrase to introduce the cited material, and place the date, in parentheses, immediately after the author's name. For a quotation, the page number, preceded by *p.* (neither underlined nor italicized), appears in parentheses after the quotation. For electronic texts or other works without page numbers, paragraph numbers may be used instead, preceded by the ¶ symbol or the abbreviation *para.* For a long, set-off quotation, position the page reference in parentheses two spaces after the punctuation at the end of the quotation.

> According to Brandon (1993), Adefunmi opposed all forms of racism and believed that black nationalism should not be a destructive force.

> As Toobin (2002) demonstrates, Joseph Lieberman unintentionally aided the Republican cause during most of 2002, playing into the hands of the administration and becoming increasingly unwilling "to question the President's motives, because he doesn't like visceral politics" (p. 43).

2. Author Named in Parentheses

When you don't mention the author in a signal phrase, give the name and the date, separated by a comma, in parentheses at the end of the cited material.

The Sopranos has achieved a much wider viewing audience than ever expected, spawning a cookbook and several serious scholarly studies (Franklin, 2002).

3. Two Authors

Use both names in all citations. Use *and* in a signal phrase, but use an ampersand (&) in parentheses.

Associated with purity and wisdom, Obatala is the creator of human beings, whom he is said to have formed out of clay (Edwards & Mason, 1985).

4. Three to Five Authors

List all the authors' names for the first reference. In subsequent references, use just the first author's name followed by *et al.* (in regular type, not underlined or italicized).

Lenhoff, Wang, Greenberg, and Bellugi (1997) cite tests that indicate that segments of the left brain hemisphere are not affected by Williams syndrome whereas the right hemisphere is significantly affected.

Shackelford (1999) drew on the study by Lenhoff et al. (1997).

5. Six or More Authors

Use only the first author's name and *et al.* (in regular type, not underlined or italicized) in every citation, including the first.

As Flower et al. (2003) demonstrate, reading and writing involve both cognitive and social processes.

6. Organization as Author

If the name of an organization or a corporation is long, spell it out the first time, followed by an abbreviation in brackets. In later citations, use the abbreviation only.

First Citation: (Federal Bureau of Investigation [FBI], 2002)

Subsequent Citations: (FBI, 2002)

7. Unknown Author

Use the title or its first few words in a signal phrase or in parentheses (in the example below, a book's title is italicized).

> The school profiles for the county substantiate this trend (*Guide to secondary schools,* 2003).

8. Authors with the Same Last Name

If your list of references includes works by different authors with the same last name, include the authors' initials in each citation.

> G. Jones (1998) conducted the groundbreaking study of retroviruses, whereas P. Jones (2000) replicated the initial trials two years later.

9. Two or More Sources in the Same Citation

List sources by the same author chronologically by publication year. List sources by different authors in alphabetical order by the authors' last names, separated by semicolons.

> While traditional forms of argument are warlike and agonistic, alternative models do exist (Foss & Foss, 1997; Makau, 1999).

10. Specific Parts of a Source

Use abbreviations (*chap., p.,* and so on) in a parenthetical citation to name the part of a work you're citing.

> Pinker (2003, chap. 6) argued that his research yielded the opposite results.

11. Electronic World Wide Web Document

To cite a source found on the Web, use the author's name and date as you would for a print source, then indicate the chapter or figure of the document, as appropriate. If the source's publication date is unknown, use *n.d.* ("no date"). To document a quotation, include paragraph numbers if page numbers are unavailable. If a Web document has no page numbers, use paragraph numbers and a heading, if available.

> Werbach argued convincingly that "Despite the best efforts of legislators, lawyers, and computer programmers, spam has won. Spam is killing email" (2002, p. 1).

12. Email and Other Personal Communication

Cite any personal letters, email messages, electronic postings, telephone conversations, or personal interviews by giving the person's initial(s) and last name, the identification *personal communication,* and the date.

> E. Ashdown (personal communication, March 9, 2003) supported these claims.

Content Notes

The APA recommends using content notes for material that will expand or supplement your argument but otherwise would interrupt the text. Indicate such notes in your text by inserting superscript numerals. Type the notes themselves on a separate page headed *Footnotes* (not underlined or italicized, or in quotation marks), centered at the top of the page. Double-space all entries. Indent the first line of each note five to seven spaces, and begin subsequent lines at the left margin.

TEXT WITH SUPERSCRIPT INDICATING A NOTE

> Data related to children's preferences in books were instrumental in designing the questionnaire.[1]

NOTE

> [1]Rudine Sims Bishop and members of the Reading Readiness Research Group provided helpful data.

List of References

The alphabetical list of sources cited in your text is called *References.* (If your instructor asks you to list everything you've read as background—not just the sources you cite—call the list *Bibliography.*) The list of references appears on a separate page or pages at the end of your paper, with the heading *References* (not underlined or italicized, or in quotation marks) centered one inch from the top of the page. Double-space after the heading, and begin your first entry. Double-space the entire list. For print sources, APA style specifies the treatment and placement of four basic elements—author, publication date, title, and publication information. Each element is followed by a period.

- *Author:* list all authors with last name first, and use only initials for first and middle names. Separate the names of multiple authors with commas, and use an ampersand (&) before the last author's name.

- *Publication date:* enclose the publication date in parentheses. Use only the year for books and journals; use the year, a comma, and the month or month and day for magazines. Do not abbreviate the month. Put a period after the parentheses.

- *Title:* italicize titles and subtitles of books and periodicals. Do not enclose titles of articles in quotation marks. For books and articles, capitalize only the first word of the title and subtitle and any proper nouns or proper adjectives. Capitalize all major words in a periodical title.

- *Publication information:* for a book, list the city of publication (and the country or postal abbreviation for the state if the city is unfamiliar) and the publisher's name, dropping *Inc., Co.,* or *Publishers.* If the state is already included within the publisher's name, do not include the postal abbreviation for the state. For a periodical, follow the periodical title with a comma, the volume number (italicized), the issue number (if provided) in parentheses and followed by a comma, and the inclusive page numbers of the article. For newspaper articles and for articles or chapters in books, include the abbreviation *p.* ("page") or *pp.* ("pages").

The following APA-style examples appear in a "hanging indent" format, in which the first line aligns on the left and the subsequent lines indent one-half inch or five spaces.

BOOKS

1. One Author

Rheingold, H. (2002). *Smart mobs: The next social revolution.* Cambridge, MA: Perseus.

2. Two or More Authors

Steininger, M., Newell, J. D., & Garcia, L. (1984). *Ethical issues in psychology.* Homewood, IL: Dow Jones-Irwin.

3. Organization as Author

Use the word *Author* (neither underlined nor italicized) as the publisher when the organization is both the author and the publisher.

Linguistics Society of America. (2002). *Guidelines for using sign language interpreters.* Washington, DC: Author.

4. Unknown Author

National Geographic atlas of the world. (1999). Washington, DC: National Geographic Society.

5. Book Prepared by an Editor

Hardy, H. H. (Ed.). (1998). *The proper study of mankind.* New York: Farrar, Straus.

6. Selection in a Book with an Editor

Villanueva, V. (1999). An introduction to social scientific discussions on class. In A. Shepard, J. McMillan, & G. Tate (Eds.), *Coming to class: Pedagogy and the social class of teachers* (pp. 262-277). Portsmouth, NH: Heinemann.

7. Translation

Perez-Reverte, A. (2002). *The nautical chart* (M. S. Peaden, Trans.). New York: Harvest. (Original work published 2000)

8. Edition Other Than the First

Wrightsman, L. (1998). *Psychology and the legal system* (3rd ed.). Newbury Park, CA: Sage.

9. One Volume of a Multivolume Work

Will, J. S. (1921). *Protestantism in France* (Vol. 2). Toronto: University of Toronto Press.

10. Article in a Reference Work

Chernow, B., & Vattasi, G. (Eds.). (1993). Psychomimetic drug. In *The Columbia encyclopedia* (5th ed., p. 2238). New York: Columbia University Press.

If no author is listed, begin with the title.

11. Republication

Sharp, C. (1978). *History of Hartlepool.* Hartlepool, UK: Hartlepool Borough Council. (Original work published 1816)

12. Government Document

U.S. Bureau of the Census. (2001). *Survey of women-owned business enterprises.* Washington, DC: U.S. Government Printing Office.

13. Two or More Works by the Same Author

List the works in chronological order of publication. Repeat the author's name in each entry.

Rose, M. (1984). *Writer's block: The cognitive dimension.* Carbondale: Southern Illinois University Press.

Rose, M. (1995). *Possible lives: The promise of public education in America.* Boston: Houghton Mifflin.

PERIODICALS

14. Article in a Journal Paginated by Volume

Kirsch, G. E. (2002). Toward an engaged rhetoric of professional practice. *Journal of Advanced Composition, 22,* 414-423.

15. Article in a Journal Paginated by Issue

Carr, S. (2002). The circulation of Blair's *Lectures. Rhetoric Society Quarterly, 32*(4), 75-104.

16. Article in a Monthly Magazine

Dallek, R. (2002, December). The medical ordeals of JFK. *The Atlantic Monthly,* 49-64.

17. Article in a Newspaper

Nagourney, A. (2002, December 16). Gore rules out running in '04. *The New York Times,* pp. A1, A8.

18. Editorial or Letter to the Editor

Sonnenklar, M. (2002, January). Gaza revisited [Letter to the editor]. *Harper's,* p. 4.

19. Unsigned Article

Guidelines issued on assisted suicide. (1998, March 4). *The New York Times,* p. A15.

20. Review

Richardson, S. (1998, February). [Review of the book *The secret family*]. *Discover,*
88.

21. Published Interview

Shor, I. (1997). [Interview with A. Greenbaum]. *Writing on the Edge, 8*(2), 7-20.

22. Two or More Works by the Same Author in the Same Year

List two or more works by the same author published in the same
year alphabetically by title (excluding *A, An,* or *The*), and place lowercase
letters (*a, b,* etc.) after the dates.

Murray, F. B. (1983a). Equilibration as cognitive conflict. *Developmental Review, 3,*
54-61.

Murray, F. B. (1983b). Learning and development through social interaction. In L.
Liben (Ed.), *Piaget and the foundations of knowledge* (pp. 176-201).
Hillsdale, NJ: Erlbaum.

ELECTRONIC SOURCES

The following models are based on the APA's updated guidelines for citing electronic sources posted at the APA Web site <http://apa.org> as well
as in the APA's *Publication Manual* (5th edition). The basic APA entry for
most electronic sources should include the following elements:

- name of the author, editor, or compiler
- date of electronic publication or most recent update
- title of the work, document, or posting
- publication information, including the title, volume or issue number,
  and page numbers
- a retrieval statement that includes date of access, followed by a comma
- URL, with no angle brackets and no closing punctuation

23. World Wide Web Site

To cite a whole site, give the address in a parenthetical reference. To
cite a document from a Web site, include information as you would for a
print document, followed by a note on its retrieval.

American Psychological Association. (2000). DotComSense: Commonsense ways to protect your privacy and assess online mental health information. Retrieved January 25, 2002, from http://helping.apa.org/dotcomsense/

Mullins, B. (1995). Introduction to Robert Hass. Readings in contemporary poetry at Dia Center for the Arts. Retrieved April 24, 1999, from http:// www.diacenter.org/prg/poetry/95-96/intrhass.html

24. Article from an Online Periodical

If the article also appears in a print journal, you don't need a retrieval statement; instead, include the label [Electronic version] after the article title. However, if the online article is a revision of the print document (if the format differs or page numbers aren't indicated), include the date of access and URL.

Steedman, M., & Jones, G. P. (2000). Information structure and the syntaxphonology interface [Electronic version]. *Linguistic Inquiry, 31,* 649-689.

Palmer, K. S. (2000, September 12). In academia, males under a microscope. *The Washington Post.* Retrieved October 23, 2002, from http:// www.washingtonpost.com

25. Article or Abstract from a Database (Online or on CD-ROM)

Hayhoe, G. (2001). The long and winding road: Technology's future. *Technical Communication, 48*(2), 133-145. Retrieved September 22, 2002, from ProQuest database.

McCall, R. B. (1998). Science and the press: Like oil and water? *American Psychologist, 43*(2), 87-94. Abstract retrieved August 23, 2002, from PsycINFO database (1988-18263-001).

Pryor, T., & Wiederman, M. W. (1998). Personality features and expressed concerns of adolescents with eating disorders. *Adolescence, 33,* 291-301. Retrieved November 26, 2002, from Electric Library database.

26. Software or Computer Program

McAfee Office 2000. (Version 2.0) [Computer software]. (1999). Santa Clara, CA: Network Associates.

27. Online Government Document

Cite an online government document as you would a printed government work, adding the date of access and the URL. If you don't find a date, use *n.d.*

> Finn, J. D. (1998, April). *Class size and students at risk: What is known? What is next?* Retrieved September 25, 2002, from United States Department of Education Web site http://www.ed.gov/pubs/ClassSize/title.html

28. FTP, Telnet, or Gopher Site

After the retrieval statement, give the address (substituting *ftp, telnet,* or *gopher* for *http* at the beginning of the URL) or the path followed to access information, with slashes to indicate menu selections.

> Korn, P. (1994, October). How much does breast cancer really cost? *Self.* Retrieved May 5, 2002, from gopher://nysernet.org:70/00/BCIC/Sources/SELF/94/how-much

29. Posting to a Discussion Group

Include an online posting in the references list only if you're able to retrieve the message from a mailing list's archive. Provide the author's name; the date of posting, in parentheses; and the subject line from the posting. Include any information that further identifies the message in square brackets. For a listserv message, end with the retrieval statement, including the name of the list and the URL of the archived message.

> Troike, R. C. (2001, June 21). Buttercups and primroses [Msg 8]. Message posted to the American Dialect Society's ADS-L electronic mailing list, archived at http://listserv.linguistlist.org/archives/ads-1.html

30. Newsgroup Posting

Include the author's name, the date and subject line of the posting, the access date, and the name of the newsgroup.

> Wittenberg, E. (2001, July 11). Gender and the Internet [Msg 4]. Message posted to news://comp.edu.composition

31. Email Message or Synchronous Communication

Because the APA stresses that any sources cited in your list of references must be retrievable by your readers, you shouldn't include entries for email messages or synchronous communications (MOOs, MUDs); instead, cite these sources in your text as forms of personal communication (see p. 572). And remember that you shouldn't quote from other people's email without asking their permission to do so.

OTHER SOURCES

32. Technical or Research Reports and Working Papers

Wilson, K. S. (1986). *Palenque: An interactive multimedia optical disc prototype for children* (Working Paper No. 2). New York: Center for Children and Technology, Bank Street College of Education.

33. Unpublished Paper Presented at a Meeting or Symposium

Welch, K. (2002, March). *Electric rhetoric and screen literacy.* Paper presented at the meeting of the Conference on College Composition and Communication, Chicago.

34. Unpublished Dissertation

Barnett, T. (1997). *Communities in conflict: Composition, racial discourse, and the 60s revolution.* Unpublished doctoral dissertation, Ohio State University, Columbus.

35. Poster Session

Mensching, G. (2002, May). *A simple, effective one-shot for disinterested students.* Poster session presented at the National LOEX Library Instruction Conference, Ann Arbor, MI.

36. Film, Video, or DVD

Jackson, P. (Director). (2002). *The lord of the rings: The two towers.* [Film]. Los Angeles: New Line Cinema.

37. Television Program, Single Episode

Imperioli, M. (Writer), & Buscemi, S. (Director). (2002, October 20). Everybody hurts [Television series episode]. In D. Chase (Executive Producer), *The Sopranos.* New York: Home Box Office.

38. Sound Recording

Begin with the writer's name, followed by the date of copyright. Give the recording date at the end of the entry (in parentheses, after the period) if it's different from the copyright date.

Ivey, A., Jr., & Sall, R. (1995). Rollin' with my homies [Recorded by Coolio]. On *Clueless* [CD]. Hollywood, CA: Capitol Records.

RESPOND ●

1. The MLA and APA styles differ in several important ways, both for in-text citations and for lists of sources. You've probably noticed a few: the APA lowercases most words in titles and lists the publication date right after the author's name, whereas the MLA capitalizes most words and puts the publication date at the end of the works cited entry. More interesting than the details, though, is the reasoning behind the differences. Placing the publication date near the front of a citation, for instance, reveals a special concern for that information in the APA style. Similarly, the MLA's decision to capitalize titles isn't arbitrary: that style is preferred in the humanities for a reason. Find as many consistent differences between the MLA and APA styles as you can. Then, for each difference, try to discover the reasons these groups organize or present information in that way. The MLA and APA style manuals themselves may be of help. You might also begin by determining which academic disciplines subscribe to the APA style and which to the MLA.

2. Working with another person in your class, look for examples of the following sources: an article in a journal, a book, a film, a song, and a TV show. Then make a references or works cited entry for each one, using either MLA or APA style.

GLOSSARY

accidental condition in a definition, an element that helps to explain what's being defined but isn't essential to it. An accidental condition in defining a bird might be "ability to fly" because most, but not all, birds can fly. (See also *essential condition* and *sufficient condition*.)

ad hominem **argument** a fallacy of argument in which a writer's claim is answered by irrelevant attacks on his or her character.

analogy an extended comparison between something unfamiliar and something more familiar for the purpose of illuminating or dramatizing the unfamiliar. An analogy might, say, compare nuclear fission (less familiar) to a pool player's opening break (more familiar).

anaphora a figure of speech involving repetition, particularly of the same word at the beginning of several clauses.

antithesis the use of parallel structures to call attention to contrasts or opposites, as in *Some like it hot; some like it cold.*

antonomasia use of a title, epithet, or description in place of a name, as in *Your Honor* for *Judge.*

argument (1) a spoken, written, or visual text that expresses a point of view; (2) the use of evidence and reason to discover some version of the truth, as distinct from *persuasion*, the attempt to change someone else's point of view.

artistic appeal support for an argument that a writer creates based on principles of reason and shared knowledge rather than on facts and evidence. (See also *inartistic appeal*.)

assumption a belief regarded as true, upon which other claims are based.

assumption, cultural a belief regarded as true or commonsensical within a particular culture, such as the belief in individual freedom in American culture.

audience the person or persons to whom an argument is directed.

authority the quality conveyed by a writer who is knowledgeable about his or her subject and confident in that knowledge.

background the information a writer provides to create the context for an argument.

backing in Toulmin argument, the evidence provided to support a *warrant.*

bandwagon appeal a fallacy of argument in which a course of action is recommended on the grounds that everyone else is following it.

begging the question a fallacy of argument in which a claim is based on the very grounds that are in doubt or dispute: *Rita can't be the bicycle thief; she's never stolen anything.*

causal argument an argument that seeks to explain the effect(s) of a cause, the cause(s) of an effect, or a causal chain in which A causes B, B causes C, C causes D, and so on.

ceremonial argument an argument that deals with current values and addresses questions of praise and blame. Also called *epideictic*, ceremonial arguments include eulogies and graduation speeches.

character, appeal based on a strategy in which a writer presents an authoritative or credible self-image to dispose an audience to accept a claim.

claim a statement that asserts a belief or truth. In arguments, most claims require supporting evidence. The claim is a key component in *Toulmin argument.*

connotation the suggestions or associations that surround most words and extend beyond their literal meaning, creating associational effects. *Slender* and *skinny* have similar meanings, for example, but carry different connotations, the former more positive than the latter.

context the entire situation in which a piece of writing takes place, including the writer's purpose(s) for writing; the intended audience; the time and place of writing; the institutional, social, personal, and other influences on the piece of writing; the material conditions of writing (whether it's, for instance, online or on paper, in handwriting or print); and the writer's attitude toward the subject and the audience.

conviction the belief that a claim or course of action is true or reasonable. In a proposal argument, a writer must move an audience beyond conviction to action.

credibility an impression of integrity, honesty, and trustworthiness conveyed by a writer in an argument.

criterion in evaluative arguments, the standard by which something is measured to determine its quality or value.

definition, argument of an argument in which the claim specifies that something does or doesn't meet the conditions or features set forth in a definition: *Pluto is not a major planet.*

deliberative argument an argument that deals with action to be taken in the future, focusing on matters of policy. Deliberative arguments include parliamentary debates and campaign platforms.

delivery the presentation of a spoken argument.

dogmatism a fallacy of argument in which a claim is supported on the grounds that it's the only conclusion acceptable within a given community.

either-or choice a fallacy of argument in which a complicated issue is misrepresented as offering only two possible alternatives, one of which is often made to seem vastly preferable to the other.

emotional appeal a strategy in which a writer tries to generate specific emotions (such as fear, envy, anger, or pity) in an audience to dispose it to accept a claim.

enthymeme in Toulmin argument, a statement that links a claim to a supporting reason: *The bank will fail* (claim) *because it has lost the support of its largest investors* (reason). In classical rhetoric, an enthymeme is a syllogism with one term understood but not stated: *Socrates is mortal because he is a human being.* (The understood term is: *All human beings are mortal.*)

epideictic argument see *ceremonial argument.*

equivocation a fallacy of argument in which a lie is given the appearance of truth, or in which the truth is misrepresented in deceptive language.

essential condition in a definition, an element that must be part of the definition but, by itself, isn't enough to define the term. An essential condition in defining a bird might be "winged": all birds have wings, yet wings alone don't define a bird since some insects and mammals also have wings. (See also *accidental condition* and *sufficient condition.*)

ethical appeal see *character, appeal based on*, and *ethos.*

ethnographic observation a form of field research involving close and extended observation of a group, event, or phenomenon; careful and detailed note-taking during the observation; analysis of the notes; and interpretation of that analysis.

ethos the self-image a writer creates to define a relationship with readers. In arguments, most writers try to establish an ethos that suggests authority and credibility.

evaluation, argument of an argument in which the claim specifies that something does or doesn't meet established criteria: *The Nikon F5 is the most sophisticated 35mm camera currently available.*

evidence material offered to support an argument. See *artistic appeal* and *inartistic appeal*.

example, definition by a definition that operates by identifying individual examples of what's being defined: *sports car—Corvette, Viper, Miata, Boxster.*

experimental evidence evidence gathered through experimentation; often evidence that can be quantified (for example, a survey of students before and after an election might yield statistical evidence about changes in their attitudes toward the candidates). Experimental evidence is frequently crucial to scientific arguments.

fact, argument of an argument in which the claim can be proved or disproved with specific evidence or testimony: *The winter of 1998 was the warmest on record for the United States.*

fallacy of argument a flaw in the structure of an argument that renders its conclusion invalid or suspect. See *ad hominem argument, bandwagon appeal, begging the question, dogmatism, either-or choice, equivocation, false authority, faulty analogy, faulty causality, hasty generalization, moral equivalence, non sequitur, scare tactic, sentimental appeal, slippery slope,* and *straw man.*

false authority a fallacy of argument in which a claim is based on the expertise of someone who lacks appropriate credentials.

faulty analogy a fallacy of argument in which a comparison between two objects or concepts is inaccurate or inconsequential.

faulty causality a fallacy of argument making the unwarranted assumption that because one event follows another, the first event causes the second. Also called *post hoc, ergo propter hoc,* faulty causality forms the basis of many superstitions.

firsthand evidence data—including surveys, observation, personal interviews, etc.—collected and personally examined by the writer. (See also *secondhand evidence*.)

fisking a term invented by Glenn Reynolds to describe a point-by-point refutation, usually online, of an argument that the writer finds inaccurate or rhetorically suspect.

flashpoint see *fallacy of argument*.

forensic argument an argument that deals with actions that have occurred in the past. Sometimes called judicial arguments, forensic arguments include legal cases involving judgments of guilt or innocence.

formal definition a definition that identifies something first by the general class to which it belongs *(genus)* and then by the characteristics that distinguish it from other members of that class *(species)*: *Baseball is a game* (genus) *played on a diamond by opposing teams of nine players who score runs by circling bases after striking a ball with a bat* (species).

genus in a definition, the general class to which an object or concept belongs: *baseball is a sport*; *green is a color*.

grounds in Toulmin argument, the evidence provided to support a claim or reason, or *enthymeme*.

hard evidence support for an argument using facts, statistics, testimony, or other evidence the writer finds.

hasty generalization a fallacy of argument in which an inference is drawn from insufficient data.

hyperbole use of overstatement for special effect.

hypothesis an expectation for the findings of one's research or the conclusion to one's argument. Hypotheses must be tested against evidence, opposing arguments, and so on.

immediate reason the cause that leads directly to an effect, such as an automobile accident that results in an injury to the driver. (See also *necessary reason* and *sufficient reason*.)

inartistic appeal support for an argument using facts, statistics, eyewitness testimony, or other evidence the writer finds. (See also *artistic appeal*.)

intended readers the actual, real-life people whom a writer consciously wants to address in a piece of writing.

invention the process of finding and creating arguments to support a claim.

inverted word order moving grammatical elements of a sentence out of their usual order (subject-verb-object/complement) for special effect, as in *Tired I was; sleepy I was not.*

invitational argument a term used by Sonja Foss to describe arguments that are aimed not at vanquishing an opponent but at inviting others to collaborate in exploring mutually satisfying ways to solve problems.

invoked readers the readers directly addressed or implied in a text, which may include some that the writer didn't consciously intend to reach. An argument that refers to *those who have experienced a major trauma*, for example, invokes all readers who have undergone this experience.

irony use of language that suggests a meaning in contrast to the literal meaning of the words.

line of argument a strategy or approach used in an argument. Argumentative strategies include appeals to the heart (emotional appeals), to character (ethical appeals), and to facts and reason (logical appeals).

logical appeal a strategy in which a writer uses facts, evidence, and reason to make audience members accept a claim.

metaphor a figure of speech that makes a comparison, as in *The ship was a beacon of hope.*

moral equivalence a fallacy of argument in which no distinction is made between serious issues, problems, or failings and much less important ones.

necessary reason a cause that must be present for an effect to occur; for example, infection with a particular virus is a necessary reason for the development of AIDS. (See also *immediate reason* and *sufficient reason*.)

non sequitur a fallacy of argument in which claims, reasons, or warrants fail to connect logically; one point doesn't follow from another. *If you're really my friend, you'll lend me five hundred dollars.*

operational definition a definition that identifies an object by what it does or by the conditions that create it: *A line is the shortest distance between two points.*

parallelism use of similar grammatical structures or forms for pleasing effect: *in the classroom, on the playground, and at the mall.*

parody a form of humor in which a writer transforms something familiar into a different form to make a comic point.

pathos, appeal to see *emotional appeal.*

persuasion the act of seeking to change someone else's point of view.

precedents actions or decisions in the past that have established a pattern or model for subsequent actions. Precedents are particularly important in legal cases.

premise a statement or position regarded as true and upon which other claims are based.

propaganda an argument advancing a point of view without regard to reason, fairness, or truth.

proposal argument an argument in which a claim is made in favor of or opposing a specific course of action: *Sport utility vehicles should have to meet the same fuel economy standards as passenger cars.*

purpose the goal of an argument. Purposes include entertaining, informing, convincing, exploring, and deciding, among others.

qualifiers words or phrases that limit the scope of a claim: *usually*; *in a few cases*; *under these circumstances.*

qualitative argument an argument of evaluation that relies on nonnumerical criteria supported by reason, tradition, precedent, or logic.

quantitative argument an argument of evaluation that relies on criteria that can be measured, counted, or demonstrated objectively.

reason in writing, a statement that expands a claim by offering evidence to support it. The reason may be a statement of fact or another claim. In *Toulmin argument*, a *reason* is attached to a *claim* by a *warrant*, a statement that establishes the logical connection between claim and supporting reason.

rebuttal an answer that challenges or refutes a specific claim or charge. Rebuttals may also be offered by writers who anticipate objections to the claims or evidence they offer.

rebuttal, conditions of in Toulmin argument, potential objections to an argument. Writers need to anticipate such conditions in shaping their arguments.

reversed structures a figure of speech that involves the inversion of clauses: *What is good in your writing is not original; what is original is not good.*

rhetoric the art of persuasion. Western rhetoric originated in ancient Greece as a discipline to prepare citizens for arguing cases in court.

rhetorical analysis an examination of how well the components of an argument work together to persuade or move an audience.

rhetorical questions questions posed to raise an issue or create an effect rather than to get a response: *You may well wonder, "What's in a name?"*

Rogerian argument an approach to argumentation that's based on the principle, articulated by psychotherapist Carl Rogers, that audiences respond best when they don't feel threatened. Rogerian argument stresses trust and urges those who disagree to find common ground.

satire a form of humor in which a writer uses wit to expose—and possibly correct—human failings.

scare tactic a fallacy of argument presenting an issue in terms of exaggerated threats or dangers.

scheme a figure of speech that involves a special arrangement of words, such as inversion.

secondhand evidence any information taken from outside sources, including library research and online sources. (See also *firsthand evidence*.)

sentimental appeal a fallacy of argument in which an appeal is based on excessive emotion.

simile a comparison that uses *like* or *as*: *My love is like a red, red rose* or *I wandered lonely as a cloud.*

slippery slope a fallacy of argument exaggerating the possibility that a relatively inconsequential action or choice today will have serious adverse consequences in the future.

species in a definition, the particular features that distinguish one member of a *genus* from another: *Baseball is a sport* (genus) *played on a diamond by teams of nine players* (species).

spin a kind of political advocacy that makes any fact or event, however unfavorable, serve a political purpose.

stance the writer's attitude toward the topic and the audience.

stasis theory in classical rhetoric, a method for coming up with appropriate arguments by determining the nature of a given situation: *a question of fact; of definition; of quality; or of policy.*

straw man a fallacy of argument in which an opponent's position is misrepresented as being more extreme than it actually is, so that it's easier to refute.

sufficient condition in a definition, an element or set of elements adequate to define a term. A sufficient condition in defining God, for example, might be "supreme being" or "first cause." No other conditions are necessary, though many might be made. (See also *accidental condition* and *essential condition.*)

sufficient reason a cause that alone is enough to produce a particular effect; for example, a particular level of smoke in the air will set off a smoke alarm. (See also *immediate reason* and *necessary reason.*)

syllogism in formal logic, a structure of deductive logic in which correctly formed major and minor premises lead to a necessary conclusion:

Major premise All human beings are mortal.

Minor premise Socrates is a human being.

Conclusion   Socrates is mortal.

testimony a personal experience or observation used to support an argument.

thesis a sentence that succinctly states a writer's main point.

Toulmin argument a method of informal logic first described by Stephen Toulmin in *The Uses of Argument* (1958). Toulmin argument describes the key components of an argument as the *claim, reason, warrant, backing,* and *grounds.*

trope a figure of speech that involves a change in the usual meaning or signification of words, such as *metaphor, simile,* and *analogy.*

understatement a figure of speech that makes a weaker statement than a situation seems to call for. It can lead to powerful or to humorous effects.

values, appeal to a strategy in which a writer invokes shared principles and traditions of a society as a reason for accepting a claim.

warrant in *Toulmin argument*, the statement (expressed or implied) that establishes the logical connection between a claim and its supporting reason.

Claim	Don't eat that mushroom;
Reason	it's poisonous.
Warrant	What is poisonous should not be eaten.

ACKNOWLEDGMENTS

Chapter-Opening Art

Part 1 (left to right): Courtesy <www.adbusters.org>; Copyright © Brian Snyder/Reuters/Corbis; Copyright © Kelly Owen/ZUMA/Corbis; Copyright © Nicholas Kristof.
Part 2 (left to right): (foreground) Courtesy General Electric; (background) John Ruszkiewicz; Copyright © Bettmann/Corbis.
Part 3 (left to right): Art Resource, NY; The Granger Collection, Office of the Counsel to the President at the White House, D.C.; Warner Brothers/Photofest; Mick Roessler/Index Stock Imagery; Courtesy McDonald's.
Part 4 (left to right): Jay Berkowitz-L.A.W.A.; Juan Castillo/AFP/Getty Images; Courtesy <www.adbusters.org>; Bill Aron/PhotoEdit, Inc.

Texts

Dave Barry. Excerpt from "Introduction" and cover photo from *Dave Barry Hits below the Beltway*. Copyright © 2000 by Dave Barry. Reprinted with the permission of Ballantine Books, a division of Random House, Inc. Excerpt from "Step No. 1: Bang Head against Wall" from *The Miami Herald* (June 30, 2002). Copyright © 2002 by Dave Barry and *The Miami Herald*. Excerpt from "How to Vote in 1 Easy Step" from *The Miami Herald* (September 13, 2002). Copyright © 2002 by Dave Barry and *The Miami Herald*. Excerpt from "The Hidden Life of Dogs" from *The Miami Herald* (December 12, 1993). Copyright © 1993 by Dave Barry and *The Miami Herald*. Reprinted with the permission of the author.
Derek Bok. "Protecting Freedom of Expression at Harvard" from *The Boston Globe* (May 25, 1991). Reprinted with the permission of the author.
David Brower. Excerpts from "Let the River Run through It" from *Sierra Magazine* (March/April 1997). Copyright © 1997 by David Brower. Reprinted with the permission of the Estate of David Brower.
Craig R. Dean. Excerpt from "Legalize Gay Marriage" from *The New York Times* (1991). Copyright © 1991 by The New York Times Company. Reprinted with permission.
Alan M. Dershowitz. "Testing Speech Codes" from *The Boston Globe Index* (2002). Reprinted with permission of the author.
Gregory Dicum. Excerpt from "GREEN Flaming SUVs: A Conversation with Convicted Ecoterrorist Jeff Luers" from *The San Francisco Chronicle* (June 22, 2005). Reprinted with the permission of Gregory Dicum.
Jennifer L. Ernst and Matthew Barge. "Abortion Distortions: Senators from Both Sides Make False Claims about *Roe v. Wade*" from <FactCheck.org>. Copyright © 2005 by the Annenberg Public Policy Center of the University of Pennsylvania. Reprinted with the permission of <FactCheck.org>.
Peter Ferrara. Excerpt from "What Is an American?" from *National Review Online* (September 25, 2001). Copyright © 2001 by *National Review*, <www.nationalreview.com>. Reprinted by permission.
Nick Gillespie. Excerpt from "Star Wars, Nothing But Star Wars" (May 19, 2005) from ReasonOnline, <www.reason.com/hod/ng051905.shtml>. Copyright © 2005 by *Reason* Magazine, www.reason.com. Reprinted with permission.

Dana Gioia. "Why Literature Matters" from *The Boston Globe* (April 10, 2005). Copyright © 2005 by Dana Gioia. Reprinted with permission.

William M. Gray and Philip J. Klotzback. Excerpt from "Forecast of Atlantic Hurricane Activity for September and October 2005 and Seasonal Update through August" (September 2, 2005), <http://hurricane.atmos.colostate .edu/forecasts/2005/sep2005/>. Reprinted with the permission of Dr. William M. Gray, Department of Atmospheric Science, Colorado State University.

Langston Hughes. "Harlem — A Dream Deferred" from *Collected Poems of Langston Hughes*. Copyright © 1994 by the Estate of Langston Hughes. Reprinted with the permission of Alfred A. Knopf, a division of Random House, Inc.

Armen Keteyian. Excerpt from "Bats Should Crack, Not Skulls" from *The Sporting News* (June 24, 2002). Copyright © 2002 by Armen Keteyian. Reprinted with the permission of the author.

Michael Lassell. Excerpt from "How to Watch Your Brother Die." Copyright © 1985 by Michael Lassell. Reprinted with the permission of the author.

James Lindgren. Excerpt from a review of Michael Bellesiles, *Arming America* from *Yale Law Review* 111 (2002). Reprinted with permission.

Dahlia Lithwick. "How Do You Solve the Problem of Scalia?" from *Slate* (March 30, 2006). Copyright © 2006 by Washington Post.Newsweek Interactive Co. LLC. Reprinted by permission of United Media.

Peggy Noonan. Excerpt from "Stand Up and Take It Like an American" from *Opinion Journal* (November 29, 2002). Copyright © 2002 by Peggy Noonan and *The Wall Street Journal*. Reprinted with the permission of William Morris Agency, LLC on behalf of the author.

Kathleen Norris. Excerpt from "Little Girls in Church" from *Little Girls in Church*. Copyright © 1995 by Kathleen Norris. Reprinted with the permission of University of Pittsburgh Press.

P. J. O'Rourke. "Mass Transit Hysteria" from *Opinion Journal* (March 16, 2005). Copyright © 2005 by Dow Jones & Company, Inc. All rights reserved.

Michael Osofsky. "The Psychological Experience of Security Officers Who Work with Executions" from *Stanford Undergraduate Research Journal* (May 2002). Reprinted with the permission of the author.

Scott Ott. "Poll: Most Americans Not in Iraq" from <www.ScrappleFace.com> (September 23, 2005). Reprinted with the permission of the author, editor/ anchor, <ScrappleFace.com>, daily news satire site.

Jon Pareles. "The Case against Coldplay" from *The New York Times* (June 5, 2005). Copyright © 2005 by The New York Times Company. Reprinted with permission.

Lynn Peril. Excerpt from "Introduction" from *Pink Think: Becoming a Woman in Many Easy Lessons*. Copyright © 2002 by Lynn Peril. Reprinted with the permission of W. W. Norton & Company, Inc.

Seth Stevenson. Excerpt from "Tangled Up in Boobs" from *Slate* (April 12, 2004), <www.slate.com>. Copyright © 2004 by Slate. Reprinted with the permission of United Media.

Margaret Talbot. Excerpt from "Men Behaving Badly" from *The New York Times Magazine* (October 13, 2002). Copyright © 2002 by Margaret Talbot. Reprinted with permission.

The Travesty. "Mundane Events Made Humorous, Entertaining by Parody News Format" and "Headline Catches Reader's Attention; Interest Wanes after Semi-

Analysis of Caption" from *Texas Travesty* (November/December 2003). Copyright © 2003. Reprinted with permission.

Illustrations

p. i: (clockwise from top left) Copyright © Royalty-Free/Corbis; Copyright © Andersen Ross/Jupiter Images; Copyright © Bob Sacha/Corbis; Copyright © Ryan Red Corn from Red Hand Media; Copyright © Webstream/Alamy; Copyright © StockTrek/Getty Images; Copyright © Joseph Sohm, ChromoSohm, Inc./Corbis; p. iv: (l–r) Courtesy <www.adbusters.org>; Bill Aron/PhotoEdit Inc.; (t) Copyright © Robin Raffer; (b) The Advertising Archives; Copyright © Bettmann/Corbis; Courtesy McDonald's, p. xiii: Copyright © Warner Brothers Entertainment Inc.; p. xvi: The Advertising Archives; p. xx: Mick Roessler/Index Stock Imagery; p. xxii: Bill Aron/PhotoEdit Inc.; p. 5: cover, *Dave Barry Hits below the Beltway*, by Dave Barry, Copyright © 2001, used by permission of Random House, Inc.; p. 6: (b) Copyright © Linda Eddy; p. 9: Copyright © Kelly Owen/ZUMA/Corbis; p. 10: Georgia O'Keeffe, *Rust Red Hills*, 1930. Oil on canvas, 16 x 30 inches. Sloan Fund Purchase, 62.02, Valparaiso University. Copyright © Brauer Museum of Art. Permission granted by the Artists Rights Society; p. 11: Stephen Jaffe/AFP/Getty Images; p. 13: Copyright © Lower Manhattan Development Corporation, 2004; p. 14: Copyright © *The New Yorker* Collection 1999 Donald Reilly from <cartoonbank.com>. All Rights Reserved; p. 16: Scala, Art Resource, NY; p. 18: Copyright © Stapleton Collection/Corbis; p. 22: Copyright © Branson Reynolds/Index Stock Imagery; p. 25: Alexander Tamargo/Getty Images; p. 26: Copyright © Bettmann/Corbis; p. 28: Copyright © Viviane Moos/Corbis; p. 30: Copyright © Alexei Kalmykov/Reuters/Corbis; p. 31: Copyright © *The New Yorker* Collection 1999 Mick Stevens from <cartoonbank .com>. All Rights Reserved; p. 34: Courtesy, *Soul Sistah*; p. 37: Courtesy Sharon Clahchischilliage; p. 38: Evelyn Hockstein/Polaris Images; p. 40: EPA; p. 41: Courtesy *Atlantic Monthly*; p. 43: Copyright © Sean John. Reprinted with permission; p. 44: BumperArt; pp. 46, 48: Courtesy <www.adbusters.org>; p. 50: Advertising created by PlowShare Group for Save the Children; p. 53: Copyright © *The New Yorker* Collection 1992 Robert Mankoff from <cartoonbank.com>. All Rights Reserved; p. 54: Copyright © Nicholas Kristof; p. 55: Copyright © Carlos Barria/Reuters/ Corbis; p. 58: (l) <StampandShout.com>; (r) Copyright © <BumperTalk.com>; p. 61: Copyright © Brian Snyder/Reuters/Corbis; p. 64: Copyright © 2004 Reprise Records; p. 66: (l) Frank Capri/Getty Images; (r) Evelyn Floret/TimeLife Pictures/Getty Images; p. 72: The Advertising Archives; p. 77: (l–r) Copyright © Kimberly White/Reuters/Corbis; Jay Laprete/AP/Wide World Photos; Kathy Willens/AP/Wide World Photos; Yves Logghe/AP/Wide World Photos; p. 79: Copyright © Bettmann/Corbis; p. 80: <www.protestwarrior.com>; p. 87: Cindy Clark and Alejandro Gonzalez/USA *Today* Copyright © 2006. Reprinted with permission; p. 89: Copyright © 2002 The Friedman Foundation; p. 103: (l) Dave Hogan/Getty Images; (r) Chris Farina/Getty Images; p. 107: Courtesy Jo-Ann Mort; p. 111: Texas Dept. of Transportation/Sherry Matthews Advocacy Marketing; p. 114: <caglecartoons .com/español>; p. 116: Shelley Eades/*San Francisco Chronicle*; pp. 117–18: Copyright © zombie; p. 122: (l) Copyright © Lionsgate Films; (r) Copyright © Warner Brothers Entertainment Inc.; p. 126: Courtesy Milena Ateya; p. 140: The Advertising Archives; p. 143: Manuscripts and Special Collections, New York State Library;

p. 145: National Archives; p. 146: AP/Wide World Photos; p. 151: Copyright © Charles Barsotti from <cartoonbank.com>. All Rights Reserved; p. 154: *Mushrooms: An Introduction to Familiar North American Species*, text by James Kavanagh, illustrations by Raymond Leung. Used by permission of Waterford Press; p. 173: Courtesy General Electric; p. 176: (t) Collection of The New-York Historical Society; (b) Copyright © David Luneau; p. 177: Cornell Lab of Ornithology; p. 180: Copyright © Robin Raffer; p. 181: National Hurricane Center; p. 183: Michael Newman/PhotoEdit, Inc. p. 189: Copyright © Bettmann/Corbis; p. 191: cover, *Epileptic*, by David B., used by permission, Pantheon Books/Random House, Inc.; p. 192: National Endowment for the Arts; p. 193: National Archives; p. 201: Mel Evans/AP/Wide World Photos; p. 203: US-Ireland Alliance; p. 220: Copyright © 2002 Brad Roberts <www.lowdiameter .com>; p. 221: (t) Copyright © Khalil Bendib/The Muslim Observer; (b) Copyright © Robin Nelson/PhotoEdit, Inc.; p. 224: Courtesy Ford; p. 225: Copyright © 2006 FOX News Network; p. 227: Copyright © Robin Raffer; p. 243: Fox Searchlight Pictures/Photofest; p. 252: Kristin Cole; p. 253: Frazer Harrison/Getty Images; p. 256: Copyright © Ron Kimball Stock; p. 260: Lucasfilm Ltd./Twentieth Century Fox Film Corp./Photofest; p. 263: Bud Freund/Index Stock Imagery; p. 264: Courtesy UTStarcom; p. 267: (l) Chris Weeks/AP Wide World Photos; (r) Copyright © Bettmann/Corbis; p. 276: Courtesy Nisey Williams; p. 281: Scott Gries/Getty Images; p. 287: Karen Kasmauski/*National Geographic*; p. 290: Mark Alan Stamaty/<slate.com> Copyright © 2006 Washington Post.Newsweek Interactive Co. LLC; pp. 294–96: <http://fightingmalaria.org>; p. 297: J Griffis Smith/TxDot; p. 299: Continental Distributing, Inc./Photofest; p. 304: <http://news.bbc.co.uk>; p. 305: Cox & Forkum; p. 329: (t) John Ruszkiewicz; (b) Glen Canyon Institute; p. 333: Courtesy, Americans for the Arts; p. 334: Copyright © Yvonne Baron Estes, *Gardening Among Deer Without Hiring a Mountain Lion*, Ponyfoot Press; p. 337: Mary Godleski/AP/WW Photos; p. 342: Courtesy San Diego Chargers; p. 343: <http:// www.sierralarana.com>; p. 344: NASA; p. 352: Photographer: Christina S. Murrey, University of Texas at Austin; p. 371: (tl) DesignPics Inc./Index Stock Imagery; (tr) ThinkStock LLC/Index Stock Imagery; (b) The Image Bank/Index Stock Imagery; p. 372: Copyright © *The New Yorker* Collection 1987 Al Ross from <cartoonbank .com>. All Rights Reserved; p. 376: Warner Brothers/Photofest; p. 385: *The Boondocks* Copyright © 2006 Aaron McGruder. Dist. by Universal Press Syndicate. Reprinted with permission. All Rights Reserved; p. 387: Lionel Cironneau/AP/WW Photos; p. 388: Reprinted by permission of *Ironic Times*; p. 395: David Kramer/<www.margaretcho.com>; p. 397: Reprinted with permission of *The Onion* Copyright © 2005; p. 400: John Ruszkiewicz; p. 402: Courtesy *Phroth*, Penn State; p. 403: Cox & Forkum; p. 404: Reprinted with permission of *The Onion* Copyright © 1998 by Onion, Inc.; p. 405: *Texas Travesty*, The University of Texas at Austin; p. 406: (back) Courtesy Scott Ott; (front) Courtesy <CNN.com>; p. 413: Copyright © Ron Kimball Stock; p. 414: (t) Art Resource, NY; (b) Copyright © Bettmann/Corbis; p. 416: (both) National Postal Museum; p. 417: (l) Mick Roessler/Index Stock Imagery; (r) AES Group. *New Liberty*, 1996, from the series *AES-Witnesses of the Future. Islamic Project* (1996–2006), digital collage, variable dimensions, variable media. Courtesy M. Guelman Gallery, Moscow, and artists. Permission granted by the Artists Rights Society; pp. 419–20: <uac-tutoring .stanford.edu/tutor>; p. 423: <www.benettongroup .com>. Reprinted with permission; p. 425: (l–r): The Granger Collection, Office of the Counsel to the President at the White House, D.C.; Courtesy McDonald's; Courtesy Philip Morris; p. 426: Copyright © 2005 Catherine Harrell; p. 429: Copyright © Ron Kimball Stock; p. 430: Copyright © 2006 SEIU, Service Employees International Union ® CTW, CLC; p. 432: Copyright © 2006 Google; p. 435: Franck Fife/AFP/Getty Images; p. 436: NASA; p. 439: National Portrait Gallery, London; p. 443: (t–b) Copyright © Daily Kos. Reprinted with permission; USDA Rural Development; Dennis MacDonald/PhotoEdit Inc.; p. 444: Courtesy IBM; p. 448: AP/Wide World Photos; p. 450: TM Copyright © 2001 FOX; pp. 454, 456, 458: Copyright © Frank Miller; p. 464: Courtesy American Legacy Foundation; p. 473: Jay Berkowitz-L.A.W.A.; p. 475: Jim MacMillan/AP/Wide World Photos; p. 477: Copyright © The New Yorker Collection 1989 George Price from <cartoonbank.com>. All Rights Reserved; p. 480: Copyright © <littlegreenfootballs.com>. Reprinted with permission; p. 485: Copyright © 2006 Google; p. 495: Office of National Drug Control Policy/Partnership for a Drug-Free America; p. 496: Copyright © The New Yorker Collection 2001 David Sipress from <cartoonbank.com>. All Rights Reserved; p. 498: Courtesy World Wildlife Fund; p. 500: Copyright © The New Yorker Collection 2001 Robert Weber from <cartoonbank.com>. All Rights Reserved; p. 502: Mike Stewart/Corbis Sygma; p. 504: Sage Stossel, The Atlantic Online; p. 507: Bill Aron/PhotoEdit Inc.; p. 510: Eric Risberg/AP/Wide World Photos; p. 515: Courtesy The Lexicomm Group; p. 516: U.S. Copyright Office; p. 518: Courtesy <www.adbusters.org>; p. 520: Doonesbury Copyright © 2002 G. B. Trudeau. Reprinted with permission of Universal Press Syndicate. All Rights Reserved; p. 530: Reed Saxon/ AP/Wide World Photos; p. 531: (l) Courtesy Vanity Fair; (r) Courtesy Tin House; p. 537: Copyright © National Audubon Society. Reprinted with permission; p. 540: Thir Khan/AFP/Getty Images; p. 543: Juan Castillo/AFP/Getty Images; p. 547: Bloomberg News; p. 551: Copyright © MLA; p. 567: Copyright © Emily Lesk; p. 570: Copyright © American Psychological Association.

INDEX